Punch and Shakespeare in the Victorian Era

Alan R. Young

Punch and Shakespeare in the Victorian Era

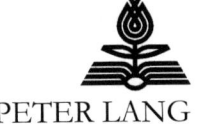

PETER LANG

Oxford · Bern · Berlin · Bruxelles · Frankfurt am Main · New York · Wien

Bibliographic information published by Die Deutsche Bibliothek
Die Deutsche Bibliothek lists this publication in the Deutsche
Nationalbibliografie; detailed bibliographic data is available on
the Internet at ‹http://dnb.ddb.de›.

British Library and Library of Congress Cataloguing-in-Publication Data:
A catalogue record for this book is available from The British Library,
Great Britain, and from The Library of Congress, USA

ISBN 978-3-03-03911-078-0

© Peter Lang AG, International Academic Publishers, Bern 2007
Hochfeldstrasse 32, Postfach 746, CH-3000 Bern 9, Switzerland
info@peterlang.com, www.peterlang.com, www.peterlang.net

All rights reserved.
All parts of this publication are protected by copyright.
Any utilisation outside the strict limits of the copyright law, without the
permission of the publisher, is forbidden and liable to prosecution.
This applies in particular to reproductions, translations, microfilming,
and storage and processing in electronic retrieval systems.

Printed in Germany

*To my family
whose love and support
helped make this possible*

Contents

Preface	9
Acknowledgments	13
Some Preliminary Notes	15
List of Illustrations	19
Chapter One *Punch* and its Readers, Writers and Artists	23
Chapter Two *Punch* and Shakspeareanity	67
Chapter Three *Punch*, Shakespeare, and the Theatre	137
Chapter Four *Punch* and Shakespeare Transposed	249
Bibliography	323
Index of *Punch* Artists Cited	331
Index of *Punch* Authors Cited	333
General Index	335

Preface

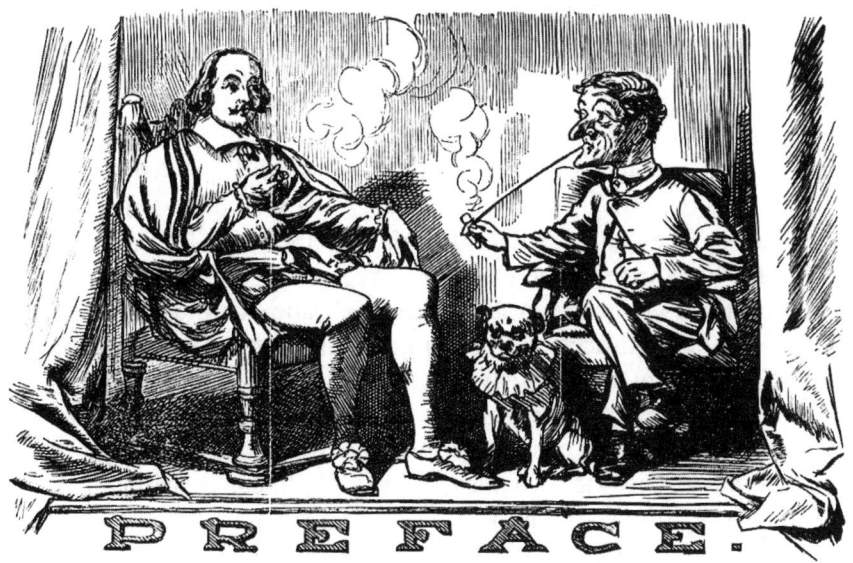

Figure 1. Unidentified artist. *Punch* (26 December 1863), 45:iii.

At the close of 1863, the publishers of the British humour magazine *Punch, or the London Charivari* gathered up the weekly issues of the previous six months in preparation for their re-publication as Volume 45. This duly appeared with a Preface dated 26 December that begins just below an engraving depicting two men and a dog. The men are comfortably seated in armchairs opposite each other, and each smokes a long-stemmed clay pipe (Figure 1). The man on the right, with his elongated nose and pointed chin, would have been instantly recognizable to all readers as Mr. Punch, and the introduction to the dialogue below confirms this:

THE SCENE represents the most unapproachable of all MR. PUNCH's deep solitudes and awful cells. He has, after a slight refection, comprising some oyster soup, a wild duck artistically sauced, and a few glasses of 'victorious Burgundy,' retired to meditate, NEC sine fume, upon his own goodness and greatness, the folly of mankind, the chances of the pantomimes being good, and other Christmas topics. To think the more profoundly, he has closed his illustrious eyes to material objects.

At Mr. Punch's feet sits his dog Toby, an equally familiar figure, one who had first appeared with his master on Richard Doyle's cover for the January 1844 issue and would remain there until October 1956. The figure at left is even more familiar. In response to Mr. Punch's post prandial reverie, so the accompanying dialogue makes clear, William Shakespeare has joined Mr. Punch to share in the fellowship of a smoke. In the course of the ensuing conversation, Shakespeare raises some questions about the forthcoming celebration of the tercentenary of his birth that will occur in the coming year, and he asks Mr. Punch to represent his interests. What these questions were and how *Punch* dealt with the tercentenary are matters that will be discussed later in Chapter Two. What is important here is the image of the relaxed familiarity between the two men, who look like old acquaintances sharing a quiet domestic intimacy. Although the picture cannot show it, there is also a great deal of mutual respect involved, for, as the dialogue makes clear, not only does Shakespeare trust Mr. Punch to represent his interests, but this latter is able to tell Shakespeare that 'I forget nothing that you wrote.' Nor will he, Mr. Punch asserts, 'while memory holds her seat in this distracted orb.' Indeed, Mr. Punch appears to know the writings of Shakespeare better than their author, who complains that he has been so distracted by the commentators that he has forgotten what he wrote.

This representation of the relationship between Punch and Shakespeare is for me emblematic of the central concerns of this book. In what follows I hope to show how *Punch* constantly referred to Shakespeare, expressing an easy familiarity with the latter's characters, his plots, and his texts. This familiarity could be used as a basis for humour and shared with readers who themselves often knew and admired Shakespeare far better than many people today. At the same time, *Punch* actively sought to increase what it at times referred to as

'Shakspeareanity' by reporting and commenting on all matters having to do with Shakespeare, by reviewing performances of his plays, by giving news of notable Shakespearean actors, by noting art works based on the plays, and by including burlesques of lines and scenes from the plays, and occasionally even burlesques of entire plays. In addition, *Punch* used Shakespeare's characters, texts, and plot situations as the basis for innumerable articles and engravings that commented on all manner of topics, ranging from relatively trivial matters of fashion and social manners to matters of great national and political moment.

In preparing this study I was confronted by a very large amount of material. Early on, I decided to restrict myself to an account of the Victorian era, beginning with the first issue of Punch on 17 July 1841 and ending with the issue of 25 December 1901. That year Queen Victoria died, the Second Anglo-Boer War appeared to be approaching its end, and *Punch*'s great cartoonist, Sir John Tenniel, retired after having worked with the magazine for just over fifty years. That same year, too, Henry Irving presented his final Shakespeare production, *Coriolanus*, at the Lyceum Theatre. *Punch* reviewed it (see Chapter Three) and so concluded a series of fourteen reviews of the beloved actor-manager's revivals of Shakespeare's plays. By examining the *Punch* output between 1841 and 1901, it is my hope that this book will contribute to our growing knowledge about the centrality of Shakespeare within Victorian culture, a topic that provided a significant subtext for my 2002 book on *Hamlet and the Visual Arts, 1709–1900*.

Within Victorian culture at large, Shakespeare's work served as a kind of literary and moral touchstone, and a copy of Shakespeare's plays could even possess in many families a status second only to the Bible. How *Punch* contributed to this state of affairs is something I hope to reveal in the successive chapters of this book. My goal is to demonstrate the ways in which *Punch* both reflected contemporary attitudes to Shakespeare and at the same time conducted a campaign to enhance and promote Shakespeare's status as the national dramatist and the unmatchable and inexhaustible fount of literary and moral inspiration.

But there are also other less esoteric issues that I hope to bring to the fore. I hope, for example, to show just how rich a source *Punch* can be to our knowledge of Shakespeare performance history. Theatre historians have, I believe, tended to neglect *Punch*; yet the magazine reported regularly on theatrical affairs and sent its writers and artists to the theatre, rarely missing any major Shakespeare production. Operas, ballets, pantomimes, and even hippodramas were also reviewed, often in a somewhat hostile fashion, but any works based on Shakespeare, whatever *Punch* may have thought of them, were usually given some consideration as manifestations of 'Shakspeareanity'. Though the *Punch* reviews, comments, and engravings can be hard to interpret (what is the reality, for example, behind some of the comic overstatements and caricatures?), the material remains a significant but barely mined source of information. Similarly, our understanding of theatrical burlesque, particularly the popular Victorian taste for burlesques of Shakespeare's plays, is immensely enhanced when we read the sometimes almost weekly burlesques of Shakespearean texts that appear in *Punch*. Again, as I hope to show, *Punch* is a significant but neglected source.

Acknowledgments

In the course of my research for this book, I incurred numerous debts to colleagues and institutions. For their help and encouragement I would particularly like to thank Peter Daly (McGill University), Clare Horrocks (Edge Hill College), Russell Jackson (University of Birmingham), Kristan Ann Tetans (Michigan State University), and Gillian Thomas (Saint Mary's University). I am also considerably indebted to Patrick Leary, whose very fine doctoral thesis on the *Punch* circle, 1858–1874, was a continuous source of information and inspiration. In our correspondence, he was especially helpful in providing information about the identification of some of the *Punch* authors and in pointing out some crucial source material in the *Punch* archives. I owe, too, a very considerable debt to Helen Walasek for help in working with the *Punch* Archives that were recently acquired by the British Library. In particular, I am grateful for her assistance in going through the *Punch* Contributors' Ledgers to identify the authors of items referred to in this book. Helen Walasek also assisted in dating specific items in the early issues of *Punch* (as noted below, volumes prior to Volume 29 in 1855, appeared without headers containing the issue dates), and she helped in locating and transcribing material having to do with Shakespeare in the Henry Silver Diary. For information about items in the Royal Academy exhibitions mentioned in Chapter Four, I am indebted to Andrew Potter of the Royal Academy Library (London). I would also like to thank Andrew Murphy (University of St. Andrews), Paul Werstine (University of Western Ontario), and A. R. Braunmuller (University of Calfornia, Los Angeles) for the opportunity to participate in their respective seminars at meetings of the Shakespeare Association of America in 2004, 2005, and 2006. These seminars enabled me to submit aspects of my work on *Punch* to the scrutiny of a number of fellow Shakespeareans. Their constructive criticisms have influenced both this book and my construction of an electronic database of all the *Punch* allusions to

Shakespeare between 1841 and 1901. I would also like to express my thanks for the generous and courteous help that I received from the following institutions: the Acadia University Library, the Arts, Languages and Literature Department of the Central Library in Birmingham, the British Library, the Broward Community College Library, the Dalhousie University Library, the Florida Atlantic University Library, and Saint Mary's University Library. Finally, I wish to thank my wife, Wendy Katz, for her patience and good humour during the gestation and birth pangs of this book.

Some Preliminary Notes

Spelling

Punch always spelled Shakespeare's name and words derived from it by omitting the 'e' that today customarily follows the 'k'. Thus, in any material quoted directly from *Punch*, readers will find 'Shakspeare', 'Shakspearian', and 'Shakspeareanity' (this last also inconsistently spelled 'Shakspereanity' and 'Shakspearianity'). In my text, I have used the generally-preferred modern spelling 'Shakespeare' and 'Shakespearean'. As will be explained below, however, I have retained the *Punch* spelling of 'Shakspeareanity'.

Dates, Volume Numbers, and Pagination

Punch was published in weekly issues that were later republished in volume form, two volumes per year. Volume One contained the weekly issues from 17 July 1841 to the end of December, and Volume Two contained the issues for January through June 1842. Thereafter, this numbering scheme continued, with the even-numbered volumes containing the issues for the first six months of the year and the odd-numbered volumes containing the issues for the last six months. The pagination in each volume was continuous, starting at page one and following the continuous pagination in the corresponding weekly issues. The citations from *Punch* used in this book are for the most part derived from a complete run of *Punch* volumes. However, the earlier volumes prior to Volume 29, July–December 1855, appeared without headers containing the issue dates. Consequently, when discussing items prior to those in Volume 29, it is often awkward to assign an exact date within the six-month period represented by a particular volume. However, each issue was dated in small print at the foot of its last page. This information has been used to date items published prior to July 1855.

Almanack

An annual feature of *Punch* that appeared each December to herald the New Year was the *Punch* Almanack (I use the spelling employed by *Punch*). It contained pages for each month, together with calendars decorated with elaborate and humorous engraved borders, amusing prophecies for the future, and all manner of humorous engravings. Because a number of engravings of Shakespearean topics appear in the Almanacks, I have chosen to include in this study a number of references to them. Although, with the exception of 1844, the Almanacks remained a separate publication, the annual Almanack was included at the beginning of each even-numbered January–June volume. However, its pages were not given numbers and were not counted in with the sequentially numbered pages of the weekly issues.

Burlesque

I have chosen to use the term 'burlesque' as a generic term to refer to the imitation of a serious work, whether in whole or in part, and the rendering of that work in a comic and debased style that inverts both form and content. Beneath this generic umbrella, I have subsumed various other terms, among them 'pastiche', 'parody', 'travesty', 'caricature', 'extravaganza', 'biretta', and 'spoof'.

Capitalization

Punch made frequent use of upper case letters for titles of all but the smallest items. Captions to engravings are also sometimes in upper case. Throughout I have chosen to retain the original use of upper case letters whenever quoting from *Punch*.

Cartoon

The term 'cartoon' is familiar today primarily as a reference to the humorous and/or satiric drawings included in many newspapers and magazines. This use of the term appears to have been the invention of *Punch* (Young 2005, 230). Originally, the word referred to a preliminary but usually full-size drawing for a work of art; a painting, a fresco, or a tapestry. In 1843, the term 'cartoon' was much in use in connection with the exhibition in Westminster Hall of large-scale drawings submitted by numerous artists in a competition to decide on fresco paintings for the new Houses of Parliament (Simpson 1994, 25–47; and Altick 1997, 674–82). In its second issue for July, *Punch* responded and began a series of six full-page engravings designed by John Leech that it ironically called 'Cartoons' in imitation of what was to be seen at Westminster. The public took to the word, and outside the *Punch* offices 'cartoon' became synonymous with a 'large cut' (see below) that was generally political in subject (Morris 1985, 31 n. 110, 34, 109 n.1, 121 n. 124). Within the offices of *Punch* itself, however, the new term was not used. Engraved designs were described as 'cuts' and the weekly full-page 'cut' was always referred to as the 'big cut' or the 'large cut', or 'the big drum' (Altick 1997, 674–675; Leary 2002, 50). The weekly 'big cut' provided a much-anticipated centre piece for each *Punch* issue. Its verso was always left blank to make it suitable for collecting in a portfolio or for framing and wall display. In this study, I have for the most part avoided the term 'cartoon' and instead used the terminology employed by *Punch*: 'big cut', 'large cut', or 'big drum'.

Shakspeareanity

The term 'Shakspeareanity' (also, as mentioned above, sometimes spelled 'Shakspereanity' and 'Shakspearianity') was a term that appears to have been invented by *Punch* (see Chapter Two). It was used to refer to awareness and appreciation of all things having to do with Shakespeare. The commonly-used modern term 'bardolatry' will not do as a substitute, since 'bardolatry' frequently implies excess or misguided adulation. There is, then, no modern equivalent for the term 'Shakspeareanity', which is not listed in the Oxford English Dictionary. With some trepidation, I have appropriated the term and used it from time to time throughout this study in connection with *Punch*'s dissemination of Shakespeare within Victorian culture at large.

Social

The term 'social' was used by *Punch* to refer to an engraving on a humorous social subject.

Names of Writers and Artists

It was customary in *Punch* for the names of authors to be omitted. In many instances, however, it is possible to identify authors from the *Punch* Contributors' Ledgers that contain records of each writer's work, although the Ledgers only begin in March 1843. Whenever an author is identified in what follows here, it is usually due to information obtained from these Ledgers. Artists are a different matter since none of their work is listed in the Ledgers except for a brief period between 11 March 1843 and 30 September 1848 when a record was kept of the designer of each weekly big cut, accompanied in many instances with the name of whoever had provided the original idea upon which the big cut was based. When engravings appeared in *Punch*, few artists signed their full names, and many used only their initials or monograms. In most cases, these artists can be identified. However, many engravings are unsigned, and in these instances, there is often no way of knowing who was responsible for the original design.

List of Illustrations

Initial letter for Chapter 1. 'D' (Hamlet and the Ghost) – *Punch* (27 November 1841), 1:232. Artist Unidentified.

Initial letter for Chapter 2. 'O' (Falstaff) – *Punch* (30 April 1864), 46:175. Artist Unidentified.

Initial letter for Chapter 3. 'D' (Titania and Bottom) – *Punch* (28 July 1866), 51:43. Artist Unidentified.

Initial letter for Chapter 4. 'T' (Macbeth with daggers) – *Punch* (4 December 1841), 1:244. Artist Unidentified.

1. John Tenniel on the birth of the Prince Imperial, Eugene Bonaparte (16 March, 1856), 'PUNCH'S ILLUSTRATIONS TO SHAKSPEARE,' *Punch* (29 March 1856), 30:130.
2. John Tenniel, 'COSTUME OF THE NOBILITY, FROM AN AUTHENTIC PORTRAIT OF HAMLET, PRINCE OF DENMARK,' *Punch* (17 March 1860), 38:113.
3. John Tenniel, 'THE ELDEST SON OF THE CHURCH,' *Punch* (8 December 1860), 39:225.
4. John Leech, 'WHO SHOULD EDUCATE THE PRINCE OF WALES,' *Punch* (2 September 1843), 5:98.
5. Unidentified artist, 'SHAKSPEAR AN EMIGRANT TO FRANCE,' *Punch* (30 November 1844), 7:247.
6. Unidentified artist, 'DESIGNS FOR A MEDAL TO COMMEMORATE THE EXPULSION OF SHAKSPEARE FROM ENGLAND AND HIS RECEPTION IN FRANCE,' *Punch* (25 January 1845), 8:48.
7. John Tenniel, 'QUEEN HERMIONE,' *Punch* (23 September 1865), 49:117.
8. John Leech, 'POET BUNN'S OPENING OF DRURY LANE THEATRE,' *Punch* (11 October 1845), 9:160.
9. William Newman, 'BUNN'S HAPPY FAMILY PATRONIZED BY ROYALTY,' *Punch* (8 May 1847), 12:196.

10. William Makepeace Thackeray, initial letter 'H' for 'THE HOUSE OF SHAKSPEARE AND THE HOUSE OF COBURG,' *Punch* (14 August 1847), 13:52.
11. Unidentified artist's depiction of George Jones for 'SHAKSPEARE'S HOUSE. – MULBERRY COLLEGE,' *Punch* (2 October 1847), 13:121.
12. Richard Doyle, 'PUNCH'S VISION AT STRATFORD-ON-AVON. THE NIGHT OF THE SIXTEENTH OF SEPTEMBER,' *Punch* (13 November 1847), 13:184.
13. John Tenniel, 'SHAKSPEARE AND THE PIGMIES,' *Punch* (30 January 1864), 46:45.
14. Unidentified artist, 'ERECTED TO THE MEMORY OF THE LONDON NATIONAL TERCENTENARY COMMITTEE, APRIL 23, 1864, BY THEIR FRIEND AND COUNSELLOR, MR. PUNCH,' *Punch* (7 May 1864), 46:193.
15. Unidentified artist, 'AWFUL APPARITION OF THE BARD AT MRS. SCRIMMINGE'S TEA-FIGHT,' *Punch* (6 February 1864), 46:60.
16. John Leech, 'DINNER-TIME AT THE CRYSTAL PALACE,' *Punch* (5 July 1851), 21:16.
17. Edward J. Wheeler, '"MODUS OPERANDI." (The Covent Garden Government, and Her Majesty's Opposition.),' *Punch* (22 June 1889), 96:301.
18. Bernard Partridge, 'FANCY PORTRAIT. QUITE TOO-TOO PUFFICKLY PRECIOUS!! Being Lady Windy-mère's Fan-cy Portrait of the new dramatic author, Shakspeare Sheridan Oscar Puff, Esq,' *Punch* (5 March 1892), 102:113.
19. Harry Furniss, 'IMMORTALITY INDEED!' *Punch* (20 October 1888), 95:185.
20. Linley Sambourne, 'PIG-HEADED ATTACK ON THE IMMORTAL BARD,' *Punch* (10 December 1887), 93:273.
21. Harry Furniss, 'PICTORIAL NOTE TO HAMLET,' *Punch* (3 January 1891), 100:11.
22. Unidentified artist, amateur actor (Tomkins) dressed as Hamlet, *Punch* (18 September 1897), 113:126.
23. G. R., 'THE MODERN PISTOL,' *Punch* (24 May 1890), 98:245.

24. Edward Tennyson Reed, 'THE LONDON COUNTY COUNCIL AND THE LYCEUM THEATRE. APPEAL OF MR. HENRY IRVING. RESULT,' *Punch* (8 March 1890), 98:109.
25. Unidentified artist, 'THE CUR-RIBS OF NEW YORK,' *Punch* (2 June 1849), 16:217.
26. John Tenniel, 'PUNCH'S ILLUSTRATIONS TO SHAKSPEARE,' *Punch* (8 September 1855), 29:93.
27. Edward J. Wheeler, 'RICHARD HIMSELF AGAIN,' *Punch* (6 April 1889), 96:157.
28. Linley Sambourne, 'PUNCH'S FANCY PORTRAITS. – NO. 75. HENRY IRVING,' *Punch* (18 March 1882), 82:130.
29. Edward J. Wheeler, 'THEATRICAL WEATHER-BOX. Irving goes in for Canada; Wilson Barrett comes out as Hamlet,' *Punch* (25 October 1884), 87:196.
30. Harry Furniss, initial letter 'M' for 'SHAKSPEARE IN TOWN,' *Punch* (12 January 1889), 96:15.
31. Unidentified artist, 'UN "CARR" D'HEURE IN THE NEW HALLÉRY GALLERY,' *Punch* (25 May 1889), 96:254.
32. Bernard Partridge, 'HIS MAD-JESTY AT THE LYCEUM,' *Punch* (19 November 1892), 103:233.
33. Unidentified artist, 'THE ACADEMY GUY'D,' *Punch* (21 May 1887), 92:251.
34. Bernard Partridge, 'GREAT ATTRACTION!' *Punch* (31 May 1899), 116:258.
35. Charles Keene, 'THE BRITISH DRAMA, 1883,' *Punch* Almanack (7 December 1882), 84:n.p.
36. Bernard Partridge, 'LOOK HERE, UPON THIS PICTURE AND ON THIS!' *Punch* (13 February 1892), 102:73.
37. Edward J. Wheeler, 'THE OPERA-GOER'S DIARY,' *Punch* (2 August 1890), 99:53.
38. Edward Tennyson Reed, 'AT THE ITALIAN OPERA,' *Punch* (31 October 1891), 101:209.
39. Edward J. Wheeler, 'OPERA-GOER'S DIARY,' *Punch* (11 June 1892), 102:280.
40. Edward Tennyson Reed, 'THE OPERA-GOER'S DIARY,' *Punch* (9 June 1894), 106:273.

41. William Newman, 'SHAKSPEARE RESTORED,' *Punch* (10 October 1846), 11:153.
42. Unidentified artist, 'BALLET OF "LADY MACBETH,"' *Punch* (2 December 1843), 5:240.
43. William Newman, 'SHAKSPEARE AT ASTLEY'S,' *Punch* (3 July 1847), 12:269.
44. John Tenniel, 'MACBETH AT ASTLEY'S,' *Punch* (10 January 1857), 32:13.
45. Unidentified artist (after Sir Thomas Lawrence), 'THE COURT AT DRURY LANE THEATRE,' *Punch* (15 July 1848), 15:32.
46. John Leech (unsigned), 'HAMLET IN THE LONDON CHURCHYARD,' *Punch* (13 October 1849), 17:147.
47. Linley Sambourne, 'MR PUNCH'S PARALLELS. NO. 7. (After a Celebrated Picture.),' *Punch* (28 April 1888), 94:194.
48. Charles Keene, 'TECHNICAL,' *Punch* (2 September 1871), 61:92.
49. Richard Doyle, 'HIGH ART AND THE ROYAL ACADEMY,' *Punch* (14:197).
50. John Tenniel, 'LITTLE VICTIMS,' *Punch* (28 August 1880), 79:91.
51. William McConnell, 'PUNCH AMONG THE PAINTERS,' *Punch* (24 May 1851), 20:219.
52. George du Maurier, 'ABOMINATIONS OF MODERN SCIENCE,' *Punch* (30 January 1892), 102:53.
53. Edward Tennyson Reed, 'ROYAL ACADEMY PEEPS,' *Punch* (8 May 1897), 112:226.
54. John Leech, 'MAC-BULL AND THE RAILWAY WITCHES,' *Punch* (18 November 1848), 15:215.
55. John Tenniel, 'KATHLEEN AND PETRUCHIO,' *Punch* (12 December 1891), 101:283.

Chapter One

Punch and its Readers, Writers and Artists

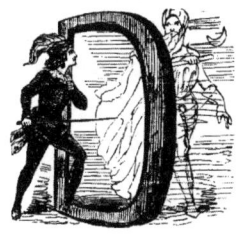uring the second half of 1841 and throughout the remaining sixty years of the Victorian era, *Punch* demonstrated a sustained and knowledgeable love of the works of Shakespeare. As the successive chapters of this study will demonstrate, the writers and artists who contributed to *Punch* took for granted that a common acquaintance with Shakespeare could be assumed among its readers. To appreciate the extent to which *Punch* in the nineteenth century both reflected and contributed to the cultural status of Shakespeare, it is first necessary to know certain features of the history of *Punch*. One needs to know, too, something about the readers of *Punch*. Who were they, and what was the level of their acquaintance with Shakespeare? One needs also to know a little about the magazine's editors, writers, and artists. Who were they, and what were their interests in Shakespeare?

The Early Years of *Punch*

The birth of *Punch, or the London Charivari* in 1841, its miraculous early survival against all odds, its rapid rise in popularity, and its transformation into a major cultural institution is one of the great success stories in the history of journalism (Spielmann 1895a; Cruse 1935, 390–408; Price 1957; Altick 1997, xvii–xxix, 1–40, 732–736). Founded in part in imitation of Charles Philipon's Paris daily *Le Charivari*, which had three pages of satirical letterpress and a single large engraving (Daumier was one of its chief artists), and using the very limited capital put up by the wood-engraver Ebenezer Landells, *Punch* brought together a heterogeneous group of aspiring writers and artists. They began by producing a prospectus for a three-penny weekly, 'A NEW WORK OF WIT AND WHIM, EMBELLISHED WITH CUTS AND CARICATURES' each issue to be of sixteen pages. The preliminary business contract was signed by Henry Mayhew, Mark Lemon, Joseph Stirling Coyne, Ebenezer Landells, and Joseph Last, the printer. Mayhew, Lemon, and Coyne were to be joint editors, and Landells, who had been a pupil of Thomas Bewick for a brief period, was to be the engraver and supply graphic items in accordance with ideas suggested to him by the editors. The artists involved were Archibald S. Henning, who designed the first cover and contributed eleven designs to the first volume, Thomas Brine, John Phillips, H. G. Hine, and William Newman. Joseph Last would be the printer, the initial publisher being R. Bryant.

When the magazine began to appear, various additional writers, most notably Douglas Jerrold, also contributed. As promised, the price per issue was 3d (special mailed copies would cost 4d), a price that remained unchanged until 1917. However, apart from an initial success with the first issue of 17 July, sales remained flat at between five and six thousand copies. To make the paper viable, something like ten thousand copies was the necessary goal. When Joseph Last withdrew from the venture, prospects took a turn for the worse. On the verge of foundering, *Punch* looked as though it would meet the fate of many another short-lived serial publication of the period.

It was at this point that the publication of *Punch*'s first Almanack at the beginning of 1842 achieved an immense instant success (Prager 1979, 42). Probably the idea of Henry Mayhew, who wrote most of it, the Almanack sold some 90,000 copies in a single week, according to a claim made by Ebenezer Landells that was later recorded by *Punch*'s rather sceptical historian (Spielmann 1895a, 33). This success, whatever the exact numbers, prompted the printing firm of Bradbury & Evans to negotiate the purchase of *Punch* during the months that followed, and, by the end of the year, this company was firmly established as the proprietor of the young publication. William Bradbury and Frederick Evans had developed a very successful printing business that made use of the latest technology (see below), including a massive steam-driven cylinder press (Moran 1973, 129; Leary 2002, 171–172, 177–178), and they were used to handling materials that involved large numbers of wood engravings. Indeed, they were ideally positioned, though they could not have anticipated it, to be the printers of the most successful and long-lasting comic magazine ever. The company had already established a sterling record as printers of works by two of the most popular of nineteenth-century writers – Dickens and Thackeray. Bradbury & Evans (though not the publishers) had already printed the former writer's illustrated monthly serials *Pickwick Papers* (1836–37), *Sketches by Boz* (1837–39), and *Nicholas Nickleby* (1838–39), together with the weekly illustrated serial *Master Humphrey's Clock* (1840–41), which contained *Barnaby Rudge* and the spectacularly successful *Old Curiosity Shop*.

The alliance of *Punch* with Bradbury & Evans, though obviously essential to the survival of the fledgling weekly, came at a fortuitous moment for Bradbury & Evans. Dickens's *Master Humphrey's Clock* was a sixteen-page weekly serial, costing 3d and well furnished with woodcuts. It thus anticipated *Punch* in both format and price. With sales that reached as high as 100,000 in response to Little Nell's death, the printers may have been only too pleased to take on *Punch* when the Dickens series ended in November 1841 (Leary 2002, 182; Patten 1978, 109–110). But Dickens's association with Bradbury & Evans was by no means at an end. In 1844, he left his former publishers Chapman and Hall for Bradbury & Evans. This latter (as both printer and publisher) then brought out *The Chimes* (1844) and three further Christmas books in subsequent years, along with *Dombey and Son* (1846–48), *David Copperfield* (1849–50), *Bleak House* (1852–53), *Little Dorrit* (1855–57), and the periodical *Household Words*, which in 1854 serialized *Hard Times*. Dickens, though a close associate of the *Punch* staff and a particular friend of Mark Lemon until 1858 (Dexter 1927, 153–154; Schlicke 1985, 144), never contributed to the magazine, though he is said to have been a frequent visitor to the *Punch* table (Dexter 1927, 100). Thackeray, however, was a regular contributor to *Punch* while at the same time having Bradbury & Evans as his prime publisher for some eleven years. During that period, the firm printed the monthly parts of *Vanity Fair* (1847–48), *The History of Pendennis* (1849–50), *The Newcomes* (1853–55), *The Virginians*

(1857–59), and (in book form) *The History of Samuel Titmarsh and the Great Hoggarty Diamond* (1849), as well as three volumes of *Miscellanies*. Clearly *Punch* was in good hands.

Technology and the Mass Production Distribution of Punch

Maintaining *Punch*'s topical immediacy and getting each new issue quickly into the hands of its readers outside London were challenges that the *Punch* owners surmounted by various means. Fundamental from the start was the decision to use wood engravings for any visual material. Wood engravings, though not capable of reproducing the fine detail and tonal nuances of copper or steel engravings, had the great advantage that they could be quick to produce. Even more advantageous was the fact that wood engravings, unlike copper or steel engravings, could be set up and printed at the same time as the letterpress text with a single pass of the paper sheets through the press. By contrast, metal plates had to be printed on a separate press so that whenever letterpress and copper or steel engravings appeared on the same page, the sheet containing that page had to pass through two different presses.

Wood engraving was even more advantageous if the designer drew directly onto the wood block, or, as was more commonly the case, transferred his drawing to the block by means of tracing paper. Most of the *Punch* artists did this (Morris 2005, 108–109), and the engraver then used this drawing as the basis for cutting away any white space to leave the lines exposed on the block. The wood blocks were made of boxwood, which was in theory sufficiently hard to be able to withstand the rigors of a long print run. However, unlike other companies producing material with long print runs, Bradbury & Evans for many years took the enormous risk of printing *Punch* directly from letterpress and wood blocks, rather than making stereotypes of the original material first and thus guarding against the particular danger of a wood block breaking. It was the time constraints under which *Punch* operated that necessitated such a risk. Only after a print run was complete did the printers pause to make electrotypes, thereby enabling the future production of reprints and the important semi-annual volumes (Spielmann 1895a, 250–251).

To further increase the speed of production, the large blocks, such as those used for the one-page weekly big cuts, were from about 1860 cut into six smaller blocks and divided among several engravers, who would then work simultaneously, drastically reducing production time (Spielmann 1895a, 249). Much later, as a development of photography, the artists' drawings were photographed directly on to the block. Then, in the early 1890s, wood blocks were replaced by metal process blocks, and the spaces between lines were cut away (etched) by acid rather than the engraver's knife. Such techniques, while serving to improve the accurate reproduction of artists' designs, also saved time and hence produced considerable financial savings (Spielmann 1895a, 251).

Allied to these time-saving and cost-saving features was the development in the early nineteenth century of high speed, power-driven printing presses, a momentous technological step that laid the foundation for mass publications that could be produced and made ready for circulation literally overnight if required. In 1833, Bradbury & Evans moved their printing works to a new location on Lombard Street and installed a steam-driven cylinder printing machine capable of producing 4,200 impressions an hour ("Mr. Punch at Dinner" 1926, 63; Leary 2002, 171). The fast production made possible by such a machine was matched by fast delivery. *Punch* was assisted in this by the new and growing system of railways throughout Britain that ensured prompt distribution to many towns and villages. To get the weekly issues on to the stalls of news agents and booksellers, *Punch* early on contracted for help with W. S. Orr & Company, the experienced London agent of Chambers of Edinburgh. Furthermore, news agents and booksellers were assisted in carrying *Punch* through the use of a 'sale or return' policy (Spielmann 1895a, 36; Price 1957, 26).

Another marketing device that helped with sales and circulation was the use of 'stamped' copies, something that began with the second issue in January 1843. This permitted copies of *Punch* that were bought stamped for a modest extra fee of 1d to be sent 'free' by post, and these same copies could then be re-mailed (and apparently often were) at no further expense, thereby adding significantly to the number of readers per copy. Though *Punch* still had to bear the tax on paper, that tax had been reduced in 1837 from 3½d to 1½d a lb. (it would be abolished in 1861). All such reductions in expenses, including a dramatic drop in the price of paper following the introduction of machine-made paper during the early 1800s (Plant 1974, 331), encouraged the creation of cheap publications like *Punch* directed towards a mass readership.

The Readership of *Punch*

But the early success of *Punch* was not just a matter of obtaining stable funding from such a well-established publisher and printer as Bradbury & Evans. Nor was it just a case of the strategic choice of production technologies. More important (and certainly more significant to the subject of this study) were other less tangible matters. First, as readers quickly discovered, *Punch* did not indulge in sensationalist ribaldry and scurrility, as had long been the tradition among comic papers (Altick 1997, xvii, 1–10). As one of its proprietors would remark at a dinner in 1862 celebrating *Punch*'s twenty-first anniversary, 'Ribaldry and dirt were inseparable from comicality until Punch came' (Ray 1955, 1:348). Indeed, as Bradbury & Evans had quickly discovered, *Punch*'s refusal to include anything offensive had given it access to drawing rooms everywhere, for this was a publication that could be placed before females and children. As early as May 1842, an advertisement for *Punch* in *Bentley's Miscellany* made this very point, noting that *Punch* 'may safely be introduced into the family circle, where it will provoke many a hearty laugh, but never can call a blush to the most delicate cheek. It is almost the first comic periodical we ever saw which was not vulgar' (quoted Altick 1997, 10). By the end of that same year, even the *Times* (27 December) was pleased to praise *Punch*'s propriety 'and the total exclusion from its pages of all that is gross, low, or coarsely personal,' while the *Somerset County Gazette* declared, 'It is the first comic we ever saw which was not vulgar. It will provoke many a hearty laugh, but never call a blush to the most delicate cheek' (quoted Spielmann 1895a, 30).

Years later, Charles Knight, a printer and publisher who from the first had greatly admired *Punch*, remarked in his autobiography that 'It is the rare merit of Mark Lemon [the first editor of *Punch*] that no impurity ever sullied the work of which he is the Editor, – that under his guidance Wit has thought it no restraint "to dwell in decencies for ever"' (Knight 1865, 2:269). Then, in the 1870 obituary for Lemon, *Punch* commented on this same matter:

> But if this Journal has had the good fortune to be credited with habitual advocacy of truth and justice, if it has been praised for abstinence from the less worthy kind of satire, if it has been trusted by those who keep guard over the purity of womanhood and youth, we, the best witnesses, turn for a moment from our sorrow to bear the fullest and the most willing testimony that the high and noble spirit of Mark Lemon ever prompted generous championship, ever made unworthy onslaught or irreverent jest impossible to the pens of those who were honoured in being coadjutors with him. (58:219)

Whether planned as a marketing strategy or not, the editorial policy referred to here of adhering to fun that kept within the bounds of acceptable decency helped ensure a much broader readership for *Punch* than it might otherwise have had. Included in that readership were generations of young people who grew up reading *Punch* in the family circle where the annual volumes of the magazine were often part of the family library. There is also some evidence that boys' boarding schools had *Punch* on the shelves of their libraries. Thus, huge numbers of young people ordinarily denied access to newspapers were given access to up-to-date commentary on modern world affairs (modern history was not taught in schools) and important domestic social and political issues (Dixon 1986, 144; Morris 2005, 244–245).

Circulation figures in *Punch*'s early years were also strengthened by its various literary 'hits', among them the publication of the instantly popular 'The Song of the Shirt' by Thomas Hood in 1843, and three very popular comic series: Jerrold's 'Mrs. Caudle's Curtain Lectures' in 1845; Thackeray's 'The Diary of C. Keames de la Pluche, Esq.' in 1845–46, which dealt with the current mania for speculation in railway shares; and the same author's 'The Snobs of England' in

1846–47. Such early successes helped establish the reputation of *Punch* as a publication of witty comic humour of the highest order. They also transformed what Bradbury & Evans may at first have considered a fairly speculative venture into a paying enterprise with a healthy-looking future. Another source of the attractiveness of *Punch* to readers, and hence something advantageous to circulation figures, were *Punch*'s political commentaries, and particularly its political big cuts that often contained caricatures of leading politicians. Initially, these tended to be the work of John Leech (he contributed his first full-page political engraving, entitled 'Foreign Affairs' on 7 August 1841) and later of John Tenniel during the last four decades of the century. Often they contained material based on Shakespeare's plays, something that will be discussed in a later chapter, but they were clearly from the first a major selling feature of the new publication.

The broad appeal of *Punch* and the composition of its readership from its earliest years can be deduced from a wide range of evidence, as Amy Cruse and Richard Altick have demonstrated (Cruse 1935, 391–408; Altick 1997, 17–29). Readers even included the Queen and Prince Consort. However, the reaction to *Punch* by the Queen was understandably a mixed one. We know that 'Though at first she liked it very well', its constant criticism of her eventually caused her to turn *Punch* 'out of the Palace' (Hodgson 1883, 58, quoted Slater 2002, 169). Other readers included members of both Houses of Parliament, lawyers, judges, clerics, frequenters of clubs and coffee houses, law and college students, schoolboys, and innumerable middle and upper class households. Regular readers also included a wide assortment of literary men and women, among them Elizabeth Barrett, Robert Browning, Thomas Carlyle, Edward Fitzgerald, the Brontës, Elizabeth Gaskell, Leigh Hunt, Charles Knight, and Charles Dodgson (Lewis Carroll). The early volumes of *Punch* were even part of the extensive libraries in the ships *Erebus* and *Terror* when John Franklin's ill-fated expedition set out in search of the north-west passage in May 1845. No doubt the copies of *Punch* provided some initial solace when the ships became tragically ice-bound during subsequent arctic winters.

It is likely also that *Punch* had its share of working-class readers, too, although concrete evidence is very scant. Aware of this, Altick engagingly fantasizes about discarded copies finding their way below stairs in middle-class households, and he alludes to an incident that Thackeray witnessed in a country inn yard where the poet Arthur Hugh Clough sat down and began 'to teach a child to read off a bit of Punch w^h was lying on the ground'. As Altick also points out, just as the London gentlemen's clubs would probably have had subscriptions to *Punch* (perhaps even multiple subscriptions), the reading rooms of the gentrified mechanics' institutes in provincial cities likely offered access to copies of *Punch* as well (Altick 1997, 35, 39; Thackeray 1945–46, 2:580). In due course, *Punch* became well-known on the Continent, and in the United States, and piracy of *Punch* (that ultimate back-handed compliment) began in 1845, a particularly egregious offender being the arch pirate, *Harper's New Monthly Magazine*. In the United States, *Punch* seems to have been regular reading material for many literary figures. Henry Wadsworth Longfellow, Ralph Waldo Emerson, Walt Whitman, James Russell Lowell, Herman Melville, Henry James, Emily Dickinson, and James Parton, for example, were all either subscribers or readers.

Collectively, all the evidence suggests that *Punch* had a very broad and loyal readership. Almost as up-to-date in its topicality as any of the daily newspapers, *Punch* itself provided a subject of conversation in tens of thousands of homes, and in other venues such as those mentioned above. Precise circulation and readership numbers are, however, difficult to specify, and estimates for weekly sales in the early decades have ranged from about 22,000 to 61,000. Readership is, of course, a separate issue, and again estimates vary. A conservative view would calculate readership at five persons per copy, but anecdotal evidence and what little we know about the availability of periodicals in coffee houses, gentlemen's clubs, and gentrified mechanics' institutes would suggest a much higher multiple would be nearer the truth (Spielmann 1895a, 28, 31, 33, 49, 251; Morris 1985, 310 n. 2; Altick 1997, 35–40; Leary 2002, 180, 210–211).

The Familiarity of the Punch *Readership with Shakespeare*

The writers and artists who worked for *Punch* appear to have assumed that those who read the magazine had a fairly close familiarity with Shakespeare. This need not surprise us. Already by 1814, Jane Austen is able to have Henry Crawford remark in *Mansfield Park* that Shakespeare 'is a part of an Englishman's constitution'. Shakespeare's

> thoughts and beauties are so spread abroad that one touches them every where, one is intimate with him by instinct. [...] His celebrated passages are quoted by every body; they are in half of the books we open, and we all talk Shakespeare, use his similes, and describe with his descriptions.

As a result, 'Shakespeare one gets acquainted with without knowing how' (Austen 1934, 3:338). Twenty-six years later, and just before the appearance of the first issue of *Punch*, Shakespeare's reputation had risen to almost god-like status. Thomas Carlyle, who himself would be a regular subscriber to *Punch* (Altick 1997, 256–257), proclaimed in 'The Hero as Poet' (May 12 1840) that Shakespeare was 'a *Prophet*', and 'a Priest of Mankind', and 'a blessed heaven-sent Bringer of Light'. According to Carlyle,

> the best judgement not of this country only, but of Europe at large, is slowly pointing to the conclusion, that Shakspeare is the chief of all Poets hitherto; the greatest intellect who, in our recorded world, has left record of himself in the way of Literature. (Quoted Taylor 1991, 167)

How all this came about and how, beginning in the eighteenth century and growing exponentially during the nineteenth century, Shakespeare's influence became deeply embedded in Western culture are matters that have been discussed elsewhere (Taylor 1991, Ch. 4; Lanier 2002, 29–49; Young 2002, Chs. 1 and 2). Central to the explanation of this phenomenon, and closely paralleling the story of *Punch*, is the way in which technical advances in printing, publishing, and distribution permitted affordable editions of Shakespeare to reach even working-class families. Although people living in London and the larger provincial cities were able to become acquainted with Shakespeare by attending stage performances, access to the texts within homes, schools, and other venues with libraries or reading rooms was possibly a far greater factor in establishing Shakespeare's pre-eminent cultural status.

This is not the place to attempt a detailed survey of the great flood of Shakespeare texts that appeared during the nineteenth century, but several matters relevant to my argument here require mention. First, given the apparent attraction of affordable publications containing visual material, *Punch* being a notable example, it is worth noting that among the hundreds of nineteenth-century editions of Shakespeare, many were illustrated. About twenty such illustrated editions had appeared in the first decade of the century and hence well before the advent of *Punch*, but as the century progressed, the numbers grew, rising to an average of about fifty in the decade of the 1850s and falling back to about twenty in the final decade of the century (Ashton 1980, iv; Young 2002, 90). By an intriguing co-incidence, one of the most popular of the illustrated editions was in the process of serial publication at the time that *Punch* first appeared. Charles Knight's *The Pictorial Edition of the Works of Shakspere* began monthly serial publication in fifty-six parts, beginning in 1838 through to 1843. Like *Punch,* Knight's edition made copious use of the cheap process of wood engraving to provide close to a thousand illustrations (Murphy 2003, 174), far more than had ever been used in any previous edition of Shakespeare. Knight also used power-driven presses and the latest technological developments in printing to establish a mass circulation at the lowest possible price (Knight 1854, 248–256). Like the proprietors of *Punch*, Knight also made use of an increasingly sophisticated retail network to market his publication throughout the United Kingdom, and, like *Punch*, Knight's publication seems to have sought after a wide audience.

Here, one cannot help wondering about another possible parallel. To what degree did those involved in the collaborative endeavour of producing *Punch* share Knight's deep-rooted belief in the power of pictorial material as an agent within 'intellectual culture' that had the potential to be 'true eye-knowledge' and that could 'add both to the information and enjoyment of the reader' (Knight 1864, 2:262, 284; 3:82; Young 202, 92)? Admittedly, the prime goal of *Punch* may have been humorous entertainment, but behind the mask of jocularity was a consistent strain of political seriousness and (especially in its earlier years) a relatively radical vision of the need for social reform. In the case of literary matters, and in particular in the case of Shakespeare, as the next chapter will show, *Punch* seems to have seen itself, like Charles Knight, the editor and publisher, as an educative agent that sought to reform and shape popular taste so that the greatest writer in the English language could be fully appreciated by the widest possible readership.

Not surprisingly, *Punch* expressed warm praise for Knight's edition when it first appeared in its final eight-volume format. Early in 1843, *Punch* included a brief letter purportedly from Edward Fitzball of Red-Fire Cottage. In it the anonymous author expressed admiration for Knight's edition and praised it for 'the taste, the learning, the industry, the rein made manifest' (4:62). A year later, Percival Leigh contributed an elaborate one-page piece (complete with graphic designs by Thackeray) that pretended to report on 'a most affecting' incident that occurred in one of the boxes at Drury Lane when Colley Cibber's version of *Richard III* was recently performed. A party, 'not having heard how Cibber had mangled Shakespeare's tragedy, had brought with them Knight's illustrated edition of the original text.' As is then explained, 'the desponding air with which they endeavoured to reconcile what they had in their hands with what they saw on the stage, was immensely impressive' (6:64). Leigh then follows this with the text of an 'Operatic Sketch' that dramatizes in full the difficulties of the party in the box, who hand from one to another the 2/6d copy of Knight (this was indeed the price of each serial part) that they have brought with them. A lady sings a recitative: 'Oh mournful times! Oh days of dark abuse – / We've got a book of not the slightest use.' An air then follows:

>While roaming in the city
>Near Paul's majestic dome,
>We saw this book so pretty –
>We said, 'Let's take it home.'
>With forms of warriors manly,
>The wondrous page was strown;
>We lik'd the face of Stanly,
>And made the book our own.

The opera proceeds in similar vein, and ironically the disgruntled and confused purchasers of Knight's work are only satisfied when they are told to shut the book and 'only mind the play'. A few months after this, Knight was again praised by *Punch* when Jerrold, a particular friend of Knight, ironically reported that Queen Victoria had made CHARLES LES KNITE' Baron of Stratford-on-Avon and had presented him with 'her portrait set in precious diamonds' for publishing Shakespeare's works' (6:220). Of course, the Queen had done no such thing, but the implication was that she should have, so important a contribution had Knight made.

Within a year of its initial publication, the images in Knight's edition were pirated in the United States, along with those of Kenny Meadows, a prolific designer and *Punch* artist, whose main body of work between 1839 and 1843 had been the design of over one thousand illustrations for a three-volume edition of *The Works of Shakspere* edited by Barry Cornwall (the pseudonym for Bryan Waller Procter). These early Victorian illustrated editions by Knight and Cornwall and the composite pirated edition across the Atlantic are particularly significant here because they catered to a readership anxious to own a copy of Shakespeare, particularly one that was profusely illustrated. As might be expected, other copiously illustrated editions followed. One was Howard Staunton's *Shakespeare's Works*, published in fifty monthly parts at a shilling per play, leading to a final three-volume format in the years 1858, 1859, and 1860. This contained over 831 wood engravings by John Gilbert, an artist who worked sporadically for *Punch* between 1842 and 1882 (Spielmann.1895a, 450–451; Young 2002, 96). Another illustrated edition designed for a broad popular market appeared a few years later. Edited by the husband and wife team of Charles and Mary Cowden Clarke (it seems clear that much of the labour was by the latter), *The Plays of William Shakespeare* appeared between 1864 and 1869 in 270 weekly parts and was then gathered into three volumes. The work was richly illustrated with over 600 wood engravings designed by Henry Courtney Selous, the portrait and landscape painter (Young 2002, 99; Murphy 2003, 175).

Knight's edition was not as cheap as he may have wished. In its completed eight-volume format, which included Knight's biography of Shakespeare, it cost £7 7s. As noted above, the theatre party described by Leigh paid 2s. 6d. for their copy of *Richard III*. Price does not appear to have been a deterrent even to that important segment of its readership composed, according to Percy Muir, of 'earnest artisans who formed the bulk of the audiences for such lecturers as Samuel Smiles and the membership of the Mechanics' Institutes that sprang up all over the country in the thirties and forties' (Muir 1971, 18). Regardless of the class status (whether artisan, lower middle, or middle class), because of the status accorded to the family copy of Shakespeare, many households must have felt it to be worth the considerable financial sacrifice necessary to make the purchase of one of the available complete editions of Shakespeare (Marder 1963, 18–19). To have a copy of Shakespeare in the home was respectable, educationally worthy, and highly desirable, as the Preface to the Cowden Clarkes's illustrated Shakespeare makes very clear:

> No household that aims at home culture can now be without a copy of Shakespeare; no domestic circle, that justly looks upon social reading aloud as a means of true happiness and improvement, can think itself duly provided without this among its books, however few the number may be to which due economy limits its cherished store. (I:vii)

As the century progressed, such aspirations were more and more easily satisfied as the costs of collected Shakespeares (whether illustrated or not) steadily declined, something dramatically reflected in the single-volume 1864 Globe Shakespeare with an announced price of 3s. 6d. Subsequent competing editions would cost as little as one shilling, and in 1890 Ward and Lock even published a *Sixpenny Shakespeare* (Murphy 2003, 175–178, 281).

Such editions as have just been mentioned deliberately sought after as wide a readership as possible. The Cowden Clarkes especially were anxious to produce a text that could be read in a family environment in the presence of both women and children. In keeping with this, their text was carefully sanitized, and anything thought to be 'coarse and unfit for modern utterance' (I:vii) was cut. Such was also the practice in another burgeoning market – editions of Shakespeare designed for schools. When Shakespeare became a regular part of the school curriculum in the latter half of the century (Murphy 2003, 181–186), a new type of Shakespeare publication developed to cater for the needs of the schools and to assist pupils prepare for public examinations. Oxford University Press's *Clarendon* series of seventeen plays, the first volume of which appeared in 1868, and Cambridge University Press's later *Pitt Press* series, the first volume of which appeared in 1890, were both extremely successful examples, and both were still being used in English schools well into the twentieth century. Like other school texts, they played a major role in familiarising successive generations with Shakespeare.

Alongside editions of Shakespeare, other types of very popular Shakespeareana contributed to the general familiarity with Shakespeare's works. Though published in 1807, for example, Charles and Mary Lamb's *Tales from Shakspear* and its various imitations, among them Caroline Maxwell's *The Juvenile Edition of Shakspeare: Adapted to the Capacities of Youth* (1828), enjoyed enormous popularity throughout the century. We know that between 1807 and 1873 there were fifteen editions of *Tales from Shakspear* and sixteen reprints in the 1880s alone (Taylor 1991, 208). Not surprisingly, the work did not escape humorous notice in *Punch* since the potential for punning jokes on the authors' surname and the first word of their title proved irresistible on at least three occasions (4:250; 96:33; 112:9). Collections of quotations, already made popular in the previous century by William Dodd's *Beauties of Shakespeare* (1752), retained their attraction. In England between 1818 and 1879, there were at least thirteen further editions of Dodd's anthology, and there were large numbers of other compilations of quotations from Shakespeare. The Folger Shakespeare Library lists some twenty-three such works published in England between 1841 and 1900. Such works helped to make familiar certain lines and passages from Shakespeare, in many instances the same ones as *Punch* often quoted or alluded to.

Particularly popular and also influential in making Shakespeare familiar were works on his heroines, among them Anna Brownell Jameson's *Characteristics of Women, Moral, Poetical, and Historical* (1832), which went through nearly twenty editions by the end of the century, Mary Cowden Clarke's *The Girlhood of Shakespeare's*

Heroines in a Series of Tales (printed serially in 1850–52), and Helen Faucit's *On Some of Shakespeare's Female Characters* (1885). Such works were often illustrated. Those by Jameson and Clarke were, and Jameson even provided fifty graphic vignettes of her own for the first edition of her work. Other publications on the same kind of subject consisted of collections of engravings, accompanied by appropriate Shakespearean quotations. Charles Heath's *The Shakespeare Gallery; Containing the Principal Female Characters in the Plays of the Great Poet* [1836–37] with its forty-five steel engravings, his second and more popular set of engravings, *The Heroines of Shakespeare* (1848), of which there were four more editions to 1883, and W. G. Standfust's *The Beauties of Shakspeare. With Fifty-Two Engravings* [n.d.] were all examples of this kind of publication, as was *The Graphic Gallery of Shakespeare's Heroines* that was published by Sampson Low, Marston, Searle & Rivington in 1888, with a further edition in 1896. Such sets of engravings clearly had a very wide circulation and were sold with a middle-class market in mind. They could be contemplated when set out on a table and kept in a portfolio, or they could be framed and used as wall decorations (Young 2002, 84).

For those living close enough to London and able to afford the entry fees, the annual London art exhibitions, particularly those of the Royal Academy and the British Institution, were another means by which large numbers of people increased their familiarity with Shakespeare. The reason for this was that the exhibitions frequently included compositions depicting Shakespearean characters and scenes. These events generated considerable interest. By the end of the century, the Royal Academy exhibitions were attracting between 350,000 and 400,000 people, and the private viewing and annual dinner before the public opening were two of the most prestigious social events of the London 'Season' (Forbes 1975, 7). Not surprisingly, the interest in the art exhibitions was then reflected in printed commentaries (and sometimes reproductions) in newspapers and magazines. *The Graphic*, *The Art Journal* and *The Art Annual*, for example, all regularly published reviews and reproductions of exhibit works. As we shall see in a later chapter, *Punch*, too, reported almost every year on the exhibitions and often included its own visual burlesques of items on display, including those with subject-matter based on Shakespeare. Not only did the exhibitions offer visual representations of Shakespearean material, but the accompanying catalogues tended to include relevant quotations from Shakespeare to provide a textual context for the paintings on display.

The above selected examples all indicate that familiarity with Shakespeare could (and was) taken for granted among the bulk of *Punch*'s readers. That familiarity could involve attendance at theatrical productions, but it was, as I have indicated, just as likely to stem from a great variety of textual sources that, apart from the plays themselves, included all manner of other works offering quotations, commentaries, and re-tellings of the plots. Collectively, these all added to the familiarity with Shakespeare that Jane Austen's character had remarked upon in the early years of the century.

The Identity of Mr. Punch

To this point, I have freely referred to *Punch,* its voice, its policies, views, and activities as a single entity. But before proceeding, a qualification needs to be registered. The journalistic convention, by no means one exclusive to *Punch* in the Victorian era, of having a single voice represent the collective product of a group of writers and (in this instance) graphic artists was something that *Punch* from the first fought hard to establish. Central to the way in which this was done was the creation of a fictional personality, Mr. Punch. The writers could refer to him at will, often using him as the supposed author of their compositions. He could, for example, be sent on assignments to report on theatrical productions; he could take holidays; and he could write and respond to letters. He could also be an instantly recognizable figure in graphic designs created by the *Punch* artists. As a puppet figure, Punch had long been familiar in England, but whereas this puppet ancestor could be rough, ribald, violent, and resistant to authority, the Mr. Punch (the 'Mr.' was a significant addition) that Victorians came to know from the pages of the comic magazine evolved within a decade or so into 'a scholar and a gentleman', and 'the incarnation of all that is best in wit and virtue' (Spielmann 1895a, 4). He was a protean figure, at home in almost any situation, as Thackeray pointed out in a piece he wrote for the December 1854 issue of the *Quarterly Review*:

> He goes into the very best company; he keeps a stud at Melton; he has a moor in Scotland; he rides in the Park; has his stall at the Opera; is constantly dining out at clubs and in private society; and goes every night in the season to balls and parties, where you see the most beautiful women possible. He is welcomed amongst his new friends the great; though, like the good old English gentleman of the song, he does not forget the small. He pats the heads of street boys and girls; relishes the jokes of Jack the costermonger and Bob the dustman; good-naturedly spied out Molly the cook flirting with policeman X, or Mary the nursemaid as she listens to the fascinating guardsman. (Thackeray 1854, 96:81)

Visually, Mr. Punch appeared in a great variety of guises, ranging from buffoon to wise, high-minded gentleman, even saint (20:136). In the early years of *Punch*, he appeared as Diogenes (9:203), as a jockey (10:214), as a physician (1:163), as an angel (11:202), as a Quaker (12:169); as the Pope (13:135), as a railway porter (14:211), as a police magistrate (18:107), and as a bootblack (20:166), to name only a few of his many different graphic manifestations (Altick 1997, 59–60). Instant recognition, whatever his current role, was provided by his recurring physiological features: his deformed pointed chin and nose, his protruding stomach, and his hunched back (Spielmann 1895a, 7–9). The gentlemanly Mr. Punch, however, in the hands of an artist like John Tenniel, had far less by way of the exaggerated physical deformity so beloved of the caricaturist; instead, Mr. Punch was a man of good social graces, a well-dressed and well-groomed figure who could converse with royalty and could when required patriotically represent the hopes and fears of his countrymen. This was the Mr. Punch who worried about raising popular tastes and encouraging familiarity with Shakespeare.

The idea that *Punch* spoke with a single voice rather than being the collaborative product of many writers and artists was encouraged by the general exclusion of authors' and artists' names since writers did not sign their work, and many graphic items were either unsigned or signed only with a monogram or the artist's initials. It is important to remain aware, however, that the univocal Mr. Punch is a constructed journalistic fiction, a clever and convenient convention that provided the publication with a uniform identity. Although in the chapters that follow I will occasionally make use of the convention and speak of *Punch* or Mr. Punch as though referring to a single voice and identity, I will also frequently identify writers and artists by name. Consequently, it is first worth saying something about those individuals who created that collective voice and identity. Two points are of particular relevance. The first concerns the manner in which *Punch* was the product of what amounted to an élite, club-like organization of men who shared a great many common interests, in spite of the conflicts that sometimes erupted among them and that led in several instances to departures from the *Punch* staff. The second point, which grows out of the first, is that among those common interests was an often passionate love of the theatre and the works of Shakespeare in particular. Who then were the members of the *Punch* circle?

The *Punch* Writers and Artists

In the early conceptual stages of *Punch*, the principal planners, Mark Lemon and Henry Mayhew, together with various potential contributors, among them Douglas Jerrold and Percival Leigh, met in a series of taverns. A little later, when *Punch* began its precarious early life, there were regular dinner meetings on Saturday, again at an inn. According to Spielmann, these meetings resulted in what became known as the *Punch* Club, whose members included Lemon, Mayhew, Jerrold, Leigh, Thackeray, Ebenezer Landells, Kenny Meadows, Albert Smith, Gilbert à Beckett, and John Leech. But this lasted only for a short time. Although a number of writers and artists who were not contributors to *Punch* often attended, the chief object of the Club, according to Landells, 'was to form a little society amongst ourselves to talk over and settle upon subjects for the paper of the coming week' (Spielmann 1895a, 93). However, when Bradbury & Evans became involved with *Punch*, regular dinners for the *Punch* staff began to be held at No. 11, Bouverie Street (the business offices of Bradbury & Evans), and then from 1867 at No. 10, where a specially-constructed dining room was set up. Initially, the dinners were held on Saturdays, when the next week's issue was made up and sent to press, but soon a change to Wednesdays was instituted, chiefly in order to permit planning and discussion of the big cut for the forthcoming issue. The artist (usually John Leech in the early years) then would have sufficient time to get his design to the wood engraver in time for the Saturday deadline. With this change, the old openness of the *Punch* Club meetings was replaced by a business and dinner meeting that Spielmann suggests was 'as exclusive and esoteric as a Masonic initiation', beside which 'the Literary Ladies' Dinner and Bluebeard's Chamber are as open to the world and free from mystery as the public streets at noon' (Spielmann 1895a, 58).

The now legendary dinner table at the *Punch* offices (it still exists) typically sat twelve to fourteen people. Seated at either end in the early years were the *Punch* proprietors, William Bradbury and Frederick Evans. The remaining seats were occupied by members of the Staff, a kind of inner cabinet of contributors, all salaried employees and all responsible (except for the Editor) for a regular weekly contribution measured in column lengths. Once both Stirling Coyne (he was let go for plagiarism) and Henry Mayhew gave up their co-editorships, a special chair appears to have been reserved for the editor, initially Mark Lemon (Spielmann 1895a, 63, 257, 272; Leary, 29). During the remainder of the Victorian era and following the death of Mark Lemon in 1870, subsequent occupants of the editor's chair were Shirley Brooks (1870–74), Tom Taylor (1874–80), and Francis C. Burnand (1880–1906).

Those who sat at the *Punch* table, in spite of their differences, were a surprisingly cohesive group, despite some at times very different views on political matters. Whereas Keene and Brooks were Tories, for example, Taylor and Du Maurier were radicals. Even so, the membership tended to change only with death and the very occasional defection, Doyle's departure on account of what he considered was *Punch*'s anti-Catholic bias was perhaps the most dramatic version of the latter kind of change. In 1855, for example, those who sat at the table included Mark Lemon (the editor), Douglas Jerrold (he died two years later), Gilbert Abbott à Beckett (he died a year later), Percival Leigh, John Leech, Thackeray, and the two proprietors (Spielmann 1895a, 65). All these had been there more or less since the beginning, but by 1855 they had been joined by Tom Taylor, who had arrived in 1844 and would stay for thirty-six years, Horace Mayhew (brother of Henry Mayhew), who had joined the table in 1845 and would stay until his death in 1872, Shirley Brooks, who had joined the table soon after his first contribution to *Punch* in 1851 and would stay until his death in 1874, and John Tenniel, who came at short notice late in 1850 to fill the gap left by the defection of Richard Doyle, and, after replacing John Leech as chief cartoonist, would stay until his retirement in 1901.

Some other prominent names that will be referred to from time to time in subsequent chapters include Henry Silver. He is best remembered now for his remarkable diary in which he recorded details of the conversations and discussions at some 350 of the weekly dinners between 1858 and 1870. He began working for *Punch* in 1848, but he did not attend a dinner until August 1857, an experience he describes in his diary (Prager 1979, 16–17). However, as he also records in his diary, his membership at the table was not confirmed until the following year (29 December 1858). During the 1860s, he was a regular theatre reviewer for *Punch*, signing himself 'Our Dramatic Correspondent' and later 'Our Theatrical Spectator.' Eventually, he ended his connection with *Punch* in 1870. Another important figure was Francis C. Burnand. Founder of the Cambridge ADC (Morley 1980, 7), and a future editor of *Punch,* he joined the table in June 1863. He was to become famous (many would say infamous) for the innumerable puns that he contributed.

Less well-known to posterity than Burnand was Edwin J. Milliken, who made his first contribution to *Punch* in 1875. During the 1880s and 90s, he held the unofficial position of *Punch* poet and joined the *Punch* table early in 1877 (Spielmann 1898a, 377). Adept in both verse and prose, he wrote the prefaces to many of the semi-annual volumes and contributed obituaries, burlesques, theatre reviews, and material for the annual almanacs. His most popular contribution was 'The 'Arry Papers', which Spielmann praises at some length (Spielmann 1895a, 378–381). In the course of his career with

Punch, he became the chief 'suggestor' regarding the subject-matter of the weekly big cuts. He appears to have been particularly familiar with Shakespeare's works, and between 1875 and his death in 1897, he contributed almost 100 items relating to Shakespeare, a third of these consisting of extended textual burlesques, written to accompany the big cuts of John Tenniel (there were twenty-four of these collaborations) and Linley Sambourne (there were seven of these).

Among the artists who will be mentioned from time to time and who sat at the table were John Leech, who was a part of the *Punch* enterprise from the very first; Charles Keene (he was a close friend of Henry Silver), who contributed some 3,000 or so designs between 1851 and 1891 and joined the table on 20 February 1860; John Tenniel (already mentioned above), who contributed some 3,900 designs between 1850 and 1901; George du Maurier, who joined the table on 7 November 1864; Linley Sambourne, who joined the table in 1871 and then succeeded Tenniel as chief cartoonist in 1901; Harry Furniss, who began contributing to *Punch* in October 1880 and joined the staff on retainer four years later; Edward Tennyson Reid, who joined the table in 1890; Bernard Partridge, who joined the table in 1892 and would become chief cartoonist in 1909; and Phil May, who joined the table in February 1895.

Maintaining the constructed journalistic fiction that a single identity – Mr. Punch – was the author/artist for the contents of the magazine required the co-operation of all these contributors. Because, as already noted, most writers and many artists did not sign their work, the individual kudos, even of contributors like Jerrold and Thackeray, was made subservient to the clever, convenient convention that provided *Punch* with its uniform face. Helping in this process was the sense of literary and artistic brotherhood shared by the *Punch* staff. The weekly ritual of the dinner, to which only an inner circle of staff were invited, encouraged a sense of exclusivity and pride in shared goals. Once admitted to the *Punch* circle, new members carved their initials into the table in the manner of schoolboys marking their desks. The ensuing fellowship around the 'Mahogany Tree' (the table was actually made of deal) was celebrated in some verses that Thackeray composed for the Christmas number early in 1847. For table members, these verses came to have the status of a school song or club anthem (*Punch* 20:13). The following extract will convey the general flavour:

> Here let us sport,
> Boys as we sit:
> Laughter and wit
> Flashing so free
> Life is but short –
> When we are gone,
> Let them sing on,
> Round the old tree.

The *Punch* dinners, which were catered, were jovial and unbuttoned affairs. When Silver attended his first dinner, he recorded in his diary 'that when dessert was on the table "Pater" [i.e. Frederick Evans, William Bradbury's partner] achieved the perilous feat of bowling a big pineapple at his partner who had asked him for a slice of it. And I feel pretty sure that not a single wine glass was broken in the transit.' As for the serious business that was the supposed reason for the dinners, it was Silver's impression on this occasion that possibly nothing would have happened had he not been there: 'Shirley [i.e. Shirley Brooks] made pretence of a debate on the cartoon "just to give the new fellow some notion of how we do it." Proposed a parody of Millais' picture which appeared next Wednesday' (quoted Prager 1979, 17). Apart from high jinks such as bowling pineapples or laughing at the effects of Percival Leigh's whoopee cushion, the dinners were notable for the cut and thrust of witty repartee and the spirit of bonhomie that was nurtured by a plentiful supply of good wine. The conversations during dinner and after business was concluded could be wide ranging. Stories were told, and songs were not considered out of place. Thackeray was known for his rendering of 'Little Billee', John Leech for his 'King Death', Tenniel for his 'The Sailor's Adieu to the Ladies of Spain', and Horace Mayhew for his musical rendering of Thackeray's 'The Mahogany Tree' (Spielmann 1895a, 74; Prager 1979, 85, 115).

Discussing suggestions for the big cut and the accompanying 'legend' or 'cackle', as it was often called, appears to have coincided with the arrival of the cigars at the end of the meal. These discussions were considered the most important business of the evening. Ideas for each big cut were 'fully and formally debated, every tussle advancing it a stage, and none finally accepted until all the others have fallen in the battledore-and-shuttlecock process to which they have been subjected' (Spielmann 1895a, 168). Once the important business of the big cut was over (when he was editor, Shirley Brooks used to throw down his knife at this point), title and legend were written on a piece of paper, placed in an envelope, and handed to the artist. Discussion of other contributions would then follow.

As Spielmann makes clear (Spielmann 1895a, 80–81), and as Henry Silver's diary confirms with many examples between 1858 and 1870, in the majority of cases the artist who went home to work on the design discussed at the dinner was not the same person as he who had suggested the subject. Another source of information concerning this collaborative process is provided by the *Punch* Contributors' Ledgers that, as John Bush Jones and Priscilla Shaw have shown, recorded for a brief period between 11 January 1845 and 30 September 1848 both the names of the artists who drew the designs for the big cuts, and the names of the suggestors (Jones and Shaw 1978, 3–14). We know, for example, that Henry Mayhew, a prolific suggestor, was recorded as the suggestor for John Leech's design for the big cut on 14 February 1846. It was based on a line in Shakespeare's *Richard III* and was entitled 'I THINK THERE BE SIX RICHMONDS IN THE FIELD' (10:79). Its subject was the current very hot Parliamentary debate concerning free trade. Another example relating to the use of Shakespearean material was the suggestion of Mark Lemon for a design (not a big cut) that appeared in January 1847. Leech was again the artist, and his design was entitled 'THE RISING GENERATION' (12:9). Part of a series so titled, the picture depicts two male youths, the one reclining on a sofa, and the other sitting in a slovenly fashion on a chair. The latter is smoking. The caption reads: '*Clever Juvenile (loq.)* "SHAKSPEARE? POOH! FOR MY PART I CONSIDER SHAKSPEARE A VERY MUCH OVER-RATED MAN."' Though obviously a general comment on the arrogance and ignorance of youth, the composition may also be read as part of *Punch*'s particular campaign to call attention to what it felt was a general lack of appreciation for Shakespeare.

There was an altogether different feature of the *Punch* dinners that no doubt helped cement the staff members' sense of belonging to a private male coterie. Behind the closed doors at Bouverie Street, the talk and jokes around the dinner table could be decidedly smutty in the manner, perhaps, of many a modern male locker-room. However, there was a decided difference between the two masculine preserves. Whereas the language and humour of the modern locker-room is increasingly mirrored by much of the open discourse in society at large and in the entertainment media, the discourse around the *Punch* table was very distinct from that of acceptable Victorian social norms. As such, the table-talk of the *Punch* staff radically transgressed the pre-determined boundaries of *Punch* itself (Prager 1979, 19, 135; Leary 2002, 59, 62–63, 109). What could never be said within the family or in a drawing room where females or children were present, and what, therefore, could never be placed in *Punch* if its carefully nurtured 'family' readership was to be kept intact, was tossed about freely in the *Punch* dining room. Silver's diary makes this clear, although even he draws the line at recording some of the details. Of the examples he does give, a handful that deal with Shakespearean material can stand as illustrations here.

When, for example, it was noted at the table on 11 April 1860 that the actor William Charles Macready, then in his sixties, had married a twenty-three-year old woman, both Frederick Evans and Henry Silver shouted out the famous line from *Henry V*: 'Once more unto the breach!' Another example is recorded in Silver's diary entry for 28 June 1860. On this occasion, the opinions of those around the table were canvassed on the question 'Was Shakespeare a b[ugger]?' a matter described as an 'Interestg. Discussion for a Debate Society'. John Leech responded by arguing that the evidence of the Sonnets indicates 'yes'. Silver wondered 'if a man with a natural passion co'd feel & write ye reverse', to which Leech replied, 'Sh. was a universal genius & co'd feel & write abt. anything.' Several years later on 7 December 1864, the same question was raised by Mark Lemon. Shirley Brooks responded with supposed affirmative proof in the form of two quotations: '& thou shalt have thy Will!' (inaccurately recalled from Sonnet 143) and 'My ventures are not in one bottom' (from *The*

47

Merchant of Venice I i 42). To these, George Du Maurier added a quotation from *Macbeth*: 'This Strange & Self Abuse' (III iv 141).

A third example of how unbridled the table conversations could be involves the discussion on 20 January 1864 of a proposed big cut by John Tenniel that would satirize the ineptitude of the National Shakespeare Committee. The members of the Committee were supposed to come up with an appropriate means of celebrating the forthcoming celebration of the tercentenary of Shakespeare's birth in April. As will be discussed in Chapter Two, the Committee hoped to erect some kind of Shakespeare memorial. What the *Punch* men proposed in order to ridicule the Committee's idea was a big cut of an enormous bust of Shakespeare, looking very much like that by Gheerart Janssen, which is situated adjacent to Shakespeare's grave in the parish church of Stratford-on-Avon. In the *Punch* version, however, which appeared on 30 January 1864 (46:45), the sculpture (unlike that at Stratford) completely dwarfs a crowd of men at its base (Figure 14). With the aid of ladders, they appear to be defacing the monument. Some are arrogantly pasting up a bill referring to the 'SHAKSPERE MEMORIAL' and the 'LONDON COMMITTEE', while others are scrawling their own names on its base. The names appear to be fictitious: 'Brown', 'Smith', 'Jones' etc., but one of them is writing the word 'ATHENAEUM'. Readers familiar with the debate surrounding the activities (or non-activities) of the Committee would have had no difficulty in recognizing that this man was probably intended to represent W. Hepworth Dixon, the editor of the *Athenaeum*, a publication often unfriendly to *Punch*. Significantly, he was also the chairman of the Committee. Entitled 'SHAKSPEARE AND THE PIGMIES', the cartoon accuses the Committee of self-aggrandizement and at the same time suggests that its members are mere pygmies alongside the genius of Shakespeare (Schoch 2002, 75–77).

This, then was what actually appeared in *Punch*, but Silver notes in his diary some quite different possibilities for the cartoon that were discussed at the dinner on 20 January 1864. One referred to the great eighteenth-century caricaturist James Gillray and what he might have drawn, perhaps depicting the Committee members as 'little dogs p__ing against the statue'. Following this suggestion, Horace Mayhew came up with a more feasible proposal that, unlike the image of

Gillray's dogs, would have been acceptable in Victorian drawing rooms: 'Shakspeare as Gulliver with Lilliputians over running him.' Then, someone else (Silver does not record the name) suggested depicting Hepworth Dixon 'whitewashing ye statue'. It was John Leech, however, who came up with the idea that was finally agreed upon. After suggesting 'Shaksp. coming to Punch "Save me from my friends"', he then improved upon his idea 'by suggesting Shaks. & the Pygmies', the concept that Tenniel then used for his big cut. A week later, Silver recorded that Leech applauded 'J[ohn] T[enniel] for the Shakspeare cut – against Ha'porth Dixon, who is said to give his Ipse Dixon' (27 January 1864).

Matching the scatological humour of Gillray's peeing dogs, there is the discussion on 7 April 1864 of possible Shakespeare mottoes for the new water closet at the Garrick Club, and on 19 March 1866, Tom Taylor's report that a picture in Manchester of Lear and Cordelia got the title 'There's life in the old dog yet!' To this the quick-witted Du Maurier responded: 'Gonnorhoea & Cordes-Lia'.

The cohesiveness and homosocial nature of the *Punch* staff, both those who sat at the table and the wider circle of those who worked as regular contributors, were further increased by a number of other factors. Thackeray, Leech, and Silver, for example, had all been students at Charterhouse, leading Thackeray to remark in a comment recorded in Silver's diary that it was 'curious how Charterhouse eventuated in Punch' (Diary entry for 21 October 1858; Ray, 259). Other former schoolfellows were Gilbert Abbott à Beckett and Henry Mayhew, who had both been at Westminster and had run away together from the school and walked all the way to Edinburgh where they hoped to join a theatre company (Price 1957, 38; Prager 1979, 41). As mentioned above, Percival Leigh and John Leech had both studied medicine at St. Bartholomew's, along with another *Punch* staffer, Albert Smith, a man detested by Jerrold and Thackeray and eventually eased off the *Punch* rota early in 1844 (Spielmann 1895a, 304–306; Prager 1979, 84). Lemon, Jerrold, and Brooks were all Freemasons, and a significant number of *Punch* men had in common a training in the law, even if only a few of them ever practised it (e.g. Gilbert Abbott à Beckett, Arthur William à Beckett, Gilbert Arthur à

Beckett, Henry Mayhew, Shirley Brooks, Tom Taylor, Francis Burnand, Thomas Anstey Guthrie, and Owen Seaman).

Ties of a different kind united a number of other *Punch* personnel. Henry Mayhew, for example, was Douglas Jerrold's son-in-law. At one time, Horace Mayhew (Henry's brother) was also about to become a son-in-law, but apparently Jerrold would not entertain the idea, declaring that 'one Mayhew is enough in the family' (Spielmann 1895a, 329). Mark Lemon's son Harry was employed as his father's secretary in the *Punch* office. Archibald Henning (an early cartoonist for *Punch*) and Kenny Meadows were brothers-in-law, as were two later artists, George du Maurier and Clement Scott. In addition, Ebenezer Landells's nephew, William Galter, was an engraver for *Punch* and two sons of Gilbert Abbot à Beckett (Gilbert and Arthur William) worked for *Punch* after their father's death, both eventually becoming table members themselves. Family links also united Charles Keene and his nephew Alfred Chantrey Corbould, who began working as an artist for *Punch* in 1871 (Spielmann 1895a, 544; Hudson, 17). Then there were those who were particularly close friends, such as Henry Mayhew and Gilbert Abbott à Beckett, Mark Lemon and Frederick Mullett Evans, and Charles Keene and John Tenniel. This latter also had close friendships with John Leech, Shirley Brooks, and Francis Burnand. Furthermore, in addition to being a close-knit group for the reasons just described, the *Punch* staff often belonged to the same societies and London clubs, often dined at each other's houses and took holidays together, and sometimes worked together on other journalistic projects. We know, too, that Leech and Tenniel were avid riders and frequently attended fox hunts together. Later, Tenniel, Burnand, and Linley Sambourne were often riding partners (Anstey 1936, 267; Morris 2005, 71–72, 81–82).

Punch Authors and Artists and the Theatre

A particular interest shared by the majority of the *Punch* personnel, and one of particular importance to this study, was the theatre. Significantly, among the members of the Dramatic Authors Society were some prominent *Punch* table members: Mark Lemon, Stirling Coyne, Francis Burnand, and the brothers Gilbert and Arthur William à Beckett (À Beckett 1903, 235–236). Mark Lemon had been writing plays before the founding of *Punch* and had had a five-act comedy performed at Covent Garden (Spielmann 1895a, 18). Benjamin Webster, the actor manager, was Lemon's close friend and is said to have produced one of Lemon's first plays at the Adelphi (Hatton 1871, 172). One of Lemon's particularly successful ventures was his adaptation of selected scenes from Shakespeare's *Henry IV* plays in *The Story of Falstaff*. In his diary, Henry Silver on 14 October 1868 mentioned that 'Mark's Falstaff began last Monday.' Silver seems to have been impressed by Lemon's theatrical skills, singling out his portrayal of Falstaff's 'shock of sorrow when banished & his crestfallen but manly bearing when sent to the Fleet.' Accompanying the entry, Silver kept press cuttings reporting the visit of the Prince and Princess of Wales on Saturday 17 October to Lemon's production at the Gallery of Illustration in Regent Street. Later, Lemon took his production on tour through England and Scotland (Hatton 1871, 5–142), Silver recording on 3 February 1869 that 'Mark has been Falstaffing in Scotland with great success,' and noting on 19 May that year that 'Mark revives his Falstaff next Monday.'

Douglas Jerrold wrote over seventy plays (more than fifty of them before he joined *Punch*). Well-known for his plays *Black-Eyed Susan* (1829) and *Time Works Wonders* (1845), he was the son of two actors, and his father was a theatre manager. His stage debut occurred as a child when Edmund Kean carried him on stage in *Rolla*. After serving in the navy, he moved to London where his mother and sisters were actresses. There he was a frequent theatre-goer and saw performances by such actors as Edmund Kean, John Kemble, and Charles Matthews. In 1818, he wrote his first play, and by the end of 1835, some thirteen of his plays had been produced at some of the better

London theatres. Not only did he produce and act in a number of them, but he was actor-manager when he and his brother-in-law, William John Hannard, jointly managed the Strand Theatre (Kelly 1972, 15–21).

Other *Punch* playwrights include Albert Smith, author of the pantomime burlesque *Harlequin Guy Fawkes; or, a Match for a King*; Stirling Coyne, author of more than fifty plays (Prager 1979, 45), and, as one historian puts it, 'an organiser of dramatists in defence of their rights' (Price 1957, 27); Tom Taylor, author of about one hundred works for the stage, most famously his comedy *Our American Cousin*, the play that Abraham Lincoln was watching when he was assassinated on 14 April 1865; Francis Burnand, already a busy comic playwright before his editorship of *Punch* and just as busy during his time as editor (Schoch 2002, 4); and Arthur William à Beckett, responsible for half-a-dozen plays before joining *Punch* (À Beckett 1903, 12). Apart from those *Punch* men known from their membership in the Dramatic Authors Society, there were still other playwrights. The elder Gilbert Abbot à Beckett, for example, was a prolific playwright before joining *Punch*, and for a short time he managed a London theatre. Over forty of his plays, some written in collaboration with Mark Lemon (À Beckett 1903, 47), were published, and twenty more can be traced in the Lord Chamberlain's collection or through playbills. Other writers who contributed to *Punch* but also wrote plays include Shirley Brooks, Henry Saville Clarke, H. Sutherland Edwards, John Oxenford, and Alfred Thompson (Ellis 1982, 142). Even, George du Maurier, though a novelist rather than a dramatist, saw his *Trilby* adapted as a play by Paul Potter at the Haymarket in October 1895 (Taylor 1989, 163).

All these selected examples collectively lend credence to Spielmann's statement in 1895 that 'the *Punch* writers, from first to last, have contributed no fewer than five hundred plays to the stage' (Spielmann 1895a, 129; Morley 1980, 7). Using some of its staff's combined talents, *Punch* itself, under the joint authorship of Lemon, Jerrold, and Henry Mayhew, even created a pantomime in 1842. Entitled *King John; or Harlequin and Magna Charta*, this was performed at Covent Garden but was not particularly successful, so the experiment was not repeated (Spielmann 1895a, 131–132). Shortly after, in June

1843, Benjamin Webster, a close friend of Mark Lemon, as noted above, and manager of the Haymarket, announced a contest with a prize of £500 for an original comedy to be performed at his theatre. *Punch* responded with two entries: 'The School for Sentiment; or, The Tar! The Tear!! And the Tilbury!!!' (17 June) and 'The Academy for Scandal' (29 July), this last by Jerrold (Altick 197, 723–724). To the chagrin of the authors, neither of the *Punch* entries was selected.

Not only were a number of key members of the *Punch* brotherhood playwrights, a significant number also acted from time to time. For example, Mark Lemon, a portly man, toured as Falstaff, as noted above. He apparently needed no padding to do so (Morley, 7), a point confirmed in an engraving of him as Falstaff by John Tenniel, who had designed Lemon's costume. The engraving appeared in the *Illustrated London News* and then provided the frontispiece for Joseph Hatton's memoirs of Lemon (Hatton 1871). Lemon also participated in the occasional benefit performance, as did Shirley Brooks, Tom Taylor, Horace Mayhew, Francis Burnand, and John Tenniel. There were, for example, benefits involving *Punch* staffers on behalf of Leigh Hunt, the bereaved family of Angus Reach (a *Punch* table member), and the widow and eight children of Charles H. Bennett (a table member from 1865 to 1867). On the program for this last, which was given in London and repeated in Manchester, was Burnand's *Cox and Box: Or, the Long-Lost Brothers*, a musical adaptation of John Maddison Morton's popular farce *Box and Cox* with music by Arthur Sullivan. Among the actors was George du Maurier. Later in the program after an address by Shirley Brooks, Tom Taylor's play *A Sheep in Wolf's Clothing* was performed, among its actors being Mark Lemon, John Tenniel, Tom Taylor, Francis Burnand, Horace Mayhew, Henry Silver, and Shirley Brooks. Then followed Jacques Offenbach's *Les Deux Aveugles*, in which du Maurier was one of the performers. In Manchester, the program concluded with an additional work, John Oxenford's farce *A Family Failing* (Oxenford had contributed regularly to *Punch* in its early years), the cast for which included Lemon, Taylor, and Silver (Spielmann 1895a, 133–134).

Punch commemorated the Manchester event by presenting John Knowles with a copy of the first volume of the magazine. Laid in the front of the volume was an albumen print by the London Stereoscopic

Company. Taken in the Adelphi Green Room, it was a group portrait of the actors, among whom were some not on the *Punch* staff, notably Kate and Ellen Terry. A wonderful record of the thespian activities of the *Punch* staff, this photograph was reproduced by Spielmann. There is also a copy in the National Portrait Gallery (Spielmann 1895a, 133; NPG x18489). Other *Punch* men of the Victorian era who also acted were three important artists: Henry Furniss, Phil May, and Bernard Partridge. All three were professional actors at some stage in their lives (Furniss 1902, 1:24; Irving 1951, 511; Morris 1985, 51).

The close association between *Punch* in its early years with Charles Dickens (the shared connections with Bradbury & Evans and the friendship with Mark Lemon have already been noted) included involvement with Dickens's amateur theatre productions and his later productions for the Guild of Literature and Art, which Dickens founded in 1851 (Spielmann 1895a, 134–135, 137; Dexter 1927, 86). The theatrical activities organized by Dickens began on the 21 September 1845 at Miss Kelly's Theatre (later the Royalty) in Soho with a performance of Ben Jonson's *Every Man in His Humour*. Apart from Dickens himself, who played Captain Bobadil, the cast included a number of *Punch* staff: Mark Lemon as both Brainworm and Cob's wife, Tib, Douglas Jerrold as Master Stephen, Percival Leigh as Oliver Cob, Gilbert Abbott à Beckett as William, and John Leech as Master Matthew. So successful was this performance that the St. James's Theatre was booked for a repeat engagement on 15 November so that Prince Albert could attend (Dexter 1927, 61; Gager 1996, 104–105), and other performances followed in Manchester on 16 July 1847, at the Haymarket on 17 May 1848, and at Knebworth on 18, 19, and 20 November 1850. A year later on 16 May 1851, at a performance at Devonshire House before Queen Victoria and Prince Albert of Edward Bulwer Lytton's *Not So Bad As We Seem*, the cast included not only Dickens, but three *Punch* men: Lemon, Jerrold, and Tenniel. During the next sixteen months, the talented group of amateurs, whose goals were to provide benevolent support to writers and artists and their families who had fallen on hard times, played at other locations in London and other cities (Morris 2005, 53–54). Lemon also acted in Dickens's production of *Fortunio* (8 January 1855*), The Lighthouse* (19 June 1855), and *The Frozen Deep* (6

January 1857). As will be discussed in a moment, a major production of Dickens's Guild of Literature and Art was Shakespeare's *The Merry Wives of Windsor* in 1848 that also included actors from among the *Punch* staff.

Punch *Authors and Artists and Shakespeare*

A number of the *Punch* staff were also involved in theatrical activities directly connected with Shakespeare. Both Gilbert Abbott à Beckett and Francis Burnand wrote burlesques of Shakespeare plays. The former wrote a burlesque of *King John* in 1837, and the latter wrote burlesques of several other Shakespeare plays (Schoch 2002, 188–189) – *Antony and Cleopatra; or, His-tory and Her-tory in a Modern Nilo-metre* (1866); *The Rise and Fall of Richard III; or, a New Front to an Old Dickey* (1868); *Our Antony and Cleopatra* (1873); and *Ariel, a Burlesque Fairy Dream* (1883). Joseph Ashby-Sterry, another *Punch* writer also contributed to the genre with a burlesque entitled *Katharine and Petruchio; Or the Shaming of the True* that was published by Clement Scott in 1870 in an anthology with the title *Drawing-Room Plays and Parlour Pantomimes*. As actors, a number of staff members took part in the performance of Shakespeare's *The Merry Wives of Windsor* at the Haymarket Theatre on 15 May 1848 under the auspices of Dickens's Guild of Literature and Art. Those participating included John Leech as Slender (like Lemon, he was a close friend of Dickens) and Mark Lemon (naturally) as Falstaff. Dickens played Robert Shallow. The goal of this amateur production, which then travelled to Manchester, Liverpool, Birmingham, Edinburgh, and Glasgow, was a matter close to the heart of the *Punch* circle – to raise funds for the endowment of a curatorship at Shakespeare's birthplace in Stratford-on-Avon (Dexter 1927, 45, 60; Gager 1996, 105–107, 375). As will be seen in the next chapter, *Punch* took a special interest in the campaign to acquire Shakespeare's birthplace for the nation when it was put up for sale and in danger of falling into the hands of unscrupulous entrepreneurs, one of whom, it was rumoured, contemplated transporting the house across the Atlantic to the United States.

But there were also other connections between Shakespeare and the *Punch* circle, apart from the fortuitous coincidence that Mark Lemon had once been landlord of a tavern named *The Shakespeare's Head*. Percival Leigh was known to his fellows at the table as 'the Professor' because of his scholarly wit and his accurate knowledge of Shakespeare and the Latin poets (Ray, 358). He was, Spielmann claimed, 'a profound Shakespearean' who 'vied with Jerrold himself in his knowledge of the Bard' (Spielmann 1895a, 301). He it was who should be credited with introducing into *Punch* a scholarly element quite new to any English comic magazine. As for Jerrold, his prodigious knowledge of Shakespeare derived from the period following his youthful service in the navy. Living with his family in London, Jerrold apparently rose early every morning to study Latin grammar and Shakespeare (Kelly 1972, 17). After he joined *Punch*, his love of Shakespeare was displayed in a number of ways, and he was responsible for some sixty items on Shakespeare topics. In 1844, for example, he wrote 'Portrait of Shakspeare,' one of eleven sketches for *Punch* that he called 'Exhibition of the English in China' (6:219). This will be discussed in the next chapter. In another series that appeared in 1842, 'Punch's Letters to his Son', a parody of Lord Chesterfield's 1774 mentoring *Letters to His Son*, the fifth letter ('On the Advantages of Being "Nothing"') included the comment that Shakespeare 'has bequeathed scenes of immortal loveliness for the human fancy to delight in – founts of eternal truth for the lip of man to drink, and drink – and for aye to be renovated with every draught' (3:79).

Another Jerrold series for *Punch* was 'The English in Little', a seven-part serial purportedly written by General Tom Thumb, the diminutive six-year-old American midget (his real name was Charles Stratton) who was brought to England in 1844 by the entertainment mogul P. T. Barnum. Tom Thumb's entertainments (he was a particularly effective mimic) were a huge success with the general public, and he was even called to the royal court on three different occasions to perform before Queen Victoria, who gave him various marks of favour that included a gold pencil case with the inscription 'T. T.' and his coat of arms (Kelly 1972, 60; and Schoch 2004, 4–10). The pages of *Punch* contain many references to General Tom Thumb, and the royal patronage he received was represented as a slight to serious

English actors and dramatists who rarely, if ever, caught the Queen's interest (see *Punch* 6:157). Jerrold's 'The English in Little' began to appear late in 1846, following several return visits of the popular entertainer (Kelly 1970, 330; Altick 1997, 375). The central conceit of the series was stated in the opening number (11:195) where it was explained that, because 'the English have idolised a dwarf', the pigmy, 'duly returning the compliment, paints "The English in Little"'. True to form, Jerrold's satire, written in Yankee dialect (Tom Thumb was from Connecticut), attacked among other things the public's and the royal family's neglect of native performers and native drama in favour of foreign imports. In the section entitled 'The General Gives Audience to Lord Mayor and Aldermen' (12:39) that appeared early in 1847, Jerrold had the General note that 'London won't let his [Shakespeare's] plays be acted, for fear of corruptin her prentices.' Elsewhere, in a section entitled 'The General Meets the Genius of Britain at the Palace' (11:239), the General reports that there is agreement in the Palace 'that we should vote the English drama and English players low'. However, as the Genius of Britain apparently has explained, 'natur wil prevail, Gen'ral – we can't help loving Shakspeare, and them as plays him best', a remark that accompanies the purported revelation that the great Shakespearean actor William Charles Macready was coming every week 'to read Shakspeare to the Queen and the Prince'.

Along with his various brief verse burlesques of passages in Shakespeare, together with his many quotations from Shakespeare, there can be no doubt that Jerrold's early studies of Shakespeare had served him well, and it is no surprise that when the famous Hungarian patriot, Lajos Kossuth, was in London, Jerrold organized a penny subscription to raise money for the purchase of a copy of Shakespeare's works that could then be presented to Kossuth to express England's esteem for him. Apparently, Jerrold was inspired by the report that Kossuth had learned English from reading Shakespeare in an Austrian prison (Slater 2002, 230). The scheme was successful, and the books were purchased, along with a specially designed case for them modelled on Shakespeare's birthplace in Stratford-on-Avon. The presentation took place at the London Tavern on 8 May 1853 when

Jerrold handed to Kossuth what he referred to as 'these word-wealthy volumes' (Jerrold 1914, 2:599; Kelly 1972, 58; Slater 2002, 230).

Reference has already been made above to the very large number of woodcut designs that Kenny Meadows supplied for Barry Cornwall's edition of Shakespeare, published between 1839 and 1843. According to Henry Vizetelly, who knew him well, Meadows 'knew all the principal passages in Shakespeare by heart long before he became an illustrator of the plays' (quoted Spielmann 1895a, 447). Two other early *Punch* artists contributed to another illustrated edition of Shakespeare. Both William Harvey, who in 1842 designed the third wrapper for *Punch* and was described by Spielmann as 'the Shakespearian illustrator' (Spielmann 1895a, 42), and Ebenezer Landells contributed work for Charles Knight's pictorial edition of Shakespeare. Knight, whose edition was lauded in the pages of *Punch*, as we have already seen, may himself have been given the special honour from time to time of being a guest at the *Punch* table, although Spielmann was unable, he says, to confirm this (Spielmann 1895a, 86). Then there was the somewhat scholarly Tom Taylor, who for two years had been Professor of English Language and Literature at London University and was also art critic for the *Times* and the *Graphic* (Price 1957, 61; Prager 1979, 16, 137). For a time he was Vice-President of the New Shakspere Society. Other *Punch* staff with especially strong interests in Shakespeare were Charles Keene and John Tenniel (Young 2005, 229–247). Because of the special importance of this latter to the concerns of this book, his work requires a measure of detailed commentary at this point.

John Tenniel and Shakespeare

Tenniel is an artist remembered today chiefly for his designs for the wood engravings that illustrate Lewis Carroll's *Alice in Wonderland* (1865) and the same author's *Through the Looking-Glass. And What Alice Found There* (1872). What is often not recognized is that many of these designs drew upon material that he had already composed for *Punch* (Sarzano 1948, 18–19; and Hancher 1985, 3–26), though this is not a topic that will be discussed here. Tenniel is also remembered for certain of his political cartoons that were originally created for *Punch* and that have regularly been used to illustrate later histories of the nineteenth century (Morris 1985, 309). He began to work for *Punch* in 1850, his first contribution being an unsigned initial letter 'L' of a horse and rider for the 30 November issue (19:224) (Grafton 1984, 51; Morris 2005, 338). On 12 July 1851, there appeared his first illustration on a Shakespearean topic, a burlesque of the quarrel scene between Brutus and Cassius in *Julius Caesar* (21:87) that was here used to comment on the visit of the Lord Mayor of London to Paris and the complaint of a City alderman that the Mayor used the occasion to generate maximum publicity for himself. The engraving, as would so often be the case regarding Tenniel's later designs, accompanied an extended textual parody of the relevant scene in Shakespeare. In the course of his long tenure with *Punch*, Tenniel would produce 164 designs based on Shakespeare, thirteen of them initial letters, fifty-three small size designs, ninety-four big cuts, and four double-page big cuts. However, his small *Julius Caesar* design for *Punch* was by no means Tenniel's first composition based on Shakespeare's works.

An ardent theatre-goer and an amateur actor of some standing even before he began work for *Punch*, Tenniel had a great love for Shakespeare and could quote extensively from his plays (Engen 1991, 4, 29–30; Spielmann 1895a, 134; Johnson 1977; Morris 1985, 12–13, and 27 n. 63). Both before and after he joined *Punch*, he used to visit the theatre and the opera with sketchbook in hand. The result was his 'Pencillings in the Pit' (1835–c. 1846) now in the Harvard Theatre Collection. This work consists of some 150 undated sketches of actors that he later mounted and identified in a small book (Knight 1928, 111–118; Morris 1985, 5–6; and Morris 2005, 24). An admirer of William Charles Macready, Tenniel made, for example, the drawings of Macready in his role as Hamlet. Other actors represented included Samuel Phelps, James Wallack, George Vanderhoff, Robert Keeley, and Charles Kean (Trewin 1967, 199; Downer 1966, fig. 8; Morris 2005, 25). Contemporaneous with 'Pencillings in the Pit' is an 1842 sketch depicting Henry Hemming, Jr., as Hamlet. Hemming was a close friend of Tenniel, and there was a Hemming family legend that the Hemmings were descended from the Danish King Hemming. No doubt the sketch of Henry as the Danish prince was a light-hearted allusion to the legend, a legend that Hemming himself did not apparently take with any degree of seriousness (Morris 2005, 32).

Another sign of Tenniel's early interest in Shakespeare was a quite different project. During the mid forties, in keeping with his love of puns and the element of the fantastic that was later to be such a characteristic of his *Alice* designs, Tenniel helped create with Thomas Barrett and Charles Keene (this latter soon to become a *Punch* artist) a book of illustrated burlesques. The joint goal of the artists was to parody contemporary gift books, particularly those very popular versions that included steel-engravings of Shakespearean topics, verse quotations, and idealized portrayals of female beauty. They titled their work *The Book of Beauty*, a clear allusion to the very popular annual gift book *Heath's Book of Beauty* that was published in fifteen volumes between 1833 and 1847. Tenniel's contributions consisted of chalk drawings. These were often based on quotations from Shakespeare that were then transformed into witty verbal and visual puns. Completed about 1846, the book was never intended for publication. In 1892 it was exhibited at the Dowdeswell Galleries in London. Thereafter, it was broken up and many of its drawings were sold (Spielmann 1895a, 467; Simpson 1994, 90–91; Engen 1991, 12–13; and Stoker, at http://oufcnt2.open.ac.uk/~gill_stoker/biog.htm).

From 1851 on, the remainder of Tenniel's works based on Shakespeare appeared in *Punch*, but there was one notable exception. Although after joining *Punch* he supplied illustrations for a number of books (including the two *Alice* books), Tenniel eventually decided to turn down further contracts of this kind (Engen 1991, 119). However, he later quietly broke his own rule to begin work on illustrations for an edition of Shakespeare, the wood engravings for which would be produced by the Dalziel brothers, a prominent firm of engravers. Sadly, this work, which the *Punch* proprietors were willing to publish, remained unfinished, no doubt chiefly on account of Tenniel's heavy workload for *Punch*. However, a number of drawings for the project have survived, along with at least two completed wood engravings by the Dalziels, and surviving proofs are now in the British Museum Print Room and in the Boston Museum of Fine Arts (Dalziel 1978, 130; Reid 1975, 26, 28; and Engen 1991, 119, 120, 198). Had Tenniel been able to complete his illustrated edition, it would perhaps have

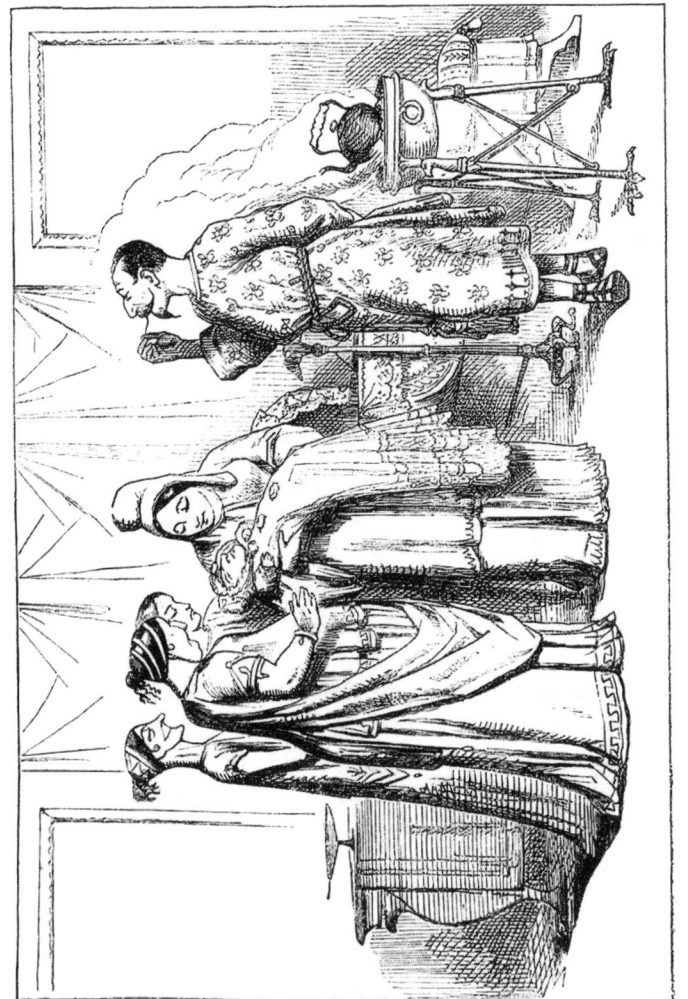

Figure 2.
John Tenniel's commentary on the birth of Eugene Bonaparte in *Punch* (29 March 1856), 30:130.

become as familiar in Victorian domestic libraries and drawing rooms as the Shakespeare editions illustrated with wood engravings of designs by Kenny Meadows in 1839–43, John Gilbert in 1857–60, and Henry Courtney Selous in 1864–69.

So far as I can tell, Tenniel's designs for his proposed Shakespeare edition were serious in character, expressive of an appropriate gravity to match the reverence Victorians accorded their complete Shakespeares; however, a Shakespeare project specifically for *Punch,* which Tenniel was involved in soon after he was taken on by the magazine, is very different. Between 7 July 1855 and 21 June 1856, with a brief hiatus between 12 January and 1 March 1856, Tenniel produced forty designs that collectively provided a weekly series entitled 'Punch's Illustrations to Shakspeare' (Simpson 1994, 122–135). During the course of this venture, there appeared at least one design for almost every Shakespeare play, the exceptions being *The Comedy of Errors, Henry VI,* Part 2, *Titus Andronicus, Measure for Measure, All's Well That Ends Well,* and *Pericles*, these being works that he continued to ignore in all his later contributions to *Punch*.

Tenniel's technique in these designs was to take a quotation from the play in question and then offer some kind of visual pun upon it that deliberately misinterpreted Shakespeare's actual meaning. This was something he had done in *The Book of Beauty* where, for example, he had used Claudius's 'And let the kettle to the trumpet speak' (V ii 275) as the basis for a chalk drawing (now in the Victoria and Albert Museum), in which a tea kettle and a trumpet are dressed as courtiers and speak to an anxious-looking cannoneer (Simpson 1994, opp. 128, and Engen 1991, 13). The readers/viewers, of course, were expected to have some familiarity with the original text in *Hamlet* so as to be able to recognize and enjoy the wit involved in Tenniel's burlesque treatment of that original.

More will be said about burlesque in Chapter Four, but it is worth noting here that, although many of 'Punch's Illustrations to Shakspeare' involve mere play upon words along the lines of that just described, others introduce a political element and refer to contemporary events, examples being relations with Austria (15 and 19 December 1855), the problem of Ireland (12 January 1856), the Congress of Paris (1 March 1856), European peace negotiations (8 March

1856), the birth of the French Prince Imperial (29 March 1856) (Figure 2), the Treaty of Paris (12 April 1856), and the Jewish Emancipation Act (3 May 1856). This more serious ingredient requires that reader/viewers recognize the topical allusions and can enjoy the wit involved in using Shakespeare's text to comment on a contemporary nineteenth-century context. As one reads through Tenniel's 'Punch's Illustrations to Shakspeare', one can trace what appears to be a growing realization on his part of the potential of Shakespeare designs to deal in a humorous and witty manner with the more serious issues of the day. Here, one might argue, one can observe him experimenting in ways that anticipate his later work from 1862 to 1901 as chief cartoonist for *Punch*.

One other project by Tenniel may be briefly mentioned. During his early student days, he had developed a particular fascination with historical costumes, arms, and armour. He studied and copied from illustrated works on these subjects in the British Museum and visited the Tower of London to study the collection of arms and armour there. As a member from 1848 of the Clipstone Street Artists' Society (later the Langham Sketch Club), he had access to the Society's costume collection (Simpson 1994, 17). When *Punch* presented a humorous burlesque of Victorian medievalism and of such widely-read and serious studies as James Robinson Planché's *The Costume of Shakespeare's Historical Tragedy King John* (1823), *The Costume of Shakespeare's Tragedy of Hamlet* (1825), and *History of British Costume* (1834), Meyrick's *Ancient Arms and Armour* (1830), and Frederick William Fairholt's more recent *Costume in England* (1842–46; rpt. 1860) (Hancher 1985, 8 and 133 n. 6), Tenniel was the obvious artist to call upon. With considerable exuberance, he embraced the opportunity to make use of the knowledge he had acquired over the years.

'Punch's Book of British Costumes,' which was illustrated with some 123 designs by Tenniel, appeared in forty-two weekly issues and presented a burlesque of English history and costume from Anglo-Saxon times to Henry VIII. Three of its chapters alluded to Shakespeare plays. On 17 March 1860, for example, Chapter 7 ('The Anglo-Danish Period'), which was written by Henry Silver, contained an illustration of a very effete Hamlet with the caption 'COSTUME OF

THE NOBILITY, FROM AN AUTHENTIC PORTRAIT OF HAMLET, PRINCE OF DENMARK' (Figure 3). A note at the foot of the page states:

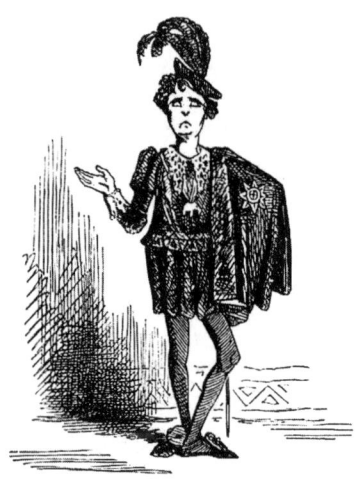

Figure 3. John Tenniel, costume for Hamlet. *Punch* (17 March 1860), 38:113.

We trust the British playgoer will bear this fact in mind the next time he ventures to see Mr. KEAN in Hamlet. By the traditions of the stage the Prince of Denmark has invariably been dressed in a black suit; whence the coarse-minded have jested about his being the Prince of Darkness, and the ignorant have fancied that he must be the Black Prince. It seems clear that Hamlet's sables should be viewed as being donned not in mourning for his father, but simply as the usual clothing of his father's son. (38:113)

Other allusions to Shakespeare occurred later in Chapter 37 (24 November) and Chapter 40 (15 December), both of which depict Richard III (39:208 and 238). Some sixteen years later in 1876, Tenniel was able to display his historical knowledge of costume in quite another way connected with Shakespeare. When making plans for his first appearance as Othello, Henry Irving persuaded the artist to design a costume for him that would represent the clothes and armour of a serving Venetian general (Irving 1951, 272).

In 1862, soon after completing work for 'Punch's Book of British Costumes', Tenniel took over from John Leech, as chief cartoonist, a responsibility that would occupy Tenniel's constant attention until he retired in 1901. Prior to taking over from Leech, Tenniel had already contributed a number of big cuts. The first appeared on 1 February 1851, and the first to employ Shakespearean material was a depiction on 8 December 1860 of Louis Napoleon as Prince Hal, trying on the Papal crown while his elderly 'father' (the Pope) lies ill in bed (39:225) (Figure 4). After his appointment in

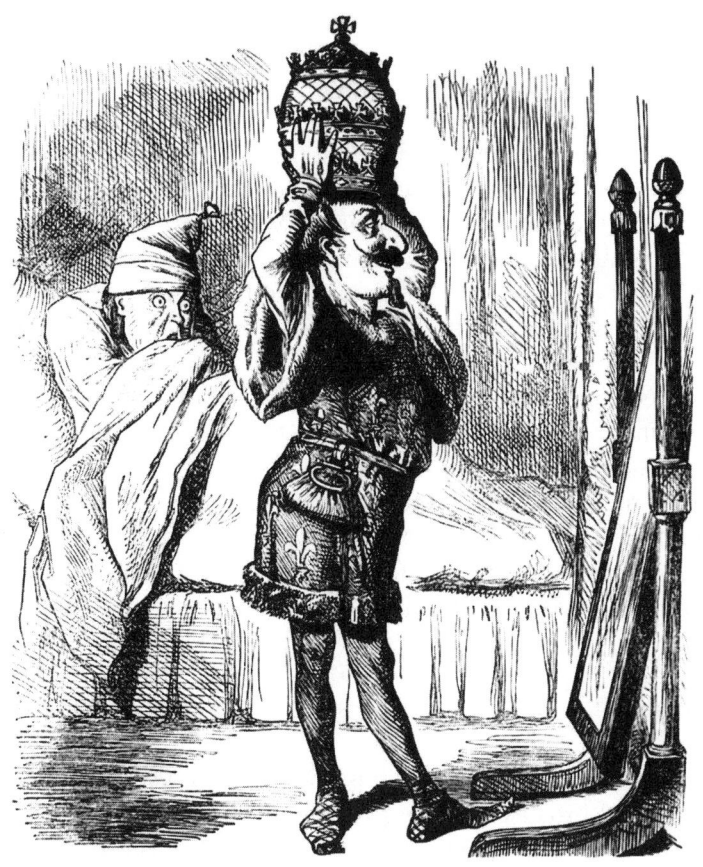

THE ELDEST SON OF THE CHURCH.

Figure 4. John Tenniel's big cut of Louis Napoleon as Prince Hal.
Punch (8 December 1860), 39:225.

1862, Tenniel barely missed a week and was responsible for almost 2,000 big cuts. These were enormously popular and influential. In 1893, Tenniel was knighted for the contribution to British culture that his work had made, and his retirement from *Punch* early in 1901 was seen as 'a national event' (*The Times,* 27 February 1914, 11). Francis

Burnand, the then editor of *Punch*, expressed in a brief article the wish that Tenniel were like Prospero and 'were simply laying aside for a while his magic art to resume it at will' ('Jackides,' *Punch*, 2 January 1901, 120:2). His designs were praised for 'swaying parties and peoples too' (Spielmann 1895b, 201), and at his death in 1914, the *Athenaeum* declared him to be 'the exponent for many years of the good sense of the nation' (*Athenaeum*, 7 March 1914, 349).

This is not the place to attempt to validate such responses to Tenniel's work. The point I wish to make here is that the veneration and attention accorded his weekly contributions to *Punch* meant that his ninety-two big cuts based on Shakespearean material (only four of these preceded his appointment as chief cartoonist) received very wide scrutiny when they first appeared, when they were re-published in the semi-annual volume format, when they were re-published in various books of collected *Punch* cartoons, and when they were displayed in exhibitions at various art galleries (Engen 1991, 202, 208–218). His was surely a very considerable and powerful contribution to *Punch*'s campaign to increase the familiarity of Shakespeare among its readers.

* * *

As I hope I have shown in this chapter, *Punch*, because of its popularity and broad cross-class readership, was uniquely positioned to both advance the knowledge and love of Shakespeare and reflect the deeply-ingrained position of Shakespeare within Victorian culture at large. It was inevitable that the collective appreciation of Shakespeare among *Punch*'s generally well-educated staff of writers and artists would show in its weekly pages in a myriad of ways. Indeed, during the sixty-year span of time with which this study is concerned, there were close to 1,300 articles and engravings in *Punch* having to do with Shakespeare. What these had to say, and what they reveal about *Punch*'s ongoing relationship with Shakespeare will be the subject of what now follows.

Chapter Two

Punch and Shakspeareanity

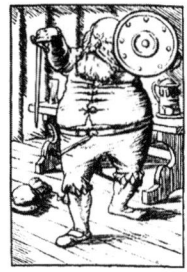
n 1 April 1844, General Tom Thumb made his second command appearance before Queen Victoria at court. Punch, which saw itself as champion of the arts and was well aware that its weekly issues went to the Queen (*Punch* Preface to Volume 12; and 12:219. Cf. Altick 1997, 17–18), launched an attack on her, wrapped, of course, in a copious sugar coating of irony:

> We had only to reflect upon the countless acts of patronage towards the arts and sciences – had only to remember a few of the numerous personal condescensions of the Queen towards men of letters, artists, and philosophers – to be assured that even Tom Thumb would be welcomed with that graceful cordiality which has heretofore made Buckingham Palace and Windsor Castle the home of poetry and science (6:157).

As if in response to Punch's jibes here and elsewhere that the court's tastes in entertainment were restricted to what was low-brow, the Queen then summoned another entertainer to court – the veteran Shakespearean actor Charles Kemble. It was announced that he would read before the court a two-hour 'compressed' version of *Cymbeline*. But this hardly satisfied *Punch*, and two of its principal satirists responded.

On 4 May, Thackeray contributed 'GREAT NEWS! WONDERFUL NEWS!' (6:189), an unsigned fourteen-stanza verse commentary, to which was added a sixteen-line verse moral. Headed by a small engraving of a very diminutive mustachioed figure captioned 'SHAKSPEARE COMPRESSED,' the verses were accompanied by marginal comments in black-letter font. The first two stanzas established the central theme:

67

> WHAT wonderful news from the Court,
> Old Will's at the palace a guest,
> The Queen and her Royal Consort
> Have received him 'a little compressed.'
>
> Who'll venture to whisper henceforth
> Her Grace loves the Opera best?
> Our QUEEN has acknowledged to the worth
> Of SHAKSPEARE a little compress'd.

The first stanza carried the marginal comment: 'Punch wondereth that Shakspeare hath at length appeared before ye Queene' and the second, alluding to the Queen's apparent preferences for imported entertainers, has the comment: 'He saith her Grace will heare no more Italians nor Almayne fiddlers, but take the right Englishe waye.' After four more stanzas in the same vein (they include an 'Away with the tiny TOM THUMB') and building on the irony of the repeated use of the word 'compressed', Thackeray then imagines the reading of *Cymbeline* by 'the last of the Royal old KEMBLES' and gives his own seven-stanza compressed version of the play. In the moral that follows, *Punch* (Thackeray) concludes by promising that he

> . . . never will jibe or will jest,
> If you'll list to our Poet immort-
> Al, and love him complete or compress'd!

A week later, Jerrold followed up on Thackeray's piece with 'DIFFUSION OF SHAKSPEAREANITY AT COURT' (6:199). Accompanied by a small engraving of Shakespeare in court dress, the article refers to Kemble's recital at court. The actor had been summoned to Buckingham Palace, we are told, 'that he then and there might enter upon the goodly work of diffusing SHAKSPEARE-ANITY through the hearts and minds of the natives abiding within the royal precincts'. Although Kemble 'found the greater number of the individuals in a very benighted condition regarding their knowledge and appreciation of the ennobling qualities of the Great Teacher, they nevertheless – the great defects of their education considered – evinced a degree of interest and aptitude, which MR. KEMBLE believes may in good time be made to produce the very best fruits'. The bulk of the article then purports to be a letter from Kemble to Mr. Punch (dated 7 May at the Garrick Club) reporting on his reception at court. According to this, there seems to be some hope that Prince Albert can be drawn away from rabbit-hunting and sitting for five hundred portraits, activities that have occupied him in the past. Perhaps he will watch something other than opera. Various other people at court are mentioned as having been converted from interest in opera and ballet to interest in Shakespeare. Throughout considerable ignorance concerning Shakespeare is comically revealed.

Two weeks later, Jerrold composed an article entitled 'EXHIBITION OF THE ENGLISH IN CHINA' (6:219–220). The original inspiration for this may have been the exhibition of Chinese artefacts that had opened in a building at Hyde Park Corner late in 1842 (Altick 1997, 615). The central conceit of Jerrold's article and the accompanying two small engravings is that an exhibition has opened in Peking on 'The Barbarian English in China.' There are numbered cases as in the Hyde Park exhibition, and there is a catalogue recording the good and bad qualities of the English. The second case contains a portrait of Shakespeare (the *Punch* engraving depicts Shakespeare as a Chinese), and the catalogue explains that 'This is the national poet, which the barbarians would, in their dreadful ignorance, compare to Confutzee.' Although the term 'Shakspeareanity' is not used, the article implies that the barbarian English worship Shakespeare like some pagan god. In the supposed catalogue entry for Shakespeare, Jerrold launches into a series of ironic statements, reiterating several of the points he had made earlier. The Chinese readers of the catalogue are told that 'It is melancholy to perceive the devotion paid by all ranks of people to this man' (6:119), but, in spite of bitter wrangles over the proper spelling of his name, Shakspeare 'is now the idol of the nation' (6:220). Furthermore,

> The house he was born in has been bought by the Government, and is surrounded by a silver rail. Whenever his plays are played, the Queen invariably goes in state to the theatre, and makes it pain of death to any of the nobility to stop away. All his relations are dead, or it is to be feared – such is the devotion of the court to SHAKSPEARE – that they would be turned into lords, and have fortunes settled upon them, like retired Ministers and Chancellors. [...] In a word, from the Queen to the peasant, all the people worship

> SHAKSPEARE. The first thing seen on approaching Dover is a statue of the poet, forty feet high, perched upon the Cliff. It is lamentable to record these things; but to fully show the moral darkness of the barbarians, it is necessary.

Punch's desire to advance what Jerrold called 'Shakspeareanity' is the theme of the current chapter and those that follow. The term appears to have been Jerrold's invention, and it was, as far as I can discern, used only sparingly in *Punch* (e.g., 13:121; 35:235; 46:49; and 46:53). As of this date, the Oxford English Dictionary does not record the word, and there is no equivalent modern noun to denote the concept of the combined knowledge and love of Shakespeare that Jerrold had in mind. The word in Jerrold's 'DIFFUSION OF SHAKSPEAREANITY AT COURT' is obviously intended as an amusing parallel to 'Christianity'. Accordingly, Kemble's letter is written in 'the Missionary style of composition'. Appropriately for such a missive, each convert to Shakspeareanity at the Palace is listed, and a brief description of each conversion is given. The resulting series of case histories attest to the effectiveness of Kemble's missionary labours at the palace and the resulting 'diffusion of SHAKSPEAREANITY throughout the court'. The imagined evangelical role of the aging actor (he was sixty-nine) who seeks to enlighten his auditors by raising awareness of the ennobling influence of the 'Great Teacher' is an amusing conceit. However, within a world in which, as Matthew Arnold maintained, 'The Bible and Shakspeare' were mentioned in the same breath and 'imposed upon an Englishman as objects of his admiration' (quoted Taylor 1991, 167), the missionary zeal displayed in Kemble's letter may not be such a comic exaggeration as it would be today. Indeed, my point in this chapter is that, even if *Punch* did not have a conscious policy of promoting Shakspeareanity, collectively its writers and artists constantly sought ways to raise the appreciation of Shakespeare, especially among those within the culture that they deemed to be as yet ignorant or indifferent regarding his near-divine status. To advance Shakspeareanity was to aspire to the highest moral truths and to give due recognition to the greatest artistic talent that England had ever produced. It was also to give due recognition to an English playwright, something especially dear to the *Punch* men's hearts.

Shakspeareanity and the Theatre Regulation Act of 1843

Advancing the cause of Shakspeareanity appears to be the subject of an 1843 engraving by John Leech of Mr. Punch as a schoolmaster (Figure 5). On the table beside him is a copy of Shakespeare's works, and the pupil who stands in front of him is the Queen's first-born son, Edward Prince of Wales (5:98). Such an image perfectly

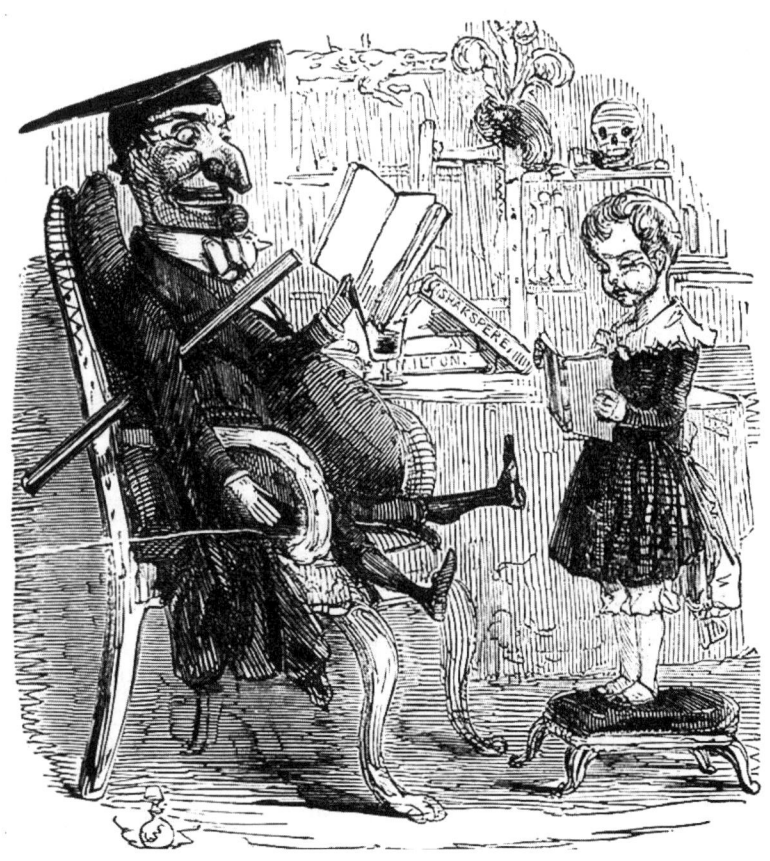

Figure 5. John Leech, 'WHO SHOULD EDUCATE THE PRINCE OF WALES', *Punch* (2 September 1843), 5:98.

represents Punch's evangelical mission to spread SHAKSPEARE-ANITY from the monarchy on down. But whereas such an image expresses an almost aggressive positivism, on many other occasions *Punch* often appears to be in a defensive mode, attempting to preserve a cultural icon that is threatened and under attack. Of deep concern, for example, were the possible detrimental effects of the Theatre Regulation Act of 1843. Whereas the Patent Houses (Drury Lane, Covent Garden, and, in the summer, the Haymarket) had been the only theatres legally authorized to put on 'legitimate' drama, the field was now wide open for the performance of serious drama (Shakespeare included) at any of the other theatres. Positive developments were Samuel Phelps and Mary Warner's establishment of a theatre company at Sadler's Wells and the many Shakespeare productions they initiated there. Positive, too were Charles Kean's Shakespeare productions at the Princess's from 1850 to 1859, although *Punch* was very critical of them, as will be discussed in the next chapter. However, at Drury Lane, Covent Garden, and the Haymarket the story was very different. At Drury Lane, for example, although Macready had succeeded in getting the Queen to attend a production of *As You Like It* in June 1843 (Downer 196, 23), his management there folded the same year. Financial difficulties were exacerbated by Macready's self-destructive management practices. His request to renew his lease was denied, and this initial attempt to establish a kind of national theatre with Shakespeare as a prime component of the repertoire then failed. The field was now open for Alfred Bunn, Macready's successor and former adversary (Jackson 1989, 246; Taylor 1989, 11), a theatrical entrepreneur who chose to seek the kind of lucrative successes enjoyed by theatres that had catered to the popular taste for melodrama, burlesques, musical spectaculars, and other forms of entertainment.

Punch, which saw the threat to Shakspeareanity inherent in the Theatre Regulation Act, made Bunn a particular target (Altick 1997, 698–707), with Jerrold as chief marksman. When the new theatre season opened in September 1844, *Punch* included a review by Jerrold of the offerings at the various London theatres, but reserved special attention for Drury Lane, where, we are told, 'An entirely new portico, under the conscientious direction of MR. BUNN, has been' erected (7:152). The unsigned engraving that accompanies Jerrold's review provides what *Punch* refers to as 'a faithful representation of the architectural novelty'. On top of the supposed new portico is a statue of Alfred Bunn that has replaced that of Shakespeare, who has now gone to Sadler's Wells. The entire structure is supported by four columns in the form of female ballet dancers, and to either side are large banners inscribed 'OPERA' and 'BALLET', clearly intended to indicate two of the ways by which Bunn hopes to make a profit. Mobs of people are besieging the theatre to gain entrance (Macready by contrast had found it very hard to fill the huge theatre for his productions, and hence his eventual bankruptcy), and, approaching the theatre, is a procession of authors bearing bundles inscribed 'MELODRAMAS', 'FRENCH PLAYS', and 'VAUDEVILLE'. These represent the other means by which Bunn intends to prosper. Included is something of an 'in' joke, since the procession is led by men bearing the banner of the Dramatic Authors Society, to which, as mentioned earlier, a number of *Punch* writers belonged, including Jerrold. Adopting its usual ironic stance, *Punch* wishes Bunn well in the coming season at the theatre made famous for its productions of Shakespeare by the managements of Garrick, John Philip Kemble, and more recently, as *Punch* readers would have been well aware, William Charles Macready:

> MR. BUNN has, for what he purposes to do, an excellent company, and we heartily wish him all success. Whilst the drama was bound hand and foot in the two patent theatres [i.e. Covent Garden and Drury Lane], we fought lustily against the injustice; but now, that Shakspere may, without let or hindrance, wander to Islington [the location of Sadler's Wells] – nay, poor fellow if whilst he is even permitted to be worried at the Victoria – we have only to commend MR. BUNN or any other manager who offers the town such entertainment as the programme for the season promises. Therefore, may good-luck rosin his bow, and – strike up fiddlers!

Coinciding with Bunn's return to Drury Lane (he had been manager there before Macready's brief tenure) was the return of this latter from a tour in America. However, Macready had no plans to perform in England, and he took his company to France. For *Punch*, this was another blow to Shakspeareanity, and late in 1844 Macready's decision was duly noted in an unsigned engraving entitled 'SHAKSPEAR AN EMIGRANT TO FRANCE' (7:247) (Figure 6).

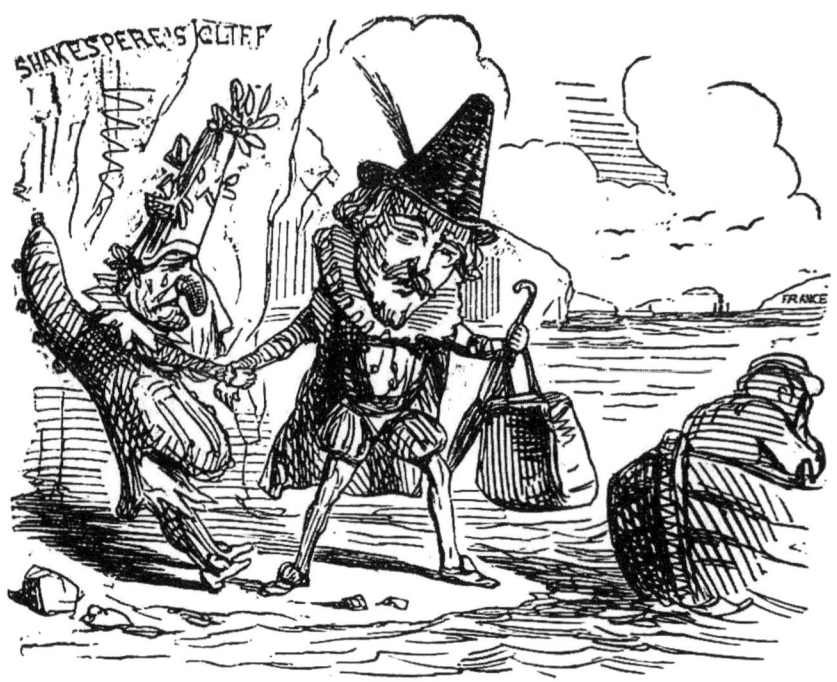

Figure 6. Unidentified artist. Shakespeare embarks for France. *Punch* (30 November 1844), 7:247.

The engraving shows Shakespeare about to board a boat for France and Punch holding his arm and attempting to prevent him from leaving. The two stand below 'Shakspere's Cliff' (at Dover). The caption below has Punch address Shakespeare ('hysterically') as follows: 'Bless you BILL! you shall never want a friend, or a good word, as long as I live.' The accompanying article purports to be a letter from Queen Victoria to the King of France (Louis Philippe) that is dated 27

November. It ironically expresses the Queen's high regard for both Shakespeare (the only thing that Queen Elizabeth had that she envies) and for the acting of William Charles Macready. She claims to have frequently attended Drury Lane during Macready's term there. She would like to decorate Macready, but her Prime Minister Peel is an obstacle. She hopes the King will decorate Macready himself.

In the new year, *Punch* continued this commentary on Macready's going to France with an engraving (Figure 7) that depicted the two sides of a medal. One side showed Shakespeare descending the steps of Drury Lane and watched by an imperious-looking Alfred

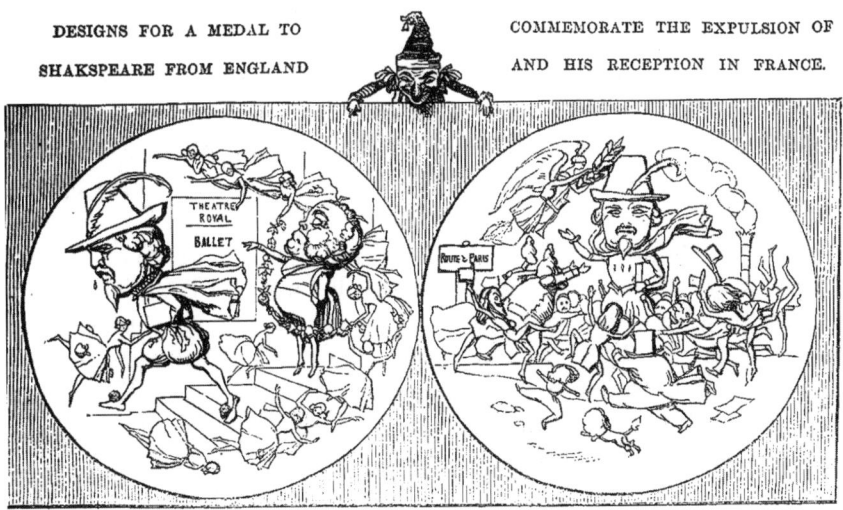

Figure 7. Unidentified artist. *Punch* (25 January 1845), 8:48.

Bunn who stands at the head of the steps. On the wall is a play-bill advertising the performance of a ballet, the kind of fare that will now be offered in place of Shakespeare's plays. The other side of the medal depicts the triumphant arrival of Shakespeare in France, greeted by rapturous crowds as he disembarks from the steamer. An angel is about to place a laurel wreath on his head. The caption reads: 'The Medal (of which the above are the designs) is to be struck by command of HIS MAJESTY the KING OF THE FRENCH. It is thought, in well-informed circles, that SHAKESPEARE'S trip to the Continent will be the means of restoring him to the boards of the Royal Theatres, as he may now be considered an importation from the French stage, and consequently has a customary right to be received in an English Theatre.'

Blame is here placed on the back of Bunn, but implied is a more general blame. English audiences appear to prefer imported entertainments rather than native products. The allusion to the supposed enthusiasm of the French king for Shakespeare is, of course, an indirect jibe at the English monarch's contrasting neglect of Shakespeare. In defence of Queen Victoria, however, and in recognition that the comments of *Punch* and other journals did not necessarily go unheeded, it should be noted that she did attend a Macready production of Shakespeare at Drury Lane (as mentioned above), and she would eventually attend his penultimate stage appearance. In 1848, she also invited Charles Kean to present a number of Shakespeare plays at Windsor Castle, and, at the same time, she pointedly ceased going to operas (Schoch 1998, 127).

Across the English Channel, Louis Philippe and the French royal family saw Macready's *Hamlet* at the Palais des Tuileries on 16 January 1845, and the King presented Macready with a bejewelled poniard (Downer 2:272; Foulkes 2002, 29). But in England there was no equivalent to this type of royal patronage, and to the staff of *Punch* it must have seemed that their various comments on the Queen's neglect of Shakespeare had little or no effect. Somewhat later, of course, her widowhood that began on 14 December 1861 resulted in her forgoing attendance at public stage performances altogether.

A respectful two years after the death of Prince Albert, *Punch* attempted to renew its campaign to obtain royal support for Shakespeare. On 7 November 1863, an article by Percival Leigh stated that the 'THE QUEEN'S loving subjects will rejoice to hear that HER MAJESTY intends to establish a theatre at Windsor Castle; a house which will be pre-eminently a Theatre Royal, entitled to be called Her Majesty's Own Theatre' (45:188). Leigh explained that

> It is plain that HER MAJESTY has resolutely determined from a sense of duty to resort to amusement as an alleviation of a grief that may be incurable, though due consideration might change it into hope, capable even of rising into joy. For such a grief, the theatre affords one of the most effectual of earthly remedies.

Quoting *As you Like It*, the article then states that '"all the world's a stage, and all the men and women merely players", tends to elevate the beholder above all the world'. The central point is that 'When the curtain has fallen on a noble tragedy, and whilst the grand words of SHAKESPEARE are still ringing in the ears, the mind looks above and beyond mortal ills; and the spectacle of a well-acted part must hint a particular consolation for a sorrow such as the QUEEN'S.'

Two years after this, when there was still no apparent alleviation in the Queen's mourning, *Punch* approached the subject again but in somewhat broader terms. Not just the theatre was at stake but her relationship with her subjects generally. At a *Punch* dinner on 12 September 1865, Mark Lemon suggested that Tenniel do a big cut of Mr. Punch 'unveiling Statue of Queen in her Court Robes to show Queen in mourning – apropos of the latter's trip to Coburg lately to 'inaugurate' another statue to the "Great & Good"' (Henry Silver Diary). What the *Punch* men had in mind was a version of the Statue Scene in Shakespeare's *The Winter's Tale* (Young 2005, 231–232, 243). In that famous scene, a curtain is drawn back to reveal a statue of Queen Hermione, whose death was announced earlier in the play. During the ensuing scene, Hermione comes 'alive', her death having been a ruse to punish her husband.

Lemon's initial idea would have symbolically shown Queen Victoria's mourning veil being removed to reveal her statue in which she is depicted as though having returned to court dress. But there were some problems associated with this. Charles Keene said that he thought 'the figure in widow's weeds should be omitted – but then t'would seem as though the Queen were dead'. There was also the matter of an appropriate caption. Lemon hunted up a copy of *The Winter's Tale* and suggested that a possible line would be ''Tis time, descend: be stone no more.' When he proposed leaving out the last four words, Henry Silver voiced an objection since 'this would hint at dethronement'. As was the usual practice, Tenniel then took these

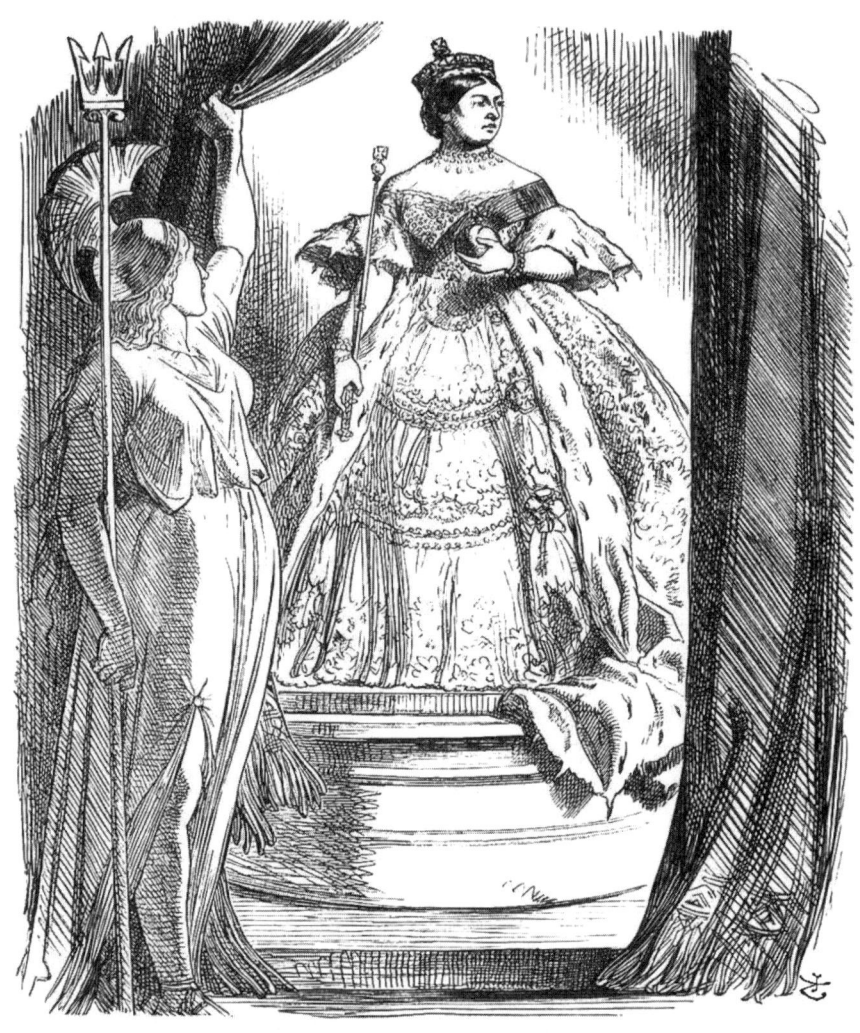

Figure 8. John Tenniel, 'Queen Hermione', *Punch* (23 September 1865), 49:117.

thoughts and suggestions of his colleagues away with him to guide him in his final design. This appeared on 23 September 1865 (Figure 8). Entitled 'QUEEN HERMIONE', it represents Hermione/Victoria standing upon a pedestal. She wears an imposing crinoline and full court dress, including crown, sceptre, and orb. There is no hint of any mourning dress or veil, and Tenniel instead uses Shakespeare's device of a curtain being drawn back to reveal the statue. In the play, the statue is unveiled by Paulina as her husband (Leontes) observes. But in Tenniel's design she is replaced, not by Mr. Punch as Lemon had originally suggested, but by a tall helmeted Britannia the identity of whom is confirmed in the caption: 'PAULINA (BRITANNIA) UNVEILS THE STATUE.' Like the readers of *Punch* in 1865, we are expected to remember the magical moment that follows in Shakespeare's play when the statue comes to life and responds to Paulina's (here Britannia's) command: ''Tis time! Descend! Be stone no more!' (49:117). Britannia is to be read as the voice of the British people urging Queen Victoria to end her self-imposed isolation and 'Be stone no more', this being in reality a plea for Queen Victoria to end her period of mourning for her beloved husband, Prince Albert.

However, *Punch*'s fantasy concerning the establishment of a theatre at Windsor remained mere imaginative speculation, and eventually the magazine appears to have abandoned its efforts to revive the Queen's enthusiasm for the theatre and to convert her to Shakspeareanity. In 1881, however, she did agree to attend a theatrical performance at Abergeldi Castle at the behest of the Prince of Wales. Command performances at Windsor, Osborne House, and Balmoral then followed during the remainder of her life (Schoch 2004, xvi). Even so, she saw little of Shakespeare, a *tableau vivant* of the statue scene in *The Winter's Tale* being an ironic exception. Presented at Osborne House on Twelfth Night in 1888, the *tableau*, in which Marcia Dalrymple and her husband Captain Dalrymple took the roles of Hermione and Leontes, was one of four unconnected creations. Later that year at Balmoral, there was another exception in the form of the character of Romeo, who appeared in a series of twelve *tableaux vivants* designed to celebrate Prince Henry of Battenberg's thirtieth birthday (Schoch 2004, 25–27). A final exception occurred in April

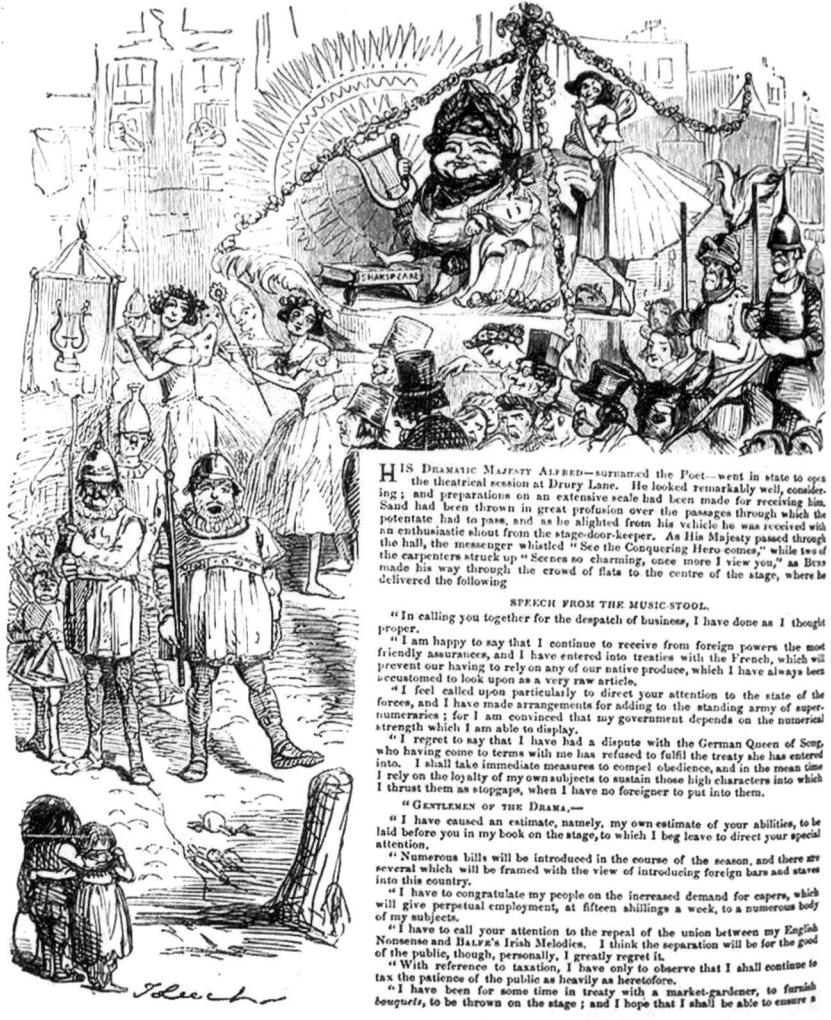

Figure 9. John Leech, 'POET BUNN'S OPENING OF DRURY LANE THEATRE', *Punch* (11 October 1845), 9:160.

when Henry Irving, Ellen Terry, and other members of the Lyceum theatre company performed the trial scene from *The Merchant of Venice* at Sandringham

But to return to Alfred Bunn. In the fall of 1845, *Punch* marked the beginning of the new season at Drury Lane with a design by John Leech, depicting an elaborate and grandiose procession in which Alfred Bunn, the wreath of Midas on his head and the lyre of Apollo in his hands, is carried through the streets of London to Drury Lane Theatre (9:160) (Figure 9). Bunn's foot is casually resting upon a volume inscribed 'Shakspeare' that serves as a footstool. Prominent in the entourage are three female ballet dancers. The accompanying article by Gilbert Abbott à Beckett ironically comments on the grandeur of the event as though describing the royal opening of a session of Parliament: 'HIS DRAMATIC MAJESTY ALFRED – surnamed the Poet – went in state to open the theatrical session at Drury Lane' etc. The commentary concludes with the following verses of 'RULE BRITANNIA' sung by the entire staff of Drury Lane after the 'king' has entered the building:

> Rule, Great BUNN, here,
> Great BUNN here rule the stage;
> SHAKSPEARE never, never, never,
> Shall be the rage.

A final example of *Punch*'s attacks on Bunn and the threat to Shakspeareanity that the manager of Drury Lane was perceived to embody appeared in the form of a design by William Newman published on 8 May two years later (12:196). At the time, Bunn had been experiencing difficulties. Having brought Jenny Lind, the immensely popular 'Swedish Nightingale', to sing in Bellini's *La Sonnambula* at Drury Lane in 1845, he had later got into a legal tussle with her when she left Covent Garden (Bunn was the lessee there as well as manager at Drury Lane) and signed a contract in 1847 with Benjamin Lumley at Her Majesty's Theatre in the Haymarket. There she had a phenomenal success. *Punch's* response to all this was to lavish praise on her (e.g. 12:197; 12:208; 13:4; 13:10; 13:71), no doubt in part to irk Bunn, while at the same time continuing its attacks on the 'desecrations' that had invaded the August precincts of Drury Lane. Among Bunn's various sins, according to *Punch*, was the presentation of an animal show, to which the Queen and Prince Albert took their children on several occasions. Attacking Bunn's crude attempt to garner revenues, and mocking his poetic talents as a librettist (Bunn wrote the libretti for a number of Michael William Balfe's operas, including the very successful *The Bohemian Girl* in 1843), *Punch* printed a full-page item by Gilbert Abbott à Beckett

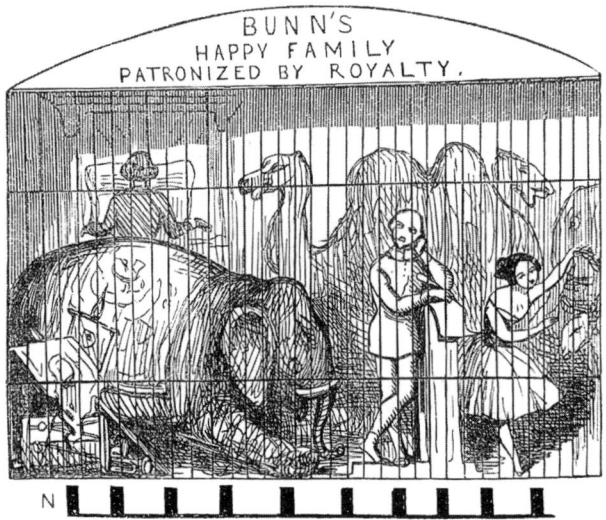

Figure 10. William Newman's portrayal of Alfred Bunn's 'happy family'. *Punch* (8 July 1847), 12:196.

entitled 'THE POET BUNN'S NEXT OPERA' (12:196). This was headed by an engraving of three exotic animals (an elephant and two camels), flanked by a cassowary and a large snake. The article below claims that the elephant's name is Jenny Lind, and, in order to give her and her fellows, satisfying roles for next year's entertainment, Bunn has decided to write the libretto for a new opera to be entitled 'THE ELEPHANT OF THE EUPHRATES; OR, THE CAMEL OF

THE CAUCASUS'. A segment of the plot is then outlined, and it is claimed that 'Jenny Lind' will dance and curtsey. Accompanying this text is Newman's engraving (Figure 10). It depicts a large cage standing before the footlights. Crowded into the cage like circus animals are the captive figures that Bunn can exploit for profit. There is a man playing the organ, an elephant ('Jenny Lind') and two camels. To the right Bunn himself appears to be seated, and there is a female ballet dancer in a tutu immediately in front of him. At the centre of the cage, is the standing figure of Shakespeare, quill in hand and leaning upon a pedestal in an obvious imitation of Peter Scheemakers's Westminster Abbey statue. Such a statue also stood over the portico of Drury Lane, so it was particularly appropriate here. However, Shakespeare's name is nowhere mentioned in the article, and the point appears to be that Bunn, though claiming ownership of him, has no intention of using him.

Before the year was out, Bunn had his revenge for the numerous attacks by *Punch* on both his artistic and entrepreneurial exploits. He sought the aid of Shirley Brooks, who had not yet joined the *Punch* staff, George Augustus Sala, an artist whose submissions to *Punch* had been summarily rejected by Mark Lemon, Ebenezer Landells, the disgruntled former engraver for *Punch,* and Albert Smith, who had been eased out of the *Punch* brotherhood. The result was the publication on 11 November of a burlesque version of a *Punch* issue entitled *A Word with Punch* (Spielmann 1895a, 227–232). Its wrapper burlesqued that of *Punch* and mockingly caricatured various members of the *Punch* staff. Among them were Thackeray, slumped against Punch's broken big drum, Douglas Jerrold in the form of a diminutive wasp, and Mark Lemon, the former publican, dressed as a pot-boy and reaching towards a tankard of ale. The wrapper also placed Mr. Punch in the pillory, and hanged his dog Toby from a gibbet. Inside its pages, the publication fiercely attacked in particular *Punch*'s 'three Puppets' – Douglas Jerrold (Wronghead), Gilbert Abbott à Beckett (Sleekhead), and Mark Lemon (Thickhead) – and their dramatic writings and acting abilities. The various failures of all three are viciously ridiculed with, one has to admit, considerable effectiveness. Bunn's burlesque, which was sold for the same price as *Punch,* was extremely successful, and a coloured 'édition de luxe' was also issued. Though the *Punch* men reportedly tried to buy up as many copies as possible, Bunn seems to have achieved his purpose in putting *Punch* in its place and even seems to have had the last word, since *Punch* uncharacteristically did not respond and maintained a diplomatically defensive silence. By this time, however, *Punch* had probably been forced to accept that Shakespeare had indeed gone from Drury Lane and that Bunn and what he stood for were not so easily vanquished. In the cause of Shakspeareanity, it was perhaps time to concentrate on other matters.

Punch and Shakespeare's Birthplace

Nothing could have served as a better alternative project regarding Shakspeareanity than the national debate that occurred when it became known that Shakespeare's birthplace in Stratford-on-Avon was to be sold, its previous owner having just died in 1846 (Fox 1948, 82). The Henley Street building was in a run-down state, and its authenticity as the actual birthplace was questionable. However, it was already an established shrine in the eyes of Victorian bardolators. In the words of the poster advertising its sale, it was 'The truly heart-stirring relic of a most glorious period, and of England's immortal bard […] the most honoured monument of the greatest genius that ever lived' (quoted Fox 1948, 79). It was a magnet for tourists (there were 2,400 in 1845 and 2,430 in 1846), who came to see such relics as the dramatist's tobacco box, the sword with which he played Hamlet, and a gold box presented to him by the King of Spain (Schoenbaum 1970, 83). In May 1847, an asking price of £2,000 to £3,000 was announced, but since neither Stratford-on-Avon nor the British government stepped forward with the funds, the property was up for grabs, the new ownership to be decided at a public auction in London on 16 September.

During the months leading up to this date, there was widespread interest, mixed with considerable anxiety among Shakespeare lovers, as means were sought to secure the property and preserve it as a national monument (Fox 1948, 82). Various fund-raising initiatives were set in motion, involving the Shakespearean Monumental Committee in Stratford-on-Avon, already charged with preserving Shakespeare's tomb, a similar committee in London, and the People's Central Committee of the Shakespeare Memorial Fund, set in motion by George Jones, the American tragedian. This last met with strong criticism and came to nothing, but meanwhile the Stratford and London committees co-ordinated their work and succeeded at the auction when their offer of £3,000 was accepted.

Up to this point, there had been a number of fund-raising ventures, including performances of *Henry IV* and *Twelfth Night*, and a musical entertainment by Joseph Stirling Coyne (formerly of *Punch*) entitled *This House To Be Sold (the Property of the Late William Shakespeare); Inquire Within*. Unfortunately, when the auction took place, the necessary sum of money had not yet been fully raised, and further fund-raising was needed. There was, for example, a benefit performance at Covent Garden on 7 December that attracted a very large audience. It consisted of nine individual scenes from Shakespeare, each featuring a different star actor. The list of those participating, a number of whom would never have agreed to act together in a single play, included Macready, Buckstone, Webster, Phelps, Helen Faucit, Fanny Kemble, Mme. Vestris, and Mrs Warner. Royal patronage was anticipated (something that helped swell the attendance), but the Queen stayed away, yet more evidence according to her critics that she neglected the English drama (Allen 1971, 112–113). The following year on 15 May the *Punch* staff and others joined in the fund-raising efforts and, as was mentioned in the previous chapter, put on a benefit performance of *The Merry Wives of Windsor* that then went on tour to five other cities, the goal being to raise money for the perpetual curatorship of the birthplace (Spielmann 1895a, 135; Gager 1996, 106–109, 375).

But what of *Punch* itself during this time when the most sacred shrine of Shakspeareanity was under threat? The first response was uncharacteristically indirect. Perhaps in hope of persuading the Queen to make some kind of intervention, presumably financial in nature, *Punch* returned to its familiar regal-indifference theme (Altick 1997, 727) and printed a long letter supposedly submitted by Stratford-on-Avon's oldest inhabitant. In reality, it was the creation of Douglas

Jerrold. Dated 29 April 1847 with a postscript dated on the 30th, the letter describes how 'QUEEN VICTORIA, PRINCE ALBERT, the PRINCE OF WALES, the PRINCESS ROYAL, and the PRINCESS ALICE have all made a pilgrimage to the birthplace of our own – the world's SHAKSPEARE; ...' (12:187). The Queen and her family, we are told, dismounted from their coach to approach the birthplace on foot. A tear fell from the Queen's eye as she crossed the threshold, and once inside 'she walked upon the floor so softly – so reverently, I may say – you'd have thought she was walking in a church.' In the chamber where Shakespeare had been born, she 'told the royal children what a great man had been born in that room; a man who had done such mighty good to all creatures; a man that they must learn to love for his goodness, and to imitate for his wisdom.' The royal party then visited Shakespeare's tomb before returning by coach to Oxford. The letter writer then concluded:

> This visit of the QUEEN to SHAKSPEARE will make tens of thousands crowd to house and tomb. Besides, the QUEEN honours herself and throne by honouring the greatest mind that ever dawned in man – and that man, an Englishman. (12:188)

There is, however, a postscript, dated the next day. In this Stratford's 'Oldest Inhabitant' reports on a newspaper item that he had read that morning:

> the QUEEN, PRINCE ALBERT and the PRINCE OF WALES, the PRINCESS ROYAL, and PRINCESS ALICE' were all at Drury Lane Theatre – all to see a show of beasts; camels, Indian ponies, and Indian elephants! This is shameful. Who invents these stories [...]?

The reality, of course, as watchers of the Court circular would have known, was that the newspaper was correct and the letter to Mr. Punch was mere fantasy and wishful thinking.

At about this time, here were also reports in the *Times* that P. T. Barnum, who had visited Stratford in the fall of 1844, was considering the idea of purchasing the house and transporting it across the Atlantic (Barnum 1967, 56; Altick 1997, 658). This is confirmed in his biography where he expresses his regret at not putting in an offer, since

> I should have made a rare speculation, for I was subsequently assured that the British people, rather than suffer that house to be removed to America would have bought me off with twenty thousand pounds. (Wallace 1959, 109)

Punch was understandably horrified with this threat to the sacred shrine, and did its best to alert its readers to the danger in an item by Jerrold entitled 'SHAKSPEARE'S HOUSE TO BE SOLD.' This was in the form of a letter supposedly from P. T. Barnum to the Mayor of Stratford. The letter is written in the same Yankee dialect as had earlier been used for Tom Thumb's epistle (see above). Its humour stemmed in part from the universal amusement that non-standard English tends to offer by way of comedy. Additionally in this instance, Barnum's language and vocabulary seem excessively brash and crude, and hence in harmony with what *Punch* hopes will seem to English sensibilities to be the outrageous idea of selling off a sacred relic to serve the financial greed of a foreigner:

> ... understand me, Mr. Mayor, SHAKSPEARE is pretty well catawampussed up in his own country by all sorts of foreign sarpints; and his nose is out of jinte, and will never be set strait agin at the English Court; and therefore, you see, Mr. Mayor, we – free Americans, children of the star-spangled banner – we, who are the only people on airth who understand English in the clear grit that 'varsal critter SHAKSPEARE writ it – we ought to possess the location in which he fust saw the light, afore any other nation under the blue canopy. SHAKSPEARE's house is a drug in England; but wouldn't it be a beauty, put upon wheels, and drawn through all the States?

After telling the Mayor to 'jist say the number of dollars that your Stratford critters want for the immortal location,' Barnum unconsciously adds insult to injury by promising 'that GENERAL TOM THUMB should act SHAKSPEARE, jist as he has acted NAPOLEON. A smartish compliment this, I think, to the ivverlastin Bard.' With Charles Knight's *Life of Shakspeare* as guide, the General will put on a re-enactment of Shakespeare's life with himself as Shakespeare. As an afterthought, Barnum wonders if Mr. Bunn could be persuaded to sell him the statue of Shakespeare 'off Drury Lane portico for the Gen'ral to rehearse by' (12:198).

Very soon after this, *Punch* continued its effort concerning the birthplace in 'SHAKSPEARE'S House' with another letter to Mr.

Punch from Stratford's 'Oldest Inhabitant' (12:219). It was dated 26 May and was again the work of Jerrold. It reported the bad omen that the martlets had failed to return to the eaves of the house, something that elicits the appropriate quotation from *Macbeth*. The old man reports that he has heard that the owners of the house are 'about to turn it into hard cash, as though it were a stack of firewood' and that a 'foreign gentleman' has 'offered money for the wondrous building, to turn it into a show somewhere across the sea'. His belief that the Queen's favour will surely protect the house has apparently been mocked, but he hopes that *Punch* will print his letter and that when that week's issue 'is laid upon the QUEEN's breakfast-table,' he hopes that it 'may catch the starry and vouchsafing eye of condescending Majesty'. He suggests that 'to save the nation from a blistering shame', the house should be 'purchased by the State'. However, the Queen was not to be so shamed into a response. She remained silent and her purse closed.

On 14 August, after reporting that six different parties were interested in buying the house (13:50), *Punch* published an open letter from Mr. Punch to Prince Albert, headed by a delightful initial letter by Thackeray in the form of Hamlet holding a skull (Figure 11). Entitled 'THE HOUSE OF SHAKSPEARE AND THE HOUSE OF COBURG' and written by Percival Leigh, the item refers to Punch's previous criticisms of the Prince but says that Mr. Punch is now happy to praise him:

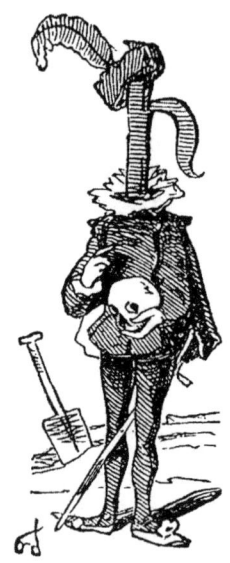

Figure 11. Thackeray's letter 'H'. *Punch* (14 August 1847), 13:121.

You cannot imagine what delight it has given me to read, in the newspapers, that you are at the head of a Committee established in order to raise a fund for the purchase of SHAKSPEARE's house; and that you have yourself contributed £250 towards this most praiseworthy object. The House of SHAKSPEARE will henceforth reflect honour on the House of Coburg. (13:52)

Aware that £250 will not go very far towards the purchase of the house, Leigh then concludes with some ironic chiding of the royal family for their general neglect of Shakespeare.

Conscious, no doubt, that it had done all that it could to prod the royal family into joining the campaign to purchase the house for the nation, *Punch* then turned its attention to one of its pet satiric targets, George Jones. This latter had earlier been associated with James Silk Buckingham's short-lived British and Foreign Institute, a somewhat bizarre establishment where, it was hoped, literary soirées and scientific enquiry could find a home. Jones had been an actor in the United States and had played Richard III and Hamlet among other roles. He was the author of some peculiar books with contents as odd as their titles, and he claimed to be a count (Altick 1997, 639–641). *Punch* seems to have viewed Jones as an arrogant, incompetent charlatan, so when Jones formed The People's Central Committee of the Shakespeare Memorial Fund to raise money for the purchase of the birthplace, *Punch*'s reaction was predictable. Not only was Jones unlikely to raise any money, but his laughable reputation and hot-air speeches were likely to detract from the serious efforts of other fundraisers. In 'SHAKSPEARE AND MR. GEORGE JONES', William Newman depicted Jones as a monkey perched on the head of Shakespeare. The accompanying article by Tom Taylor talks about The People's Central Committee, describes him as 'a sort of Human Blue-Bottle, that buzzes about, and fly-blows great memories', and mocks one of Jones's publications, an 'utterly absurd and intolerable, 'oration' on SHAKSPEARE' (13:84). The especially savage attack concludes that Jones 'must not be allowed to paw the revered head of the Poet – to bring his pinchbeck near the touch-stone of SHAKSPEARE's truth. There is a desecration in it ...'

After brief notices expressing alarm about the now imminent sale (13:97), and after pointing out that the Lord Mayor of London (Sir Peter Laurie) had not made a donation, in spite of proposing to set up a statue of Shakespeare (13:113), the day of the auction arrived, and on 16 September at Robin's London auction house, the property was purchased for the nation, though £2,000 was still needed to finalize everything. An article by Douglas Jerrold recorded the event in 'SHAKSPEARE'S HOUSE – MULBERRY COLLEGE', in which it is suggested, not altogether facetiously, that a new college be built beside the birthplace with collegians who would strive 'to do honour to the World's Poet, and to diffuse Shakspeareanity throughout all classes' (13:121). After including yet another ironic comment on the Queen's patronage of the arts (or lack of it), Jerrold concluded with a shot at Jones, who, we are told, stopped for refreshment on the way to the auction, got 'Hocussed,' and fell into a profound sleep after sending for a copy of his *Oration* on Shakespeare. This concluding section is accompanied by a delightful unsigned engraving that depicts the recumbent Jones, one elbow resting upon a fat volume inscribed 'ORATION – SHAKESPEARE' (Figure 12) The reader/viewer, however, is expected to recognize that he is a burlesque version of Bottom in *A Midsummer Night's Dream* and that the air-borne Punch, who is about to place an ass's head upon him, is a version of Shakespeare's Puck.

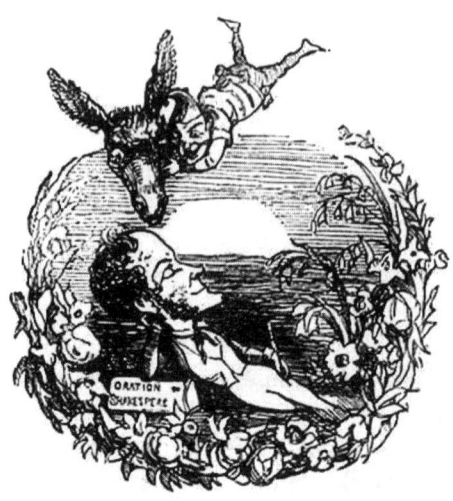

Figure 12. Unidentified artist's portrait of George Jones. *Punch* (2 October 1847), 13:121.

But *Punch* had not quite finished with making an ass of Jones and his bid for the house. A letter from 'Fast Man' (Percival Leigh) that was included in a later issue praises Jones's fund-raising efforts and derides *Punch* for sneering 'at JONES for mixing up his name with that of SHAKSPEARE.' George Jones is an equal to Shakespeare, for, like this latter, he goes in for clap-trap. After all, Shakespeare, like the present Alfred Bunn, was involved in theatre merely to make money. Hamlet was composed 'merely on spec,' and the Ghost introduced into that play only for effect. Having set up its straw man, *Punch* then responds in a concluding editorial note and argues that Shakespeare, even had he written in contemporary times, would 'still have illustrated human nature. We surmise that his

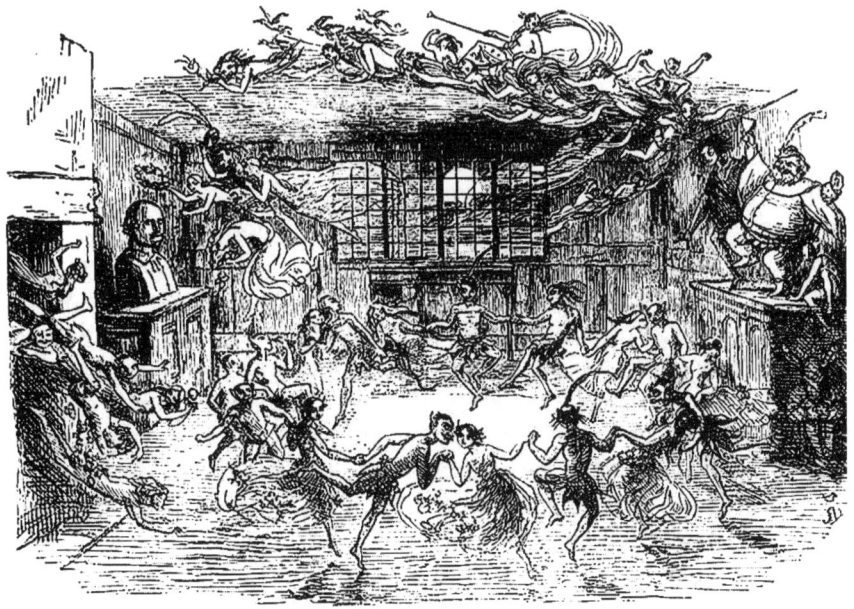

Figure 13. Richard Doyle, 'PUNCH'S VISION AT STRATFORD-ON-AVON', *Punch* (13 November 1847), 13:184.

productions would still have glowed with poetry, and been pregnant with wisdom, and would not have been replete either with commonplace absurdities or crimes.'

Now that the birthplace was safe from profiteers like Barnum and Jones, *Punch* concentrated on efforts to secure the remaining sum needed. Two reports by Jerrold, each chiding the aristocracy for not contributing sufficiently, noted that the original £2,000 required was now down to £1,400 (13:152; 13:161). Then in the 13 November issue (13:184) and somewhat belatedly for no apparent reason, there appeared 'PUNCH'S VISION AT STRATFORD-ON-AVON. THE NIGHT OF THE SIXTEENTH OF SEPTEMBER' (Figure 13). This consisted of a fanciful half-page engraving designed by Richard Doyle, accompanied by some verses supplied by Tom Taylor. It depicted a host of fairies who have returned to the room in which Shakespeare was born. Some dance in a circle around the room, while others fly around the ceiling. One figure, possibly Titania, places a wreath on the bust of Shakespeare. On the opposite side of the room, Falstaff, seated beside what appears to be Hamlet, raises a glass in honour of Shakespeare and in celebration of the successful purchase. Seated in the shadows below Falstaff, and looking rather glum, is Bottom in his ass's head, an allusion to George Jones perhaps. The verses record the vision of someone who went from London to visit Stratford and fell asleep in the room. According to the verses, among the figures who appeared (not all of whom can be found in Doyle's design) were Othello ('Jealousy, with black lips'), Ophelia ('Madness looked sweet, but tore its hair, And fell on sudden trances'), King Lear ('an old king, left by his daughters bare / To the world's chances'), Lady Macbeth ('One wrung her hands – walking, all wan, / In nightrail'), and Hamlet ('One curiously a skull did scan'). All have come to 'their great master's home' to mark the setting free of his dwelling 'From shameful desecration, / And made o'er SHAKSPEARE'S house, a shrine to be / For SHAKSPEARE'S nation!'

Just under a month later in the issue for 11 December, *Punch* more or less concluded its thread of items on the birthplace drama with a lively piece by Jerrold entitled 'THE SHAKSPEARE NIGHT' (13:221). This was based on an actual event, a benefit performance of various scenes from Shakespeare's plays that had been put on at the Royal Italian Opera House, Covent Garden, four days earlier (Fox 1948, 84). Continuing his critique of the royal family's apparent failure to give proper recognition to Shakespeare, Jerrold mentions ironically that there is 'reason to believe that HER MAJESTY was most unwillingly absent'. In spite of all the appropriate arrangements having been made for her to travel by train from Osborne House on the Isle of White, the trip was cancelled because the 'the wife and child of the favourite stoker of the royal train being very poorly indeed with the prevailing malady, the man could not, as a husband and a father, leave his partner and his infant, ...' According to the *Court Circular*, or so we are told, the Queen and the Prince instead 'took a hand at cribbage'.

Jerrold's fantasy takes full flight a little later when he describes the unexpected arrival of Shakespeare himself with his wife, the late

Anne Hathaway. Despite a slight disturbance when a 'man named JONES would run by the carriage, and insist upon SHAKSPEARE taking the copy of an *Oration*', Shakespeare was graciously received by his editors, Charles Knight and John Payne Collier, who each presented to him a copy of their respective editions. Mary Cowden Clarke was also present. A Shakespeare scholar of some note, she had published her *Complete Concordance to Shakespeare* in 1844–45 (Young 2002, 98). Upon recognizing her, Shakespeare asked 'But where is *your* book, MISTRESS MARY CLARKE? Where is your *Concordance?*' After bestowing such compliments upon Shakespeareans of whom *Punch* clearly approved (Collier's forgeries had not yet come to light), Shakespeare then watched the various performances: Macready as Henry VIII, John Pritt Harley as Lance, John Baldwin Buckstone as Speed, Mrs. Butler as Queen Katharine, William Farren as Shallow, Helen Faucit as Juliet, Mrs. Glover as the Nurse, Webster as Petruchio, Mrs. Nesbitt as Katherine, Miss Addison as Miranda, Priscilla Horton as Ariel, and Bennett as Caliban.

More such benefits occurred at other English theatres, and in the following year on 15 May, as already mentioned, some of the *Punch* staff were participants in the Guild of Literature and Art benefit production of *The Merry Wives of Windsor*, the principal object for which was to aid the endowment fund for a perpetual curatorship of the birthplace (Spielmann 1895a, 135). Thereafter, *Punch* appears to have set aside its concern for the birthplace, believing no doubt that enough had been done to preserve it for future generations, although in actuality it was not finally paid for in full until 1856 (Fox 1948, 85). In 1891, there was passed the Shakespeare Birthplace [...] Trust Act, an act that incorporated the Trustees and Guardians of Shakespeare's birthplace, vesting in them the birthplace as well as the New Place estate, which had been bought through public subscription in 1862 (Fox 1948, 86; Halliday 1964, 64). The critical threat to one of Shakspeareanity's most sacred shrines was finally laid to rest.

Punch and the Shakespeare Tercentenary

After the struggle to save Shakespeare's birthplace, no issue affecting the progress of Shakspeareanity would subsequently garner a similar amount of public attention until the great debate over the appropriate way to mark the tercentenary of Shakespeare's birth on 23 April 1864. Accounts of the Tercentenary have been given elsewhere by a number of scholars (Halliday *Cult*, 148–161; Trewin 1957; Spencer 1964; Foulkes 1984; Foulkes 2002, Ch. 3), so it is not necessary to provide more than an outline here. In Stratford-on-Avon at the dinner of the Shakespeare Club in 1859, the actor Harries Tilbury warned that the tercentenary would soon occur and there was general agreement that something on a large scale should be done. The following year, it was agreed that something should be planned that would have a worldwide significance and appeal. Nothing much was done, however. A Tercentenary Committee was formed on 22 July 1861, but there was no draft program until 23 April 1863. Thereafter followed a certain amount of bickering among the citizens of the town, and at their instigation, it was eventually agreed that, along with plans for such things as university scholarships for students from the Grammar School, the laying out of New Place garden, an art exhibition, and the erection of a building for such festival events as performances of plays and Handel's *Messiah*, a key part of the celebrations would also be a memorial statue. Under the leadership of the highly energetic Mayor, Edward Fordham Flower, fund-raising began but with limited success, and in the meantime a rival project arrived in the form of the London-based National Shakespeare Committee, the organizational body that eventually emerged to combine the efforts and initiatives of at least three other committees. The National Shakespeare Committee, as already noted, was led by W. Hepworth Dixon, editor of the *Athenaeum*, and its chief goal (as with the Stratford campaign) was a statue of Shakespeare.

Punch first commented on the coming Tercentenary on 5 October 1861 in 'FRIENDS AT THE SWAN' (41:135). The article mentions that various 'Gifted Intellects' are proposing 'to erect a

Monument in token of their veneration for that great and good Poet, WILLIAM SHAKSPEARE.' A plea for donations is then made and a comical list of donors to date is given, the most generous donor being Mark Lane, no doubt a joke at the expense of Mark Lemon, the editor of *Punch*. Two years later, two suggestions related to the Tercentenary appeared in *Punch*, both of them purportedly from Shakespeare himself. The first was penned by Tom Taylor. It appeared in the issue for 5 December in the guise of a letter from the ghost of Shakespeare to *Punch*. In it, Shakespeare argues 'that the best monument of SHAKSPEARE would be a theatre where good plays would be well and worthily put forth' (45:233). In a theatre devoted to his honour, not only his plays would be performed but rather such plays as 'are most akin to mine' and 'as are fullest of the living spirit of their time, and most in tune with the hearts and pride of Englishmen'.

The second proposal purportedly from Shakespeare, though in reality written by Shirley Brooks, appeared when the volume of issues for the latter half of 1863 was bound up in December. As we have already seen, a preface was added in which Punch and Shakespeare discussed the forthcoming celebrations. In the course of the two-page discussion that accompanies the engraving of the two men having a quiet smoke together, Shakespeare suggests that his proposed London memorial statue be situated in Temple Garden beside the Thames. *Punch* readers who knew their Shakespeare would have recognized that this was the location of the famous scene in *Henry VI*, Part 1, in which Somerset, Plantagenet and others pluck either white or red roses, an event that signified the beginning of the War of the Roses and was therefore of 'national interest for every Englishman' (45:iv).

Having offered two reasonably constructive ideas to the ongoing debate as to how the Tercentenary should best be celebrated (see also 45:73), *Punch* then began a series of comments of a very different tenor. The general thrust that these would take is apparent in a letter from Brooks to Percival Leigh, dated 18 January 1864. In the letter, of which there is a transcript at the end of the Henry Silver Diary, Brooks expresses his own views and mentions those of his *Punch* colleagues when he says

> I have all along held that the idea of a memorial was foolish. The real memorial is in the fact that England thinks and talks Shakespeare. It would be almost as reasonable, to speak with due reverence, were we to propose to erect a memorial to the Author of the Bible, for fear He should be forgotten. I think, however, that Theodore Martin, Tom Taylor, and yours truly, who are like the Three Anabaptists in the 'Prophète', have done a good deal in the way of hindering downright bosh, prize poems, 'special services', and the like, and we are not without hope of showing the General Committee that there is no time to prepare a worthy memorial. (Layard 1907, 210)

Punch was thus against the Committee's plan for a monument, but it had other doubts about the arrangements being made for the coming Tercentenary. Of particular concern to *Punch* at this time, and one noted later in Brooks's letter, was that one of its own, Thackeray, had been excluded from the National Shakespeare Committee's list of Vice-Presidents, a list that included Charles Dickens and Sir Edward Bulwer Lytton. The cause of this snub appears to have been the pre-existent antipathy between Thackeray and the *Athenaeum*. Thackeray had been angered by some negative statements in an *Athenaeum* review of his daughter Anne's novel, *The Story of Elizabeth*. As Richard Foulkes has pointed out in his account of the incident, 'Thackeray's hostility towards *The Athenaeum* and its editor was irremediable and inevitably extended towards the National Shakespeare Committee' (Foulkes 1984, 18). Various attempts by certain Committee members to reverse the decision were ongoing when to the consternation of all, Thackeray quite unexpectedly was found dead in his bed on the morning of Christmas Eve. At the next meeting of the Committee on 4 January, a motion was passed that expressed regret at what had happened. *Punch* recorded the motion in its issue of 16 January: 'That the General Committee deeply deplore the premature decease of MR THACKERAY, and regret that circumstances should have occurred to prevent the enrolment of his name in the list of Vice-Presidents' (46:30). The following week, *Punch* quoted part of the report of the Committee concerning its treatment of Thackeray and explained that the 'disingenuous passage has been *Rejected*' by another vote of the General Committee (46:40).

Having sufficiently noted the tactless and even vindictive behaviour of some members of the National Shakespeare Committee towards Thackeray, behaviour that some felt may even have contributed to his death, *Punch* shifted its attack to two other matters: the general incompetence of the Committee and Hepworth Dixon in particular, and the Committee's plan to erect some kind of national monument in London. In the final January issue of 1864, *Punch* included four items on these topics. On one page are some verses ('MR MILTON MODERNISED') which exclaim that Shakespeare is in no need of the money that people like George Jones are attempting to raise. Nor does Shakespeare need a 'HEPWORTH-DIXON pyramid' (46:43). Below is a small engraving showing the beleaguered and diminutive figure of Shakespeare. He is defended by Mr. Punch, who carries a large baton, from the impending assault of Hepworth Dixon, who holds an umbrella. Punch's words to the assailant are 'Let him alone.' Two pages later is the big cut by John Tenniel, already described in Chapter One (Figure 14). Entitled 'SHAKSPEARE AND THE PIGMIES,' it depicts an exceptionally large bust of Shakespeare, which is being defaced by a group of tiny figures at its base. Among the 'Pygmies' so dwarfed by the giant genius of Shakespeare is Hepworth Dixon.

Four pages later, Shirley Brooks contributed a small item entitled 'More SHAKSPEAREANITY'. This lists from the pages of the *Athenaeum* the decidedly unimpressive persons (they include 'the Beadle of the Burlington Arcade') who 'have given their consent to have their names added to the National Shakspeare Committee' (46:49). Then, on the very next page, one finds another item by Brooks entitled 'THE NATIONAL SHAKSPEARE COMMITTEE'. This refers to a recent 'crushing condemnation' of the Committee and its plans by the *Times*, and it also mentions the resulting departure from the Committee of a number of members. Their letter of resignation had been included in the *Times* on 20 January, and among the signatories were two familiar *Punch* staffers: Tom Taylor and Shirley Brooks. As far as *Punch* is concerned, the Committee is now moribund, and the 'Memorial absurdity is at an end' (46:50). Or so those who sat at the *Punch* table may have believed.

But the National Committee was not dead yet, so *Punch* continued its assault. In the very next issue of 6 February appeared Henry Silver's 'THE SHAKSPEARE INCAPABLES.' This discusses the

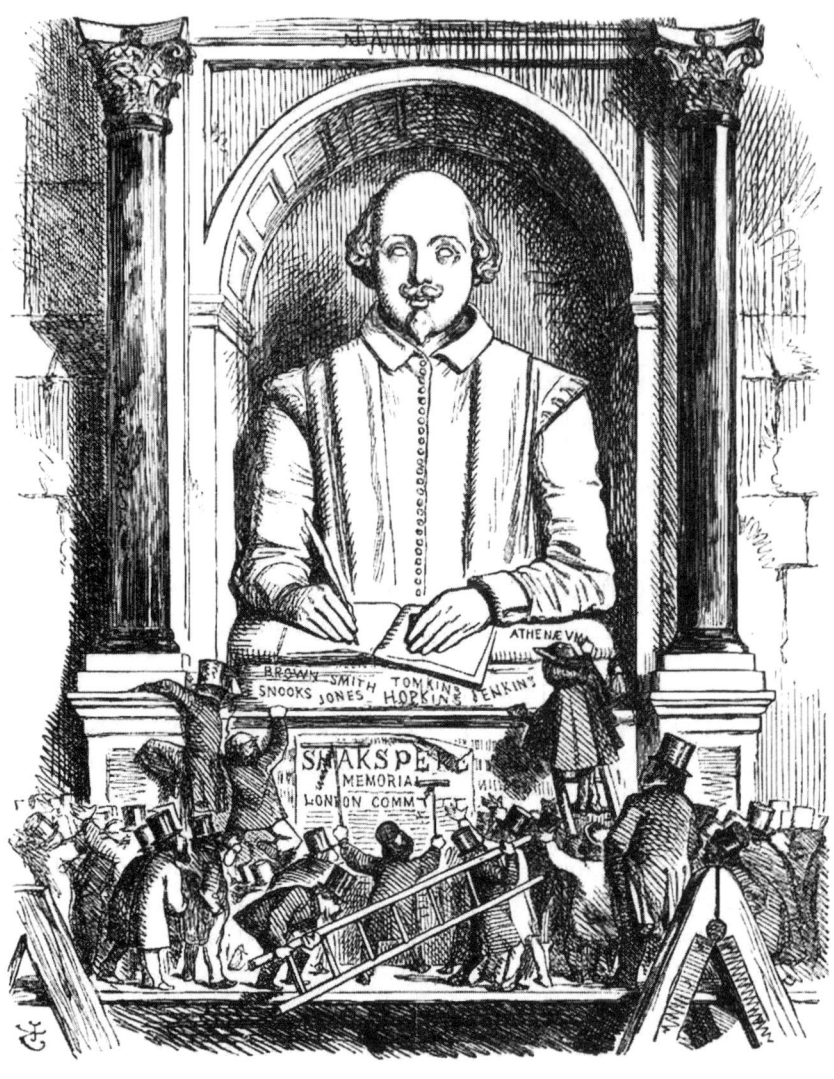

Figure 14. John Tenniel, 'SHAKSPEARE AND THE PIGMIES', *Punch* (30 January 1864), 46:45.

national loss of confidence in the Committee and argues that 'SHAKSPEARE needs no statue' (46:51). A few pages later appeared a letter supposedly from Christopher Sly (the principal character in the induction to *The Taming of the Shrew*) on the subject of madness and the Committee (46:57), and, upon turning that page, readers discovered a letter from 'A Retired Hamlet' (it was contributed by Francis Burnand), suggesting to the Committee various possible ways to commemorate the Tercentenary, all of them laughable (46:59). A small accompanying unsigned engraving depicts a clown carrying a bust of Shakespeare on his shoulder, a caricature of Hepworth Dixon, whose derisory nickname appears in the title: 'A GOOD HA'PORTH.' Over the page was yet another kick at the Committee (by Henry Silver) in the form of 'An Apology to Shakspeare. *Apropos of all the Blundering of the "National Committee"*' (46:60):

> FORGIVE, blest Shade, the tributary sneer
> With which this trading on thy fame we hiss;
> Nor think we less thy honoured name revere,
> Because we shrink from snobbishness like this!

During the remainder of February and on through March and early April, *Punch* continued to hold Hepworth Dixon and the National Shakespeare Committee to the fire. On 13 February, for example, *Punch* printed an interchange of verses between Hepworth Dixon and Shakespeare, punning on the former's nickname and the word 'halfpence' and deriding Hepworth Dixon and the 'National Monument mullers' in the process (46:63). On 27 February appeared the punning suggestion by Leigh that the proposed memorial be a monumental brass rather than a statue and that the gentlemen of the Committee furnish the 'brass' themselves (46:88). Then, *Punch* in another item by Leigh introduced an idea already put forward to the Committee by Benjamin Webster that an appropriate memorial would be the building of a college for retired and indigent actors (Shakespeare's 'poor players') (46:89). In yet another item, Leigh criticized the language of an advertisement for the proposed London Shakespeare memorial that would consist of 'a monument embracing a bronze statue placed under a decorative canopy in the style of the Poet's period' (46:134. Cf.

46:174). The same joke was later employed in the special Shakespeare Tercentenary issue that *Punch* published on 23 April. This contained an unsigned engraving 'Respectfully Dedicated to the Shakspeare Committee' (page 2). It depicted Shakespeare leaning against a stone column in the manner of the Scheemakers memorial and being embraced by a tall stone pyramid, the caption being 'Design for "a Monument Embracing a Bronze Statue"'.

On 2 April some three weeks prior to the date of the celebration itself, Leigh made fun of a notice that had appeared in the *Athenaeum*, announcing the performances of various plays by Shakespeare as part of the Tercentenary celebrations. The list of plays, as quoted by *Punch*, included *Venus and Adonis* and a play with the title *Bunkum*. Of this last, *Punch* recalls that 'this is by no means the first time that our contemporary [i.e. the *Athenaeum*] has somehow mixed Bunkum up with SHAKSPEARE; and we should not mind predicting that it will not prove the last' (46:140). The following week, and now only two weeks from the Tercentenary, *Punch* notes in an article by Shirley Brooks that Green Park is supposedly the National Committee's proposed site for the memorial statue; however, the design has not been prepared, sufficient funds have not been collected, and nothing in connection with the memorial will actually occur on 23 April: 'There, ladies and gentlemen, that is what your Executive has done for you' (46:152).

The first issue of *Punch* to appear after the celebrations contained various items related to the Tercentenary (46:178 [2]; 46:185), but of particular interest here are the reports of the difficulties Edward Flower had encountered in Stratford when two possible performances of *Hamlet* were cancelled and a leading actress (Helen Faucit) withdrew her services (46:183; 46:185; and Foulkes 1984, 14–16). Charles Fechter had originally agreed to play Hamlet, but at one stage Samuel Phelps believed that he had been invited to do the performance. Both men were angered by the apparent mismanagement, and both decided to stay away. Phelps had already been angered earlier when he had been invited to play what he considered the minor role of Iachimo in *Cymbeline*, whereas Fechter was apparently asked to play the title role in *Hamlet* (Allen 1971, 296). For her part, Helen Faucit cancelled her appearance because she had not been given the part of Juliet in *Romeo and Juliet*. An article by Henry Silver, who had gone to Stratford on 27 April, refrained from criticizing Flower and instead suggested that the private jealousies of the respective actors had 'hurt the public cause' and (using the language of flowers) that *'London Pride'* was unseemly since 'the Flower Show at Stratford was meant solely for *Sweet William*' (46:183).

We know from other sources, however, that Stratford's celebrations were a great success and included (on 23 April) an inspection of the site intended for the future memorial, a banquet in the specially-built wooden Pavilion, and fireworks. The next day, a Sunday, there were two services in Holy Trinity Church, and the week following offered a range of activities: various properties associated with Shakespeare, including, of course, the birthplace, were open to the public; there was an exhibition of art works, pride of place going to twenty-eight portraits of Shakespeare and Sir Thomas Lawrence's portrait of John Philip Kemble as Hamlet; there was a performance of Handel's *Messiah*; a concert of music associated with Shakespeare; and there were performances in the Pavilion of *Twelfth Night, The Comedy of Errors, As You Like It,* and *Romeo and Juliet*.

The following week, the celebrations continued with a pageant, more music, and performances of *Othello, Much Ado About Nothing*, and the Trial Scene from *The Merchant of Venice* (Foulkes 1984, 27–38). *Punch*'s one comment about all this appeared on 14 May in a letter to Mr. Punch from 'Vagabundus' (Henry Silver) that was entitled 'A PILGRIMAGE TO STRATFORD' (46:199). Using the religious language elsewhere used of Shakspeareanity, the letter-writer describes his pilgrimage to Stratford 'to pay his homage at the shrine of SHAKSPEARE', and to see the many 'relics of St. Shakspeare' that have been put on view to excite veneration. Vagabundus explains that he found the relics of little interest, but the birthplace pleased him greatly and he remembers Mr. Punch's role in helping to secure it from general decay and 'the penknives of the pilgrims, who, if permitted, long ago would have chipped it up for snuffboxes, and put it in their pockets'. While at Stratford, Vagabundus attended neither the celebratory banquet nor the ball, but he did visit Charlecote Park and Ann Hathaway's house, besides attending a performance of *As You Like It*.

Punch had little to say about the London celebrations, which included a tree-planting on the southern slope of Primrose Hill, various concerts, an Actors' Supper, and a viewing of the Chandos portrait at the National Portrait Gallery (Foulkes 1984, 39–45). There were also a number of play productions, among them *Twelfth Night* at the Haymarket, *The Merchant of Venice* at Sadler's Wells, *Romeo and Juliet* at the Princess's, *Henry VI*, Part Two, at the Surrey, and a revival of Joseph Stirling Coyne's entertainment about Shakespeare's birthplace (see above) at the Adelphi. This last was performed on the 23 April, as one might expect, but then proved to be very popular and was performed for 123 nights. About the London dramatic fare, *Punch* was silent. Only the Drury Lane production of *Henry IV*, Part One, with Samuel Phelps as Falstaff (though with the omission of the 'Crown and Cushion' scene), received a review. In it, Henry Silver used the opportunity to reiterate that a theatre for the performance of Shakespeare's plays 'would be the noblest monument that England could erect, and one that SHAKSPEARE, were he living, himself would most approve of' (46:175).

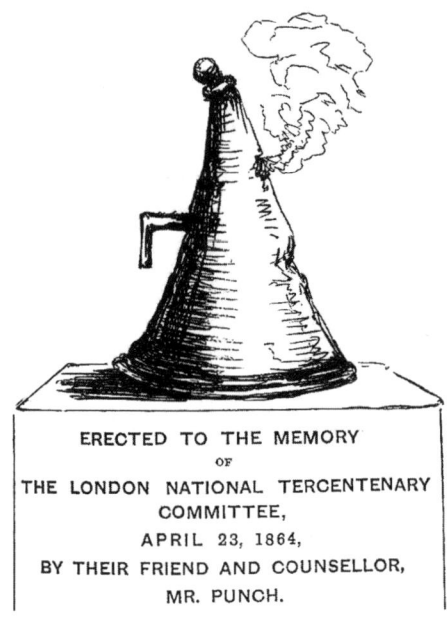

ERECTED TO THE MEMORY
OF
THE LONDON NATIONAL TERCENTENARY COMMITTEE,
APRIL 23, 1864,
BY THEIR FRIEND AND COUNSELLOR,
MR. PUNCH.

Figure 15. Unidentified artist's comment on the National Tercentenary Committee. *Punch* (7 May 1864), 46:193.

It seems that the National Shakespeare Committee was not the prime instigator in any of these events, so *Punch* appears to have decided to end its baiting of the inept organization. However, to lay things to rest, *Punch* first offered one last insult. This was an unsigned engraving of a monument that was published in the issue for 7 May (46:193). It depicted a steaming kettle on a large base, on which was an inscription (see Figure 15). *Punch's* last word is very clear. The boastful assertions and grandiose plans of the Committee and its leader, W. Hepworth Dixon, when put to the test, had proved to lack any more substance than the hot vapours from a kettle. Indeed, the Committee's efforts (or lack of them) never did produce a memorial statue. There was to be no Tercentenary statue in Stratford either. However, there at least the general success of the festival, the tourist interest in the buildings associated with Shakespeare, and above all the performances in the Pavilion all combined to encourage the establishment of Stratford as the central shrine for future bardolators.

Even more significant, perhaps, was the impetus given in Stratford-on-Avon to the dream of a permanent theatre. Charles Edward Flower, the son of the tercentenary organizer, donated a site beside the Avon, fund-raising began, and on Shakespeare's birthday in 1875, the foundation stone was laid. Four years later to the day, the Shakespeare Memorial Theatre opened its doors and annual Shakespeare festivals began with a production by Barry Sullivan's company of *Much Ado About Nothing*. The event was warmly welcomed by *Punch* in its issue of 26 April (76:190), and no doubt many Stratfordians took particular pleasure in the irony that Helen Faucit, who had left them in the lurch in 1864, appeared for the 1879 event in order to play Beatrice.

The Tercentenary Issue of *Punch*

One further matter needs to be added to the account of *Punch*'s response to the Shakespeare Tercentenary. Long before 1864, the publishers of *Punch* had had a number of successes with special issues on such topics as '*Punch*'s Watering Places', '*Punch*'s Valentines', '*Punch*'s Holidays', and 'Records of the Great Exhibition, Extracted from *Punch*'. Much later would appear a special Paris Exhibition number in celebration of the Exhibition of 1889, and when John Tenniel died in 1914, there was a special issue in his honour. For the Shakespeare celebrations of 1864, as mentioned briefly above, the publishers issued 'Punch's Tercentenary Number'. It was, of course, published on 23 April.

Twelve days prior to this on 11 April, a special meeting was held to discuss the Tercentenary issue, and details of the meeting are recorded in Silver's diary. All manner of ideas were launched concerning possible visual material. Though he had apparently sneered at the idea of a special issue, John Leech suggested the 'joke of representing the Queen as one of the Merry Wives of Windsor'. Henry Silver and Percival Leigh, who had sent in their suggestions a few days before, by coincidence had 'both hit on Diz [Disraeli] as Shylock'. Silver, who admits that he is more up to suggestions involving Shakespeare 'than to great cuts generally', then recorded a string of suggestions that he made at the meeting whereby various persons would be represented as characters from Shakespeare. They included the Prime Minister (Viscount Palmerston) as Prospero, Earl John Russell (the Foreign Secretary) as Ariel, Garibaldi, who that day had made a triumphal entry into London, as Coriolanus, the Northern and Southern American states, which are so alike, as the two Dromios, Abraham Lincoln as the Gravedigger, the Shakespeare Tercentenary Committee as Bottom and company, Louis Napoleon as Richard III, Francis Burnand as Falstaff, and John Delane, the editor of the *Times,* as Hamlet, saying 'The Times are out of joint'. Somehow, this hodge-podge was worked up by John Tenniel into a double-page big cut that was given pride of place in the special issue.

Tenniel's design, which, according to Silver, was displayed to some acclaim at the dinner on 20 April, depicted Shakespeare seated in a triumphal chariot, driven by Mr. Punch as Touchstone and drawn by twin Pegasi. A procession follows, and among those in it are a variety of people represented as Shakespearean characters, many of them identical to those suggested at the planning meeting, and others quite different. An elaborate two-page key (contributed by Mark Lemon) identifies each figure and provides an apt accompanying quotation from a character in Shakespeare. Those represented include the *Punch* editor, Mark Lemon as Prospero (the identity, however, is listed as John Bull in the accompanying key on page one), Britannia as Miranda, Earl Russell as Ariel, and a malignant organ grinder as Caliban (John Leech had a particular, even pathological, hate of organ grinders). Among the various statesmen and monarchs represented as Shakespearean characters are Lord Palmerston (Ajax), the Earl of Derby (Hotspur), Gladstone (Ulysses), Disraeli (Iago), Peel (Pistol), Lincoln (Richard III), Garibaldi (Coriolanus), John Bright (Brutus), Victor Emmanuel (Falconbridge), and Louis Napoleon (Julius Caesar).

As noted, Henry Silver had suggested that this last be represented as Richard III, but at the planning meeting Percival Leigh had suggested the switch to Julius Caesar, quoting the description of Caesar in the play: 'Why, man, he doth bestride the world like a Colossus.' Members of the Shakespeare Tercentenary Committee are shown towards the front of the procession 'in habits of the period, BLOWING THEIR OWN TRUMPETS', and at the rear are two figures from the *Standard* and the *Morning Herald*, here in the form of two of the Witches (Mesdames Gamp and Harris) in *Macbeth*. 'Characters Round the Corner' (i.e. not actually depicted in the engraving but listed in the key) included the North and South States of America (the two Dromios), the poet Martin Tupper (Cinna the poet), the actors Charles Fechter (Glendower) and Charles Kean (Benedick), and the theatre manager Benjamin Webster (Hamlet). Lemon's commentary makes clear that the procession depicted in the engraving is *Punch*'s response to the 'bungling and bother about the Tercentenary celebrations'. Mr. Punch has now taken matters in hand and 'arranged a Procession worthy of the occasion' that will start from Buckingham Palace and make its way to Fleet Street and the *Punch* offices.

Other visual material for the Tercentenary Number was contributed by Charles Keene, George du Maurier, and a new-comer, A. R. Fairfield. As the *Punch* Contributors' Ledgers reveal, the textual material for the Tercentenary Number was the work of Shirley Brooks, Francis C. Burnand, Percival Leigh, Mark Lemon, Henry Silver, and Tom Taylor. Brooks, for example, contributed a full-page item entitled 'TO CORRESPONDENTS', which offered witty responses to a series of letters regarding Shakespearean matters that had supposedly been sent to *Punch* (p. 4). Burnand's contribution ('SHAKSPEARIAN MSS') was a two-page burlesque play that, it is argued, may be in Shakespeare's handwriting (p. 9). Leigh contributed seven items, among them 'HOW TO COOK A RUMP STEAK (from

Macbeth)', the text of which stated: 'If it were done, when 'tis done, then 'twere well it were done quickly' (p. 10). Henry Silver provided a set of verses ('A VISIT FROM QUEEN MAB'), in which he recounts a dream in which he was transported to Stratford-on-Avon and there met a succession of Shakespeare's characters. A final example from what was a light-hearted and generally frivolous publication was Tom Taylor's verse squib concerning the successful commercial exploitation of the Tercentenary by the citizens of Stratford-on-Avon – 'Two Faces under one Laurel-wreath':

> As *Vates* in Latin means prophet and poet,
> So in English identical should be the name:
> And Stratford-on-Avon hopes shortly to show it,
> By proving her *poet* and *profit* the same. (p. 10)

One wonders whether anyone at the *Punch* office noticed the irony here since the Tercentenary Number carried a considerable number of advertisements for books on Shakespeare, many of them published to coincide with the Tercentenary. The London publisher Booth, for example, announced a facsimile of the Shakespeare First Folio of 1623, a photographic reproduction of *The Shakespeare Gallery*, and a similar reproduction of *The Seven Ages of Man* as originally depicted by Robert Smirke at the beginning of the century. Also advertised were Smith, Elder, & Company's *On Shakespeare's Knowledge and use of the Bible* by Charles Wordsworth; the *Shakespeare Commentaries* by G. G. Gervinus; *Shakespeare Characters* by Charles Cowden Clarke; and *Shakespeare: His Birthplace and its Neighbourhood* by John Wise. Other advertised books included *Shakespeare: A Biography* by Thomas De Quincey; *The Cambridge Shakespeare*, of which four volumes had been published to date; and *Cassell's Illustrated Shakespeare*, which was edited by Charles and Mary Cowden Clarke and currently appearing in serial form. Included too was an advertisement of the Stereoscopic Company for photographs of Shakespeare's death mask. It would seem then that *Punch*, like the citizens of Stratford-on-Avon, also made its own attempt to profit as fully as possible from public interest in the Tercentenary celebrations, not only by selling a special issue of the magazine but by soliciting advertisements for it.

Punch, Shakspeareanity, and Visual Icons of Shakespeare

Punch seems always to have been well aware that the campaign to encourage Shakspeareanity possessed a powerful tool in the form of two instantly recognizable visual icons of Shakespeare. One was the bust (properly speaking a half-length figure) by Gheerart Janssen in the Stratford church. This was widely known through engravings, and, once the railway reached Stratford in 1860, it was seen *in situ* by ever-growing numbers of tourists. The other icon was Peter Scheemakers's statue of Shakespeare, erected by public subscription in 1740 and unveiled early in 1741 in Westminster Abbey where anyone in London could see it. This was also frequently reproduced in engravings and has remained one of the most familiar likenesses of Shakespeare (Dobson 1992, 141). It was also the model for Louis-François Roubiliac's 1758 bust of Shakespeare that was commissioned by David Garrick for his Temple of Shakespeare at his villa on the Thames. Garrick then bequeathed it to the British Museum in 1779. In 1769, at the time of the Stratford Jubilee, Garrick had also commissioned a copy by John Cheere of a revised version of Scheemakers's statue that the sculptor had produced for the Earl of Pembroke. This Garrick had donated to the new Stratford Town Hall. It is still on display there in a niche on the exterior wall of the building (Kimberley 1989, 11). As has already been noted, a Scheemakers replica stood over the portico at Drury Lane. Later, in 1873, when Albert Grant acquired Leicester Fields, he commissioned Signor Fontana to reproduce Scheemakers's statue to serve as the centre-piece of Leicester Square, thereby providing another publicly accessible image of Shakespeare (Foulkes 1986, 7; and see *Punch* 97:161). *Punch* celebrated Grant's renovation of Leicester Square in 1874 in some verses by Tom Taylor that refer to five statues, the chief of which was that of Shakespeare, part of the centre-piece fountain (67:11):

> In this fair space these statues five,
> Should mighty memories revive
> For all its gates who enter:
> Wisely, the marble fount to crown,
> SHAKSPEARE, our Greatest, gazes down,
> Jet-circled, in the centre.

Of course, both the engraved image by Martin Droeshout in the First Folio (and that volume's three subsequent seventeenth-century successors) and the Chandos portrait, which was presented by the Earl of Ellesmere to the National Portrait Gallery in March 1856, were also well known from reproductions, but neither image appears to have imprinted itself in the public consciousness as strongly as the memorials at Stratford and Westminster.

Prior familiarity of its readership with the image of Shakespeare is probably something that *Punch* took for granted, beginning with its earliest visual representation of Shakespeare in an engraving that depicted George Stephens, the editor of the *Church of England Quarterly Review*. Stephens is shown looking down into the River Avon at Stratford where he sees the reflection of Shakespeare rather than himself. Stephens had recently published a dramatic poem entitled *The Hungarian Daughter*. This was then re-titled for stage performance as *Martinuzzi; or, The Patriot* and performed in August 1841 at the English Opera House (the Lyceum Theatre) under the auspices of a 'Syncretic Society' formed by a group of dramatists. The theatre was renamed the Dramatic Authors' Theatre for this production, and the leading actors were Samuel Phelps and Mary Warner.

Punch was particularly scathing about the production and about its sponsors in a number of items (e.g. 1:100, 106, 111, 112–113, 124–125. See Altick 1997, 722). The *Punch* engraving with the image of Shakespeare, which was very much akin to that of the Stratford bust, was designed to accompany a mocking analysis of Stephens's work and to satirize Stephens's apparent narcissistic pride in his own authorial genius (1:86). Although only a relatively small number of readers/viewers may have been familiar with Shakespeare's bust or engravings of it, many more would have become familiar with his facial features from a host of other derivative sources. Indeed, one type of source provided the subject for *Punch*'s next visual depiction of Shakespeare. In 1842 in an ongoing series entitled 'LONDON INTERIORS,' *Punch* included 'THE BACK PARLOUR OF MR. SNOOKS'S RESIDENCE IN AMWELL-STREET, PENTONVILLE.' This consisted of a satiric description of the interior of Mr. Snooks's house. Included in the description, and shown in one of the accompanying engravings, is a bust of Shakespeare that stands at the centre of Snooks's mantel (2:152). However, the owner is not certain whether it represents Shakespeare or Milton. *Punch*'s prime point is that poor Snooks's aspiration to appear cultured when he bought the bust from a travelling Italian salesman has merely revealed his ignorance; he should have been able to recognize Shakespeare, but he failed. As *Punch* was aware, a bust of Shakespeare was a common decorative feature in many houses. During the months just prior to the Tercentenary, *Punch* indirectly alluded to this in an engraving of 6 February entitled 'AWFUL APPARITION OF THE BARD AT MRS. SCRIMMINGE'S TEA-FIGHT' (46:60). This shows what appears to be Shakespeare in nineteenth-century dress interrupting a tea party. The caption explains:

> BUT IT WAS ONLY YOUNG FLARROP, FROM THE NEXT DOOR, LARKING WITH THE BUST OUT OF THE LIBRARY; AND IT BEING THE FASHION TO MAKE FUN OF DEAR OLD SHAKSPEARE JUST NOW, THE JOKE TOOK IMMENSELY.

Other busts, some real and some imagined, appear in *Punch* engravings in a variety of locations. An 1843 description of the Drury Lane Theatre, part of a series by Douglas Jerrold entitled 'THE GRATUITOUS EXHIBITIONS OF LONDON', besides describing the statue of Shakespeare over the portico of the theatre, also included an engraving of the head and shoulders of Shakespeare close to the Box Office, an area open to the public during daytime hours (4:255). It is not clear, however, whether this engraving is of an actual bust or whether it is an inaccurate representation of the head and shoulders of a full-length statue of Shakespeare (based on Scheemakers's original) that stood in the Rotunda, close to John Edward Carew's 1833 full-length marble of Edmund Kean as Hamlet.

In another engraving entitled 'STATE OF COVENT GARDEN', Mr. Punch (and Toby) survey from behind a barrier various theatrical artefacts that appear to be no longer in use and are now for sale. They include props for a number of Shakespeare plays and a bust of Shakespeare (11:254). Two years earlier, in an allegorical fantasy, *Punch* had included an engraving of Colley Cibber, hammer and chisel in hand, standing on a chair reworking a bust of Shakespeare. As with the depiction of the sale of Shakespearean artefacts at Covent Garden, the general theme is the detrimental effect of the Theatre Regulation Act and the replacement of serious drama, especially the work of Shakespeare, with lesser fare (6:95). Even when something Shakespearean was performed at Drury Lane, as *Punch* had reported earlier, what the audience was given was Cibber's mangled version of *Richard III* (6:64). Other busts appear in representations of the room in which Shakespeare was born (13:184); a room occupied by two members of the Northern Shakespeare Society (91:159); and the interior of the Garrick theatre (98:97). There is also a fanciful satiric story concerning Edwin Forrest, the American actor who had gained notoriety for insulting Macready in 1849, thereby causing the tragic Astor Place riots (Moody 1958; Downer 1966, 29–31). In the Fall of 1849, *Punch* published a small item penned by Jerrold and entitled 'SHAKSPEARE IN AMERICA'. This was an imaginary report that a penitent Forrest had ordered 500 casts of the bust of Shakespeare in the church in Stratford-on-Avon. The busts were to be shipped to New York and distributed among the men hired by the actor to 'pelt and put down MACREADY' (17:195).

As we have already seen, as part of its commentary on the National Shakespeare Committee's handling of the tercentenary preparations, *Punch* published a big cut by John Tenniel that showed an immense bust of Shakespeare modelled on that at Stratford though not with regard to size. Some years earlier in the second issue of 1850, there appeared an engraving of the Stratford bust. So far as I know, this is the most faithful representation of the Stratford effigy to appear in the Victorian issues of *Punch*. It depicts Walter Belville standing in the church in front of the memorial. He holds his hat on the end of his cane and addresses the subject of the bust: 'IMMORTAL BARD, INDEED ! ! I SHOULD JUST LIKE TO KNOW WHERE

YOU WOULD HAVE BEEN, MY BUCK, IF I HADN'T – BUT NO MATTER. *Exit growling*' (18:24).

Scheemakers's statue also served the cause of Shakspeareanity by providing an immediately recognizable image of Shakespeare. The depiction in *Punch* of a caged Shakespeare in Bunn's Drury Lane menagerie (12:196) has already been discussed. Two years before, on 13 September 1845, as part of its ongoing efforts to jog the conscience of Queen Victoria into giving appropriate recognition to Shakespeare, *Punch* published an item by Douglas Jerrold entitled 'QUEEN VICTORIA'S STATUE OF SHAKSPEARE'. The article recounts that Queen Victoria, who recently travelled to Germany to participate with the King of Prussia in the dedication at Cologne of a memorial statue of Beethoven, was so impressed that on her return to England she wished to have erected a large statue of Shakespeare on the Shakespeare Cliff at Dover (*Punch* had first jokingly mentioned such a statue the year before, see, 6:220). The dedication of the Dover statue will occur, we are told, as part of the forthcoming celebration of Shakespeare's birthday. As the article goes on to explain, 'there is something grand in the choice of the site. It is wisely and well determined that the image of the tutelary genius of England shall stand a sea-mark to all nations.' Passing ships will 'lower their sails, like wild swans stooping in their flight, to the image of him who has cast 'a girdle round about the world' – a girdle made of the triple cord of love, and gentleness, and truth!' (9:118). An accompanying engraving by Richard Doyle depicts the imagined dedication ceremony and shows the statue, which is modelled on the Scheemakers monument, atop a tall white cliff, presumably the Shakespeare Cliff, so named because it was thought to be the 'fearful and dizzy' place described by Edgar in *King Lear*. At its base in the *Punch* representation stands a crowd of cheering people, including the royal family. On the shoulder of Shakespeare sits a diminutive Mr. Punch, who places a laurel wreath on the poet's head. At the foot of the cliff is a large group of Shakespearean characters, many of them with banners inscribed with the titles of Shakespeare's plays.

A few years after the comic proposal that England's national poet be honoured at Dover, a statue of Shakespeare by John Bell stood in the British Nave of the Great Exhibition in 1851 (exhibit number 83).

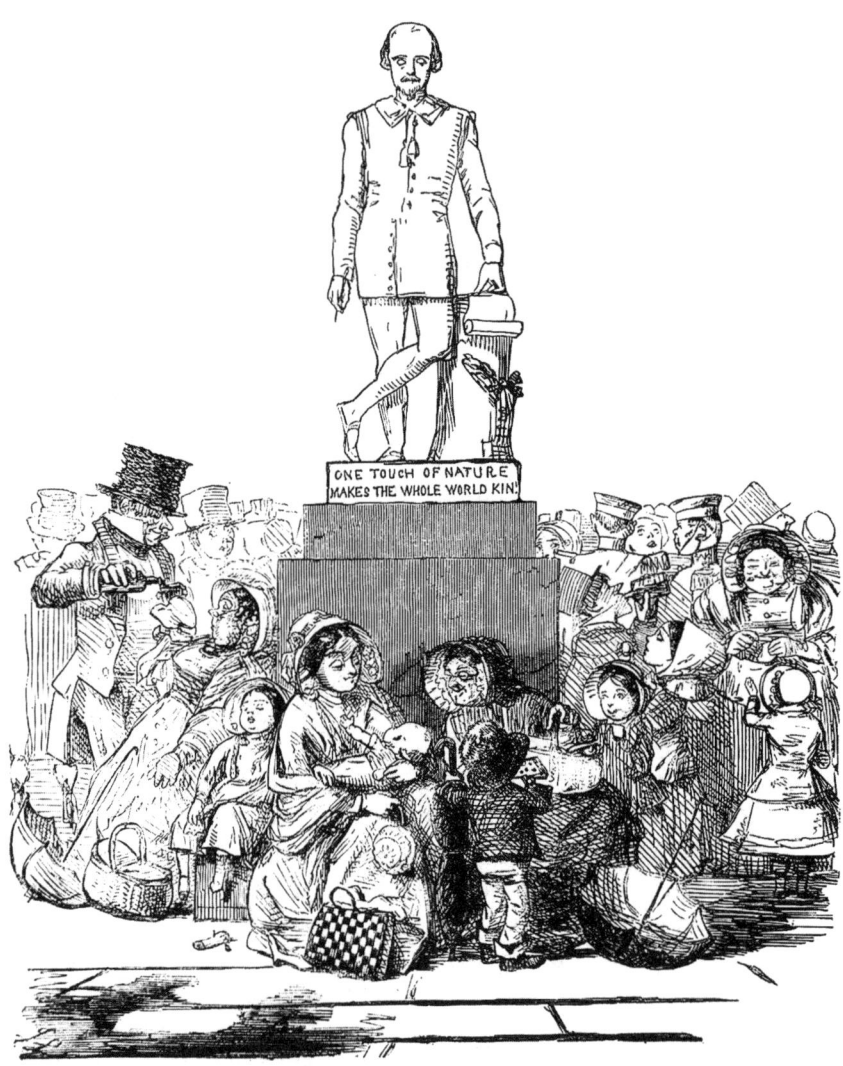

Figure 16. John Leech's depiction of Bell's statue of Shakespeare. *Punch* (5 July 1851), 21:16.

The exhibition took place in Hyde Park, London, the centre-piece being Joseph Paxton's enormous iron and glass exhibition building that became known as the Crystal Palace (the name was Douglas Jerrold's coinage, see Slater 2002, 296), a wonderful innovative creation that was later moved south of London to Sydenham. Bell's statue, which was one of many other representations of Shakespeare displayed at the exhibition, was listed in the official catalogue as 'unfinished statue of Shakspeare, from the Stratford bust' (Pettitt 2003, 61), but its full-length format and its placing of Shakespeare leaning against a plinth, his hand upon a scroll and one leg crossed over the other, suggests that it has been modelled on the statue by Scheemakers.

In July 1851, *Punch* included a full-page cartoon by John Leech entitled 'DINNER-TIME AT THE CRYSTAL PALACE' (21:16) that depicted Bell's statue (Figure 16). Around its base is a broad assortment of people, most of them working class and many of them eating or drinking. There is even a Hogarthian touch in the form of a woman breast-feeding a baby. The monument itself is inscribed 'ONE TOUCH OF NATURE MAKES THE WHOLE WORLD KIN' (see *Troilus and Cressida* III iii 175), an inspired addition, so far as I can tell, to Bell's original. Leech, in showing the working class crowd casually eating their picnic meals against the base of Shakespeare's statue, was undoubtedly conscious of the manner in which the plan to use Hyde Park for the exhibition had generated heated opposition because it was a site close to fashionable Belgravia and the site also of Rotten Row, a favourite rendezvous for the horse-riding gentry (Altick 1997, 621). Plans had gone ahead, however, and working class visitors turned out to be no threat to peace and order and were further encouraged to come when the Commissioners reduced the entry price from 2s. 6d. to 1s., Monday through Thursday. Indeed, the figures sitting around the base of the statue that Leech depicted may not have been the offspring of a caricaturist's fantasy, for in his diary Gideon Mantell recorded as the exhibition approached its end that in the British Nave 'many dirty women with their infants were sitting on the seats giving suck with their breasts uncovered' while 'others ate their packed lunches' (Mantell 1940, 273, quoted Auerbach 1999, 155). The levelling of class boundaries (cf. Leech's later 'THE POUND

AND THE SHILLING', 20:247) and the sense that Shakespeare belongs to all is very effectively evoked in Leech's cartoon, which can be seen as one of the most hopeful of *Punch*'s statements concerning Shakspeareanity and the democratization of Shakespeare.

In the latter two decades of the century, *Punch* obviously felt assured that its readers knew the Scheemakers image of Shakespeare well enough for it to become the object of burlesque. In 1884, for example, *Punch* included a portrait by Linley Sambourne of Tommaso Salvini, the Italian Shakespearean actor. Salvini was placed in the pose employed for Shakespeare in the Scheemakers sculpture. In this instance, however, the head of Shakespeare, which now rests at the foot of the monument, has been replaced by that of the actor. This latter points to a paper scroll that hangs down at the front of the work just like that in the original; however, here it is inscribed with three play titles: *King Lear, Othello,* and *Macbeth*. These represent three works in which Salvini played the title roles. Below is a caption consisting of a quotation from *Cymbeline*: 'COME, I'LL GO SEE THIS ITALIAN!' *Punch*'s response to Salvini, contrary to its frequent hostility to 'foreign' performers, was generally very laudatory (see, 68;181 and 68:255), and the Italian was even described as a worthy successor to Macready. High praise indeed! Sambourne's design is thus intended as a playful tribute rather than a satiric suggestion that a foreign import has now 'put down' Shakespeare.

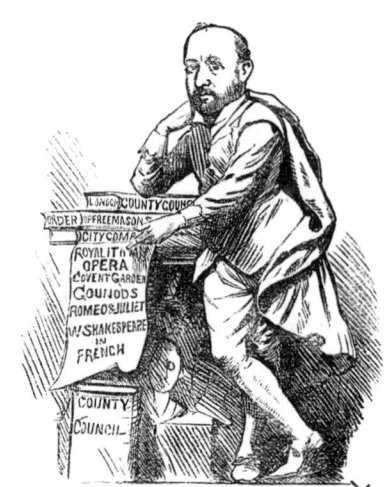

" Take him for all in all, we shall not look upon his like again."
Suggestion for a Statue to be erected in the R. I. O. C. G.

Figure 17. Edward J. Wheeler's burlesque of Scheemakers's statue of Shakespeare. *Punch* (22 June 1889), 96:301.

Five years later, as part of *Punch*'s long-standing concern about popular preferences for opera and other 'imported' entertainments, the issue of 22 June 1889 contained another burlesque engraving by Edward J. Wheeler of Scheemakers's statue (Figure 17). The accompanying article is punningly entitled '"MODUS OPERANDI" *(The Covent Garden Government, and Her Majesty's Opposition.)*'. It comments on the performance in French of Gounod's *Roméo et Juliette* with Nellie Melba and Jean de Reszke in the title roles (96:301). The caption to Wheeler's design is based on Hamlet's words to Horatio: 'Take him for all in all, we shall not look upon his like again.' To this is added the comment: 'Suggestion for a Statue to be erected in the R. I. O. C. G' (i.e. the Royal Italian Opera Covent Garden). The pedestal upon which the figure of Shakespeare leans has a pile of books. The top one has the label 'LONDON COUNTY COUNCIL.' A sheet of paper hangs down. On it is playfully inscribed 'ROYAL ITALIAN OPERA COVENT GARDEN. GOUNOD'S ROMEO & JULIET. W SHAKSPEARE IN FRENCH.' Although the production is praised, the engraving, its inscription, and its caption collectively remind reader-viewers that at Covent Garden, at least, Shakespeare is not as he was; he remains subservient to a foreign art form and an alien language.

Some three years later, *Punch* published yet another burlesque of Scheemakers's statue in an 1892 design by

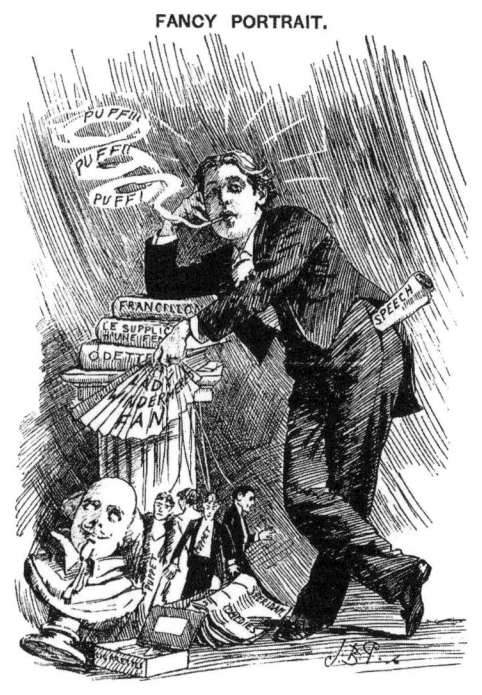

Figure 18. Bernard Partridge's portrait of Oscar Wilde. *Punch* (5 March 1892), 102:113.

Bernard Partridge (Figure 18). In this, the place of Shakespeare, whose head is at the foot of the plinth, is taken by Oscar Wilde. Entitled 'FANCY PORTRAIT. QUITE TOO-TOO PUFFICKLY PRECIOUS!! *Being Lady Windy-mère's Fan-cy Portrait of the new dramatic author, Shakspeare Sheridan Oscar Puff, Esq*' (102:113). Wilde is shown in the familiar pose that Scheemakers gave Shakespeare, but he is smoking a cigarette. From his pocket protrudes a paper inscribed 'SPEECH', and he leans with his elbow upon several books by French authors, holding in his hand a fan inscribed 'LADY WINDERMERE'S FAN'. In the same hand he holds the strings that lead down to a group of puppets who appear to be fellow aesthetes. At his feet, beside the discarded bust of Shakespeare, are a box of cigarettes and a volume inscribed 'SHERIDAN COMEDIES'. A quotation from the *Daily Telegraph* makes clear what provided the inspiration for Partridge's amusing design: 'He addressed from the stage a public audience, mostly composed of ladies, pressing between his daintily-gloved fingers a still burning and half-smoked cigarette.' Aware of Wilde's talents as a comic dramatist, Partridge (himself very much a man of the theatre) is not satirizing Wilde for arrogantly displacing Shakespeare. Instead, as in a number of earlier works in *Punch* dealing with the Aesthetic movement (82:58; 92:202; 100:11), the design expresses a bemusement and mock horror at the challenges to social and artistic norms embodied in the behaviour and attitudes of one of the movement's chief proponents.

Two years later, in 1894, *Punch* published a review by Francis C. Burnand of Augustin Daly's production of *Twelfth Night* at Daly's Theatre. The production receives high praise and is accompanied by two engravings designed by Bernard Partridge. In one of these, he repeats the visual joke employed in his portrait of Wilde by depicting Daly in a pose that again burlesques Scheemakers's Shakespeare. The small column on which Daly leans is inscribed 'MANAGER DALY'S TROUPE OF AMERICAN COMEDIANS', and below is the caption: 'Shakspeare à l'Américaine'. This time, as with Sambourne's engraving of Salvini, the artist's comment is entirely laudatory. However, unlike Sambourne and unlike what he had done in his portrait of Oscar Wilde, Partridge leaves out the head of Shakespeare entirely. The pose is clearly deemed a sufficient visual clue for reader/viewers to recognize and enjoy a burlesque of Shakespeare as depicted by another artist, a burlesque that offers sincere flattery to the man who here stands in place of Shakespeare. In 1898, four years after the representation of Daly as Shakespeare, *Punch* used the Scheemakers model once more. Having reported that a number of Shakespeare's plays had been translated into Japanese, *Punch* published a design by L. Harrison that is entitled 'SHAKSPEARE JAPANNED'. The small engraving depicts Shakespeare (in Scheemakers's pose) as a Japanese.

There were in the course of the latter half of the century other public statues of Shakespeare erected in the environs of London. There was, for example, a large sculptural group by John E. Thomas of a seated Shakespeare attended by Tragedy and Comedy. The plaster model of this subject had been shown at the International Exhibition of 1862 (*Illustrated London News,* 28 June 1862; Kimberley 1989, 23–25). In 1864, the Tercentenary year, it was erected in the grounds of the re-situated Crystal Palace in Sydenham *(Illustrated London News*, 30 April 1864; Foulkes 1984, after page 48). However, widely-known as it must have been, it was never, so far as I am aware, referred to in *Punch*. Other public works that *Punch* readers may have come across but that were not referred to in the magazine's pages include Charles Bacon's Tercentenary bust that was then reproduced the following year as the frontispiece to John H. Heraud's *Shakspere: His Inner Life* (1865); the marble sculpture by Henry Hugh Armstead for the podium of the Albert Memorial; the 1871 sculpture by William Hamo Thornycroft for the Poets' Fountain in Park Lane; and the 1896 bust by C. J. Allen in the churchyard of St. Mary the Virgin in Aldermanbury.

One sculptural representation that *Punch* did take notice of, however, was the much talked about work created by the Scottish aristocrat, Lord Ronald Gower. The idea of creating some kind of Shakespeare memorial first occurred to Gower in 1877, the year in which the foundation stone for the Memorial Theatre was laid in Stratford. The project underwent a lengthy genesis (Kimberley 1989, 10–28), and most of the work was done in Paris. In 1881, Gower exhibited a plaster model of his design at the Paris Salon (he had exhibited his planned figure of Prince Hal at the previous year's Salon), and this was then moved later that year to the Crystal Palace.

It was surmounted by the figures of Comedy and Tragedy crowning with laurel a bust of Shakespeare that Gower had endeavoured to make as 'authentic' as possible by using the Stratford bust and the Kesselstadt Death Mask as his models. These figures were placed upon a tall and very grand edifice. Arranged around its base were various Shakespearean character portraits (Prince Hal, Hamlet, Lady Macbeth, and Falstaff). The whole structure was on a relatively massive scale, offering itself as the model for a national monument. Gower planned that the various figures would eventually be in bronze and the remainder would be in granite.

In the years following, he created the bronzes for some of his figures, but no site for his project was determined until Queen Victoria's Jubilee in 1887 when an American donor gave Stratford a fountain and a clock tower in Rother Market. It was then that Gower, after having earlier approached the town unsuccessfully, obtained a site in the gardens in front of the Memorial Theatre and facing the parish church where Shakespeare was buried. The finished monument was then unveiled on 10 October the following year. What must have startled some who attended, among whom was Oscar Wilde, was that a radical change of design had occurred in the representation of Shakespeare. No longer a rather static funerary bust, the monument now consisted of a six foot, four inch, full-length seated but energetic-looking figure, pen and paper at the ready, and left arm draped confidently over the back of the chair. Tragedy and Comedy have disappeared to leave the viewer's eye no opportunity to wander from the dominant central figure. Stratford now had both a theatre and a monument worthy of its famous son.

Understandably, *Punch* responded to the Stratford unveiling of Gower's gift. No one from the *Punch* staff appears to have been present at the event, so the magazine's chief source of information was the report in the *Times* the day after on 11 October. According to that report, Shakespeare 'is here represented as seated, with a quill in his right hand, and his left carelessly thrown over the back of a chair and holding a roll of manuscript' (10). These descriptive details are mocked by *Punch* in its 20 October issue as simplistic and obvious pieces of symbolism, and the same vein of criticism is also applied to the character figures, the 'comic and tragic masks', and the various 'emblematical plants, fruit, and flowers cast in bronze'. The estimated value of Lord Gower's generous gift, according to the *Times*, is several thousand pounds. *Punch* laughs at this too, but then (not very subtly) begins to reverse the general thrust of its commentary by suggesting that the value is priceless.

The article, the work of Burnand, points out that 'Parisians now possess a statue of the "Divine WILLIAMS."' This was a bronze of Shakespeare by Paul Fournier and presented by William Knighton, the Vice-President of the International Literary Association (*Times*, 15 October, 5). It was unveiled at the junction of the Boulevard Haussmann and Avenue de Messine only four days after the unveiling of Gower's work. 'Can anything more be done to prevent Englishmen forgetting SHAKSPEARE?' Burnand exclaims. 'No. The Bard has been chiselled by Lord RONALD GOWER, and his Immortality is at last assured' (95:185). Offsetting this concluding note of seriousness, however, is an accompanying

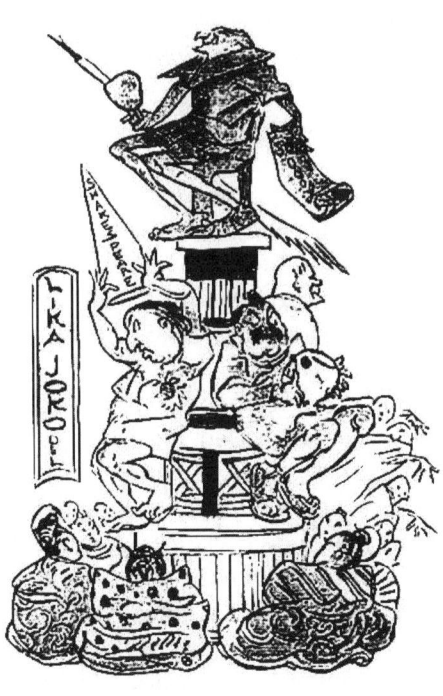

Figure 19. Harry Furniss's burlesque of Gower's statue of Shakespeare. *Punch* (20 October 1888), 95:185.

engraving (Figure 19). This depicts the seated Shakespeare (here with the head of Mr. Punch) on top of a tall stone base, an enormous quill in his right hand, his left arm draped over the back of his chair and holding a manuscript scroll. Around the base of the structure are burlesques of three of Gower's Shakespearean characters, here transformed into Japanese. The Prince Hal figure, instead of holding a crown above his head, holds a dunce's cap inscribed 'SHAKE-SPEARE', the Hamlet figure in an ungainly pose holds a large skull, and partially visible in the rear is the Falstaff figure, who stares into the distance. Seated around the base are a number of Japanese viewers. To one side is a banner, inscribed 'LIKA JOKO', and the caption below reinforces the Japanese references: 'Lika Joko's idea of the Gower Shakspearian statue after reading the *Times* report.' The design is the work of Harry Furniss, an important *Punch* artist who began working for *Punch* in 1880, one of his most distinctive contributions being a striking series of 'Japanneries' that he produced under the *nom de crayon* Lika Joko.

A week later, *Punch* followed up its 'Japannerie' on Gower's monument with an item (again by Burnand) entitled 'DIVINE SHAKSPEARE AND THE GREAT SCOTT' (95:197). Accompanying an engraving designed by John Priestman Atkinson that shows Shakespeare and Sir Walter Scott in conversation is an article that suggests leaving off the second 't' of the novelist's name. The intention is that the reader should then think of another Scot – Lord Ronald Gower. There follow some verses in ballad form that ironically remind the reader that both Stratford and Paris have a Shakespeare monument, whereas London, which saw only the model of Gower's, has none. At the end of the year, however, *Punch* was able to report that London did receive a specific benefit from Gower's twelve-year labours. On 22 December appeared a small article by Burnand entitled 'A NEW CAST FOR DRURY LANE' (95:289). 'Last Saturday', we are told, 'that gay young buster, Lord RONALD GOWER, presented a gigantic plaster (of Paris) cast of SHAKSPEARE's head and shoulders to DRURIOLANUS MAGNUS.' Presumably, what London got was related to the earlier version of Gower's monument, the plaster model of which he had put on display in Sydenham.

Stratford's enthusiastic acceptance of Gower's gift represented an apparent change of mind regarding the erection of a sculptural monument. To some degree, the new attitude was undoubtedly a reflection of the increasing realization that it was Stratford rather than London that in the future would be the Mecca for Shakespearean pilgrims, the principal site for what *Punch* chose to call Shakspeareanity. Anything that would help to consolidate Stratford's pre-eminent position, whether a new theatre, a new drinking fountain, or a grand monument, was now welcome. As the booming influx of tourists had already proved, Shakespeare was a commercial asset the like of which no other small English town would ever share. However, as one scholar has pointed out (Kimberley 1989, 21), there was possibly a particular reason for Stratford's willingness to erect Gower's monument on account of the outbreak between 1886 and 1888 of an old threat – a questioning of the authenticity of Shakespeare as author. In the face of this, Gower's powerful portrait was a forceful icon that would attest to the 'reality' of the Stratford author.

Punch and the Authorship Debate

The questioning of Shakespeare's authorship was long-standing. The theory that someone else wrote the works attributed to Shakespeare goes back to the eighteenth century, and in the Victorian period the idea blossomed, with a number of authors independent of each other coming to the opinion that Shakespeare was not the author. Among such pioneers of the anti-Stratfordian heresy were Joseph C. Hart, Nathaniel Holmes, William Henry Smith, and Delia Bacon. These last two both argued that Francis Bacon was the true author. Between 1856 and 1884, so Gary Taylor has estimated, the authorship debate gave rise to more than 250 books, pamphlets, and articles (Taylor 1989, 211).

Punch appears not to have paid much attention to the issue. However, in 'GAMMON OF BACON' (20 December 1856), a short item by Percival Leigh, *Punch* did allude to Smith (31:247), the Harley Street recluse, who in September 1856 had circulated privately a pamphlet in which he asked 'Was Lord Bacon the Author of Shakespeare's Plays?' Then in the following May, Leigh responded in another short piece to the publication of Delia Bacon's near impenetrable *The Philosophy of the Plays of Shakspere Unfolded*. An American, Delia Bacon had come to England in 1853 to research and propagate her theory. She met with an incredulous Thomas Carlyle and spent time at St. Albans (Bacon's home) and Stratford. At both locations she failed to get permission to open the respective tombs of the two men who figured so prominently in her thoughts. Eventually, with Emerson's assistance, she published her theory in the January 1856 issue of the New York magazine, *Putnam's Monthly*. With the help of Nathaniel Hawthorne, at that time the American consul in Liverpool, her 675-page book was published the following year (Schoenbaum 1970, 534–538, 550–553). Reactions were almost universally derisory, and *Punch*'s sexist dismissal of her efforts was typical. Leigh's article was entitled 'THE SWAN OF AVON A GOOSE'. Through him, *Punch*, the faithful organ of Shakspeareanity stated:

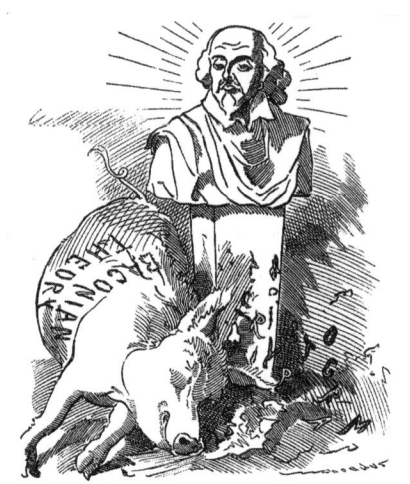

PIG-HEADED ATTACK ON THE IMMORTAL BARD.

Figure 20. Linley Sambourne's comment on the authorship debate. *Punch* (10 December 1887), 93:273.

A MISS DELIA BACON has written a book, entitled, *The Philosophy of the plays of* SHAKSPEARE *Unfolded*. That philosophy, as unfolded by MISS BACON turns out to be not SHAKSPEARE'S at all, but to belong to RALEIGH, to MISS BACON'S namesake of Verulam and the *Novum Organon*, and to others than the divine WILLIAMS. MISS BACON had better fold SHAKSPEARE'S pages than attempt to unfold his philosophy; she is evidently unable to read him, and should shut him up. Let her henceforth confine herself to the unfolding of table cloths and other linen maters more fit to be unfolded by feminine posers than those sheets which contain the philosophy of SHAKSPEARE. (32:179)

Following this brief outburst, *Punch* left the heretics alone apart from a passing allusion in 1878. (67:187), but in 1887 something changed, and for a short time *Punch* once more confronted the anti-Stratfordian theory. On this occasion, he who bore false witness was another American, Ignatius Donnelly. His long-lasting contribution to the authorship debate was the suggestion that Bacon had left behind cryptographic messages in what were known as Shakespeare's plays. Their purpose was to record that Bacon was the real author. The task at hand was therefore that of decoding Bacon's cryptograms, hence Donnelly's extremely long Baconian book, *The Great Cryptogram: Francis Bacon's Cipher in the So-Called Shakespeare Plays*. In his book, he claimed that he had decoded the cipher that Bacon had supposedly planted in the First Folio. The book appears to have been published in 1888, the date recorded for the copies in the Harvard Library, the Folger Shakespeare Library, and the British Library; however, *Punch* seems to have had access to a copy in December of the previous year. In the issue for 10 December, a small engraving by Linley Sambourne (his signature is upside down) depicted a plinth surmounted by a bust of Shakespeare (Figure 20). Various letters appear to be falling from the side of the plinth but spell out the word 'CRYPTOGRAM'. Leaning against the plinth, and perhaps responsible for dislodging the letters, is a pig, upon the back of which is inscribed 'BACONIAN THEORY'. The engraving has no caption, but it does have a striking title: 'PIG-HEADED ATTACK ON THE IMMORTAL BARD' (93:273).

The accompanying text (by Horace Frank Lester), entitled 'A DISPUTED WILL', consists of a series of letters to the editor that supposedly support Donnelly's 'wonderful discovery' that Bacon is 'the author of all SHAKSPEARE'S plays'. The various authors, it soon becomes apparent, have found their own cryptograms that both support Donnelly and prove, for example, that the works of certain other authors (Milton and Thackeray among them) were written by someone else, and that Queen Elizabeth was really Anne Hathaway. Over the page was another allusion to the authorship issue ('The Shakspearian Question'). An actor expresses his view 'in a strictly professional cryptogrammatic style' by saying, 'SHAKSPEARE written by a chap called BACON, my boy? Very likely; I always found "lots of fat" in it' (93:274). Also recorded is the opinion of a mariner, who, confusing Bacon with someone else with the same last name (Arthur Bacon), doubts that this individual could have written Shakespeare.

In the next issue of 17 December, *Punch* continued the attack on Donnelly's theory in three separate items. The first is entitled 'A RASHER THEORY OF BACON' and offers a ridiculous interpretation of Milton's 'What needs my SHAKSPEARE for his honour'd bones?' and uncovers a cypher in *A Midsummer Night's Dream* (93:278). It then goes on to maintain that Bacon and Shakespeare jointly authored a play called *Picoviccius*, an extract from which is then appended. Eight pages later are some verses with crude puns on 'side of Bacon' and 'gammon', and, over the page, in 'BACON AGAIN', readers are told that an 'erudite student' has informed *Punch* that 'the crest of SHAKSPEARE'S mother's family was a boar, so that there is something Baconian about the Immortal Bard' (93:288). In the next issue, continuing the all-too-obvious 'Bacon' puns, a 'Baconian writes to ask if there isn't sufficient proof of SHAKSPEARE'S affinity to BACON in Ham let alone?' (93:289).

As the year concluded and the issues for the preceding six months were gathered up to make Volume 93, *Punch* took one more swipe at Donnelly by devoting the entire Preface to the authorship question. An engraved headpiece by Charles Keene depicts the shades of Shakespeare at left, Mr. Punch in the centre, and Francis Bacon to the right. They stand in a kind of fog, representing 'a snug and sequestered if cloudy corner of the Elysian Fields'. Shakespeare and Bacon have been reading 'MR. DONELLY'S egregious lucubrations, not without such mild and mitigated mirth as becomes the locality', and they have just been joined by Mr. Punch, who is merely making a visit In the dialogue by Edwin James Milliken that follows, they discuss the writings of Ignatius Donnelly, beginning with a brief parody of one of the encounters between Hamlet and Polonius:

> *Mr. P.* What do you read, Sir?
> *Shaks.* 'Words, words, words!'
> *Mr. P.* 'I mean the matter that you read.'
> *Shaks.* 'Slanders, Sir.' For the coney-catching rogue – one DONELLY – says here – but of course you know *what*. (93:iii)

After laughing at Donnelly's theory, mocking his *Atlantis, the Antediluvian World* (1882), an attempt to argue that the island of Atlantis once existed opposite the Straits of Gibraltar, Bacon speaks out. Taking his cue from Mr. Punch's suggestion that Shakespeare and Bacon are quite separate entities ('Let the Great Brethren of British Genius be brethren still – twins, if you please, but twain.'), Bacon responds: '... the language of the Realm of Phantasy – WILL'S own world – the speech of Arcady, of Arden, of shadowy Elsinor, of *Prospero's* enchanted Isle – WILL'S native tongue – passeth many a league-long step beyond the 'neatness' of the judgment-seat, or the 'fulness' of the *Novum Organum Scientiarum'* (93:iv). All agree upon Donnelly's folly, and his book is doubly damned as being dull as well. When Shakespeare asks if Mr. Punch can offer Bacon and him a substitute, Mr. Punch presents the newly-bound Volume Ninety Three. Reluctantly having turned his back upon Elysium, he then leaves 'the two Illustrious Shades, prone side by side and cheek by jowl upon an asphodel bank, eagerly and diligently perusing' the work in question. A delightful engraving by Keene of this fantasy then concludes the Preface.

With that, *Punch* let the matter rest, with the exception of two small items in the course of the following year, and another in 1889. On 12 May 1888, *Punch* included a letter from 'Much Ado About Nothing' (Arthur William à Beckett). This claims to have found a cypher in Mary Cowden Clarke's *Concordance* that when decoded reads: 'Donnelly is a fool' (94:265). Then, on 10 November, in an item by Milliken entitled 'DOWN ON DONNELLY; Or, Crushing the Cryptogram', there appeared a discussion of Gerald Massey's *The Secret Drama of Shakspeare's Sonnets* (1888), a book which, among other things, uses the Sonnets to prove that Ignatius Donnelly's theory of authorship is wrong and that Shakespeare was the author of the poems and the plays. In response to Massey's book, an enlargement of his earlier six-hundred page *Shakspeare's Sonnets Never before Interpreted: His Private Friends Identified: together with A Recovered Likeness of Himself* (1866), *Punch* (Milliken) offers some verses that attack Donnelly rather than expose the follies of Massey. The verses describe Donnelly as a '"Moon-Raker" gone frantic / Who hunts for mare's-nests under the Atlantic', an allusion to Donnelly's 1882 book on Atlantis. Under 'MASSEY'S mace he [Donnelly] must have wilted / Like the pricked bladder that he is'. For his part, Massey is assured that all who read him

> ... will track with grateful heart and eye
> Your slaughtering of that colossal Sham
> Egregious DONNELLY'S Great Cryptogram! (95:221)

Finally, a year later, Henry Lucy contributed an article to the series 'ESSENCE OF PARLIAMENT. EXTRACTED FROM THE DIARY OF TOBY, M.P.'. This included a burlesque of cipher finding. In this instance, however, there was no direct reference to Bacon and Donnelly's theories. Instead, Lucy applied some of the bizarre methods of the cryptologist to Shakespeare's Sonnets (particularly Nos. 12, 16, 38, 45, and 65) and argued that the 'W. H.' (the only begetter) must be W. H. Smith, the Secretary for War (97:24).

Punch and the Exhumation of Shakespeare

Although the authorship debate raged on throughout the remainder of the century, *Punch* seems to have let it alone, confident, one assumes, that it posed no real threat to Shakspeareanity. Nor did *Punch* have anything much to say about the related issue of the exhumation of Shakespeare's remains and anything else that might be in his tomb to prove or disprove his authorship. In September 1856, Delia Bacon had entered the Stratford church at night with a small shovel. She was in search of documents and other relics, to which she had been led by her decipherment of the hieroglyphics of Bacon's letters (Schoenbaum 1970, 537). Her lack of adequate tools and, in the end, her lack of resolve left Shakespeare's tomb intact. By the time of Delia Bacon's nocturnal adventure, however, stories had already circulated that the grave had been opened and that the skull had been taken or the vault had proved to be empty. Serious proposals were made in 1864, 1876, and 1883 that the vault be opened and the skull examined in the interests of the so-called science of phrenology, but public sentiment was so strongly against the idea that nothing was done, and whatever was in the tomb – if indeed there was anything – remained untouched (Schoenbaum 1970, 471–473).

Punch commented on the matter on 15 September 1883. This followed the publication that year of Clement Mansfield Ingleby's *Shakespeare's Bones. The Proposal to Disinter Them, Considered in Relation to Their Possible Bearing on His Portraiture: Illustrated by Instances of Visits of the Living to the Dead.* Some twenty years or so previously, Ingleby had been the principal figure in the exposing of John Payne Collier's infamous forgeries regarding Shakespeare. He was a respected Shakespeare scholar, one of the original Birthplace trustees, and a vice-president of the New Shakspere Society. He thus spoke with some authority and could not be lightly dismissed. Furthermore, Ingleby's proposal to exhume Shakespeare in order to examine his skull was supported by Samuel Timmins, the Birthplace Librarian, and by the Reverend George Arbuthnot, the custodian of the grave (Halliday 1964, 242; Schoenbaum 1970, 473). *Punch*'s brief allusion to the proposal must therefore be seen as part of the storm of public protest that ultimately persuaded the Stratford authorities (both the town and the clergy) to leave Shakespeare in peace. The comment occurs in 'SHAKSPEARIAN REMAINS', an item by Francis C. Burnand that is principally concerned with the matter of burlesques based on works by Shakespeare, a topic on which he was, of course, well-qualified to speak. John Dryden's version of *The Tempest*, which has recently come to the attention of the magazine in the newly-published fourth volume of Sir Walter Scott's edition of Dryden's works, is not a burlesque, *Punch* argues, even though the literary scholar George Saintsbury had called it a 'Shakspeare Travesty'. Nonetheless, and referring indirectly to Ingleby's tract, the author of the *Punch* article then exclaims, 'Bones of SHAKSPEARE! Glorious JOHN at least made no bones about disturbing SHAKSPEARE'S literary remains' (85:130).

Apart from this remark and the obvious interpretation that any reader would give the title of the article, *Punch* gives only two further brief allusions to the debate going on in Stratford. Regarding the proposed exhumation, *Punch* offers a rather back-handed compliment to the Stratford authorities, who, *Punch* assumes, will withhold permission for the opening of Shakespeare's grave while taking advantage of the debate to raise funds: 'of course the Shakspearian Mayor, and the Shakspearian Vicar, who cleverly seizes the opportunity for letting the public know how badly he is off for funds for his Church's restoration, won't allow SHAKSPEARE'S bones to be exhumed.' A few years later on 30 July 1887, *Punch* made one further passing allusion to the issue of exhumation when it reported, in an article by Percival Leigh that a tomb in the Middle East had been opened in spite of an inscription on it discouraging such an act. The parallel to the situation of Shakespeare's tomb then elicited a brief comment (93:46).

Punch and Critical Works on Shakespeare

In its campaign to advance and defend Shakspeareanity, *Punch* occasionally referred to some of the very numerous Victorian publications connected with Shakespeare. The lengthy and often bizarre titles and subject-matter of many of the books on Shakespeare led *Punch* to include an item entitled 'SHAKSPEARIAN STUDIES' on 27 October 1877, the author of which is not listed in the *Punch* Contributors' Ledgers. This article contained brief notices of books that the editor of the new magazine, *The Year After Next,* has arranged to publish. The titles of the books burlesque 'scholarly' books on Shakespeare. The first is entitled 'An Enquiry into the Religious Principles of the Second Grave-Digger in *Hamlet*' (73: 184). Another example is entitled 'Extraordinary Revelations of the Infernal Practices used by Mother Prat of Brentford, aunt to *Mistress Ford's* maid in the *Merry Wives of Windsor*.' Other supposed titles deal with *As You Like It, Romeo and Juliet, King Lear, Richard III, The Tempest, Antony and Cleopatra*, and *Troilus and Cressida*.

In commenting on actual books, *Punch* gave considerable praise, for example, to Charles Knight's edition (see Chapter One), and forty-four years later, *Punch* included a laudatory review by Francis C. Burnand of a new edition of Shakespeare by Henry Irving and Frank Marshall (93:244). On the other hand, as we have seen, Delia Bacon's and Ignatius Donnelly's authorship theories were scornfully derided. Somewhat surprisingly, perhaps, few books are mentioned specifically. Possibly, the opportunities they offered for humorous comment were limited, and besides, as we shall see in the next chapter, *Punch* seems to have preferred to concern itself more with theatrical productions, no doubt in the belief that its readers were more likely to have seen what was currently on stage than to have read whatever new book on Shakespeare had found its way to the bookseller's shop.

However, in 1881 *Punch* briefly referred to Clement Mansfield Ingleby's *Shakespeare, the Man and the Book* (80:94), and on at least two occasions, and as already noted, *Punch* made punning allusions to Charles and Mary Lamb's ever-popular *Tales from Shakespear* (4:250; 96:33; 112:9). One of these allusions, that dated 19 January 1889 and titled 'LAMBS AT THE LYCEUM', offers an intriguing comparison between Ellen Terry's current performance as Lady Macbeth at the Lyceum theatre and the character-portrait of Lady Macbeth in the *Tales*. While doing so, the *Punch* author (either Burnand or Milliken – the Contributors' Ledgers are not clear) reminds his readers that the 'LAMBS' Tales were written for our innocent lambkins, and it is from this charming collection that so many of us, when children, have learnt the plots of SHAKSPEARE'S plays, and the character of the persons who figure in them'. *Punch*'s readers are urged to engage in a 're-perusal of their [i.e. the Lambs'] story of *Macbeth*'. Ellen Terry is urged to do the same thing:

> If Miss TERRY has considered the LAMBS' work as mere child's play, I should advise her to read it over carefully, for there is so much in their view of Lady Macbeth's character which so entirely accords with a part of her own view of it, and so much which her genius will at once adopt as representing the stern and repulsive side of the character.

If the *Punch* readership is presumed to have first garnered an acquaintance with Shakespeare's plots and characters by reading *Tales of Shakespear* during childhood, that same readership is also assumed to have read something of Shakespeare's biography. Jerrold's burlesque version of the details (legendary and otherwise) of Shakespeare's early life in 'EXHIBITION OF THE ENGLISH IN CHINA'

(6:119) depends for its comic effect upon the reader knowing something about this topic:

> He [Shakespeare] was originally a carcass butcher, and was obliged to fly from his native town because he used to slip out at nights, kill his neighbours' deer, and then sell the venison to the poor for mutton. [...] He went to London, and made a wretched livelihood by selling beans and wisps of hay to the horses of the gentlemen who came to the playhouses. Thinking that he could not sink any lower, he took to writing plays, out of which – it is awful to relate – he made a fortune.

The supposed Chinese author of the catalogue entry that *Punch* is quoting refers to having gathered his facts 'from the last two or three authentic lives lately written'. Significantly, Collier's *The Life of William Shakespeare* appeared in 1844, the same year as Jerrold's article, while Knight's *William Shakspere: A Biography* had appeared the year before in the eighth and final volume of the *Pictorial Shakspere*. However, as Samuel Schoenbaum has demonstrated in such captivating detail, other accounts of Shakespeare's life (often derivative) routinely appeared throughout the nineteenth century in books, pamphlets, encyclopaedias, periodicals, and biographical dictionaries, as part of the prefatory material for editions, and even (in fictional form) in plays and novels (Schoenbaum 1970, 251, 298–299, 309, 311, 315–327, 365–380).

In spite of their number, however, only one Shakespeare biography seems to have been singled out for comment by *Punch*. William John Birch's *An Inquiry into the Philosophy and Religion of Shakspere* was published in 1848. Rather than attempting to find in Shakespeare's works evidence of the details of his private life – a favourite form of Victorian biography – Birch attempted to inquire into something very different though equally dear to Victorian hearts. What interested Birch was Shakespeare's religious persuasion. Where others set out to show that Shakespeare was an Anglican, or a Puritan, or a Roman Catholic, Birch attempted to prove that Shakespeare was an atheist. *Punch* objected strenuously to this idea in a brief article by Douglas Jerrold that appeared in August 1848. Birch is described as a 'benighted' and 'unfortunate individual,' who is 'guilty of begetting' a book for which he should be punished by being birched. Where various contemporaries have 'abused BIRCH at length', *Punch* suggests the following response: 'we would turn him adrift in a washing-tub upon the Avon; and whereas BIRCH has thrown his dirt at the Swan, he should be piloted by congenial geese. After this, we would have it most significantly proved to BIRCH that he deserved nothing short of himself' (15:84).

Punch and Other Shakespearean Matters

As with its occasional allusions to writings about Shakespeare, *Punch* from time to time demonstrated an interest in other Shakespearean matters. In 'MUGGLETONIAN MECHANICS' INSTITUTION', for example, *Punch* mocked Mechanics' Institutes (there were over 300 by 1841) and their attempts to provide educational experiences to artisans and industrial workers (Kelly 1962, 125). Given *Punch's* supposed desire to spread Shakspeareanity as widely as possible, this 1843 composition by Gilbert Abbott à Beckett was perhaps somewhat hypocritical; however, it was nonetheless in harmony with a fairly sustained vein of *Punch* satire aimed at the popular education movement as represented by the Society for the Diffusion of Useful Knowledge (founded in 1825), the Working Men's Colleges begun in 1854 by F. D. Maurice, and other organizations and societies (Harrison 1954, 10–11; Altick 1997, 635–642; Foulkes 2002, 84). In 'MUGGLETONIAN MECHANICS' INSTITUTION', *Punch* made fun of the kind of esoteric-sounding lecture that often appeared on the programmes of both mechanics' institutes and learned societies. This instance consists of a report on a Mr. Frisby's 97th lecture on the 'Genius and Grammar of Shakspeare' (5:226). The supposed lecture is a parody of academic excesses in interpreting Shakespeare's text. Unintentionally comical interpretations are given by Frisby of lines from *Julius Caesar* (III ii 175), *Macbeth* (IV i 112), and *Othello* (I iii 87). One example will suffice here. Quoting Antony's 'See what a rent the envious Casca made', Frisby argued that Casca must have been a landlord and 'looked probably rather sharp after his tenantry'.

131

In 1844, and also concentrating on matters to do with Shakespeare's text, *Punch* humorously demonstrated in Percival Leigh's 'CIBBER DETECTED' how Colley Cibber's text of *Richard III* was found to be uncomfortably far removed from that in Charles Knight's recent edition of the play (see above). Some forty-five years later, *Punch* was still pointing out the distinction between stage versions of *Richard III* and the authentic Shakespeare text when a small item (probably by Burnand) was given the title 'Familiar Line from Cibber-Shakspeare's Richard the Third' (112:321). Adapting Cibber's most famous textual addition to Shakespeare's play, *Punch* offers the following version of the line in question, here 'Adapted to the Present Time and Fashion' in order to comment on a common problem at theatres:

> *Irritable Sight-seer (whose view is blocked by a lady's hat).* 'Off with her .... hat! So much ...' *(Gives the necessary directions.)*

In a quite different vein, *Punch* attacked Samuel Bailey, the author of an 1862 book in two volumes, entitled *On the Received Text of Shakspeare's Dramatic Writings and its Improvement*. In 'SHAKSPEARE RESTAURATUS', which appeared on 8 March 1862, *Punch* (Percival Leigh) described Bailey as 'of logical and limited intellect' (42:98). His offence is to have proposed an amendment or 'improvement' to Shakespeare's text whereby Hamlet's line 'Or, to take arms against a sea of troubles' in his 'To be, or not to be' soliloquy would be changed to 'Or, to take arms against *the seat* of troubles', and the following line 'And, by opposing, end them' be changed to 'And, by a *poniard*, end them'. Whereas Bailey thinks that 'The emendation is not inferior in tone of thought or force of expression to what it displaces', *Punch* thinks otherwise. Hamlet's 'a sea of troubles' has come to be a stock expression in English for a reason, *Punch* insists. Bailey is a 'stolid pedant', and divesting Hamlet's speech of Hamlet's poetry is like leaving Hamlet out of *Hamlet*.

Recognizing the seeming perversity with which editors and students of Shakespeare felt free to suggest emendations to Shakespeare's text, *Punch* in 1853 published 'HINTS FOR A NEW EDITION OF THE DRAMATISTS,' an item contributed by Gilbert

Abbott à Beckett. This consisted of some examples from the supposed notes of a clever scholar who planned an edition of some plays. Among the plays is Shakespeare's *Julius Caesar*. Taking the line 'See what a rent the envious Casca made', the would-be editor says that what is revealed here is that Casca either made money through charging high rents for lodgings or that he derived a considerable income from landed tenants. Recycling a joke made ten years before, à Beckett has the supposed scholar develop the idea at some length to provide an interpretation of the much-neglected character of Casca (25:43).

Much more succinct but equally foolish is another example of *Punch*'s mockery of the plethora of emendations and reinterpretations that appeared in the course of the century. This time the text is that of *Hamlet*. Entitled 'NEW SHAKSPEARIAN READING', a letter from 'A YOUNG COMMENTATOR' (in reality Shirley Brooks) asks: 'When did *Hamlet* express a desire to become a member of the Hebrew persuasion?' Answer: 'When he wished that his too too solid flesh would resolve itself into a Jew' (46:19). Towards the end of the same year, and again playing with words and their sounds, *Punch* offered yet another suggested emendation, Brooks again being the author. This time the source came directly from Elysium in the form of a letter to Mr. Punch dated 11 November from Shakespeare himself. In the letter, Shakespeare asks his old friend to call in at the Drury Lane Theatre 'where they are playing something like my *Macbeth*' (47:207). Shakespeare would like Punch to alter the prompter's copy. Of the lines 'Letting "I dare not" wait upon "I would," / Like the poor cat *I' the Adage*', Shakespeare says:

> What rubbish have you been setting down for me all these years? There is an Italian river into which a mediaeval cat fell, and to which, of course, I alluded. I mean to describe a helpless sort of state, and what can be more helpless than a cat in a river? Ask MISS FAUCIT [i.e. Helen Faucit] to be good enough to say, 'Like the poor Cat *I' the Adige.'*

In addition to being aware of contemporary attempts, many of them misguided and unconvincing, to establish Shakespeare's text, *Punch* also derived amusement from some of the better-known Shakespearean mysteries. Two items in particular illustrate this point. Both concern matters that were widely discussed and that *Punch* could therefore assume many of its readers were familiar with. The first has to do with the scholarly puzzle concerning the appearance of a third murderer in *Macbeth* III iii, even though Macbeth in III i had commissioned only two with the task of slaying Banquo. The topic had been raised in *Notes and Queries* on 11 September and 13 November 1869 by Allan Park Paton. E. Hills responded in *Notes and Queries* on 2 October 1869. Then on 30 October, 1869, still in *Notes and Queries*, T. S. Baynes maintained that he had anticipated Paton. In *Nineteenth Century* in April, 1877, Henry Irving put forward his own theory, and there was a response to Irving by Moy Thomas in the *Athenaeum* on 14 April, 1877. That same day, *Punch* issued its own explanation in the form of a dramatic scene by Francis C. Burnand that was set on the stage of the Globe Theatre in 1606 following a performance of *Macbeth*. The characters in the scene include Richard Burbage and William Shakespeare. An actor playing the part of Attendant complains that his part is too small. He says that in III i he has only one line, and then he is 'at once ordered off the stage by *Macbeth*, and told to stay outside the door until he and the two Murderers call' for him (72:160). An obliging Shakespeare then goes to the prompter's table and alters the play copy to make the Attendant also double as one of three murderers, Burbage having objected to an earlier suggestion of having a fourth witch.

Somewhat similar to the conundrum posed by the third murderer in *Macbeth* is that which arises from Gertrude's assertion that Hamlet is fat. This too was a familiar topic of discussion and one likely to have been known to most readers of *Punch*. In its own commentary on this issue, *Punch* did not this time offer any explanation for why Shakespeare had used the word. Instead, we have the suggestion in 1880 that tragic actors, in keeping with their heavy roles, should themselves be heavy. Even Hamlet, we are reminded in an article contributed by Burnand, was 'a trifle inclined to obesity', an indirect allusion to Gertrude's remark that Hamlet is 'fat, and scant of breath' (78:29). A different comment was offered by Harry Furniss in 1891. Below the title 'PICTORIAL NOTE TO HAMLET', he depicted two engravings, each of a very fat Hamlet. The first illustrated Hamlet's 'O that this too too solid flesh would melt!' and the second (obviously seen as

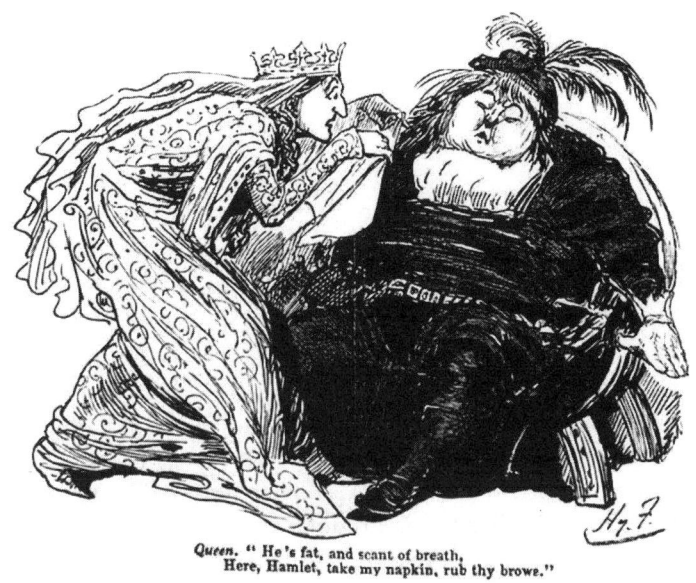

Queen. "He's fat, and scant of breath,
Here, Hamlet, take my napkin, rub thy brows."

Figure 21. Harry Furniss, 'PICTORIAL NOTE TO HAMLET',
Punch (3 January 1891), 93:273.

linked to the first) showed Gertrude offering a napkin to Hamlet, who has collapsed breathless into a chair (Figure 21). The caption consists of Gertrude's comment 'He's fat, and scant of breath, / Here, Hamlet, take my napkin, rub thy brows' (100:11). A year later appeared an engraving designed by Bernard Partridge that depicted a confrontation between two actors dressed as Hamlet. One is Herbert Beerbohm Tree and the other, a short fat figure, is named H. Kemble. This latter argues that it is he who should be playing Hamlet and that he has Shakespeare's authority: 'Oh, that this too too solid flesh would melt', and again, 'Fat and scant of breath!' To this Beerbohm Tree replies: 'All right, my dear Kemble. Quite true what you say; and, any night, I am unable to play, you shall be my double!' (102:73). Elsewhere, *Punch* offers a comic pun on the awkward line. In response to the question 'WAS HAMLET FAT?' a 'great Shakspearian actor' (*Punch* does not name him) replies: 'Fat! Of course he was fat. [...] In my time I have played many parts, and I tell you, my dear boy, that

135

Hamlet is one of the "fattest" parts going. Why, *Hamlet* is all "fat"' (116:281).

* * *

Attempts by *Punch* and its staff of writers and artists to propagate what they referred to as 'Shakspeareanity' have provided the main subject for this chapter. As we have seen, the magazine's constant allusions to matters having to do with Shakespeare assume a readership that has more than a passing interest in Shakespeare's works, that cares about the places in England associated with him, that has an interest in proposals for memorializing him, that is conversant with the authorship and exhumation debate, and that is aware of ongoing discussions about textual matters. But the materials presented in this chapter are only a small part of the total picture. Omitted so far are several other large pieces of the cultural phenomenon that provides the subject for this book, the study of the relationship between *Punch* and Shakespeare. These additional segments will be the focus for subsequent chapters, beginning in the next chapter with what proved to be a topic of consuming interest for *Punch* and presumably for its readers – the performance of Shakespeare's plays.

Chapter Three

Punch, Shakespeare, and the Theatre

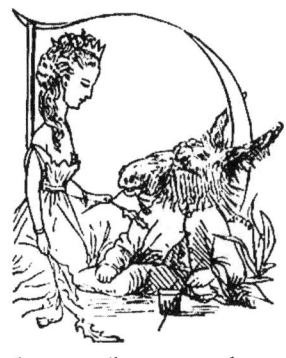

During the Victorian era, *Punch* offered its readers a steady stream of commentary on all matters having to do with the theatre. Given the theatrical interests of the *Punch* staff, this is no surprise. In making theatre a central interest, the magazine was thoroughly in tune with contemporary culture. Theatre attendance was an important part of the London and provincial social calendar. From the Queen on down to working-class people, theatre (however loosely defined) occupied a place in the cultural landscape equivalent to the dominant situation of television and film today. Recognizing this, the pages of *Punch* are full of talk about the theatre.

In *Punch*'s view, because Shakespeare's plays represented an ideal against which all other theatrical entertainment might be judged, particular attention was given to Shakespearean actors and the performance of Shakespeare's plays in England and abroad, whether by English or foreign actors. As *Punch* became more and more aware of itself as a national institution and potential arbiter of public taste, it tended to focus attention upon the fare at certain selected theatres. That is not to say that the contemporary love of melodrama, burlesque, and the sensational went unnoticed. However, in line with *Punch*'s desire to cultivate a respectable, predominantly middle-class family readership, the so-called minor theatres and their often rough and raucous audiences received far less notice in *Punch* than the former patent theatres (Covent Garden, Drury Lane, and the Haymarket) and such theatres as Sadler's Wells (site of a brave experiment by Samuel Phelps and Mary Warner to promote Shakespeare), the Lyceum (during Henry Irving's tenancy), the Princess's (particularly during Charles Kean's tenancy), Augustin Daly's Theatre in the 1890s, and Her Majesty's (during Herbert Beerbohm Tree's occupancy from 1897).

Theatrical Titbits and Gossip

Punch maintained a constant commentary on Shakespeare theatre productions throughout the Victorian era and reviewed all kinds of other theatrical entertainments. Such commentary was part of an even broader context that could range from mere titbits of news and gossip to discussions of more serious issues having to do with the theatre. Whatever the topic, however, Shakespeare's name and work was likely to be invoked. Typical, for example, was a report in 1862 that a London actor had allowed himself to be carried on the back of Charles Blondin as this latter walked a tight rope (43:136). For those who knew their Shakespeare, the title of the item burlesqued a line from one of Ariel's songs: 'On the bat's back I do fly.' A few years later, *Punch* reported on a performance of *Henry IV* by deaf and dumb students in a Manchester asylum. Sign language 'familiar to the pupils' was used and 'was easily followed by the other spectators', something that led *Punch* to suggest that perhaps some London theatre manager should take the hint so that 'one could see a play of SHAKSPEARE'S, without hearing SHAKSPEARE'S language mumbled, mouthed, or murdered otherwise' (49:255).

Then there was the short article entitled 'HAMLET AT VIENNA' about a Viennese actor named Archer who was imprisoned after being accused of mimicking M. de Schmerling. *Punch* suggests that the actor should have followed Hamlet's advice to the Players concerning Polonius: 'Follow that lord; and, look you, mock him not.' At Vienna, *Punch* surmises, 'the theatre is some way from Liberty Hall' (48:185). In 1880, *Punch* published a description contributed by Arthur William à Beckett of a visit to Madame Tussaud's wax works. Various of the famous persons represented are humorously described,

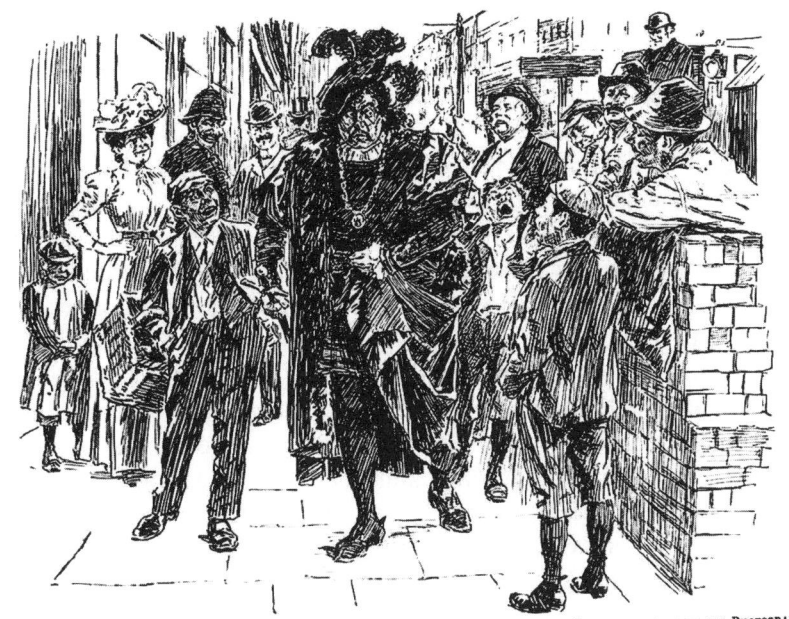

TOMKINS, WHO HAS RECENTLY MADE HIS APPEARANCE *EN AMATEUR* AS THE MELANCHOLY DANE, GOES TO HAVE HIS PHOTOGRAPH TAKEN "IN CHARACTER." UNFORTUNATELY, ON REACHING THE CORNER OF THE STREET, HE FINDS *THE ROAD IS UP*, AND HE HAS TO WALK TO THE DOOR! TABLEAU!!

Figure 22. Unidentified artist. Amateur actor dressed as Hamlet. *Punch* (18 September 1897), 113:126.

among them Charles Dickens, Lord Byron, Walter Scott, several British politicians, and a number of well-known international figures. Among the many wax effigies is that of William Shakespeare, the one dramatist mentioned. *Punch* included in its article a small engraving of the wax works effigy. Designed by John Priestman Atkinson, the engraving shows that the wax work was posed as in Scheemakers's statue but here possessed an abundance of hair on either side of an otherwise bald head. The accompanying text then remarks that Shakespeare would probably have 'given many more works to Posterity had he not seemingly, from this presentment of him "in the habit as he lived", spent three-quarters of his waking hours in the arrangement of his hair!' (79:169).

A final example of such trivia (Figure 22) is an invented report concerning an amateur actor, one Tomkins, who recently made his debut as Hamlet and then went to have his photograph taken 'in character.' 'Tomkins' was a generic name, usually employed by Victorians to denote an ordinary and often inept male representative of the urban middle class. In this instance, an engraving depicts Tomkins dressed as Hamlet in long dark coat and plumed bonnet. He is walking along a street before the amused gaze of a number of onlookers in contemporary dress. As the caption explains, because of some road works, Tomkins was forced, no doubt to his great embarrassment, to walk in the open street for the last part of his trip to the photographer's studio (113:126). As *Punch* and its readers knew well, it was common for leading actors to be photographed 'in character'. Given the prestige attached to the role of Hamlet, it was almost *de rigueur* for an actor playing the role to then have his or her (there were a great many female Hamlets) photograph taken. The *Punch* cartoon would thus appear to be a satirical commentary on the pretentiousness and vanity of a mere amateur who both took on the role of Hamlet and then had his photograph taken to commemorate the occasion.

Trials and Tribulations of the Theatre-Goer

Because many of the staff at *Punch* were themselves theatre-goers, it is not surprising to find comments on a number of issues, trivial in retrospect, perhaps, but considered to be of sufficient collective interest to be featured in the pages of the magazine. On 1 February 1851, for example, Gilbert Abbott à Beckett contributed 'THE PASSAGE OF THE HAYMARKET PIT. A Lay of Modern Babylon.' Below an engraving depicting the procession of kings that the three witches present to Macbeth (he is here transformed into Mr. Punch) are verses describing the very uncivilized crush of people attempting to get from the street to the box office window for one of the farewell performances of the eminent tragedian, Macready (20:51). There they must exchange money for a token and then get to their seats in the pit. Because seats, except for boxes, could normally not be reserved in advance, and because they were not numbered, undignified crushes and tussles to get into the theatre were not uncommon, especially for some special attraction such as that referred to here.

In addition to the struggle to obtain entrance and get a good seat, once inside the theatre, there was also the issue of ticket price. When a number of West End theatres underwent renovations (the Haymarket was a notable example in 1843), the managements reduced their seating capacity, and generally attempted to make theatre going a more genteel and physically comfortable experience, with such modifications as the introduction of comfortable stalls in place of pit benches and the addition of backs to the pit benches. The introduction of gas lighting was another added expense, as Webster at the Haymarket noted (Odell 1921, 2:243). As a result, ticket prices increased considerably. On 1 January 1881, in a series entitled 'PLAYERS AND PAYERS' that was contributed by a writer listed as 'Morris' in the Contributors' Ledgers, *Punch* included a letter from 'Oliver Twist'. It was headed by Iago's advice to Roderigo: 'Put money in thy purse.' The supposed letter is an extended complaint about the high costs of theatre seats and especially the cost of 10s. 6d. for a stall seat (79:301).

Two weeks later, the same series voiced a complaint that in addition to high ticket prices, patrons in certain theatres were also expected to pay 'fees' (i.e. tips). These were hard to avoid because they have 'been commonly entrusted, with a fiendish cunning, to the hands of a lovely woman, against whom no man, though persecuted beyond all control, may venture to lift his hand, save it is for the purpose of putting sixpence in hers'. This, *Punch* exclaims, is to 'be plundered under the guise of courtesy, with a smiling face, and a pretty welcome' (80:41). Elsewhere, in a burlesque by John Hollingshead of some lines from *Hamlet* (80:226), *Punch* suggests that the sense of being financially exploited is exacerbated by the knowledge that a significant number of seats were given out for free, either by individual actors or by the management. Known as 'orders', these were frequently a cause of resentment. Managements did not necessarily like them either but saw no way of avoiding them, particularly in the case of members of the press (Jackson 1989, 254–255).

Once in the theatre, there were other potential annoyances. These might include the size of women's hats and the subsequent problem of seeing the stage, or so one audience member (Arthur William à Beckett) reported in 1898 after attending a performance of *Hamlet*: 'NOTHING could be finer than the scenery, so far as I could judge. I frankly confess that, instead of the ramparts, I saw one lady's picture-hat, and lost half of the graveyard act, thanks to the *chapeau à la Française.*' His only hope is 'that some day female head-dresses, like children in arms, will not be admitted' (114:48). Then there was the problem encountered in 1865 by Francis Burnand when he attended a performance of *Henry IV*, Part One, at the Standard Theatre. The play was repeatedly disrupted by the noise of passing trains, and Shakespeare's lines as performed by William Creswick, John Ryder, and Sarah Thorne were 'discordantly interrupted by the Lines of the North London Railway' city extension (49:222).

More common, perhaps, was the disruptive noise of audiences that had no compunction about talking during a performance. As one 'Will Waddle' (the actual author's name is not recorded in the Contributors' Ledgers) complained in 1867 concerning both plays and operas, 'It is not pleasant in the middle of a noble scene by SHAKSPEARE to hear the twitter of JOCASTA, or the twaddle of BELINDA, and when a gentleman has paid a guinea for a stall, the chance is he would rather hear the melodies of MEYERBEER than the gabble he could gratis listen to at home' (52:221). A few years later on 10 December 1870, the same issue was referred to in some sexist verses complaining about a female audience member:

> PERCHED in a box which cost her not a *sou*,
> GIGLINA chatters all the evening through,
> Fidgets with opera-glass, and flowers, and shawls,
> Annoys the actors, irritates the stalls.
> Forgive her harmless pride – the cause is plain –
> She wants us all to know she's had champagne. (59:242)

Such chatter was not, of course, confined to female audience members, and the ease with which events on stage might be ignored in favour of private conversation among those in the auditorium remained an issue even near the end of the century (Booth 1991, 62).

A somewhat darker issue is referred to in 30 January 1864 when *Punch* bluntly charged that 'Another victim has been sacrificed to the grinning Moloch. Another young girl has been burned to death to make an evening's show. MARIA CHARLES, a dancer at the Pavilion Theatre, is the sacrifice. Her dress caught fire from some unprotected gas-lights used in the Pantomime, and she has since expired.' Stricter safety rules, enforced by government inspectors, are needed, *Punch* argues, to 'prevent these oft-recurring burnt sacrifices'. Something of this kind would mean that 'English mothers in the boxes, with their laughing children, would be spared the thought that when the scene is the most brilliant, the chance is greatest that a shriek will announce that someone else's child is in the agony of burning.'

Another type of fire hazard was referred to in 1881 in the 'PLAYERS AND PAYERS' series by Morris referred to above. As the author explains, theatres 'though tolerably easy to get into', are 'uncommonly hard to get out of'. As was widely recognized, many theatres were fire traps, but, as the author explains, government inspections are supposed to occur twice a year, and precautions against fire are supposed to be taken, 'But what they may be, I don't know, nor what the penalty of their violation; the latter I take to be some such as honest *Dogberry* instructed his watchmen to enact.' The author, who happens to have a copy of the Official Circular detailing the supposed regulations, then discusses as an example the requirement that 'all gangways, passages, and staircases, intended for the exit of the audience, are to be kept entirely free from obstructions, whether permanent or temporary'. This rule, he explains, is constantly and recklessly disregarded 'whenever some lucky hit happens to draw the town in larger numbers than the architect bargained for'. Because the law is not enforced, managers confronted with a 'visitor with money in his hand' find the temptation to admit extra persons irresistible 'so long as any hole or corner can be found in which to stow him' (80:41).

The dangers of fire in theatres were well known and were given special emphasis in a pamphlet referred to by the author of the *Punch* article – *Fire in Theatres* (1876) by Captain Eyre M. Shaw, Chief of the London Fire Brigade. Between the advent of *Punch* and the appearance of the *Punch* article, at least six theatres, including Covent Garden in 1856, had been lost to fire in London and twenty-six theatres in the provinces. Six years later, the particular disaster feared by the author of the article occurred, not in London but at the Theatre Royal, Exeter, when a fire destroyed the building and took a hundred and fifty lives, something that prompted public outrage and fresh precautions against the ever-present danger (Jackson 1994, 209; and Booth 1991, 68–69).

Legislation and the Theatre

Punch was, as might be expected, well attuned to the effects of any legislation regarding the theatre. As pointed out in the previous chapter, the Theatre Regulation Act of 1843 had far-reaching consequences. The following year, in 'A WORD OR TWO ON THE PLAYHOUSES' by Douglas Jerrold, *Punch* suggested that 'The wisdom of Parliament having all but destroyed the drama, has declared it free! This is the humanity of a barbarian, who, having wellnigh starved his victim to death, gives him, whilst in *articulo mortis*, his unconditional liberty' (6:95). Macready, it is lamented has gone on tour in North America, Covent Garden has become 'a house of call for fiddlers', Drury Lane offers an 'opera there one night, and CHARLES KEAN'S tragedy another', the Haymarket is conducting an open competition for writers of comedies, and other theatres offer nothing suitable for the discriminating theatre-goer. As for Shakespeare, his future is uncertain.

Late in 1844, as mentioned in the previous chapter, *Punch* published an engraving entitled 'SHAKSPEAR AN EMIGRANT TO FRANCE' that depicted the dramatist embarking for France. A few years later, when Alexandre Dumas came to London to present a series of French plays at Drury Lane, *Punch* published an engraving designed by William Newman that showed Shakespeare leaving Drury Lane Theatre. Significantly, it was entitled 'SHAKSPEARE AN ALIEN' (14:246). The legislation that potentially freed Shakespeare from the constraints of the patent theatres was a disaster, or so *Punch* appears to have at first believed. However, as will be seen in a moment, the concern that Shakespeare's plays would no longer be accessible to London theatre goers unless they braved the wilds of Islington to see Samuel Phelps's productions was short-lived. Even so, it was real enough during the first few years after the Act was passed.

A very different issue was that of copyright. This was a perennial problem in England, even after copyright legislation began to be introduced. Douglas Jerrold's *Mrs. Caudle's Curtain Lectures* provides a clear example. An important 'hit' for *Punch*, the series was pirated by at least six country papers (Slater 2002, 162), prompting a vigorous response by Jerrold in *Punch* on 19 July 1845 entitled 'Punch and the "Pickers and Stealers"' (9:33). Numerous instances of alleged piracy of *Punch* material occurred as the first few decades of the magazine's life unfolded, although *Punch* was often itself accused of stealing material that had originated elsewhere (Spielmann 1895a, 151–159). Almost twenty years after the thefts of the *Curtain Lectures*, issues of literary theft and copyright were still very much alive. According to *Punch* on 14 March 1863, a certain playwright who had adapted a fifty-year-old novel had claimed copyright for his play, including the original dialogue and incidents taken from the novel. In the article discussing this matter, which was contributed by Henry Silver and was no doubt of considerable interest to the playwrights among the *Punch* staff, it is suggested that

> if old novels be held by any law Court to be the property of any dramatist who happens to lay hold of them, the same rule might apply with equal justice to old plays, and a copyright in Shakspeare, say, be claimed by any writer who might 're-arrange' the incidents, and make some little alteration in the dialogue and plot (44:105).

To show the absurdity of such a situation, Silver then offers a burlesque of the final scene in *Othello* that is composed of lines from that play and lines imported from other plays.

Far more serious was the matter of American piracy since British authors' and publishers' rights had long been unprotected under American law. Jerrold's *Mrs. Caudle's Curtain Lectures*, for example, was pirated by New York publishers, and during the early years of *Punch,* the Philadelphia publisher Carey & Hart stole *Punch* material by W. H. Wills, Gilbert Abbott à Beckett, Albert Smith, Percival Leigh, and above all Jerrold (Altick 1997, 24). As already mentioned in Chapter One, *Harper's New Monthly Magazine* also engaged in piracy of *Punch* material. Relief seemed in sight in 1890 when hopes were pinned upon what became known as the Chace Act (1891) that gave protection to authors from outside the United States, provided that their work was printed in the United States. However, *Punch* was very cynical regarding any legislation designed to deal with piracy. On 24 May 1890, it published an engraving designed by G. R. and entitled 'THE MODERN PISTOL' (98:345) (Figure 23). This depicted an 1890s American version of Shakespeare's Pistol, wearing the stars and stripes on his costume and standing in front of the Capitol building and an American flag. Beside him on the ground is a heap of books, variously inscribed 'CHEAP EDITION', '25 CENTS', and 'ENGLISH NOVELS'. Beneath Pistol's foot is a document inscribed 'COPYRIGHT ACT. PAYMENT TO BRITISH AUTHORS'. However, the caption below, a quotation from *Henry V*, makes clear what the literary thief really thinks and what presumably *Punch* expects to be the effect of the legislation in the future: 'BASE IS THE SLAVE THAT PAYS!'

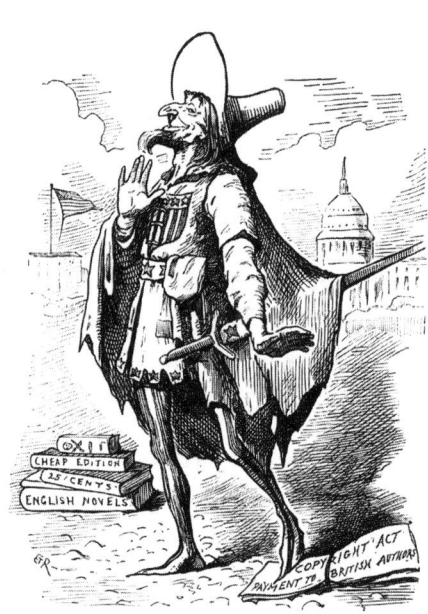

Figure 23. G.R., 'THE MODERN PISTOL', *Punch* (24 May 1890), 98;245.

Two other legal issues also drew comments from *Punch*. In 1889 in an article entitled 'THE DRAMA IN AMERICA' that was probably written by Burnand, *Punch* alluded to a move by American actors to protect their profession by banning English actors (96:39). As will be seen later in this chapter, English actors such as Macready and Irving were able to enjoy lucrative tours in the United States and banning them would no doubt have appealed to some native American actors. The *Punch* article then takes matters further and suggests that American playwrights are about to follow the American actors and attempt to ban British plays, including three by Shakespeare. The article goes on to toy with the fantasy of how some of Shakespeare's plots could be re-worked by American writers to create such works as *Three Gentlemen of Chicago; The High Falutin Dane, or the United State of Denmark; The 'Cate Thane of Cawdor, or the Bustin up of Duncan; Bosworth Dick, Duke of New York; The Venetian Nigger, or the Kentucky Cuss on the Spree*; and *The Blizzard* (i.e. *The Tempest*).

Such ideas were probably never a serious threat at all. Closer to home, however, was the very real threat to London theatre that occurred in 1890 when the London County Council threatened to impose a stamp duty on theatre tickets. This occasioned a strong response from Henry Irving (Irving 1951, 546). That same year on a slightly different topic having to do with the Council, *Punch* published 'THE LONDON COUNTY COUNCIL AND THE LYCEUM THEATRE. APPEAL OF MR. HENRY IRVING. RESULT. (*A not impossible Extract from Next Year's Morning Papers.*).' The article (by Thomas Anstey Guthrie) imagined a situation in which the London County Council had failed to renew the Lyceum Theatre's licence with the result that the manager, Henry Irving, is forced to appear before the L.C.C.'s Theatres Committee to appeal the decision.

Having described the various plays that he put on, Irving is then questioned by members of the committee. A Mr. Hecklebury ascertains from Irving that *Hamlet*, a play in which the actor had many times appeared, has a plot in which 'the chief character in the play drives his *fiancée* to madness and suicide by his cruelty, slays her father and brother, together with his own step-father, and procures the death of two of his school-fellows'. A Mr. Fussler then read various passages from *Othello* that he felt were not suitable for public declamation but which were nonetheless used in Irving's production of that play, and a Mr. Medlam got Irving to admit that 'the hero in *Othello* is

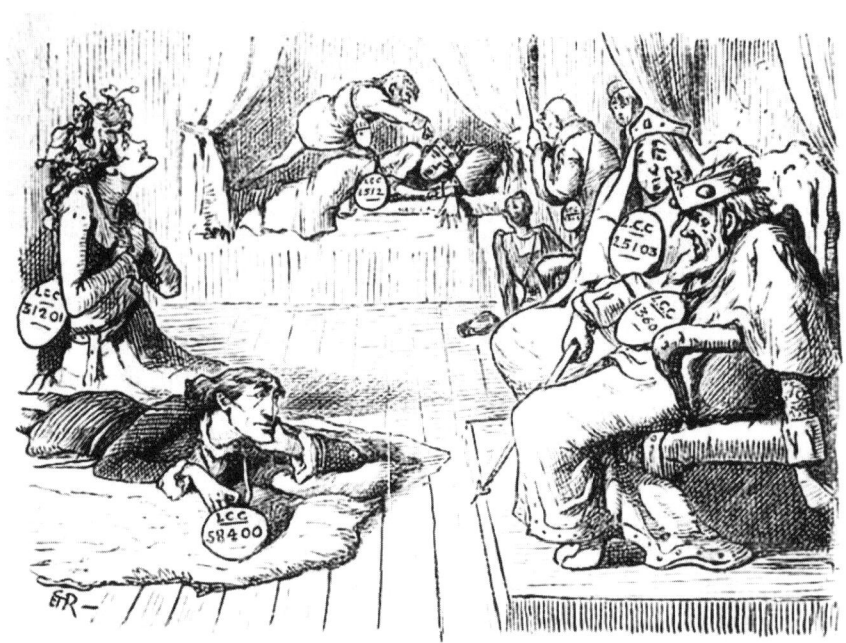

Figure 24. Edward Tennyson Reed, Irving and Terry before the L.C.C. *Punch* (8 March 1890), 98:109.

not only a murderer but a suicide.' Another committee member, a Mr. Parseeker, then got Irving to admit that he had fought duels in *Romeo and Juliet* and *Hamlet*, had fought a hand-to hand combat in *Macbeth*, and had committed a murder in this last-named play. More evidence is then established in support of the committee's idea that in putting on certain of Shakespeare's plays at the Lyceum, Irving had made the Lyceum 'a School of Murder,' something quite detrimental to public morals.

This humorous mockery of attempts to censor certain kinds of theatrical entertainment is accompanied by an engraving of the Play Scene in *Hamlet* at the moment when the murderer (Lucianus) pours the poison into the ear of the victim (Gonzago) (Figure 24). Irving as Hamlet is at left, lying on the floor upon a large fur rug. Behind him, Ellen Terry as Ophelia sits upright, and, clasping her hands to her breast, looks upward. At right, sitting upon a raised dais, are Claudius and Gertrude. Attached to almost every character is a disk with the letters 'L. C. C.' (London County Council) and a number. The caption below states:

> 'This is what the County Council's Licensing Bill for Places of Entertainment did not intend, as, according to the latest authoritative explanation, the L. C. C. does not consider Theatres as coming under the head of 'places of entertainment.' Rather hard on the Theatres!'(98:109).

Theatre Notices and Reviews

As indicated earlier, the most significant and valuable portion of *Punch*'s material on actors and the theatres was its steady stream of reviews of Shakespeare productions. Not only did the magazine review the principal productions in London, but it also reviewed a number of university productions at Oxford and Cambridge, productions by English companies on tour abroad, the productions of visiting foreign companies who came to London, and on occasion productions by foreigners in other countries. The total amount of material is considerable, and it offers the theatre historian a rich and largely neglected source of commentary on nineteenth-century Shakespeare production. In what follows here, I can offer only a limited consideration of the *Punch* notices and reviews, beginning with those dealing with the performances of William Charles Macready and Samuel Phelps.

Notices and Reviews: William Charles Macready

When *Punch* first came into being, there was no clear indication that serious drama would be of future and abiding interest within its pages. During 1841, only two Shakespeare productions were reviewed – Charles Kean's *Romeo and Juliet* at the Haymarket with Miss

Beerbohm Tree as Juliet (1:24) and Graham's *Macbeth* at the Surrey with Mrs. H. Vining as Lady Macbeth (1:36). *Punch* gave both a negative reception. Kean is compared unfavourably as an actor to J. William Wallack, while Graham (only his last name is given) as Macbeth is criticized for being weak-voiced and is dismissed by the reviewer as being 'entirely out of his element' in the part. As will be seen later in this chapter, hostility to Kean in the pages of *Punch* would in time become vociferous, even vicious. Unfortunately, because the *Punch* Contributors' Ledgers do not begin until 1843, it is not possible to identify the reviewer(s) of these two productions.

It is surprising in retrospect that the early issues of *Punch* contain no account of Macready's Shakespeare productions during his two-year management at Drury Lane that concluded in the Spring of 1843. Macready's carefully staged and scenically mounted *The Merchant of Venice* that opened on 27 December 1841, his *Two Gentlemen of Verona* that opened two days later, his *As You Like It* that opened on 1 October during the next season in 1842, and his *King John* that opened on 24 October all received generally very positive reviews (Odell 1920, 2:226–232), but *Punch* ignored the productions, even when the Queen attended *As You Like It* in 1843 (Macready played Jaques). During the remainder of the season, Macready put on *Hamlet, Othello, Macbeth, Cymbeline, Much Ado About Nothing, Julius Caesar*, and *The Winter's Tale* (Odell 1920, 2:205), but still there was no note of them taken in the pages of *Punch*.

This neglect of Macready's work may have had something to do with the brief but fierce antagonism between Macready and Jerrold. Macready had rejected Jerrold's play *The Spendthrift* at the beginning of 1839 as 'a hopeless affair' (Toynbee 1912, entry for 8 January 1839), while Jerrold had then prefaced a very positive review of Macready's revival of *Macbeth* at Drury Lane on 22 January 1840 with some vicious comments on the subject of Macready's vanity and self-indulgence (Slater 2002, 117). We know from an entry in Macready's diary on 12 February 1842 that Mark Lemon sent him a copy of the first volume of *Punch,* but, according to Macready, the volume contained 'copious abuse' of himself (Toynbee 1912, 2:158), a charge that seems to have been a gross exaggeration (Altick 1997, 30). In March that year, Macready put on Jerrold's *The Prisoner of*

War at Drury Lane. This ran very successfully until mid April as a three-act afterpiece to a lavishly staged production of Handel's opera *Acis and Galatea*, but then in August 1842, Macready no doubt ruffled *Punch*'s (and Jerrold's) feathers when he turned down *Punch's Pantomime, or Harlequin King John*, an entertainment written by Mark Lemon in collaboration with several *Punch* staff, including Jerrold (Toynbee 1912, 2:182).

In September 1842, Macready complained that Jerrold had placed his latest play, *Gertrude*, at Covent Garden, thereby breaking a pledge that he would write his next play for Drury Lane (Slater 2002, 130–131). That same month, Macready complained further in his diary about 'a paltry impertinence' in *Punch,* perpetrated 'by a set of low-mannered, ignorant, and ill-conditioned men, who rejoice in the miserable Jerrold as their captain' (Toynbee 1912, 2:183). He was referring to an item that had appeared on 13 August. In it, despite asserting that 'Mr. Macready is certainly our chief tragedian in the present state of the stage', *Punch* had jokingly suggested that the actor might consider studying music. He could then obtain the £400–£500 nightly fee that he would get if he sang a title role in an opera at Covent Garden. No doubt *Punch*'s gibe stung the always querulous Macready because Covent Garden, now under the management of Macready's enemy, Alfred Bunn, was the chief rival house to Drury Lane where Macready was endeavouring against considerable odds to establish something akin to a national theatre, with Shakespeare plays as a central part of the repertoire.

In September 1845, Macready attended the amateur performance of Ben Jonson's *Every Man in His Humour*, in which Charles Dickens, Daniel Maclise, Mark Lemon, John Leech, and Jerrold all appeared. Macready was generally favourable, but of the last named he said: 'Jerrold very bad in Master Stephen' (Toynbee 1912, 2:304). As his diary records, however, he was quite happy to have dinner with a group that included Jerrold, Lemon, and Leech on 21 October, and he appears to have had no objection to Jerrold visiting his dressing room after the performance of *Othello* the following month (Toynbee 2:307, 310). However, when Macready attended an amateur performance of *The Elder Brother*, and Jerrold appeared in an afterpiece,

Macready remarked in his diary, 'As Macbeth says – *No more sights!'* (Toynbee 2:320).

Perhaps Macready kept his opinions on Jerrold's acting abilities to himself, because relations between Jerrold and Macready became increasingly more positive. During 1846, Macready's diary records his attendance at dinner parties where Jerrold was also a guest, and there is no sign of any hostility to Jerrold. The following year on 30 May, Jerrold attended a Macready evening party, and on 24 July, Macready attended a dinner at Jerrold's house (Toynbee 2:367, 371). We know, too, that when Jerrold became President of the Whittington Club, he recruited Macready as one of his Vice-Presidents (Slater 2002, 208). Simultaneously, whenever *Punch* made fun of others, and after its scattered but generally positive reviews of his work began to appear, Macready adopted a much more positive attitude to the magazine, as can be observed in a number of later entries in his diary from 1847 onwards (Toynbee 1912, 2:297, 315, 323).

The corresponding change in *Punch* to a more positive attitude towards Macready is probably related to a cessation by Jerrold of any jibes directed at Macready, but it also may in part have been due to the effects of the Theatre Regulation Act. The realization that ending the monopoly on the spoken drama held by the three patent theatres might result in fewer rather than more opportunities for the performance of works by national dramatists, including Shakespeare, may have made *Punch* cautious about mocking the most eminent English tragedian. This shift in attitude, whatever the precise causes, parallels a new vein of seriousness in *Punch*'s treatment of the theatre after 1843. Although in the future there might be mockery of the lack of discrimination and the poor taste of audiences and managers alike at many of London's theatres, serious productions of Shakespeare and the work of important Shakespeare actors would henceforth be reviewed. What is more, the reviews (those of Charles Kean, as will be seen, are a notable exception) would generally be respectful and constructive in their criticism. Though nowhere stated explicitly as a policy, this seems to have become a key part of *Punch*'s campaign to encourage Shakspeareanity.

As was noted in the previous chapter, following the financial collapse of his Drury Lane venture in June 1843, Macready left

England to tour in North America and then on his return went to France for the 1844–1845 season. This apparent abandonment of England for France led to a strong reaction in *Punch*. Shakespeare, it seemed had now become almost synonymous with Macready whose great contribution to Shakspeareanity lacked proper appreciation in his own land, something that necessitated his exile (along with that of Shakespeare) to a country where he was appreciated (7:247; 8:64; 8:48). So it was that *Punch* first reviewed a Shakespeare performance by Macready at the opening of the 1847 theatre season in London.

'PUNCH AT THE PLAY', contributed by Douglas Jerrold, begins with a discussion of the coming season and fancifully suggests that the Queen has purchased new horses for conveying the royal family from Windsor to the theatres, since the old horses always shied at anything but Italian opera. *Punch* then confesses that it 'has of late neglected the theatres. But – *Punch* is a courtier. All the world knows that. Therefore, as his QUEEN determines to smile upon the English Drama, *Punch* – like certain other patrons – will patronize it too', although this will be dependent upon *Punch* getting an order (i.e. a free ticket) or the free use of a private box for the entire season as payment for its reviews (13:141). Passing on from this dig at the way reviewers' good opinions were often 'bought' by theatre managements, Jerrold then makes some encouraging general comments about the offering at the Haymarket Theatre before turning to Shakespeare at the Princess's, a theatre owned since 1843 by J. M. Maddox: 'SHAKSPEARE – though sophisticated SHAKSPEARE – is mighty at the Princess's', Jerrold exclaimed before briefly, and in very general terms, praising the performances of Macready as Macbeth ('especially in the fifth act') and of Charlotte Cushman as Lady Macbeth ('first-rate'). Also briefly but positively reviewed is Macready's production of *Othello*. Miss Montague, 'the new *Desdemona*', is given special praise as 'a charming actress, with a dove-like manner, and a voice of magical sweetness – a voice that would draw a suit out of Chancery'. The scenic effects of both *Macbeth* and *Othello* are, however, ironically mocked. *Punch* expresses 'the intensest admiration of his [Macready's] scenery – it is so primitive, so perfect'.

Two accompanying engravings make the point by showing scenes from *Macbeth* (the exterior of Dunsinane Castle, and Lady

Macbeth's sleep-walking scene) upon completely bare stages. Although *Punch* was often disdainful of elaborate scenic effects, in this instance, the Princess's appears to have been rather limited in what it could offer Macready. So for once, it is the poverty of the sets that comes under fire in *Punch*. It is also not without significance, however, that the review concludes with a dig at attempts at historical verisimilitude that were to be such a feature of Charles Kean's productions and a fashionable feature of Shakespeare stage productions that *Punch* tended to denigrate. We are told that James Robinson Planché, President of the Antiquarian Society, 'has very recently discovered in Brokers' Row a complete set of tea-spoons of the fourteenth century, and is now engaged on a drama of "stirring interest" to introduce them'.

The following year in July, *Punch* published an account by Jerrold of a performance of *Henry VIII* at Drury Lane. Macready had played Wolsey in this play in October 1847 and again in February 1848 during his engagements with Maddox at the Princess's Theatre (Downer 1966, 278). Now, he performed it at Drury Lane at a royal command performance before the Queen and the Prince Consort. Macready appeared as Wolsey, Charlotte Cushman as Queen Katherine, and Samuel Phelps as King Henry. The Queen wanted only the first three acts so that there would also be time for another play, *The Jealous Wife* (Downer 1966, 288). According to *Punch*, the performance was attended by members of the court, members of the House of Commons, who occupied the pit, and residents of the fashionable districts of Mayfair and Belgravia, who were crushed into the first tier and the private boxes respectively. Of the actual performance Jerrold says little. However, according to his ironic commentary, the Lord Chamberlain, whose task was to license plays but who boasted that he never attended the theatre and never read plays, was heard to say of Wolsey's famous speech to Cromwell, 'Upon my life, extremely good!' In similar fashion, 'Many of the Court seemed a little startled at the beauty of the language.'

At the conclusion of the performance, the Queen, 'to prove the high honour in which she held the actor's art in its noblest development', summoned Macready and knighted him, bestowing on him the orders of the Knight of the Fleece and the Garter, and Commander of the Bath' (15:32). Obviously, this part of the report is a fantasy aimed at nudging the Queen to attend more performances of Shakespeare and to recognize in more tangible fashion the merits of England's pre-eminent actor, Macready. Jerrold no doubt remembered that the Queen had commanded Macready's production at Drury Lane of *As You Like It* on 12 June 1843 (Downer 1966, 23), but this was not an honour that had since been repeated regarding any of Macready's Shakespeare productions. As for knighthood, no English actor was to receive one (Kean would desperately attempt to obtain one) until 1895 when to great acclaim the Queen knighted Henry Irving. If Macready had any hopes of receiving such an honour, he would surely have been dismayed to learn that the Queen recorded in her journal that *Henry VIII* was 'not well acted, or produced' (quoted Schoch 2004, 130).

Queen Victoria's decision to command a performance by Macready may have had more to do with politics than some newly developed cultural awareness on her part of the skills of Macready and the splendours of Shakespeare. The summer of 1848 saw considerable fear in England that a revolution could occur as it had in France. The Queen recognized that she should build stronger bonds with her subjects. Taking cognizance of the general love of the theatre, and on the advice of her husband and the Prussian ambassador, Baron Christian von Bunsen, she immediately ceased attending the opera and its foreign fare, a point mentioned in the previous chapter. Instead, on 3 July, she attended Charles and Ellen Kean's benefit performance at the Haymarket and, exactly a week later, the performance of Macready in *Henry VIII* before the actor left for a tour of the United States (Schoch1998, 127; Davis and Emeljanow 2001, 197). That same month, she arranged for Charles Kean to organize court theatricals at Windsor Castle during the next Christmas season (Folger Shakespeare Library, Y.c. 393 [169a–c], quoted Schoch 1998, 128).

As part of the Windsor theatricals, Macready would later act once more before the Queen. On 1 February 1850 at Windsor, he played Brutus (Kean played Mark Antony) in *Julius Caesar*. Never happy to share the limelight, he evidently very much resented having to work under the management of Kean (Downer 1966, 312). What were Macready's feelings, one wonders, when Kean, who played

Mark Antony, stood victorious over the corpse of Brutus at the end of the play?

When Macready began his last tour of the United States in 1848, he arrived in Boston on 24 September and opened with *Macbeth* at the Astor Place, New York, on 4 October. He then played in various southern states. Following his arrival in New Orleans in February 1849, *Punch* obtained a copy of the local newspaper, the *Daily Picayune*. In the copy issued on 15 February, there was a review of Macready's *Othello*, 'upon which the critics shower roses', so *Punch* proudly reports in an item by Jerrold entitled 'OTHELLOS IN NEW ORLEANS'(16:133). According to the *Picayune*, 'We have never yet seen anything so brilliant: such acting would redeem the vices of the stage, were they tenfold what they are.' The same reviewer also remarks: 'What could we say of MACREADY, but that he carried into his personation of the Moor, the same elaborate study, matchless elocution, and consummate art, which we have admired before?'

Such comments tell us little about the specifics of Macready's performance, nor is it necessarily important to the theatre historian to know that 'the house was full and radiant with beautiful women'. However, after turning to other pages in the newspaper, Jerrold introduced a whole new vein of commentary. Included in the newspaper, so he had discovered, were 'columns filled with advertisements of runaway slaves and of slaves to be knocked down by the hammer'. There was clearly a huge irony apparent here when such advertisements should be 'in the same sheet, with glowing commendation of the black of the actor'. Macready's performance consequently strikes Jerrold as being highly subversive since they must surely be 'so much incitement to the black blood of New Orleans to decamp or rebel'. To drive home the point, Jerrold comes to the following conclusion: 'We think every Slave State should consider this, and forbid the personation of *Othello* by MR, MACREADY; unless, indeed, he should choose to "reverse the character", playing the Moor as a white man.'

When Macready went back to New York, there was soon something else to report that was also deleterious to the English view of Brother Jonathan. When he opened with *Macbeth* on 7 May, Macready became the victim of what *Punch* considered was a hostile attack planned by the American tragedian, Edwin Forrest. There was some history involved here. In 1845, Forrest had been hissed while performing Macbeth in London. He blamed Macready, and when Macready performed Macbeth in Edinburgh, Forrest hissed Macready. During the initial stages of Macready's 1848–1849 American tour, James Oakes, a friend of Forrest, had published a lengthy article in the *Boston Mail* that outlined Forrest's various grievances concerning his earlier treatment by Macready in London in 1845. Further to this, when Macready had performed in Philadelphia, Forrest had organized a claque to disrupt the English actor's opening in *Macbeth*. Forrest had also pointedly played the same series of characters as Macready at a rival theatre, and he had continued with further published attacks (Downer 1966, 292–293).

In New York a tragic outcome ensued, beginning with orchestrated disruptions of Macready's opening in *Macbeth* on 7 May. This is recounted by *Punch* in an article by Jerrold entitled 'THE CUR-RIBS OF NEW YORK.' It reports on the confrontation that occurred when supporters of Forrest attempted to ruin Macready's performance by throwing rotten eggs and a stink bomb consisting of a bottle of asafoetida onto the stage of the Astor Place Opera theatre. The title reference to 'Cur-rib' puns on the word 'cur' (dog) and 'carib' (aboriginal) and refers to an accompanying engraving by John Leech that depicts Forrest as a native Indian named Edw Inf Or Rest (or Whitefeather) (Figure 25). Between his legs on the ground is a tomahawk inscribed '[undecipherable] of Shakspeare.' Beside him on the ground is a bucket of eggs (16:217). Jerrold's

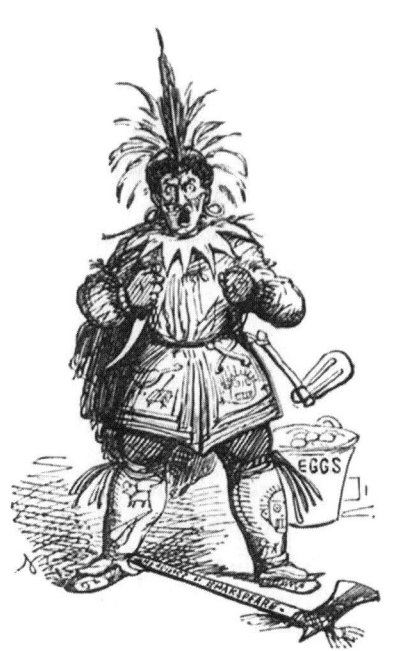

Figure 25. Unidentified artist's representation of a 'Cur-rib'. *Punch* (2 June 1849), 16:217.

article develops the conceit that Forrest (Whitefeather) is the chief of the tribe of Cur-ribs and that he 'believes in an old Indian superstition; namely, that to kill a man of genius, is to become the possessor of his departed power'. Hence Forrest's attack on Macready. Quoting a New York newspaper, Jerrold then details the yelling, the showers of rotten eggs, the stink bomb, the shouting at Macready's Lady Macbeth, and then (on Macready's return to the stage) the hurling down of a heavy piece of wood from the upper tier of the theatre. That Forrest was not even present was, Jerrold suggests, 'the worst of cowardice', and he then quotes the New York *Courier and Enquirer* that said of Forrest:

> He is safe for ever, not only from rivalry, but from that envy from which it often springs. He succeeded last night in doing what even his bad acting and unmanly conduct never did before, – he inflicted a thorough and lasting disgrace upon the American character.

In a subsequent issue, *Punch* reiterated its view of the attack on Macready:

> The New Yorkers have stumped us with their stools, bottles, and other missiles, to which we may give the title of American opinions; and, as the last new Americanism, we may venture to say that there are men in New York whose opinions are so strong as to be capable of knocking anybody down. (16:237)

As is well known, Macready's presence in New York and the vicious reaction of Forrest and his supporters led a few days later to violence on the streets between rival factions. Matters were so bad that the so-called Astor Place riot resulted in some seventeen to twenty deaths (the accounts differ as to numbers). As already noted in the previous chapter, in the Fall of 1849, *Punch* published a small item by Jerrold entitled 'SHAKSPEARE IN AMERICA'. This was *Punch*'s final comment on the American actor's conduct. It appeared in the form of an imaginary report that a penitent Forrest had ordered 500 casts of the bust of Shakespeare in the church in Stratford-on-Avon. These were to be distributed among the men whom Forrest had hired to 'pelt and put down MACREADY'. The busts were also to be considered as an act of contrition for 'the injuries committed upon the Bard by MR. FORREST himself'. Every bust, says Jerrold, has been inscribed with the following couplet: 'Good folks when this you see / Oh, *don't* remember me' (17:195).

Concerning the actual details of Macready's performances in New York, we thus learn very little from the pages of *Punch*, and the same can be said of the actor's final performances in London in 1851. Macready's last Shakespeare performance at the Haymarket, where he played King Lear before the Queen and Prince Consort on 3 February, does not receive a proper review. Years before in 1839, when he had played Lear before the Queen at Covent Garden, he had pointed directly at her during his 'poor naked wretches' speech, a gesture bordering on the offensive, though timely, given the sufferings of many of her impoverished subjects (Schoch 2004, 157). There is no indication that such histrionics were repeated this time around.

Of Macready's final benefit performance as Macbeth at Drury Lane on 26 February, his farewell to the stage, *Punch* printed an anticipatory fantasy by Jerrold, announcing that the shades of Shakespeare, Garrick, Kemble, and Kean (Edmund Kean, that is) 'will be at Drury Lane on Wednesday next, the 26th, on the farewell performance of MACREADY' (20:82). *Punch* expresses the intention of being present in order to say farewell to Macready 'and, – no, we will not despair – to SHAKSPEARE'. But if a representative from *Punch* was present, no report or review was forthcoming. However, when Macready died on 27 April 1873, *Punch* included a verse obituary by Tom Taylor in the issue for 10 May. Aware that Macready had left the stage over twenty years earlier and that many current readers of *Punch* would not have seen his work, Taylor states:

> We were boys then, and, with young hearts aglow,
> Followed his hand, that bravely led along
> Through *Prospero*'s glamour, *Lear*'s colossal woe,
> *Hamlet*'s brain-sickness, and *Othello*'s wrong.

Not only had Macready done much to inspire appreciation of Shakespeare but 'most of good our Stage can boast to-day / Came from *his* labour, who is now no more' (64:189). However, there is a sad postscript to this. A few years later in the Spring of 1881 during Booth's English tour, Macready's style of Shakespearean performance (along with that of Booth and Phelps) has become synonymous in *Punch* with an out-dated style that compares unfavourably with the work of the current eminent tragedian – Henry Irving (80:149, 225).

Notices and Reviews: Samuel Phelps

When Macready's management at Drury Lane failed and when the Theatre Regulation Bill passed both Houses of Parliament on 22 August 1843, London actors of the formerly 'legitimate' drama were faced with a bleak prospect. Macready was to go to the United States; Bunn took over Drury Lane once more with the intention of doing only operas, ballets, and spectacles; the English Opera House alternated between concerts and melodramas; the Olympic concentrated on presenting French translations; the St. James's presented plays in French; the Princess's produced opera; and Webster at the Haymarket switched for the time being from five-act plays to shorter, lighter works of the kind favoured by the minor theatres (Allen 1971, 79). At the same time, the minors showed no sign of changing their popular general menu of farce, burlesque, melodrama, and romance. To abandon London for the Provinces seemed to many actors the best course for the coming 1843–1844 season, but an excess of out-of-work London actors then created a whole new set of difficulties that had to be overcome by anyone wishing to eke out a living on the stage.

This set of circumstances proved to be a motivating factor in persuading Samuel Phelps in 1844 to accept an invitation by Thomas Greenwood, lessee of Sadler's Wells Theatre, to become a co-lessee, with Mrs. Mary Warner as his partner and leading actress. Prior to this and after early critical successes in a number of Shakespeare roles, Phelps had had a difficult time when Macready had engaged him at Covent Garden during the 1837–1838 and 1838–1839 seasons and at Drury Lane between 1841 and 1843. Life for Phelps had also been difficult when he had played alongside Macready under Webster's management at the Haymarket in the summer of 1839 and in March and April 1840. The problem was that Macready's behaviour as both actor and manager displayed a pattern that was inimical and frustrating to Phelps. Whenever the audiences and critics praised Phelps, Macready could not control his envy and anger. Repeatedly, Macready would then deliberately place Phelps in minor roles and cut short the repetition of productions in which Phelps had excelled (Allen 1971, 34, 37–38, 39, 56, 58, 59–60). However, once free of Macready, Phelps had been able to give full outlet to his considerable talents during the 1843–1844 season in Liverpool and Bath, playing major roles that included Richard III, Macbeth, Shylock, and Hamlet. In the same plays under Macready, he had been limited to King Henry VI (in the Colley Cibber version of *Richard III*), Macduff, Antonio, and the Ghost. In addition, while out of London, Phelps had gained some experience of management. In 1844, he was now ready for a startling new venture at Sadler's Wells, one that did an enormous service to Shakspeareanity, as *Punch* would acknowledge. With Greenwood responsible for theatrical management, Phelps took on the role of stage manager, what today we would call 'director'.

Before the opening night on 27 May, handbills appeared that printed a statement by Phelps and Mary Warner outlining their plan to make Sadler's Wells 'what a Theatre ought to be; a place for justly representing the works of our great dramatic poets' (quoted Phelps and Forbes-Robertson 1886, 64; Allen 1971, 82). Apart from this notice, which was aimed primarily at local residents, the opening with *Macbeth* on 27 May received no announcement in the major newspapers. The seemingly remote location of Islington in north-east London, a relatively expensive cab ride away from central London, meant that the opening six-night run was ignored by many drama critics. However, both the *Athenaeum* and the *Theatrical Journal* published positive reviews on 1 June, and there was no mistaking the enthusiasm of the audiences. On 29 May, the *Times* printed a brief notice of the production and remarked that the house was 'crowded in every part', though 'To play one of Shakespeare's tragedies at this place is a bold undertaking' (p. 5).

Following *Macbeth*, Phelps presented *Othello* for a week, and thereafter he began to add a variety of plays by other writers. Then, on 24 June, *The Merchant of Venice* was added, and on 29 July, Phelps undertook *Hamlet*. Eventually, *Punch* took notice of what was happening. In 'DEAR SHAKSPEARE' by Percival Leigh, published in the issue for 13 July, *Punch* informed readers that 'SIX or Seven weeks ago, MRS. WARNER and MR. PHELPS took Sadler's Wells Theatre, therein to enact, with some chance of success, the plays of WM. SHAKSPEARE' (7:32). Phelps and Warner are congratulated 'for the zeal which has impelled them thus to consecrate a temple to the Drama in the remote waste of Islington'. Leigh then notes the relatively inexpensive ticket prices at Sadler's Wells that have made access to performances so available to the people of Islington.

About six weeks later, Jerrold on behalf of *Punch* made the trip to Islington and, we are told, he

> has seen plays so excellently put upon the stage – has beheld an audience so possessed and delighted by the admirable acting of the scene, – that he would be false to himself and to the town (whose guide, philosopher, and friend he is), not to counsel the said town – or those members of it who delight in the glories of a good play well acted – to make a pilgrimage towards merry Islington, made all the merrier by the high entertainment now proffered to all comers. (7:125).

Jerrold's article begins by discussing the manner in which the 'Shaksperian monopoly' was destroyed by the Theatre Regulation Act. As a result, the legitimate drama (and Shakespeare's plays in particular) have been hard to find. Charles Kemble's reading of *Cymbeline* ('a little compressed') stands out as an exception, but the remark is ironic, given opinions expressed elsewhere in *Punch* concerning Kemble's reading (see previous chapter). At the same time Alfred Bunn's management of one of the former patent theatres has led only to 'the blandishments and endearments of ballet and opera'. Now, however, Warner and Phelps,

> to the edification and amusement of thronging audiences, have for weeks past been playing SHAKSPERE, BEAUMONT and FLETCHER, SHERIDAN, and such folks, who – it was sorrowingly predicted – had been destroyed for ever and ever by a recent statute.

The article then heaps further glowing praise upon the Sadler's Wells venture:

> Assuredly it is a pleasant reproof to those despairing folks who sighed over the hopeless condition of the Drama, to witness its robust vitality at Sadler's Wells. SHAKSPERE may have been banished from Drury Lane and Covent Garden; but then he has found the snuggest asylum near the New River. There, at nights, is he heard in all the might of his passion and the tenderness of his thoughts, [...]

To accompany this tribute to the achievements of Sadler's Wells, there is an unsigned engraving depicting Shakespeare, 'in sweetest, laziest mood', sitting on the parapet of a bridge over the New River fishing. Behind him is a poster advertising the Sadler's Wells production of *Hamlet*. At long last, Jerrold's article implies, Shakespeare has found a home.

A few weeks later on 30 September, Phelps began a new production of *King John*. This received very favourable reviews from the London critics, and its success brought increasing numbers of playgoers from central London. It was now clear that Sadler's Wells, for the moment at least, had established itself as the epicentre for the legitimate drama in London. Rather than reviewing the production, however, *Punch* used the situation for yet another attack on the Queen's failure to nurture serious national theatre. On 19 October appeared a satiric fantasy by Jerrold, which described a visit of the Queen and King Louis Philippe to see a performance of *King John*. The Queen is ironically compared to Louis Philippe. Both are said to have 'a passionate fondness for the theatre', and both lose 'no opportunity of lavishing favours upon its professors, actors as well as authors'. This may have been true of the French king, but, as we have seen elsewhere, it was decidedly not true of the Queen, who to date had shown little interest in the serious national drama. To rub the point home, Jerrold reports that at the conclusion of the performance, the French King addressed Phelps: '"It gives me", said his Majesty, "infinite pleasure to find that even in the suburbs of London, the mighty genius of the immortal SHAKSPERE can be so finely illustrated, as I have this night witnessed it. I am much gratified"' (7:172). As a token of his appreciation, he then gave Phelps the Legion of Honour. The hint to the Queen, who had nothing of her own to contribute, is obvious.

The following Spring, on 20 February 1845, Phelps bravely challenged current theatrical tradition by presenting *Richard III* in a version close to Shakespeare's original text. Abandoned was the beloved version by Colley Cibber that omitted the central character of Margaret (now played in Phelps's production by Mrs. Warner) and the characters of Edward IV, Stanley, Clarence, and Hastings. Abandoned, too, were the interpolated scenes taken from *Henry VI* so that the play now began with Richard's famous soliloquy ('Now is the winter of our discontent'). Richard's famous line (invented by Cibber and beloved by both audiences and actors) – 'Off with his head, so much for Buckingham' – also vanished. For the first time, Victorian audiences encountered the powerful figure of Margaret and were able to see a tent scene that included the apparitions that appear to Richmond. As the playbill put it,

> In order to meet the spirit of the present age, so distinguished for illustrating and honouring the works of Shakespeare, and with at least an honest desire of testing truthful excellence over all attempted improvements, this restoration is essayed, in lieu of the alteration, interpolation, and compilement of Colley Cibber, which has so long held possession of the stage. (Quoted Odell 1920, 2:268–269).

Audiences and most critics responded enthusiastically to Phelps's work, and the production played for a total of twenty-four performances through March and April (Allen 1971, 228–230).

On 15 March, *Punch* presented its own review. Heavily ironic, *Punch* fictionalized its account, which was written by Tom Taylor, as though it were a letter addressed to Mr. Punch from an 'Old Actor', one who had played the Cibber version many times to great acclaim on 'not less than twelve country circuits' (8:125). The Old Actor's 'Off with his head', for example, invariably secured him 'nine rounds, and an invitation to dinner from the Mayor'. Phelps's

> *Richard* may be SHAKSPEARE'S *Richard*, but it isn't KEAN'S; it isn't FRED. COOKE'S; it isn't GARRICK'S. Why, Sir, PHELPS' *Richard* is a tame part [...] I doubt if there's a good start or a decent scowl from beginning to end of it. Besides, there are at least half-a-dozen parts in his version that kill *Richard's* business. I don't think he has the stage to himself in a single scene.

As Taylor realized, Shakespeare's original was a far more complex drama than Cibber's version, which was very much a 'one-man show' for the actor playing Richard. In conclusion, Taylor then suggested that Kean did things very differently and that Phelps was contributing to the demise of the drama. Readers, of course, were expected to recognize the irony and conclude that in *Punch*'s opinion Kean was the enemy to drama and Phelps the heroic defender and innovator:

> I should like you to hear CHARLES KEAN'S opinion of the Sadler's Wells play. He's been starring with us the last week. There is a great creature, with proper notions of the actor's dignity. You won't catch him restoring any of your humbugging 'texts', as they call 'em. No: he goes in a good one at the regular *Richard* business, and I'll be bound gets nine rounds to PHELPS' one. It's really sickening in these days to see a manager hastening the decline of the Drama, by cutting the ground from under the actors' feet in the style they are doing at Sadler's Wells. (8:125)

In the Fall of 1845, *Punch* published on 27 September what purported to be the 'Report of the Managers of Sadler's Wells for the Diffusion of Shakspereanity'. Written by Jerrold, it was supposedly signed by Phelps and Warner. Its central conceit is that whereas 'the natives of the immediate neighbourhood and surrounding villages' had been 'in a lamentable state of darkness as to the existence and humanizing purposes of WILLIAM SHAKSPERE', now they 'are very constant in their attendance at Sadler's Wells to listen to SHAKSPERE: they are, moreover, very attentive, and seemingly much edified by what they come to witness'. What is more, 'the night charges at the various police-stations of the neighbourhood have sensibly diminished; and men – before considered irredeemable bacchanals – are now nightly known to bring their wives and little ones to listen to the solemn and sportive truths of SHAKSPERE, in the pit and gallery' (9:138).

The success of the Sadler's Wells venture in converting the natives of Islington to Shakspeareanity was in reality more complex than Jerrold implied. Modern theatre historians have increasingly recognized as mere myth the idea that Phelps transformed a barbaric, working-class audience at Sadler's Wells into an attentive, appreciative one that grew to love Shakespeare in place of an earlier diet of aquatic spectacles and melodramas. The best-known manifestation of this myth occurs in an article entitled 'Shakespeare and Newgate' that appeared in *Household Words* on 4 October 1851 (4:25–27). In it, Dickens, in collaboration with R. H. Horne, discussed the transformation of Sadler's Wells from a rough venue of low entertainment into a home for the 'legitimate' drama. Crucial to his account is the suggestion that Phelps was able to reclaim 'one of the lowest of all possible audiences'. When Phelps took over Sadler's Wells, so the article claimed, the theatre was 'like the worst part of the worst kind of Fair in the worst kind of town'. The interior of the theatre was even worse: 'it was a bear-garden, resounding with foul language, oaths, catcalls, shrieks, yells, blasphemy, obscenity, – a truly diabolical clamour. Fights took place anywhere, at any period of the performance' (quoted Jackson 1989, 29–30). Crucial to Dickens's myth-making is the account of the way in which on the opening night of Phelps's tenure, the noisy, drunken, obscene-tongued audience for *Macbeth* was gradually tamed by Phelps. Within a month, repeated victories by Phelps over those who sought to disrupt the performances led to a state of affairs that permitted a five act tragedy to be heard without a single interruption (Jackson 1989, 32). Repetitions and elaborations upon the Dickens/Horne story have strongly affected later histories of Victorian drama. Jerrold's 'Report of the Managers of Sadler's Wells for the Diffusion of Shakspereanity', which anticipated Dickens's 'Shakespeare and Newgate', reveals that *Punch* subscribed to the Phelps as Orpheus myth. Indeed, *Punch* probably played a major role in propagating that myth years before Dickens wrote his fanciful article.

Actual reviews of the early productions at Sadler's Wells, together with comments by Phelps's nephew and Phelps himself, show that the audiences for Phelps's productions were not at all like those described by Jerrold and Dickens (Allen 1971, 84–87, 94–97, 137–141, 247–250; Taylor 1989, 19; and David & Emeljanow 2001, 100–105). Although the exact demographics remain a matter for debate, the audience was drawn from those living close to the theatre and from further away. It was made up of a faithful cadre of the middle classes, working men, tradesmen, shop girls, and clerks (Allen 1971, 96, 97), whose respectful, well-informed, and attentive behaviour might serve as an example to the more privileged classes elsewhere who were quite capable of conversing among themselves throughout even the most serious of plays. On this theme, *Douglas Jerrold's Weekly Newspaper* noted on 1 August 1846 that 'there are shop-girls whose genuine enjoyment of the fine dramas produced here would put to shame the corrupted taste of some even of the very highest ladies in the land' (quoted Allen 1971, 127).

As Phelps's reputation grew, Sadler's Wells became, in one writer's view, 'a sort of pilgrim's shrine to the literary men of London, to the younger members of the Inns of Court, and to those denizens of the West in whom poetic taste still lingered' (Marston 1888, 2:36). Drama critics who initially had stayed away began to attend on a regular basis. Even so, reviews of Phelps's Shakespeare productions in *Punch* are frustratingly few. In the late 1840s, *Punch* paid far more attention to Macready's work and to Charles Kean's Shakespeare productions at Windsor than to the by then established menu of Shakespeare plays at Sadler's Wells. In the 1850s, the pattern was the same with Kean's productions at the Princess's Theatre receiving the bulk of attention from *Punch*.

For whatever reason, following the *Punch* review of Phelps's *Richard III*, there is nothing detailed to be found concerning Shakespeare productions at Sadler's Wells until the 1853–1854 season when *A Midsummer Night's Dream* is reviewed by Douglas Jerrold (Phelps and Forbes-Robertson 1886, 129–131). In 'BULLY BOTTOM,' which appeared in the issue for 15 October, Jerrold not only provided an very laudatory account of Phelps's innovative performance as Bottom but used the occasion for a comment on Phelps's achievement in nurturing theatrical performances of Shakespeare. Phelps is described as 'a man with a real vital love for his art', who 'has now for many seasons made his theatre a school; and more, has never wanted attentive, reverent, grateful scholars' (25:165). By this, Jerrold seems to have had in mind on the one hand the steady stream of actors who served unofficial apprenticeships under Phelps's tutelage just as other aspiring actors 'trained' in the Provinces before trying their luck on the London stage. At the same time, Jerrold appears also to have been thinking of the audiences at Sadler's Wells, who often struck visitors as being particularly knowledgeable about Shakespeare, having conned the texts that they took with them to the theatre, having returned again and again on a regular basis, and having participated in the animated discussions of the plays that took place in the intermissions (Allen 1971, 139). No one, it is implied, has done more for Shakspeareanity than Phelps.

It is disappointing, however, that Jerrold does not comment on the many innovations in Phelps's production, which gave audiences a performance fairly faithful to the original text, one that was free from the heavy dependence upon music and dance that had often made productions of *A Midsummer Night's Dream* seem closer to opera, and one that above all was endowed with a new focus upon poetic fantasy. However, Jerrold does note that Phelps's Bottom was no longer the crude and farcical ass of 'dull tradition', but a more subtle portrait of a conceited man, who is transformed into the 'purest, airiest SHAKSPERE'. Jerrold's review then concludes with the hope that the Queen, who has never visited Sadler's Wells, will at the very least command a performance of *A Midsummer Night's Dream* at Windsor. This did not happen, but Phelps was not ignored by the Queen. On 10 November, shortly after Jerrold's review, the Sadler's Wells production of *Henry V* was transported to Windsor (Allen 1971, 135). Jerrold was delighted, and in *Lloyd's Weekly London Newspaper,* he proclaimed on 13 November:

> The Kean monopoly has been broken through. Mr Phelps performed *Henry V* at Windsor Castle on Thursday last. He has been the first to find a north-west passage to the palace. [...] The difficulties of the passage no one can conceive, [except] those who have had to steer through the immense blocks of ice which Mr. Charles Kean has thrown in the way of his brother managers. (Quoted Schoch 2004, 57).

Later in the season and following in the spirit of Jerrold's suggestion that a royal visit to Islington should happen, Dickens actually attempted to persuade the new Master of Revels to arrange a royal command performance at Sadler's Wells, but the difficulties, as he explained in a letter to Phelps on 25 February 1854, proved to be 'unsurmountable' (Phelps and Forbes-Robertson 1886, 390).

A number of years later, for the 1861–1862 season, Phelps revived an earlier production of *Henry IV*, Part Two, in which he doubled the roles of King Henry and Justice Shallow. His son played Prince Hal, which made for a moving extra dimension in the reconciliation scene just prior to the King's death. *Punch* published a very positive review by Henry Silver on 5 October. Included within the review was an apology for *Punch*'s recent neglect of the Sadler's Wells venture:

> I know that Sadler's Wells is accessible from Regent Street for an eighteen-penny fare, and I know moreover that whenever I have gone there I have invariably been pleased with my evening's entertainment: and yet with all this knowledge I go there very seldom, and why I don't go oftener I'm sure I cannot say. Every time I come away I make a firm resolve to go again within a month; but somehow this intention always goes to fill a gap in the infernal pavement. (41: 139)

In reviewing the production itself, Silver particularly singled out 'the scene in the fifth act with the old King and his son'. He describes the scene as 'replete with touching pathos and nobly written lines', and goes on to say: 'I think few more telling pictures have been seen upon the stage than the confronting of young HARRY with his dying father; who first upbraids, then listens, then pardons and embraces, and retires to die content.' Like other critics, Silver notes the effect of having Phelps act with his son, Edmund: 'both sustained their parts as well as any actors living could have represented them'. Even so, it was the comic material in the play that Silver found especially pleasing. Phelps is particularly praised for his Justice Shallow and the 'quick versatility' with which he exchanged the role of the calm, majestic, old king for 'the fussy fatuous justice'. Of this latter, Silver remarks:

> The trembling nervous hands and feeble hesitating voice, seemed fit signs of his senility and of his shallow pate: and while he prattled on with garrulous complacence of the freaks of his hot youth, one felt how many *Shallows* still are extant in Society, and how fond they are of boring you with the wild deeds which, by Jove, Sir, they did when they were boys.

In his review of Phelps's *Henry IV*, Silver also notes of the Sadler's Wells productions in general that they are free of the vice of a theatre system in which it is common to hire 'farthing dips' who then 'stand about the stage, so as to heighten the effulgence of some bright particular "Star", whose brilliancy is deemed to be enough to fill the house.' By contrast, Phelps's productions have strong casts, and 'minor parts are carefully attended to, and no unnatural excrescence spoils the general effect'. The review then offers a revealing comment about the Sadler's Wells audiences. Shakespeare's ghost, it is suggested, would be very content to see how his plays 'are relished by that audience, and how reverently it listens to each one of SHAKSPEARE'S words'. Attentiveness 'is the order until the curtain drops, and not a sneeze or snuffle grates upon the ear, indeed (except when moved to laughter or applause) the house is all so silent you might hear a playbill drop'. Finally, and perhaps with an indirect dig at the kind of production that London audiences had experienced when Charles Kean was manager at the Princess's Theatre in the 1850s (see below), the review concludes by saying that the audience's behaviour is proof that at Sadler's Wells 'good plays still are cared for, if they are but acted evenly, and mounted not with gorgeous splendour, but simple natural good taste'.

Shortly after his 1861 production of *Henry IV,* and after not having put on *A Midsummer Night's Dream* for five seasons, Phelps revived this latter production and received an especially warm plaudit from *Punch* on 2 November 1861. After noting that London was currently blessed with four different productions of Shakespeare – by Gustavus Brooke, Edwin Booth, Charles Fechter, and Samuel Phelps – the *Punch* author, Henry Silver in this instance, singles out Phelps:

> MR. PHELPS at Sadler's Wells has appeared again as *Bottom*, and they who have not seen him are advised hereby to go. On the whole I like it best of his Shakspearian conceptions, and rank it far above all other actings of the character that I have ever seen. The mingled 'cuteness and obtuseness of this very prince of clowns, his dense dull-brained stupidity and important self-conceit, are admirably shown by MR. PHELPS'S rendering: while the languor that pervades him in his love-scenes with *Titania* fitly carry out the notion of his being in a dream. I think his exit on awaking, when his ass's head has been removed, is one of the best bits of comic by-play ever acted. (41:175).

The following month, the *Punch* reviewer (probably Silver) went to see Charles Fechter's *Othello* at the Princess's Theatre. While generally liking Fechter's performance in the title role, he claimed that Phelps's performance at Sadler's Wells was superior, particularly with regard to the declamation of Shakespeare's verse (41:241). Later, that same season on 22 February 1862, Silver was back at Sadler's Wells to review Phelps's *Macbeth*. First, however, he comments on the eagerness and attentiveness of the Pentonville playgoers, who 'go to see the play, and not to flirt and chatter' and for whom 'the falling of a pin would doubtless be resented as an outrage by the pit'. He finds the reverence for Shakespeare among the audience particularly impressive in 'these sensation-craving times, when murders by moonlight in the midst of splendid scenery, and ships on fire, and slave sales, and great headers are so sought after'. Here, he says, is 'a theatre where SHAKSPEARE is still popular, and is loved and revered for his own intrinsic sake, and not by reason of the adjuncts which the paint-pot can supply' (42:73). Implicit here is criticism of Charles Kean's *Macbeth*, with its emphasis upon scenic effects ('the gorgeous up-getting supplied at the Princess's a season or two since') that detractors maintained often took preference over the play itself. That said, however, Silver notes the loss of former members of the cast – Isabella Glyn and Henry Marston – and he remembers what a fine Macduff Phelps made when he played the part in Macready's farewell performance. Phelps's son, Edmund, cannot rival this in the current production. Even so, 'although at times too ponderous and dragging in his speech (in soliloquy especially is this defect observable)', Phelps senior 'is really now the only English actor (your pardon, MR. KEAN; no, I have *not* forgotten you) who can fitly play a SHAKSPEARE tragic part'.

Less than three weeks after *Punch*'s review of *Macbeth*, Phelps quietly transferred his lease of Sadler's Wells to Catherine Lucette. He returned briefly at the beginning of the 1862–1863 season and gave what in effect were unannounced farewell performances of plays that included *Hamlet, Othello, The Merchant of Venice*, and *Julius Caesar*. Only on the final night was there a notice that he was making his final appearance at Sadler's Wells. Such reticence was typical of Phelps, though in this instance it seems to have verged on the excessive.

Punch commented on 29 November: 'Here is Mr. Phelps retiring from Sadler's Wells in such a modest quiet way that people knew nothing about it until the thing was done.' An important opportunity seems to have been lost: 'Mr. Phelps slips out of sight with neither flummery nor fuss, and so modestly takes leave of us that we have scarce the opportunity to say how much we liked him' (43:225).

Regular visitors to Islington during the eighteen years of Phelps's tenure could have seen productions of thirty-two of Shakespeare's plays, a number of them with restored texts that were something of a revelation to those who experienced them for the first time. Only *Richard II,* the three parts of *Henry VI, Troilus and Cressida*, and *Titus Andronicus* were excepted. His was an extraordinary legacy that *Punch* was well aware of, although actual reviews of Phelps's Shakespeare productions by *Punch* were relatively few. Following his departure from Sadler's Wells, Phelps unwisely signed a contract to work under Fechter's management at the Lyceum. There, he was subjected to the same kind of treatment that Macready had practiced, and he was at first not given even a minor role, let alone a major part. After three months, Fechter deigned to offer him the role of the Ghost in Hamlet. Phelps interpreted this as an insult and arranged to be released from his contract. The dispute between the two actors was later to be played out again, as we have already seen in the previous chapter, in the arrangements for the Shakespeare Tercentenary celebrations in Stratford-on-Avon when Fechter was invited to play Hamlet and Phelps was asked to play what he considered a relatively minor role, Iachimo in *Cymbeline. Punch* briefly commented on the *Hamlet* affair at the Lyceum by suggesting that Fechter and Phelps should alternate the two roles (44:241), but Fechter, one assumes, would never have considered such a solution.

After breaking with Fechter at the Lyceum, Phelps then played six consecutive seasons at Drury Lane, where he was engaged as director of dramatic productions by the current lessees, Edmund Falconer and F. B. Chatterton. This was a bold attempt to revive the fortunes of Drury Lane and make it once more *the* centre for serious national drama. For a time, the plan seemed to be succeeding, but before long other types of entertainment began to take prominence (Odell 1920, 2:258; Davis and Emeljanow 2001, 206–208). Unaware of what the future had in store, the *Times* was able to assert late in 1864 that 'Drury Lane is now indisputably the house of the poetic drama. [...] The revival of a tragedy at Drury-Lane is now anticipated as an important event by hundreds of persons who not long since would have regarded it with utter indifference. A *prestige* is restored that has much of the practical virtue of a patent' (7 November 1864).

Central to the project and its success was Phelps, and central to the repertoire were the plays of Shakespeare. Among those that Phelps put on were both parts of *Henry IV, Othello, Cymbeline, Macbeth, The Comedy of Errors, Henry VIII, The Merchant of Venice*, and *King John*. Of these, Part One of *Henry IV* was reviewed in *Punch* by Henry Silver on 30 April 1864. Hotspur, played by Walter Montgomery, is applauded 'for his gallant speech and bearing', and Phelps's Falstaff is praised, though with some reservations (46:175). 'If he were more unctuous', Silver claims, 'he would more be the fat knight.' Silver is particularly troubled that the famous 'royal crown and cushion bit of merriment' has been left out, but he praises Phelps's restoration to the text of both the 'Glendower scene and Welsh song'. Silver then complains, probably tongue-in-cheek, that the armour 'is certainly not strictly "of the period", as a glance at *Mr. Punch's History of Costume* will clearly serve to show'.

In November that year, *Punch* included a passing reference to the production of *Macbeth*, but the chief point of the piece was to play upon one of Helen Faucit's lines in the part of Lady Macbeth (47:207). A year later, *Punch* included a brief review by Burnand of the major production for Phelps's third season at Drury Lane – *King John*. The article, '"KING JOHN" IN PRIVATE', which appeared in the issue for 25 November 1865, was intended as a comic disquisition on the experiences of its author when playing a minor role in a private amateur production of *King John*. Having prepared his role, he 'went to Drury Lane to see what was done with the drama in *that* place' (49:213). However, we learn very little about the production, apart from the view that James Anderson and Barsby were 'capital' in their roles, and that Master Percy Roselle as Prince Arthur 'is the best Prince that ever I saw, and so powerfully did he appeal to the sympathies of his audience, that I know more than one member of the male sex present who was obliged to use his opera-glasses every other minute and blow his nose violently'.

After Phelps finished his six seasons at Drury Lane, he spent the 1869–1870 season touring the provinces. On returning to London in the spring of 1870, he began a short engagement at Astley's in a production of *Othello*, with Hermann Vezin as Iago and Vezin's wife as Desdemona (Phelps and Forbes-Robertson 1886, 304–305). Astley's, as will be seen in the next chapter, was famous for equestrian performances, including equestrian versions of Shakespeare. On 19 March 1870, this provided *Punch* with an opportunity for comic fantasy rather than serious review. Burnand, the author of 'SHAKSPEARE AT ASTLEY'S', after remarking that '*Othello* with MR. PHELPS and MR. AND MRS. HERMANN VEZIN has been highly successful at the celebrated Amphitheatre' (58:108), admits that he himself has been unable to witness the performance. He then offers 'a few notes for stage-business' involving the use of horses, the whole accompanied by two engravings by Linley Sambourne. Though mildly amusing, it is perhaps a pity that this constituted *Punch*'s final commentary on Phelps's very considerable contribution to Shakespeare performance.

However, when Phelps died in November 1878, *Punch* honoured him with a verse obituary by Tom Taylor that portrayed him as 'the last of the brave troop who fought' to re-establish 'Great plays of old, presented with new power' (75:219). Taylor appears to have in mind Macready and the earlier Drury Lane venture to establish a national theatre. This quickly waned, we are told, and 'when the chief of that foiled enterprise / Laid down his truncheon', Phelps fearlessly 'With smaller force, and in less stately guise' managed 'To hold the same good fight for many a year'. The verses then develop the by now familiar mythology of Phelps 'taming' the rude and rough audience at Islington for eighteen years with 'SHAKSPEARE'S magic spell'. Phelps is then praised as a Shakespeare actor, particular mention being made of his portrayals of Bottom and Falstaff. In spite of this late acknowledgment of Phelps's extraordinary achievement, one senses that *Punch* had never been completely comfortable with the manner in which Phelps managed to popularize Shakespeare. He perhaps did more that anyone in his age to advance the cause of Shakspeareanity, but *Punch* was never fully whole-hearted about acknowledging the point. In this matter, the *Punch* critics were not alone, though given their expressed concerns to promote Shakespeare, the somewhat benign neglect of Phelps's achievements is hard to excuse or explain.

Notices and Reviews: Charles Kean

Passing reference has already been made to *Punch*'s generally negative attitude to Charles Kean, an important contemporary of both Macready and Phelps. Kean's contributions to the performance of Shakespeare were considerable in his roles as actor, as theatre manager, and as Master of the Revels at court; yet *Punch* persistently ridiculed and belittled him. It seems very likely that this sustained attack on one who made such a significant contribution to Shakspeareanity was, as already mentioned, largely the work of Douglas Jerrold. According to Jerrold's biographer, the source of Jerrold's antipathy to Kean can be traced back to January 1838 when Macready's touchiness about rival actors was inflamed as a result of Kean's considerable success in *Hamlet* at Alfred Bunn's Drury Lane (Slater 2002, 242). Just prior to this, Kean had declined an offer to join Macready's new company at Covent Garden (Schoch 1998, 24). That he should then have gone over to Macready's rival and enemy at Drury Lane would have been particularly galling to Macready, and that he should then have received great acclaim for his performance of the prized tragic role of Hamlet must have been impossible to accept. Thereafter, Macready's friends and admirers, particularly Forster, Dickens, and Jerrold (despite Jerrold's brief antagonism to Macready mentioned above), rallied to Macready's support and collectively assailed Kean.

The first sign in *Punch* of this animosity appeared in the second issue of 24 July 1841. In an item entitled 'THE DRAMA: ROMEO AND JULIET', Mr. Punch reports that he recently ensconced himself 'in a box at the Haymarket Theatre to witness the fourth appearance of my rival puppet, Charles Kean, in Romeo' (1:24). Ironic praise is then heaped upon Kean's performance:

He *is* an actor! What a deep voice – what an interesting lisp – what a charming whine – what a vigorous stamp, he hath! How hard he strikes his forehead when he is going into a rage – how flat he falls upon the ground when he is going to die! And then, when he has killed Tybalt, what an attitude he strikes, what an appalling grin he indulges his gaping admirers withal!

A few issues later in a letter purportedly from a fellow Eton alumnus of Kean's (1:53), *Punch* is chastised for criticizing Kean. The author of the letter then heaps praise upon Kean for his delivery of a couplet that was slow enough to permit the letter-writer to leave the theatre, down a dozen oysters and a bottom of brandy, place a bet on the St. Leger, and return in time for the final word in the couplet.

Two years after this, *Punch* included a small column-filler by Jerrold entitled 'AN "INSANE" QUESTION'. It began what was to become a repeated joke about Kean's 'murdering' Shakespeare: 'As there can be no doubt that *Hamlet* has in his character a considerable touch of *insanity*, ought not Mr. Charles Kean, when appearing in the part, to be allowed to *Murder* Shakespear with impunity?' (4:106). The following year in 1844, *Punch* reported in another piece by Jerrold that a wax effigy of Kean was being prepared for Madame Tussaud's. *Punch* then comments: 'The actor has unquestionably won the distinction by his many Shaksperian murders, and will therefore hold a prominent place among Madame T.'s celebrated criminals' (6:116). Much later, on 19 March 1859, the same joke appeared in yet another guise. In 'MURDER WILL OUT', *Punch* notes that the claim has been made that 'whereas no actor had ever been executed for a great crime, there was no crime punishable by death of which a clergyman had not been guilty' (36:120). *Punch*'s riposte is 'that for one murder by a churchman, a thousand have been committed by actors. Who has seen Mr. Never-Mind-Whom in *Macbeth*?'

More general, but no less damning, was *Punch*'s comment early in 1844 that 'The National Drama, we are sorry to say, has, since the engagement of Mr. Charles Kean, gone down to zero' (6:57). Nothing seemed to change *Punch*'s view, so that when in 1859 John Cole published his obsequious, two-volume *Life and Theatrical Times of Charles Kean, F. S. A.*, the magazine responded with an item by Tom Taylor that stated: 'The passionate enthusiasm of MR. COLE has deluged the hero of his idolatry with such a *douche* of laudation as few men could have stood up under and breathed. Luckily, MR. CHARLES KEAN is case-hardened. He has gone through such a course of puffery, that nothing in the way of superlatives can tell upon him much' (37:101). More damning was Taylor's ensuing argument that throughout his career Kean has been 'weakly and unwisely susceptible' to his critics and has 'lost no opportunity of conciliating, cajoling, or otherwise influencing such as he *could* influence in his favour.' Kean is criticized for not taking note of what had been done before him 'with better taste and less pretension, [...] by MR. MAC-READY and MR. PHELPS.' In spite of Kean's industry, good business practices, and 'attention to proprieties of costume, place, and period', *Punch* 'must still be allowed to think MR. CHARLES KEAN a very bad actor'. Furthermore, that Kean 'has done anything to raise the literary character of the stage, *Mr. Punch* must take leave to deny'.

Punch's attacks on Kean were sustained throughout the actor-manager's two most important ventures, his series of theatricals at Windsor from 1848 to 1857 and his tenure at the Princess's Theatre between 1850 and 1859. The Queen's choice of Kean to manage the Windsor performances was first referred to in *Punch* in August 1848. In an unusually guarded notice by Jerrold, *Punch* is careful to be positive about the Queen's apparent conversion to the cause of Shakespeare: 'The QUEEN herself proposed to take SHAKSPEARE by the hand, and lift him on his legs again. This is very commendable; and the noble influence of high example will of course be felt throughout high places' (15:98). Refraining from any irony, Jerrold goes on to state:

> that the QUEEN, even at a somewhat late hour, should order a theatre to be built in her palace, that she may hold a review of the players, is a very grateful self-assertion, on her part, against the folks who accuse the House of Hanover of a coldness of heart towards the Drama and letters in general.

Kean himself escapes virtually unscathed, except for the joking suggestion that he will be knighted for his work. In this Jerrold was surprisingly prescient since some years later, as will be discussed below, Kean was rumoured to be in line for a knighthood.

Early the next year, in 'THE WINDSOR CASTLE SHAKE-SPEARE' by Gilbert Abbott à Beckett, *Punch* criticized Kean for excluding the Gravedigger from *Hamlet* at a performance before the Queen. By so doing, the comedy of the Gravedigger's removal of multiple waistcoats, Hamlet's business with Yorick's skull, and Hamlet's dramatic jumping into Ophelia's grave were all lost (16:1). Two further items in the same issue (16:4 and 16:16), one by Jerrold and one by à Beckett, refer respectively to a performance of *The Merchant of Venice* and the ways in which the Rubens Room at Windsor is somewhat different from a 'real' theatre; however, in neither instance is Kean mentioned. Later there are allusions by Jerrold on two occasions to performances at Windsor of *Hamlet, Julius Caesar*, and *Henry IV*. In one, *Punch* again chooses not to even mention Kean, but in the second, the tragedian is depicted as a kind of bogey man who causes the royal children to become 'still as mice' if they are at all refractory and are then told '*Hamlet's coming*!' (16:68; 18:29). If Kean got off fairly lightly regarding his work at Windsor, *Punch* took a very different stance regarding his series of Shakespeare productions at the Princess's Theatre between 1850 and 1859.

Early productions in this important venture included *Twelfth Night, As You Like It, the Merry Wives of Windsor, The Merchant of Venice, Hamlet,* and *Henry IV, Part 2*. However, it was with the revival of *King John* on 9 February 1852 that Kean began a memorable series of productions that were to earn him a considerable measure of fame and that were to capture a large and enthusiastic audience for Shakespeare. Completely without irony, Kean's strongest apologist, John Cole, noted that *King John* was a turning point in Kean's career and the start of 'a complete revolution in the dramatic system by the establishment of new theories and the subversion of old ones'. According to Cole, the time had now arrived

> when a total purification of Shakespeare, with every accompaniment that refined knowledge, diligent research, and chronological accuracy could supply, was suited to the taste and temper of the age, which had become eminently pictorial and exacting beyond all former precedent. The days had long passed when audiences could believe themselves transported from Italy to Athens by the power of poetical enchantment without the aid of scenic appliances. (Cole 1859, 2:26)

Punch appears, however, to have ignored *King John*, and of *Macbeth*, the second major revival, which opened at the Princess's on 14 February 1853 (it was performed at Windsor a week earlier), *Punch* says little. This reticence was possibly because Jerrold by this time had written two plays for Kean, *Heart of Gold* and *St Cupid; or Dorothy's Fortune*. The former was eventually produced at the Princess's in October 1854, but it was quickly followed by an extended quarrel between Jerrold and Kean that had overflowed into the pages of *Lloyd's Weekly Newspaper* (Jerrold had been appointed editor in April 1852). The quarrel even stirred up vigorous ripostes in various other publications (Cole 1859, 2:68–93, 95–99; Slater 2002, 250, 258). Jerrold's *St Cupid*, which had earlier received a royal command performance at Windsor on 22 January 1853, played in repertory at the Princess's with *Macbeth* (Slater 2002, 257; Schoch 2004, 57).

However, the momentary reticence in *Punch* regarding Kean does not mean that his *Macbeth* passed completely unnoticed. The little that *Punch* does have to say consists in part of an amusing engraving, designed by Thomas Harrington Wilson, and a brief accompanying comment by Horace Mayhew. The engraving depicts Kean adjusting his makeup off stage during the murder of Duncan (25:224) while an assistant holds the two daggers which Kean will need when he returns to the stage. This makes no direct comment on the production, and its depiction of Macbeth's costume fails to show the radical changes Kean introduced when, as he explains in lengthy detail in his play bill essay, he dressed his title character in 'the tunic, mantle, cross gartering, and ringed byrne of the Danes and Anglo-Saxons' of the eleventh century. The accompanying article by Mayhew lists various non-Shakespearean plays at the Princess's that are supposedly novelties but clearly are not. Only at the conclusion does he say anything about Kean's *Macbeth*. In his final sentence, which is full of irony, he states: 'There can be no fear as to the acting, when the principal parts will be performed by MR. CHARLES KEAN himself.'

Kean's *Macbeth* is also the subject of 'THE MACBETH MUSEUM' (26:95) by Shirley Brooks. This comments on an article in the *Morning Chronicle* concerning excavations in Scotland at the supposed site of Dunsinane. Although nothing of any significance has been found, Brooks humorously lists a series of items that have since surfaced, among them the 'rattle and coral of the baby *Lady Macbeth* speaks of', the 'goblet *Macbeth* let fall when he saw the Ghost', and the 'ring *Duncan* sent to *Lady Macbeth* as a small token of respect and esteem for her cookery'. We are then told that in 'the hopes of obtaining them, MR. CHARLES KEAN is already writing a learned and voluminous fly-leaf to his play-bill'. The chief object of *Punch*'s amusement here is, of course, the attempt by Kean in many of his major productions, particularly those at the Princess's, to be historically authentic. Attempting to serve the Victorian quest to re-create history, Kean went to unprecedented lengths to provide antiquarian detail in his stage sets, costumes, and stage properties. To be archaeologically 'correct' in every way was a prime goal of his productions of such plays as *King John, Macbeth, The Winter's Tale, Richard II, Henry V*, and *Henry VIII*. While many who attended Kean's productions were thrilled at the effect of being transported in time, there were many who felt very differently. *Punch* was thus not alone in its hostility to what Kean was attempting to do. Even with regard to such a small matter as the bear in *The Winter's Tale*, *Punch* could not resist a quip: 'MR. PUNCH has it upon authority to state that the Bear at present running in Oxford Street in the *Winter's Tale* is an archaeological copy from the original bear of Noah's Ark' (30:190).

Equally ridiculous to his detractors were Kean's play bills that often consisted of highly detailed commentaries on his attempts at historical accuracy in such matters as costume (as in the play bill for *Macbeth* mentioned above), the panorama of London in 1533 employed in *Henry VIII*, the paintings copied from a manuscript in the British Museum to decorate John of Gaunt's bedroom in *Richard II*, the interpolated spectacle (only described in the original text of *Richard II*) showing the respective entries into London of Bolingbroke and King Richard on horseback accompanied by a host of supernumeraries, and his substitution of Clio, the muse of history, for the Chorus in *Henry V*. The materials that Kean issued with his play bills from *Macbeth* on were used as introductions to the printed texts of his theatre productions. As Odell once sarcastically noted, every playgoer was informed of the scholarly reasons why the spectacle was clothed and built in exactly the manner visible on stage. The whole disquisition fairly bristled with the names of long-forgotten worthies, classical, mediaeval and renaissance. It was as good as going to school, or, better, attending a present-day popular lecture. (Odell 1920, 2:329)

In Shirley Brooks's 'THE PRINCESS'S SPECTACLE', an item that appeared in the issue for 28 March 1857, *Punch* mocked Kean's play bill essays and the archaeological goals they represented by providing some paragraphs that had supposedly been omitted from the play bill for *Richard II*. The additional text points out that the paper for the play bills is made up entirely of 'fly-leaves from old folio editions of the *History of England*, and the ink is from a receipt discovered in a "chapel" (whence the printing-office is so called) in Westminster Abbey' (32:123). Throughout each play bill, 'the small capitals are most judiciously inserted, while the infusion of italics leaves nothing to be desired'. Among other details, *Punch* reports that the 'character of the refreshments provided for consumption during the *entr'acte*, has also been studiously attended to, and the bottles of imperial pop, elegantly labelled "hippocrass", in old English letters, form quite a feature in the entertainment'. A few pages later in the same issue, Jerrold further mocked the *Richard II* play bill, specifically its statement that John Wycliffe, '"the morning star of the Reformation", made himself heard amidst the angry roar of contending passions: and in the hearts of fiery and seditious men sowed the seed, which, after a growth of one hundred and fifty years, was destined to expand into the STANDARD RELIGION OF OUR COUNTRY'. Such playhouse authority must be comforting to the English bishops, Jerrold suggests, but 'if the "standard" religionists are the chosen, what – we ask MR. KEAN, as an actor and a man – what is to become of the "ranters?"'(32:128).

Macbeth, complete with the restoration of the Locke-Davenant balletic and operatic material that Phelps had carefully removed, was Kean's principal Shakespeare production of 1853, and it played for sixty performances during twenty weeks (Odell 1920, 2:288). Its successor a year later was the resurrection of Colley Cibber's *Richard III*, nine years after Phelps had restored the original, and this was followed in 1855 by the 100-night run of *Henry VIII*, presented with a spectacular wealth of costumes and scenic effects, including the moving panorama of London mentioned above. *Richard III*, which opened on 20 February 1854, did not receive a full review in *Punch*; however, inserted into a blistering review of Kean's *Faust and Marguerite*, a melodramatic adaptation from a French work by Michel Carré, was a brief comment on *Richard III*. The review by Jerrold of Kean's adaptation of Carré's work, itself based on Goethe's *Faust*, had the demeaning title 'POODLE MEPHISTOPHELES AT THE PRINCESS'S' and contained such vicious comments as the following: 'MR. KEAN [...] had no more subtlety in his speech than the waiter at the Dog Tavern; nothing more scorching in his looks than might flash from brass buttons. There was boldness, but no burning.' Mid way through and with scathing irony, Jerrold suggests that when Kean enters Elysium, Shakespeare himself will 'step forward and embrace him for his acting of SHAKSPERE, with every conceivable and inconceivable scenic effect', just as 'GOETHE might hug and thank MICHEL CARRÉ for his "low-art fabrication" (his low cutting of the jacket of the poodle)'. In this way, Shakespeare will 'embrace MR. CHARLES KEAN for *his* fabrication with very low cuttings of CIBBER'S *Richard the Third*. Wonderful must be the sources of gratitude in the Fields of the Blest!' (26:189).

Later, Jerrold again referred to Kean's *Richard III* (together with *King John* and *Macbeth*) in 'THE LAST STAGE OF PUFFING', in which it was suggested how advertisements (puffs) could be inserted into the texts of Shakespeare's plays. After demonstrating how this might be achieved in Clarence's account of his dream, Jerrold, presumably with Kean in mind, vituperatively suggests that the example given 'will be sufficient to afford a hint to those town or country Managers, who, looking on the stage as a legitimate source of making money, are prepared to take advantage of any and every mode of increasing the receipts of a theatre' (28:201).

Comment on the production of *Henry VIII* seems to have been largely avoided, although when news got out that Kean had begun rehearsals, *Punch*, in a piece by Jerrold, announced the formation of a Society for the Protection of Shakespeare. The immediate cause for this has been 'the alarming report' that Kean plans to put on *Henry*

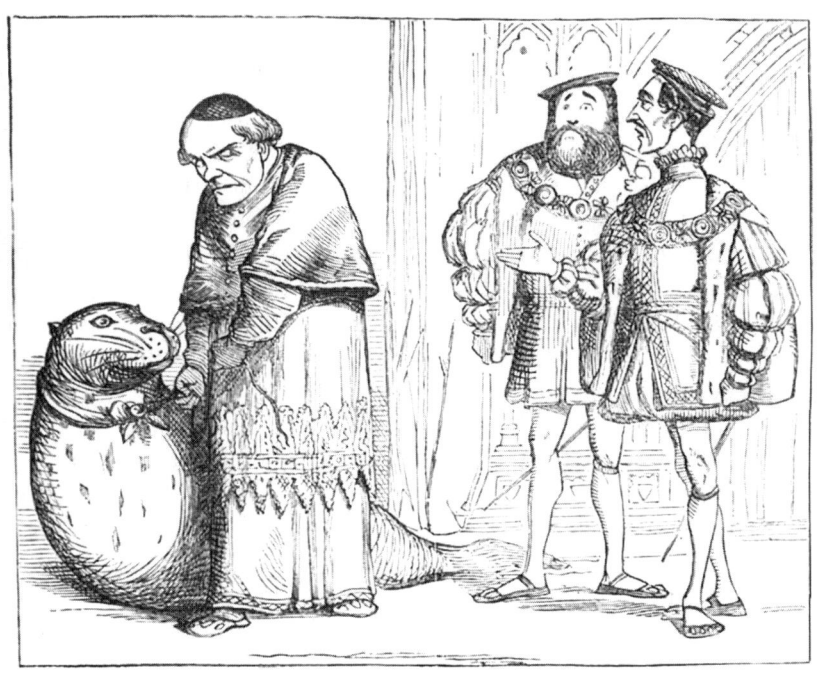

Figure 26. John Tenniel's depiction of Charles Kean as Cardinal Wolsey in *Henry VIII*. *Punch* (8 September 1855), 29:93.

VIII, so members of the new Society have 'determined to act with all the vigour demanded by the extremity of the case' (27:226). The lack of a full review following the opening of the production was perhaps because the pages of *Punch* in 1855 were already well peppered with references to Shakespeare in the form of John Tenniel's series of 'Illustrations to Shakspeare' (see Chapter Two). Three of these, however, depicted scenes from *Henry VIII*. One of them (Figure 26) – that depicting Wolsey being ordered to surrender the Great Seal – mocks Kean by portraying him as Wolsey holding on to a very large seal of the sea mammal kind.

When Kean's *The Winter's Tale* appeared on 28 April 1856, *Punch* responded on 17 May with a lengthy review by Shirley Brooks. Its approach is heavily ironic, for it purports to praise everything about the production that *Punch* in reality disapproved of in the performance of Shakespeare. The opening sentence sets the tone: 'AN exceedingly splendid Ballet-Spectacle, partly suggested by an old play of SHAKSPEARE, and partly by a fiction of SIR THOMAS HANMER, has been produced by MR. KEAN with a success to which *Mr. Punch* hastens to bear testimony' (30:198). As will be seen in the next chapter, *Punch* considered ballet to be a decadent import from France. This is the point behind the second sentence, which explains that the play at the Princess's 'Is called the *Winter's Tale*, and one only regrets that the usual custom of affixing a French name to a ballet has been departed from, as *Le Conte d'Hiver* would perhaps have been more appropriate'. Brooks then praises the manner in which Kean has preserved a 'Shakspearian *aroma*' in the ballet and the manner in which 'the personages, incidents, and purpose of the original have been dexterously subordinated to, and indeed fused into, the Terpsichorean element' of the production.

Brooks then praises Kean's changing the Bohemia settings (for which Shakespeare supposed a sea-shore location) to Bithynia, something that is in accord with a suggestion first made by Thomas Hanmer, a matter commented upon in Kean's play bill essay (Odell 1920, 2:339). He even pretends to like the new Asia setting, 'for the spectator is conducted among an entirely new race of people, of whom SHAKSPEARE had no idea, and whose manners, and customs, and costumes are in the strongest and most artistic contrast to any comprised with the comparatively limited range of his conception'. The thread of Shakespeare's original story has, however, been 'cleverly retained, and it serves to connect the beautiful effects for which this theatre is celebrated'. With mounting irony, Brooks then describes the elaborate dance sequences, the 'vast number of young ladies in the costume of Greek warriors', the second act 'pictorial illustration of a lady's apartment in classic times, and the furniture and accessories, down to a child's toy', the Greek theatre represented in the third act, the Bacchanalian revel in the fourth act, with its 'charmingly painted scene, worthy of CLAUDE', and 'the gem of the spectacle', which consisted of an allegory of Luna and Phoebus that was 'in no way indebted to SHAKSPEARE'. Kean is then praised for preserving, 'perhaps with a little pardonable archaeologic hankering – some of the language of the old poet'. However, we are assured that this has not been done

> offensively; the so-called poetry being cut down to the scantiest dimensions, and delivered with the utmost rapidity, and with no intrusive attempt at acting, except where the necessities of the stage require carpenter's scenes. Indeed there never was a piece from which what is called acting was so carefully excluded. (30:198–199)

Punch firmly believed that Kean's pictorialism and his emphasis upon scenic splendour, his devotion to archaeological 'accuracy', and his considerable cutting of Shakespeare's text (essential to free up time for his elaborate spectacles) were distractions that substituted for good acting and for the poetic power of Shakespeare's texts. In 'PLAYHOUSE PAROXYSMS', for example, Jerrold noted that the wildly enthusiastic crowds attending *Richard II* were spectators, not an audience. Although 'there can be no doubt that the pageant is very fine, and the scenery beautiful' (32:113), the 'frenzy of delight' that one London newspaper attributed to those in attendance should really be a matter, Jerrold suggests, for the Commissioners of Lunacy. Elsewhere, in 'SINGERS IN THE SAWDUST' (30 May 1857), Henry Silver made disparaging comments about Kean's use of horses in *Richard II* in the interpolated scene of the entry into London of Bolingbroke and Richard, drawing a parallel with the hippodramatic spectacles common at Astley's (32:222). A dig at Kean's use of horses is also made in Jerrold's 'PLAYHOUSE PAROXYSMS', which concludes by suggesting that if Kean does not receive a knighthood for his efforts, he could be made Master of the Horse (32:113).

Some two years later, *Punch*'s criticism remained unrelenting. Kean and his supporters are accused of forgetting 'that there really was a MR. MACREADY who, some years ago, produced, both at Covent Garden and Drury Lane, the plays of SHAKSPEARE and others, with every necessary accessory of scenery and costume' (37:52). Elsewhere, Kean, as a Shakespearean actor, was unfavourably compared in 'Two Actors' with his father, Edmund Kean, whose

Shakespeare performances Coleridge in *Table Talk* had famously associated with flashes of lightning:

> THE father – eye with genius bright'ning –
> Read SHAKSPEARE as by flash of lightning:
> The son, who lets all meaning slip,
> Reads SHAKSPEARE as by farthing dip. (37:90)

In Tom Taylor's review of John Cole's *Life and Theatrical Times of Charles Kean, F. S. A.*, a work already mentioned above, it is stated 'that there never was an actor who has been so unduly puffed and panegyrised'. (37:101). Then, a few pages later, noting that Kean's tenure at the Princess's had come to an end, *Punch* published a lengthy and heavily ironic puff of its own by Henry Silver in the form of a testimonial to the actor-manager's supposed achievements, something that permitted a review of all the features of Kean's career (including the play bills) that *Punch* most deplored. Silver's article then concluded with the tentative plan to present Kean with a gift set of *Punch*, 'with an index to the jokes' which had been made at this great actor's expense. (37:105).

In addition to attacking Kean's Shakespeare productions at the Princess's Theatre, *Punch* also mocked Kean for his hope of being the first actor to receive a knighthood. Rumours that he was to receive such an honour began to circulate in 1856 when the Queen asked for a photograph of the Keans that she could place in her personal collection (Schoch 1998, 60; and Schoch 2004, 173). No doubt Kean was encouraged to believe that some special honour was pending. After all, he had been singled out to superintend the Windsor court theatricals, the Queen had presented him with a diamond ring and accorded him a personal interview on 21 February 1849, and she had later annually retained a box at the Princess's and had made a series of visits to his productions (Cole 1859, 1:348, 2:13), even taking her children on occasion.

In June 1857, Mrs. Kean (Ellen Tree), hoping to turn rumour into reality, even wrote first to the Prime Minister's wife and then three weeks later to the Queen directly, but to no avail (Schoch 2004, 174–176). While the *Illustrated London News* was in favour of some 'special mark of distinction and respect' being awarded to Kean to demonstrate the esteem in which he was held by the 'people from amongst whom [...] Shakespeare sprang' (10 May 1856. Quoted by Schoch 1998, 62), *Punch*, as might be expected, was of a very different opinion. Citing hints in the *Post* that Kean merited 'some higher tribute to his genius', *Punch* in the issue for 10 May then mockingly describes the actor as 'now busily employed in rehearsing the ceremony' that accompanied a knighthood (30:190). Furthermore, we are informed, 'When the act of Knighthood has been graciously performed by the Sovereign, it will be duly represented at the theatre', accompanied by 'A Moving Panorama from Oxford Street (the address of the Princess's Theatre) to Windsor Castle.' Further to this, in March 1857, *Punch* cruelly quipped in a piece by Jerrold that a 'knighthood has hitherto been spoken of as the final reward of MR. KEAN'S scenic and decorative spirit; but after *Richard II*, it is not reasonably supposed that he will escape with less than a baronetcy' (32:113).

Douglas Jerrold died in June 1857, but there followed no apparent lull in the hostility of *Punch* towards Kean, as several items from *Punch* attest, some of them cited above (37:52, 90, 101, 105). A year and a half after ending his tenure at the Princess's Theatre, for example, Kean appeared in *Hamlet* at Drury Lane in February 1861. *Punch* at first grudgingly admitted that he was 'a good actor (of some parts)' but then went on to argue that in 'the present dearth of talent he may hold a higher rank than is properly his due'. Kean's Wolsey and his Benedick are accorded a measure of praise, and the critic, who is not named in the Contributors' Ledgers, further acknowledges that Kean is 'a most painstaking actor, and in a certain sort of melodrama he is clever and artistic'. However, this is all somewhat deceptive, hiding what is to follow when we are told that Kean is not, contrary to anything the critics may have said, a great tragedian. He is not a consummate artist 'when he plays in SHAKSPEARE parts'. Moreover, his *Hamlet* is not a 'masterpiece of art' nor is it 'as high in the list of histrionic triumphs as any personation that was ever achieved in this or any other country'. Such judgements, *Punch* maintains, are 'clearly a burlesque of criticism, which should provoke our laughter only less than our regret' (40:83).

Not long after, the *Punch* critic (again, he is not named in the Ledgers) once more attacked other critics who continued to praise the actor and his performance as Hamlet: 'Why I chiefly blame such writers is, that the course they are pursuing is degrading to the press, which must cease to be looked up to for integrity or taste. To applaud without a word of censure such a *Hamlet* as CHARLES KEAN'S, is to show a thorough lack of judgment and experience, such as clearly must unfit a critic for his post' (40:125). This was *Punch*'s last word on Kean as a Shakespearean actor. Not long after, in July 1863, Kean left England for a world tour that took him to Australia, then, California, and then the Atlantic states. He eventually returned to England in 1866 but died two years later.

Notices and Reviews: Charles Fechter and Others

Accounts of nineteenth-century theatre often seem to suggest that following the work of Phelps at Sadler's Wells and Kean at the Princess's there was a period of cultural drought with regard to Shakespeare productions until Henry Irving burst upon the London scene with his appearance as Hamlet in 1874. However, as already noted Phelps continued to appear in Shakespearean roles in the 1860s and F. B. Chatterton attempted to transform Drury Lane into a National Theatre with Shakespeare figuring prominently in the repertory. As we also saw in the previous chapter, the 1864 Shakespeare Tercentenary provoked a heightened interest in Shakespeare and was the inspiration for attempts to establish a permanent theatre in Stratford-on-Avon where Shakespeare could be regularly performed. It is not that Shakespeare disappeared from theatres in London and the Provinces. Quite the contrary. But what was missing, perhaps, was the enterprising leadership of any actor-managers the like of Phelps or Kean. Not until Irving assumed the management of the Lyceum Theatre in 1878 was there an heir of their stature. In the mean time, the gaze of media like *Punch* was attracted in the early 1860s to the figure of Charles Fechter, who came to England from France in 1860 and performed Ruy Blas in English at the Princess's Theatre now under the management of Kean's successor, Augustus Harris.

Fechter's performance as Hamlet at the Princess's, which opened on 20 March 1861, was a startling novelty and revelation to many who saw it, and it elicited a full-length commentary in *Punch*. What struck those who saw Fechter in the role was first of all his physical appearance. 'After the fashion of the German stage' (*Times*, 22 March 1861, page 5), he wore a blond wig to suggest Hamlet's Scandinavian origin, something matched by the Nordic medieval costumes used in the play. But more than mere appearances startled those who attended his performances. Hamlets' lines were delivered in an 'easy, natural, and conversational tone', according to the *Era* for 24 March. He came across as a polished and refined gentleman, capable of pleasing and amicable informality when talking with other characters, most of whom in the play are his social inferiors (Hapgood 1999, 30–32). This was a meditative and thinking Hamlet. As one commentator suggested, 'The stronger passions intrench as little as possible upon his solitude, and he is chiefly occupied with a play of intellect. The birth of his thoughts is more visible than the influence of his emotions' (*Times*, 22 March 1861, p. 5).

When the *Punch* reviewer (it was probably Henry Silver) attended Fechter's performance and recorded his response on 20 April, he stressed above all his delight with Fechter's skills as an actor:

> As we don't get a new *Hamlet* once in a score of years, or, at any rate, not one who is worth a second looking at, I may perhaps revisit the Princess's ere my next, and speak a little more in detail of the merits that I mark. Meanwhile, I would advise all those who like good acting, untrammeled by tradition, to enjoy the present chance. (40:165)

The 'untrammeled by tradition' is a particular attraction, and the reviewer asks his readers: 'Without descending to superlatives, will you not agree that you have never seen a more original conception, and scarce ever one more carefully and perfectly worked out?' Dismissed are any concerns that Fechter is a foreigner, that he speaks English with a noticeable accent, and that he 'dares disturb the old traditions of our stage, and to read the part afresh by the light of his own intellect, without looking for enlightenment to the actors whose bright genius has thrown lustre on the past'. Instead, readers are advised that when they go to see Fechter's performance they should 'keep their eyes upon their opera-glass, rather than their book'. In order to fully appreciate Fechter's Hamlet, viewers must look at the actor 'all the while that he is listened to'. Those who go to the Princess's must 'observe the facial play that gives meaning to each word, and note the graceful ease of attitude and gesture'. To this, the enthusiastic reviewer, implicitly dismissing all that Macready, Phelps, and Charles Kean had achieved in the part, adds: 'Not since the elder KEAN has there been seen upon our stage a *Hamlet* with an eye; and if MR. FECHTER lacks the lightning-flash of genius, his eye is ever shining with an intellectual light.'

Fechter's Hamlet was highly successful and had an unprecedented run of 115 performances (Odell 1920, 2:253). Horace Mayhew could not resist noting in the issue for 1 June that whereas 'a certain HAMLET', Kean, had lost a fortune at the Princess's,

> At the present day, the fortune of the Princess's Theatre is (thanks to MR. FECHTER, who, like a true CELLINI of his art, adorns everything he touches) being made by another *Hamlet*. It would seem as though it had been written down in the Book of Fate that it was to be the lucky destiny of the one *Hamlet* to pick up the fortune that had been lost by the other. (40:221)

On 10 August, *Punch* (the Ledgers identify the reviewer as Silver on this occasion) paid a further visit to the Princess's. The season in London was coming to a close but at the Princess's 'MR. HAMLET – otherwise known as M. FECHTER – still continues to attract. When I looked in the other evening there was scarcely a stall vacant.' Silver then reiterated his praise by saying that Fechter's 'is a performance which bears seeing bit by bit, and I think that one enjoys it all the more for doing so. Well-nigh every line has its appropriate look or gesture, and very many of the points are so carefully minute that one's attention need be fresh to appreciate them properly' (41:60).

After his great success as Hamlet, Fechter took on the role of Othello, which opened at the Princess's on 23 October 1861. Initially, *Punch* declined to comment, not having sent anyone to see the play. However, in the issue for 2 November, Silver ventured to predict that, because *Hamlet* had been so successful, 'curiosity alone will cram the theatre till Christmas' (41:175). In the issue for 14 December, the *Punch* critic reported that he had now attended a performance of *Othello* at the Princess's. It appears, however, that like many other critics at the time, he found Fechter's performance in the role inferior to his Hamlet. His chief concern was that the character of Othello is very different in nature from Hamlet. Thus, 'the delicate bye-play' that Fechter employed with such effect for Hamlet 'is of very little service in a part such as *Othello*'. In essence, 'The brave and fiery Moor, a soldier not a scholar, is not the man to mark his varying emotions by the shrugging of a shoulder, or the curling of a lip.' Furthermore, 'he is not a man of intellect but action; and the subtleties employed by M. FECHTER in the part are scarcely natural to the nature which he would present' (41:241).

Also criticized is Fechter's French accent. Where it had been barely a concern in his very colloquial Hamlet, it is irritating and wearying in connection with the impassioned language and poetry of Othello. It robs the poetry 'of half its beauties'. Silver then briefly digresses to praise Phelps's portrayal of Othello before returning to quarrel with Fechter's treatment of the fifth act. He notes that Fechter has modified his performance and 'has had the good sense to listen to advice, and no longer drags his wife across the stage before he smothers her'. However, Fechter is seen to be at fault in that he has abandoned the theatrical tradition of having the murder done out of sight of the audience, behind the curtains at the back. He complains that Desdemona's touching 'Willow' song has been reallocated to make it a street ballad, sung 'by a company of Waits'. In addition, he objects to the way Othello speaks his line ('It is the cause, it is the cause, my soul') as he contemplates an image of himself in a mirror, a piece of stage business that makes his skin colour rather than his wife's presumed adultery the chief focus. Having got these matters off his chest, Silver then makes clear that he finds much more to praise than blame in Fechter's performance, and he lists some of the details concerning 'the fine touches that embellish every scene, and so much enhance the naturalness of everything he does'. In conclusion, Fechter is praised for 'turning his thoughts […] to other parts besides his own', and thereby delivering 'a deadly blow at the odious "Star" system'.

Following the review of Fechter's *Othello*, there is little mention in *Punch* of his Shakespeare productions prior to his departure in 1869 for the United States where he died ten years later. There is a complaint by Percival Leigh in 1864 that Fechter's *Hamlet* at the Lyceum, where he is now manager, lacks the Prayer Scene (46:257), and there is a brief earlier allusion by Leigh (44:241) to Phelps's refusal to play the Ghost in Fechter's production (see above). At the time of the Shakespeare Tercentenary celebrations, there is also an allusion (see Chapter Two) to Phelps's refusal to perform in Stratford-on-Avon because Fechter had also been invited (46:183), and there is a depiction of Fechter in John Tenniel's large celebratory engraving in 'Punch's Tercentenary Number'.

After reviewing Fechter's initial productions of *Hamlet* and *Othello*, *Punch* appears to have found no one Shakespearean actor of sufficient calibre to be worth following. This did not mean that Shakespeare productions were ignored. On 2 November 1861, for example, *Punch* noted that in addition to Fechter's *Othello* theatre-goers in London had the choice of various other productions to choose from – Phelps's *A Midsummer Night's Dream* at Sadler's Wells, Edwin Booth's *The Merchant of Venice* and *Richard III* at the Haymarket, and Gustavus V. Brooke's Shakespeare performances (including an *Othello*) at Drury Lane (41:175). During the Shakespeare Tercentenary year, *Punch* mentioned the performance of J. B. Buckstone as King Lear and Paul Bedford as Edgar at Drury Lane (46:184) and the Phelps *Macbeth* with Helen Faucit as Lady Macbeth also at Drury Lane (47:207). The following year on 8 July, Tom Taylor contributed a short note of praise and encouragement to Alfred Wigan, manager of the Olympic, who stepped away from his usual repertory (*Punch* alludes to 'sensation-drama and the burlesque') and presented *Twelfth Night* with a company not used to acting Shakespeare.

Then, in the issue for 1 June 1867, the *Punch* reviewer (probably Henry Silver) informs his readers that 'few contrasts are more grateful than to enjoy the entertainment of an evening spent with SHAKSPEARE, after suffering the penance of sitting through a stupid piece'. It turns out that 'Will Waddle', as the reviewer signs himself, has been to see the production of *Antony and Cleopatra* at the Princess's Theatre, with Isabella Glyn and Henry Loraine in the title roles.

Perhaps with Kean's earlier excesses in mind, the reviewer remarks of Shakespeare:

> What ample scope he gives for scenery and decoration, yet how little he requires them to make a play attractive! Who feels the need of scenery, that hears the glowing poetry wherein *Enobarbus* paints the voyage of *Cleopatra*? What artist could so vividly depict her pomp and grandeur?

Even so, the production apparently had 'great scenic attractions, but they only show that SHAKSPEARE was the greater scene-painter'. Referring to Glyn's previous performances of the role at Sadler's Wells and how in the past she showed 'great skill in her conception of the character', the reviewer concludes by suggesting that 'she now brings her maturity of judgment to improve it, and represents the queen most worthily in all her vanity and petulance, her passion, anguish, and despair' (52:221).

That same summer, noting that four or five London theatres were still open, in spite of the season having ended, Silver points out in the issue for 17 August that Shakespeare 'may still be seen in London, though nearly everybody else of any consequence is out of it' (53:63). At the Adelphi Theatre, we learn, *Much Ado About Nothing* is playing. Kate Terry, the elder of the talented Terry children and the Viola in the 1865 Olympic production, performed the role of Beatrice (Henry Neville was her Benedick) 'as prettily and cleverly' as Shakespeare himself could wish. Her performance is given high praise: 'It is rare to see an actress with such natural play of feature, and subtle power of expression, not in voice-tone merely but in gesture and in look.' Furthermore, 'She appears to hold the floodgates of her heart in her command, and to have the power at will to flush or blanch her cheek.'

After 1867, there is something of a hiatus in *Punch*'s reviews of Shakespeare productions, the exceptions being comments on Phelps's performance of Macbeth at Astley's (already discussed above) and a production of *The Taming of the Shrew* at the Globe. Mr. Punch (Burnand was the actual author) reported on this latter in the issue of 26 November 1870. In search of a comfortable seat, he had tried several theatres, ending up in 'an elegant and capacious stall' at the Globe, with 'plenty of room for his hat and his legs' (59:219). So comfortable was he that he slept through almost the entire performance. Like Christopher Sly, whose role had been cut, he was only awakened at the end of the play. Consequently, he has nothing of consequence to report, although he does mention that in his opinion the role of the shrewish Katherine was played too gently. Even so, in spite of the paucity in *Punch* at this time of reviews of Shakespeare productions, there is no abatement in allusions to Shakespeare and his works. Among these are a report of the discovery of a second copy of *The Passionate Pilgrim* in 1867 (53:144), a review in 1869 of Ambroise Thomas's opera of *Hamlet,* some verses in September 1869 complaining about the current popular preference for melodramas over plays by Shakespeare (57:91), and some verses in 1874 in praise of certain female actresses who have excelled in such roles as Ophelia, Rosalind, and Juliet (66:264). Later in 1874, Henry Irving made his London debut as Hamlet at the Lyceum and achieved an instant popular success. Within a short time, the *Punch* reviewer was finally off to see a Shakespeare production, one that his pen would accord a detailed two-page review.

Notices and Reviews: Henry Irving

Prior to his 1874 London appearance as Hamlet, Irving had performed the role a number of times in various provincial theatres where, like many actors, he first learned his craft. He had also played seven of the other characters in *Hamlet*, something that provided him with the opportunity to observe closely various other Hamlets. He had, we know, played Laertes to Edwin Booth's Hamlet when Booth visited Manchester in 1861, and he had also played Laertes to Fechter's Hamlet in Birmingham in 1865. In 1864 in Manchester, Irving had participated in a series of *tableaux vivants* devised by Charles Calvert to mark the Shakespeare tercentenary. Irving's contribution, recorded in a photograph (reproduced in Young 2005b, 4), was an imitation of John Philip Kemble's Hamlet as represented in Sir Thomas Lawrence's famous portrait of 1801 (Irving 1951, after 98, 113; Young 2002, 248–250). Two months later, and perhaps inspired by his static and silent appearance as Hamlet in the Graveyard Scene,

Irving played Hamlet for the first time for his benefit performance. Receiving mixed but encouraging reviews, he gave two further performances in Manchester, together with performances in Oxford that summer, and Bury the following year. Irving's legendary success in the role did not begin, however, until 1874 when he appeared in the part in a production at the Lyceum Theatre in London under the management of the American impresario, H. L. Bateman. This production, which opened on 31 October 1874, was a huge success and ran for two hundred nights, breaking Fechter's record of 115 performances at the Princess's in 1861 and Booth's 100 performances at the Winter Garden in New York in 1864.

Punch's first response to the excitement being generated at the Lyceum was a joking reference in the issue of 14 November to the unfortunate wording of the playbill advertising Irving's performance. Meeting 'the eye upon every hoarding in London' was the announcement, according to *Punch*, of a farce, 'Fish Out of Water'. This title was then followed by the announcement of 'Mr. Irving in the Part of Hamlet' (67:209). No doubt realizing that Irving was proving to be anything but a fish out of water, *Punch* published a review by Tom Taylor of the Lyceum *Hamlet* on 28 November (67:224–225). The lengthy review begins by pointing out that after more than two hundred and fifty years *Hamlet* is still the most discussed play wherever English is spoken. 'Physicians, metaphysicians, and psychologists are still discussing its problems, as actors are still pondering its points.' It is 'the drama which the galleries know best, and follow with the keenest sympathy', and Hamlet is the part that 'every aspiring novice first studies and dreams of making his *début* in'. The play itself 'is the greatest work of dramatic – if not of all imaginative – creation; and its interest for public, actors, and critics has the inexhaustibleness which belongs to life, and like life, carries in it the germs of perpetual renewal'. Following this rather grand overture, Taylor then focuses on Irving, upon whom he bestows what for *Punch* reads like unprecedented praise. Irving is given credit for 'having worked one of those periodic *Hamlet*-galvanisms' and is credited with having outmatched all the Hamlets within living memory, including Macready and Fechter: '*Mr. Punch* can recall none whose impersonation, as a whole, has displayed, to his thinking, more consistent conception, and more sustained intention, with more intelligent mastery of the utterance, demeanour, and action of this many-sided character.'

In what followed, Taylor raised a number of questions about the production, in spite of the extremely positive overview with which he had begun. 'Mr. P.', as he refers to himself, explains that he 'least liked, and least went along with' Irving's 'dealings with the *Ghost*'. Irving just did not seem to believe that the Ghost was a real ghost. But even before Hamlet's first encounter with the Ghost, the impact of the opening scene, in which the Ghost is seen by Marcellus, Barnardo, and Horatio, was lost because the scene was played close to the footlights as a 'front scene.' The castle, as the promptbook copy now in the Harvard Theatre Collection confirms, was a painted drop in the second grooves. Mr. P. compares this arrangement unfavourably with that employed in a production at the Crystal Palace the previous year. For this earlier production, 'the whole stage was opened [...], at the cost of a brief closing of tableau-curtains, before the Great Hall was discovered' for the first appearance of the full court (including Hamlet) in I ii. Even stronger is Mr. Punch's/Taylor's objection to the arrangement of I v, when the Ghost led Hamlet from the castle 'to a nook among cliffs with a blasted tree'. This departure from tradition strikes the reviewer as distracting and without purpose: 'To take the apparition out of the wintry hold on the sea-cliff, is to break the thread both of the imagination and the action. The alteration [...] looks like a change made for the sake of change.' Significantly, in his later revival of the play, Irving changed things, and, as the promptbook that is now in the Shakespeare Memorial Library (Stratford-on-Avon) reveals, the Ghost appeared on a rocky crag above the sea. Irving was not, it would seem, deaf to the reviewers' responses.

In Taylor's review, more negative criticisms then follow. Taylor worries about the lack in Irving's interpretation of 'all that SHAKSPEARE has indicated of the surging up of a wild, hysterical, half insane mirth, mingled with horror, which follows the disappearance of the *Ghost*'. This is attributed to Irving's aim of 'bringing out the pathetic and more gentle side of the Prince'. Equally questionable, according to the reviewer, was Irving's suppression or softening of Irving's outbursts when he swears Horatio and Marcellus to secrecy, when he vents his wrath on Ophelia in the 'Get thee to a nunnery' scene, when he 'rises to the top tide of passion in the scene with his Mother' (the Closet Scene), and when he 'outraves *Laertes* at the grave of *Ophelia*' (67:224). Taylor also had a very negative response to Irving's startling innovation in the Closet scene when Hamlet forces his mother to compare the portraits of his father and step-father. Where most productions either employed two wall paintings or two portrait miniatures (one around Gertrude's neck and one around Hamlet's), Irving's Hamlet pointed into empty space, forcing his mother to 'conjure up with him brain-pictures of the King that was and the King that is' (67:225). Among Taylor's other objections were the blocking of the Play Scene that resulted in Hamlet having his back to the play-within-the-play (something that Irving changed four years later) and Hamlet's rather tame and colourless delivery in the Graveyard Scene after the funeral procession has appeared.

Having done his critical duty by listing his reservations, Mr. Punch/Taylor then praises Irving for his soliloquies,

> for his tender agony of separation from *Ophelia*, and his piteous passion of remonstrance with his Mother; for the kindly courtesy and ease of his scenes with the players; his wild and whirling storm of frenzied emotion after the play; and his scornful dealings with *Rosencrantz* and *Guildenstern*.

Praise is also given to Thomas Mead's performance as the Ghost and Isabel Bateman's as Ophelia. Though lamenting the production's 'wilful and wanton deviations from the verbal and scenic indications of the immortal text', Taylor insists that 'all cavil and question apart, let *Mr. Punch*'s estimation of MR. IRVING'S performance be measured by the space he has given to it, and the fulness and freedom with which he has pointed out the things in it to which he takes most exception'.

Irving's 1874 *Hamlet* was the prelude to a further eleven Shakespeare dramas that he was to appear in at the Lyceum, some of which (*Hamlet* is a good example) he presented in more than one production. Indeed, one might argue that there were some seventeen different productions between the 1874 *Hamlet* and the 1901 *Coriolanus*, this last corresponding with the bankruptcy of the Lyceum and the approaching conclusion of Irving's career. The only Shakespeare play he appeared in after *Coriolanus* was *The Merchant of Venice*, which featured prominently in his farewell tour in 1904–1905. Of the Lyceum productions, *Punch* reviewed thirteen, missing only the 1876 *Othello*, and the 1877 and 1896 *Richard III*. Irving's performances in this last play were not, however, completely ignored. Following the 1877 production, *Punch* (Burnand) jokingly alluded to Edwin Long's portrait of Irving as Richard III, which was exhibited at the Royal Academy in 1877 (74:265), describing the painting in a mock exhibition catalogue entry as 'Decidedly E-long-ated.' On 10 December 1881, to accompany an article by Burnand on Irving's attempts to persuade the ecclesiastical authorities that attending theatre performances such as those at the Lyceum would be no sin, *Punch* included a small engraving depicting Irving as Richard III standing between two bishops, an allusion to an incident in III vii of Shakespeare's play (81:273). Then, in a review of Richard Mansfield's production of the play at the Globe Theatre in 1889, Mr. Punch (Arthur William à Beckett in this instance) states that he has vivid memories 'of the performance of my talented friend, HENRY IRVING'. The review is accompanied by several engravings, one of which depicts Richard Mansfield as a diminutive Richard (Figure 27). His immense shadow on the wall behind him, however, is that of Irving (96:157)

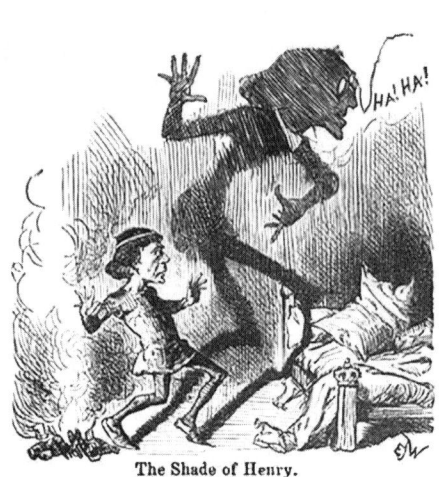

Figure 27. Edward J. Wheeler's depiction of Richard Mansfield as Richard III. *Punch* (6 April 1889), 96:157.

During the long run of *Hamlet*, which ended on 29 June 1875, H. L. Bateman, the manager of the Lyceum, died. His wife then assumed his responsibilities, but Irving increasingly took charge of productions, although at times he was frustrated by Mrs. Bateman's managerial decisions (Irving 1951, 253). Eventually, in August 1878 he would, not without a degree of acrimony (Hughes 1981, 23), assume the role of manager himself, following the path of such earlier Victorian actor-managers as Macready, Kean, and Phelps. His first Shakespeare play under Mrs. Bateman's management was *Macbeth*, which opened on 25 September 1875 and ran for eighty performances. Where Mrs. Bateman's daughter, Isabel, had played Ophelia to Irving's Hamlet, another daughter, Kate, now played Lady Macbeth. *Punch* reviewed the production on 9 October. The reviewer, Tom Taylor, was willing to concede that Irving's performance was acceptable, 'if not as consistent with the text of SHAKSPEARE as it stands, at least as within the limits of fair psychological and histrionic interpretation' (69:138). In this respect, Taylor shared the fairly widespread critical coolness towards Irving's portrayal of Macbeth. Rather than seeing the character as a great man who falls but struggles hard against the irresistible forces that destroy him, Irving presented a man weak from the outset, a coward and a liar, who is chiefly responsible for all that happens. Wife and Witches are only appendages to his own moral failure. Irving's is a Macbeth who is 'pale and haggard in face, meagre almost to emaciation in frame, shrill and high-pitched or hollow of voice, feverish and restless of movement, and hysteric of temperament'. His physique and temperament, Taylor acknowledges, are not up to embodying 'a rude, stalwart, fierce, fighting, northern warrior'. Implied, perhaps, is the suggestion that Irving should not be attempting the part and that his interpretation, though suited to his physique and acting style, is wrong-headed.

As in the review of *Hamlet*, Irving is criticized for expunging 'those passages of the text which he found in the way of his interpretation'. The introductory scene, in which Macbeth's warlike feats are extolled, is, for example, completely cut so that the audience is denied any image of Macbeth as a mighty warrior. By contrast, Kate Bateman's Lady Macbeth, apart from some cautions about her elocution, is warmly praised by Taylor for its 'many points of high excellence' (69:139). Bateman's 'strong marking of the different moods of the wicked woman', we are told, 'from the intense determination of the First Act to the breaking strength and failing spirit of the Third, was both original in conception, and powerful in execution'. Also praised, without any hint of Irving's possible involvement, was Mrs. Bateman for 'her courage in getting rid of the chorus of witches, even at the cost of MATTHEW LOCKE'S music, and bringing back the weird sisters to the original mystic three – The Fates of *Macbeth* – the Eumenides of modern tragedy'. However, in spite of the mixed reviews that the Lyceum *Macbeth* received, it continued, as already mentioned, for eighty performances, bringing to London audiences a radically different interpretation of its title-character.

Later in the season, beginning on 14 February, Irving attempted the role of Othello, four months after Salvini had been widely praised for his London performances of the part. Where Salvini had presented a powerful portrait of a noble African transformed into raging and violent passion, Irving downplayed Othello's race by wearing a lighter make-up and by replacing the traditional turban and moorish robe with a Venetian-style general's uniform designed by John Tenniel. Audiences were bewildered by what Irving did with the part, and, although the production ran for forty-nine performances, it was not very well received. *Punch*, which had earlier praised a pre-season performance of the play by Salvini (see below), chose not to review Irving's version. The magazine also passed on Irving's *Richard III*. This opened on 29 January 1877 and ran for two hundred performances. This production was surely of considerable interest in that it discarded the Colley Cibber arrangement in favour of something closer to Shakespeare's original, though it cut almost 1,600 lines, omitted a number of minor characters, and greatly reduced the part of Queen Margaret, played by Kate Bateman (Isabel Bateman was Lady Anne). Just why *Punch* ignored Irving's performance, which those who saw it generally found novel and persuasive (Irving 1951, 282–285), remains unclear.

In August the following year, Mrs. Bateman transferred the lease of the Lyceum to Irving, who would now have autonomy in such crucial matters as casting. This permitted him to drop the Bateman sisters, whose abilities he had always questioned. Indirectly, this would lead to the start of his acting partnership with Ellen Terry, perhaps the most successful theatrical liaison of the century. Once he became manager of the Lyceum in 1878, the first fruits of his new artistic freedom were displayed in his opening production of the new season – *Hamlet*.

This revival opened on 30 December, and *Punch* attended and reviewed it in the issue for 11 January 1879. The reviewer, Tom Taylor, appears to have been present on the opening night, since he tells how Irving, at the end of the four-hour performance, stood 'before a crowded house, thrilling with enthusiasm, and tumultuous with applause' and told the audience 'that this was what he had been working for all his life – not meaning the applause, of course, but the opportunity, of producing *Hamlet* in a theatre under his own whole and sole management'. Mindful of his earlier strictures about the Lyceum's 1874 production, Taylor notes that the Ghost is now given 'the full range of the platform of Elsinore for his martial stalk, in the opening Scene'. He still disapproves of the Ghost appearing outside the castle in the scene where he is alone with Hamlet, but admits that the Ghost's appearance on the 'dreadful summit of the cliff' provides 'an impressive and effective stage-picture, and is an immense improvement on the close glen shut in by mountains which it replaces ...' He complains again about Hamlet sinking down when the Ghost leaves him, and once more protests 'against the absence of visible pictures in the Closet Scene' (76:9), this last being a feature of Irving's performance that would provide the theme of an extended joke by Burnand in a later issue of the magazine (78:28). *Punch* also objected to the fencing scene being placed in a gallery overlooking a garden. Curiously, the revised blocking of the Play Scene that is evident in the production promptbook receives no comment, even though it corrected what Taylor had suggested was an error in the 1874 production.

The acting of Georgina Pauncefort (Gertrude), William Henry Chippendale (Polonius), and Samuel Johnson (the Gravedigger) is praised, but Taylor could find nothing positive to say about the actors of the remaining secondary parts. However, their inadequacy seems to have been more than compensated for by 'the two pillars of the play', Irving as Hamlet and Ellen Terry as Ophelia. Though he criticizes Irving's elocution and physical deportment, he claims at the same time that it would 'be difficult to find a better Hamlet, in conception'

(76:10). Whereas the praise for Irving is bound up with qualifications, that for Ellen Terry is virtually unbridled:

> In ELLEN TERRY'S hands the execution of the part – but for the fright that on the first night almost strangled her singing in both mad scenes, and weakened the effect of the second – was as consummate, as its conception was subtle and complete. It was an ideally beautiful presentment jarring in no point of look, movement, or speech with the ideal called up by SHAKESPEARE'S exquisite creation.

Taylor particularly admired 'the great scene of the Third Act, in which *Hamlet* does his best to wrench the love of her out of his heart, and breaks hers in the effort'. For the reviewer, Terry's Ophelia was a 'revelation for which we have to thank the new management of the Lyceum,' for if 'anything more intellectually conceived or more exquisitely wrought out has been seen on the English stage in this generation, it has not been within *Punch*'s memory'. *Punch*'s enthusiasm was widely shared, and Irving's revival of *Hamlet* played to great acclaim for ninety-eight nights. From this time on, with Ellen Terry as Ophelia, the play became a standard and renowned feature of Irving's repertoire both in England and on his tours of North America until, bowing to age, he played his final Hamlet at age forty-seven on 8 May 1885.

Following the enormous success of his partnership with Ellen Terry in *Hamlet*, Irving kept her as his leading lady throughout the remainder of his time at the Lyceum. She was Portia to his Shylock, Desdemona to his Othello, Juliet to his Romeo, Beatrice to his Benedick, Lady Macbeth to his Macbeth, Cordelia to his King Lear, Imogen to his Iachimo, and Volumnia to his Caius Marcius. In *Twelfth Night*, she played the leading female role (Viola), while he played what at the time was considered the leading male role, Malvolio, and in *Henry VIII* she played Queen Katherine, while he virtually stole the play with his magnificent Wolsey. It is not my intention here to give detailed comments on the *Punch* reviews of these productions. It is my hope, however, that the brief survey that follows will make clear that *Punch*, in faithfully reviewing all of Irving's Lyceum productions of

Shakespeare (apart from the exceptions already mentioned), was anxious to support Irving as a leading proponent of Shakspeareanity

After the great success of *Hamlet*, Irving presented in the next season a much anticipated new production of *The Merchant of Venice*, with himself as Shylock and Ellen Terry as Portia. As with his *Hamlet*, he had generated interest in the production and made his intentions clear in advance by publishing an acting version of the play prior to opening night. The hope was, perhaps, that critics would have had time to digest any quibbles concerning cuts (Irving dropped four scenes) or changes to the text (the concluding Lorenzo-Jessica romantic night scene was much cut). This stratagem may have worked in the case of the *Punch* reviewer, Burnand. The play opened on 1 November 1879, and, when Burnand reviewed it in considerable detail two weeks later, there were no complaints about cuts, and even the exclusion of the Prince of Arragan's scene (II ix) was ignored. With few qualifications, Burnand heaped praise on Irving, admiring especially the frightening power of his hatred, cloaked by the dignified bearing that he was able to evoke in the Trial Scene, and the ensuing powerful sympathy he earned in the concluding part of the scene once he fell into the legal trap set by Portia.

In praising Irving's complex portrait of the wronged Jew, Burnand sided with those critics, who, following Hazlitt's lead, saw Shylock as a once noble figure whose deep hatred and desire for revenge are the result of the accumulated injuries he has suffered from the racist Christian community in the past (Hughes 1981, 224–225). As for Terry's Portia, Burnand is equally enthusiastic. She had already performed the part at the Prince of Wales Theatre in 1875 with Charles Coghlan as Shylock, but, according to Burnand, 'her performance there was but as the sketch of which this at the Lyceum is the perfect picture' (77:225). Even an apparent lack of dignity in the Trial Scene that was criticized by some reviewers is defended as being in character. Like *Hamlet* (the 1878 revival had played for a 100 performances), Irving's *Merchant of Venice* was an enormous success. It played for 250 performances, and Irving kept it in his repertoire to the end of his acting career.

The following season, while Irving at the Lyceum continued to establish his hold on the London theatre-going public, Edwin Booth, the American tragedian, was struggling at the Princess's Theatre where he had to overcome poor facilities (much had changed since Kean's time), a weak cast of supporting actors, and a cheapskate manager. London theatre gossips expected a vicious rivalry between Booth and Irving, especially when the American dared to play Hamlet in the same city as Irving. But, contrary to expectations, the two actors developed a mutually respectful friendship, and as the end of Booth's guest season approached in the Spring of 1881, Irving invited Booth to perform with him in *Othello*, alternating with him the parts of Othello and Iago. Ellen Terry would play Desdemona. Doubling the usual ticket prices for the more expensive seats (Irving 1951, 374), Irving gambled on attracting well-filled houses anxious to compare the two principal male actors. He was not disappointed, and the twenty-one performances of the play between 2 May and 17 June earned over £8,000. Burnand was present and his review appeared in the *Punch* issue for 14 May. On this occasion, Booth played Othello, and his performance was dismissed by Burnand as being 'as stagey as ever, in the old-fashioned Macready-Phelps style' (80:225). Clearly, Irving's more naturalistic theatrical style had successfully gained ground if the *Punch* reviewer now found the once lauded Macready and Phelps to be *passé*. This impression is reinforced by the praise that is then accorded Irving's performance as Iago. Though still deprecating Irving's mannerisms, Burnand claims that 'MR. IRVING has never been seen to greater advantage than as *Iago*.' His performance 'is a masterpiece' and 'a real triumph'. Ellen Terry's Desdemona is also praised, but Burnand complains that the text has been cut in such a way that the audience does not see enough of her. Consequently, the audience does not 'grow so fond of her as to shed tears over her sad end behind those private-theatrical bed-curtains' (Irving had her murder occur out of sight behind the curtains as a sop to his audience's sensibilities).

Oddly, however, Burnand's chief focus is upon the comic moments that Irving created. These are amusingly illustrated by four engravings designed by Harry Furniss, and this emphasis upon the comic even extends to the punning title of the review: 'TWO STARS; OR, BOOTH TOGETHER'. The influence here of Burnand, who had replaced Tom Taylor as editor the year before, is unmistakable.

Notorious for his puns and keen to inject more liveliness and fun into the pages of *Punch* (Spielmann 1985a, 366), Burnand, on becoming editor, had hired Furniss, who subsequently achieved a considerable reputation for his comic portraits of Parliamentarians. During his fourteen years with *Punch*, Furniss designed some forty or so comic engravings that employ allusions to Shakespeare. Most of these accompanied comments on the affairs of Parliament, but a few, among them the designs based on *Othello,* employed Furniss's legendary skills at sketching likenesses of actors in current theatre productions. Thus, while this remained a serious review (there is a paragraph discussing cuts that have taken away from the possible motivations that Iago may have had), the emphasis on the comic introduces a new note that Burnand doubtless wanted as a means of keeping *Punch*'s theatre reviews consistent with the broadly comic tone and goal of the magazine. It is also worth noting that *Punch*'s tendency in the 1880s and 90s to spare Irving any severe negative criticism may relate to the friendship that existed between Burnand and Irving. Furthermore, there was also a business relationship to be considered since Irving had solicited work from Burnand (Irving 1951, 437, 492–493). It might be argued, then, that it was in Burnand's best interests to maintain cordial relations with Irving and to write supportive reviews.

The kinds of changes that were apparent in the 1881 review of *Othello* are not repeated in the review of Irving's *Romeo and Juliet* by Edwin James Milliken the following year. This production, which opened on 8 March, is highly praised as 'a series of stage pictures', a tribute to the scenic craft of Hawes Craven, William Cuthbert, and William Telbin, who by all accounts created an unprecedented series of eighteen beautiful stage settings, made all the more effective through the use of novel lighting effects. But, as the opening line of the *Punch* review notes, 'c'est magnifique, mais ce n'est pas – l'amour'. The problem, according to Milliken is that Irving (now aged forty-four) fell short as Romeo, while Ellen Terry as Juliet lacked 'the warm impulsiveness checked ever and anon by girlish misgivings, which we naturally look for in the youthful daughter of the Capulets' (82:121). Even so, the reviewer finds much to his liking, including the acting of the other characters (Fanny Stirling as the Nurse is particularly singled out). Whereas Milliken clearly did all he could to present the production in as positive a light as possible, a prelude to the review in the issue for 18 March had already noted in a humorous way that Irving had miscast himself. An engraved design (Figure 28) by Linley Sambourne depicted the moonlit balcony scene with the adoring Irving (Romeo) gazing up at Ellen Terry (Juliet) (82:130). The caption read: 'ROMEO! ROMEO! WHEREFORE ART *THOU* ROMEO!' A note below states: 'But had the DIVINE WILLIAMS [a frequent *Punch* sobriquet for Shakespeare] witnessed the performance, he might have been able to satisfy his own query.'

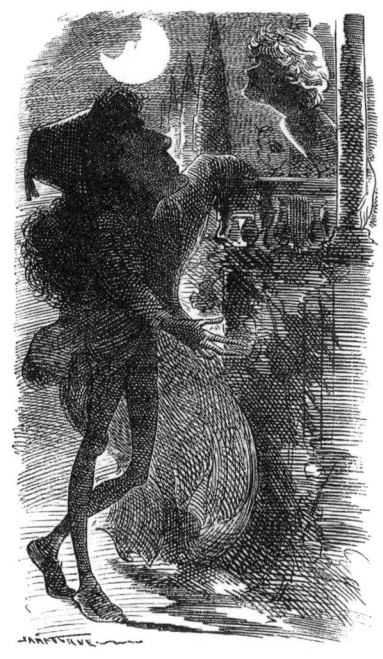

Figure 28. Linley Sambourne's design of Irving and Terry in *Romeo and Juliet*. *Punch* (18 March 1882), 82:130.

Then, following the review, the issue for 15 April contained 'A SHORT SHAKSPEARIAN CATECHISM', contributed by Burnand, on the subject of *Romeo and Juliet*. The question and answer format permitted comments on the unrealistic plot of the play and provided the opportunity to suggest that Romeo is a nincompoop and that Johnston Forbes Robertson came closest to Shakespeare's original by playing Romeo 'like a modern effeminate aesthetic young man'. No doubt readers would have remembered that Forbes Robertson, with Helena Modjeska as Juliet, had performed in *Romeo and Juliet* the year before and that *Punch* had included a review on 9 April (80:165). In answer to the question in the 'CATECHISM' 'What do you think of MR. IRVING as Romeo?' the respondent offered the following defence:

> I think that he does his best with a part, which the Author, 'had his own opportunities been brought up to the level of our own time', – to quote MR. IRVING'S own preface, – would never have chosen for him, in spite of the advantages offered by the 'fuller development of our present stage'. (82:173)

Further comments concern the character of the Nurse and 'Mrs. STIRLING'S marvellous impersonation of the character' and the objectionable nature of the Capulets, old Capulet being 'the very type of the good-hearted jolly old Father, who is so sociable and pleasant "before company", and such a tyrant and bully within his own family circle'.

A central feature of the article, as with the earlier review of *Othello,* are three engravings designed by Edward J. Wheeler. Hired by Burnand at the same time as Furniss, Wheeler contributed numerous humorous designs on theatrical subjects, many of which accompanied *Punch*'s reviews of Shakespeare productions. Those accompanying the 'CATECHISM' depict a demure Terry (Juliet) being berated by her Capulet father and mother; the Nurse (Fanny Stirling); and Terry and Irving in the final tomb scene. Two of the engravings have captions containing puns. One describes the Nurse as 'A Sterling Actress', and the other showing Romeo and Juliet confronting each other in the Capulet tomb has 'All our own Vault'.

The Lyceum *Romeo and Juliet,* in spite of the general view among critics that Irving failed as Romeo, was well attended and ran for twenty-four weeks. However, after being briefly revived at the beginning of the next season, it was, like Irving's *Othello,* quietly dropped from his repertoire. No such fate awaited Irving's next Shakespeare venture, *Much Ado About Nothing,* which opened on 11 October 1882 and had a first run of 212 performances. In the part of Benedick, Irving was able to reveal a remarkable talent for comedy, and as Beatrice, which she had already played elsewhere, Terry found a perfect outlet for her beauty, charm, and wit. None of the principals' acting partnerships were more successful than this, and the production received almost universal praise (Irving 1951, 403–404). The play remained a popular item in the Lyceum repertoire until 1895, and, beginning with the year after it was first introduced, it was also well received on Irving's tours in America.

Punch joined in the initial general acclaim. On 21 October, it reported that the production was 'the most thoroughly successful of all the pieces yet put on this stage under the management of MR. HENRY IRVING, who, as far as he himself is personally concerned, has never been seen to greater advantage' (83:184). *Punch*'s comments, which were accompanied by a humorous engraving designed by Wheeler, were the prelude to a full-length review by Burnand that appeared the following week. 'MUCH ADO AT THE LYCEUM' begins with something of a plot summary, perhaps because the play was less well known at the time than other Shakespeare comedies. The review then praises almost every actor in the cast. Irving and Terry are surprisingly given relatively little attention, but Burnand leaves no doubt about his opinion of their contribution: 'Mr. IRVING'S *Benedick* and Miss ELLEN TERRY'S *Beatrice* are everything, about whom there will be much ado for some time to come, [...]'

Accompanying the review are five designs, again by Wheeler, of characters in the play. Each engraving has a joking caption, the church scene in which Hero 'dies', for example, being captioned 'Extraordinary Scene in a Church; or In-a-Mess at Messina'. By now, Burnand's policy of lightening the tone of *Punch* was clear, and even what reads as a straightforward serious review may well be accompanied by playful and humorous graphic designs, often mildly irreverent in their effect. These counterbalance any textual solemnity and help maintain *Punch*'s character as a humour magazine, but no reader would be so distracted by them as to believe that the reviews themselves were not serious critiques of what *Punch* felt were important Shakespeare productions.

At the end of the 1882–1883 season, Irving did his customary tour in the provinces and then on 11 October embarked for the United States where he would tour for six months. Among the plays he presented were *Hamlet, Richard III, The Merchant of Venice*, and *Much Ado About Nothing. Punch* included the occasional report on his activities, most notably an article by Horace Frank Lester on 24 May 1884 entitled 'EXTRACTS FROM "GETTING ROUND AMERICA"'. This was allegedly written by 'Benedick Hamlet, Esq., of the Lyceum,' and consisted of extracts from a supposed two-volume account of the actor/author's tour in the company of Miss

Ellen Merry (86:245). On his return, Irving introduced a new production of *Twelfth Night* on 8 July, in which he played Malvolio and Terry played Viola. Burnand reviewed it on 19 July (87:28–29). Ellen Terry's Viola is praised, but Irving's Malvolio is questioned. First, the dominance of his performance obscured the principal comic characters (Sir Toby, Sir Andrew, Maria, Feste), and secondly, he played the role as tragic melodrama, matching Irving's Shylock in the eventual plea for sympathy.

Two graphic designs by Wheeler admirably underline these two concerns. The first depicts the four principal comic characters, alongside the dominating figure of Irving as Malvolio. They all stand upon a large cake. The caption below reads: 'Twelfth Night Characters on the Lyceum Cake'. The second engraving shows Irving in bed. Standing beside the bed is the ghost of Shakespeare who holds up a notice inscribed: 'WILL YOU PLAY MALVOLIO IN A-MERRY-KEY?' (i.e. will you lighten the tone you use for the part, a punning way of also asking whether Irving planned to perform the role in America) (87:28). Apparently, Irving did tone down his performance and he did perform the play in America, though only on four occasions (Irving 1981, 190). The production having been generally considered something of a failure in England, Irving then dropped it.

The allusion to America in Wheeler's graphic design had to do with Irving's second tour there. This began in Canada where he arrived that September before moving on to the United States. While Irving was away, *Punch* kept jealous watch on theatrical affairs in London, commenting in particular on two Shakespeare productions. First, there was the production of *Hamlet* at the Princess's Theatre in October by the young and relatively inexperienced Wilson Barrett (Odell 1920, II:380–381, 398–400). He began a 110-performance run in an obvious challenge both to Irving's earlier 108-night run and to the older actor's pre-eminence as the English Hamlet. Then, at the Lyceum, Mary Anderson put on *Romeo and Juliet* in November. A renowned beauty, she played Juliet opposite William Terriss, a handsome young Romeo who had recently been Irving's Orsino in *Twelfth Night*. The production was elaborately staged with many of the scenes painted by Hawes Craven, Irving's artist, the entire production having been designed by Lewis Wingfield. The elaborate staging was similar to the kind of effect aimed at by Irving. The productions by Barrett and Anderson invited, perhaps deliberately, comparisons with the absent Irving's work. *Punch* responded by reviewing each, but shaping the reviews in the form of letters addressed to Irving in America, entitled 'LETTERS TO SOME PEOPLE'.

That on Barrett's *Hamlet* was published in the issue for 25 October. The letter, contributed by Burnand, was purportedly from 'Nibbs' to Irving and commented in some detail on Barrett's production (87:196–97), noting aspects wherein it differed from Irving's production. There were four accompanying engravings by Wheeler, the principal one depicting a weather box, a type of weather indicator that customarily shows two figures who make alternate appearances from the box, depending upon the state of the weather (Figure 29). The two figures in this instance are Henry Irving at left and Wilson Barrett at right. Both are in costume as Hamlet (87:196). Irving is shown entering the box labelled 'H. I. Canada', while Barrett emerges from the box labelled 'W. B. London'. On the gable of the weather box is a sign: 'October 1884'. The caption below states: 'THEATRICAL WEATHER-BOX. Irving goes in for Canada; Wilson Barrett comes out as *Hamlet*.'

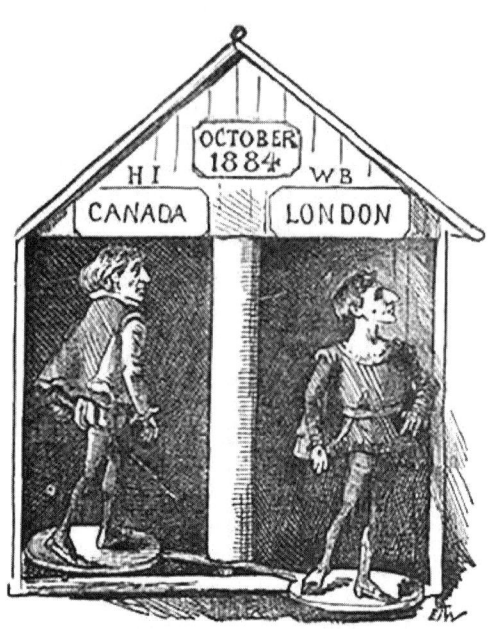

Figure 29. Edward J. Wheeler, 'THEATRICAL WEATHER-BOX.' *Punch* (25 October 1884), 87:196.

210

However, though the engraving may have implied that Barrett was taking Irving's place in the sun, Burnand's text told a very different story:

DEAR HENRY IRVING,
W. B. HAS done it. WILSON B., like JOEY B., is 'sly, devilish sly', and he only waited till your back was turned in order to play *Hamlet.*
When IRVING's away,
WILSON BARRETT will play.
And now that he *has* done it, I write at once to quell any natural anxiety on your part. Don't you be afraid; it's all right; your position is secure. *Hamlet* Junior has not caught you up, or come any way near you, as far as I can judge from a first night's performance, either as Actor or Stage-Manager.

The letter goes on to make particular note of Barrett's young age in its generally negative review, one that misses many of the intriguing details of Barrett's production (see Odell 1920, II: 380–81, 398–400). Two weeks later, *Punch* took up this same theme. To accompany a brief article entitled 'A YOUNG HAMLET', it included a small engraving designed by Wheeler that playfully depicted a very youthful-looking Barrett, posing with a cricket bat and Yorick's skull (in place of a ball) (87:221).

Mary Anderson's production of *Romeo and Juliet* at the Lyceum opened on 1 November. The *Punch* review by Burnand in the issue for 15 November is clearly ill-at-ease (as were other contemporary reviews) with the stress upon scenic effects and fine costumes (Odell 1920, II:381, 402, 434–435): 'All that decorative Art and archaeological learning could do for it, has been done; ...' Among other matters, the reviewer discusses some of Anderson's innovations, such as substituting cloisters for the Friar's cell; the introduction of a marriage ceremony that occurs in a private chapel, 'with a Maltese cross and two lighted candles on an altar'; Juliet's 'violent gymnastic header into, or rather, right over the bed', which 'was sufficient to have brought down the house, – which it did'. Burnand's two-page review is accompanied by eight small humorous engravings by Wheeler to illustrate the production. These include Juliet jumping on to her bed; the poorly-cast Herbert Standing as Mercutio, a portly figure whom

Burnand compares to Henry VIII; and two stage hands dragging the bed off stage with Juliet collapsed upon it (87:232–233).

When Irving returned to England in the Spring of 1885, he opened the season at the Lyceum with his ever-popular *Hamlet*, an attempt, perhaps, to re-establish his authority as the pre-eminent English Hamlet. For the next two years, he then made a huge investment in time and money in a dramatic version of Goethe's *Faust*. There were his customary tours of the provinces, a tour in Germany, and another visit to the United States. Not until 29 December 1888 did he present a new Shakespeare production in the form of a totally revised *Macbeth*. Ellen Terry was reluctantly cajoled into taking on the role of Lady Macbeth, a decision soon to be immortalized in John Singer Sargent's famous portrait, in which she wears the costume designed for her by Alice Comyns Carr. The production ran for 151 performances. Much was changed since Irving's earlier *Macbeth* some thirteen years before, but it was still not a version that would be considered viable today. Irving did restore the bleeding Sergeant and hence the early allusions to Macbeth as heroic warrior, but the on-stage murder of Banquo was cut, as was that of Lady Macduff, something that is possible because these events are described elsewhere.

Significantly, Irving's interpretation of his role was different. Now Macbeth was much more the bloody-minded villain and a moral coward virtually devoid of conscience. He had thought about murder, it is clear from his first entrance, even before he encountered the Weird Sisters. Lady Macbeth had changed too. Whereas Kate Bateman had depicted a strong-minded wicked woman who, more assertive than her husband, drives him to commit murder, Ellen Terry is the loving wife who supports her husband and urges him not to be afraid. When she is first seen reading the letter from her husband, for example, she is seated by a fire in a comfortable, very domestic sitting-room. Ignoring any incongruity with the text, she maintained the pose of the gentle, loyal housewife, one who forced herself to behave unnaturally to serve her husband's wishes. Her later madness and death was to be attributed to loneliness and a broken heart, caused by the loss of her husband's love (Hughes 1981, 93–8).

The opening night of Irving's *Macbeth* had been much anticipated, and *Punch* had even published an article by Burnand one week earlier that purported to quell some of the supposed rumours about the new production (95:292). When the play finally opened on 29 December, Harry Furniss and Burnand were both present, and the resulting illustrated review on 12 January covered two full pages (96:15–16). Burnand finds the production 'admirable' but criticizes Irving for first appearing on stage not as the victorious Chieftain, but 'as though he were brooding over a defeat'. No thought of murder enters Macbeth's head until he meets the three Witches, and, we are told, without the promptings of his wife, Macbeth would never have gone ahead. For her part, Terry is not 'the awful Tragedy Queen' normally associated with the play but her husband's 'dearest chuck'. The reviewer feels that her gentle exterior works in the scenes where she is with Macbeth, but 'a horror-struck, nervous *Lady Macbeth*, listening for the result of her husband's murderous visit to *Duncan*'s bed-room is not SHAKSPEARE'S *Lady Macbeth*, but *Lady Macbeth* Terry-fied' (96:16). Terry's performance in the sleep-walking scene also failed to impress Burnand. She remained the 'dearest chuck.' But 'she must be the tiger-cat as well as the purring domestic cat; and when alone the tiger-cat only. Velvet and iron is *Lady Macbeth*.'

To this very mixed response, Furniss added seven drawings. The first is a fascinating half-page initial letter 'M' that depicts the interior of the Lyceum (Figure 30). Mr. Punch is visible in the audience, and on stage we observe the ghost scene. Beneath his design, Furniss included the caption 'First night Sketch, by Our Lightning Artist, in the dark'. In the ghost scene, Irving used a trick seat from which the bloody Banquo emerged. Furniss includes a small drawing of this seat, a second humorous drawing showing Banquo's sudden appearance, akin to that of 'Jack-in-the-Box', and a third design (also deliberately comic) showing Irving seated on the closed seat with the caption: 'Macbeth rushes up, presses down lid, and sits on it, "Why, being gone, I am a man again!"' Two other designs illustrate two different versions of Lady Macbeth. 'The Dearest Chuck' of the past depicts a tall, imperious Lady Macbeth (Kate Bateman?) staring down at a diminutive and pleading Macbeth, while the 'Dearest Chuck' of the present shows Irving and Terry in a near embrace, looking into each other's eyes.

Burnand, who was on friendly terms with Irving, was aware that following the opening performance there had been rumours that Terry would give up the part. He had then written to Irving to tell him that two items about the production were about to appear in *Punch*. Perhaps he was preparing Irving for the negative comments that were

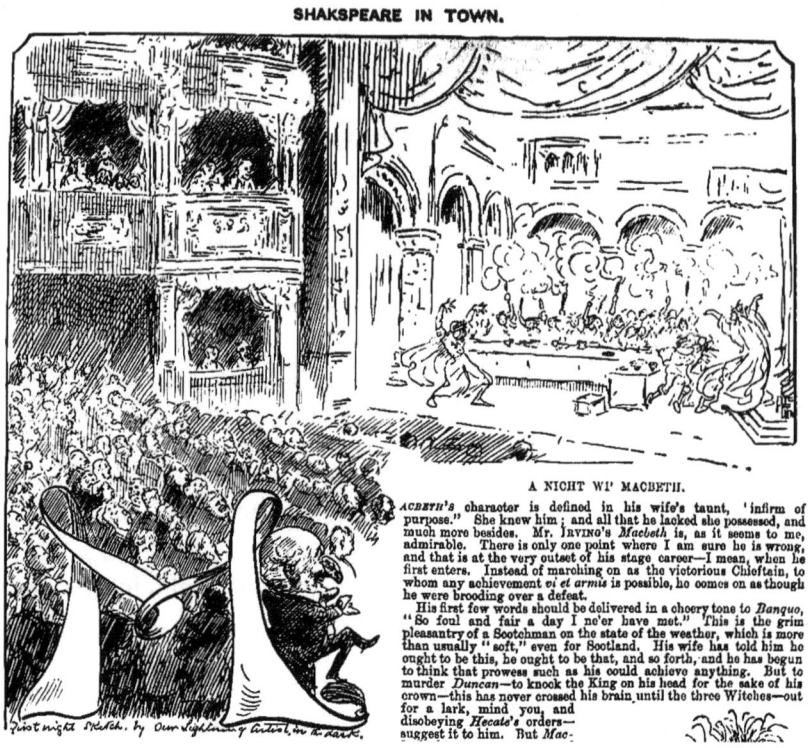

Figure 30. Harry Furniss, initial letter 'M' showing interior of Lyceum Theatre and Irving as Macbeth. *Punch* (12 January 1889), 96:15.

about to be published. He must surely have been somewhat disarmed, then, by Irving's reply to him the day before the review in *Punch* was published. It began 'I shall read with great interest and I am sure pleasure, tomorrow's *Punch*. Of course you are with us – and with the public too. Ellen Terry has made the hit of her life. She really begins

214

to like her Ladyship and plays it wonderfully' (quoted Irving 1951, 506). What Irving thought the next day when he opened his copy of *Punch* we can only guess at.

The second item Burnand had referred to in his letter to Irving appeared a week later in the issue for 19 January. It can be read as a polite critique of Terry's interpretation of Lady Macbeth. Entitled 'LAMBS AT THE LYCEUM', it quotes Charles and Mary Lamb's *Tales from Shakespeare* and their views of Lady Macbeth. It is suggested that Terry read over the Lambs' work. She will find that much is in accord with her own view, but there is 'so much which her genius will at once adopt as representing the stern and repulsive side of the character' (96:33). The problem with her performance, the reviewer argues, is that she 'has made one "blend" of *Beatrice, Ophelia*, and *Lady Macbeth*, in which the awful characteristics of the last have been toned down'. But this was not all that *Punch* had to say about Irving's *Macbeth*. Two pages later, Furniss was given a whole page for a collage of nine sketches in which the 'old' and 'new' styles of *Macbeth* were depicted. The old style is represented by a warrior Macbeth and a fierce Lady Macbeth carrying two daggers. The new style is represented by the central sketch that depicts a loving Lady Macbeth seated on her husband's lap. With what may have been a deliberate *double entendre*, the caption reads: 'The Homely Style. Lady Macbeth encourages Mac to do the deed.'

The following May, *Punch* offered one more comment on the new *Macbeth*. Discussion of it properly belongs in the next chapter, but it can be mentioned here because it directly relates to Ellen Terry's Lady Macbeth. Soon after the opening of Irving's new production, John Singer Sargent painted his now famous portrait of Terry as Lady Macbeth. The work, which today hangs in the Tate Gallery (London), was an instant success and attracted a great deal of attention when it was shown at the New Gallery. It portrays Terry with long braids that are almost knee length and wearing the magnificent costume designed for her by Alice Comyns Carr. She holds her crown with both hands and lifts it above her head after Macbeth's exit at the end of the banquet scene. This piece of stage business was originally introduced by Samuel Phelps in 1857, but it was never actually used by Terry, who did not hold the crown in this way in the production. According to her notes and other sources, 'as Macbeth departed she took off her crown, staggered to the vacated throne, held the crown in her hand, and laughed as the curtain fell' (Altick 1985, 318; Manvell 1968, 198–202, 261). Ironically, however, it is Sargent's portrait that remains as the most familiar memento of her part in Irving's production. In the issue of 25 May, *Punch* included a small unsigned engraving that parodied Sargent's picture (Figure 31). In place of the crown above her head, Terry holds up a heavy steel bar. Her braids are transformed into a heavy chain at each end of which is a metal ball. In addition, the voluminous sleeves of her dress are each inscribed '100,000 lbs.' Appropriately, the caption says of this amazing weight lifter: 'Athletics. Strong Woman performing her *tour de force*' (96:254). One wonders whether the *Punch* artist was aware that Terry was particularly sensitive about weight and always refused to wear anything that was heavy, even if it was true to the period (Marly 1982, 108).

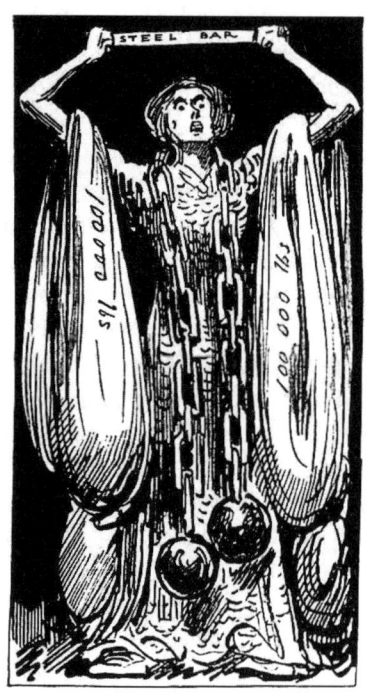

Figure 31. Unidentified artist's burlesque of John Singer Sargent's portrait of Ellen Terry as Lady Macbeth. *Punch* (25 May 1889), 96: 254.

Two years later on 5 January 1891, Irving revived *Much Ado About Nothing* as part of the Lyceum's Christmas offerings. This was heralded by *Punch* on 27 December with a supportive 'puff' composed by Burnand that must surely have pleased Irving. *Much Ado About Nothing*, it is announced, in 'all its memorable glory of costume and scenery', will be presented at the Lyceum Theatre over Christmas. This will be 'a Shakspearian revival well worthy to be reckoned as among the foremost of all the attractions offered by the theatres this Christmas' (99:305). However, though expressing eager anticipation of the revival, *Punch* seems not to have reviewed it. This was not the case with Irving's next Shakespeare revival, a production of *Henry VIII*, which opened on 5 January 1892 and ran until 30 July for a total of 172 performances. This was the most lavish and expensive of Irving's Shakespeare productions, and the immense investment in costumes, spectacular scenery, and supernumeraries, who were required for crowd scenes and processions, resulted in financial loss (Odell 1920, II:445–6; Irving 1951, 546; Hughes 1981, 17).

Burnand reviewed the production on 16 January, remarking on the expenses involved but acknowledging the scenic splendour. Irving's Wolsey and Terry's Queen Katharine are strongly praised, but the review concludes with a back-handed compliment intended to question Irving's emphasis on scenic splendour and historical recreation: 'This revival is bound to have a long – it may be an unprecedentedly long – run. All of us dearly love a show. Moreover, 'tis education; and the School Board should issue an Examination-paper on the history of HENRY THE EIGHTH and his times as exemplified by Mr. IRVING & CO. at the Lyceum' (102:33). As had now become the pattern, Burnand's review was accompanied by a group of engravings. On this occasion there were four of these by Edward Wheeler. That of Irving as Wolsey is typical of their generally comic tone. It shows him in his magnificent costume but deliberately exaggerates the length of his train, which is supported by two small page boys. The caption, probably the contribution of the inveterate punster Burnand, is 'The Cardinal's *Train de Luxe*'.

In November 1892, Irving undertook yet another challenge, *King Lear*. The first night was something of a failure largely because Irving attempted to use a particular voice style that turned out to be virtually inaudible to the audience and in any case impossible to maintain for the entire play. Even so, the *Times* critic praised the production the next day (11 November), stating that the production ranked 'in some respects as one of the greatest and most memorable' (quoted Odell 1920, II:446). However, other critics were less positive, a number of them finding fault with the play itself. Burnand reviewed the production for *Punch* on 19 November in 'HIS MAD-JESTY AT

THE LYCEUM', referring to Shakespeare's work as 'a strange weird play; much for an audience, and more for an actor, all on his own shoulders to bear' (103:233). The play is criticized for showing too little of Cordelia, and the guarded conclusion of the review was that *King Lear*, as Irving in his before-curtain and after-play speech had termed it, is a titanic play and that 'OUR HENRY has his work cut out for him'. While 'the gods' (i.e. those in the upper levels of the theatre) 'very much applauded what he'd done', the reviewer notes somewhat ambiguously that 'the gods of old were not quite so favourable to "Titanic work" generally, and punished eternally Titanic workmen'. *King Lear* was less well known to audiences than the other tragedies that Irving produced. It was a play that some thought was unstageable or flawed and incoherent. Irving's efforts seem to have done little to change this, and although there were many reviews that were largely encouraging and positive, Irving recognized that there was a problem, and, after the play ran for seventy-six performances, he never revived it or took it on tour (Hughes 1981, 117–118).

Other reviews of Irving's *King Lear* mentioned the scenic grandeur of the play and the impressive opening when Lear makes his first appearance. Burnand referred to this latter when he gave the following somewhat ambiguous description:

> never has he [Irving] been so curiously and wonderfully made-up as now, when he represents *Lear*, monarch of all he surveys. Bless thee, HENRY, how art thou transformed! Sure such a *King Lear* was never seen on any stage, so perfect in appearance, so entirely the ideal of SHAKSPEARE'S ancient King.

For his production Irving had commissioned scenic designs from the Pre-Raphaelite painter Ford Madox Brown and had been greatly influenced by this latter's *Cordelia's Portion* (1875), now in the Southampton Art Gallery. From this painting, Irving copied details of posture, costume, make-up, and furniture, as can be seen when the painting is compared to a depiction of Irving as Lear by Bernard Partridge that appeared in the *Illustrated London News* on the very same day as the *Punch* review (Robertson 1931, 168; Hughes 1981, 123–5; Altick 1985, 121).

Partridge was also the artist who provided the two designs that appeared with the *Punch* review. These deliberately seek a comic effect that further adds to the ambiguity of the review. One of the designs depicts William Terriss as Edgar in his first disguise. Captioned 'Mr. Terriss as the Good Fairy', this accompanies the comment in the text concerning the moment when Edgar first appears on stage in his newly-assumed disguise as the mad Poor Tom:

> To those unacquainted with this play, MR. TERRISS'S sudden appearance in somewhat anti-Lord-Chamberlain attire, as he bounded on, with a wand, and struck an attitude, was suggestive of the Good Fairy in the pantomime; and his subsequent proceedings, when he didn't change anybody into Harlequin, Clown, and so forth, puzzled the unlearned spectators considerably.

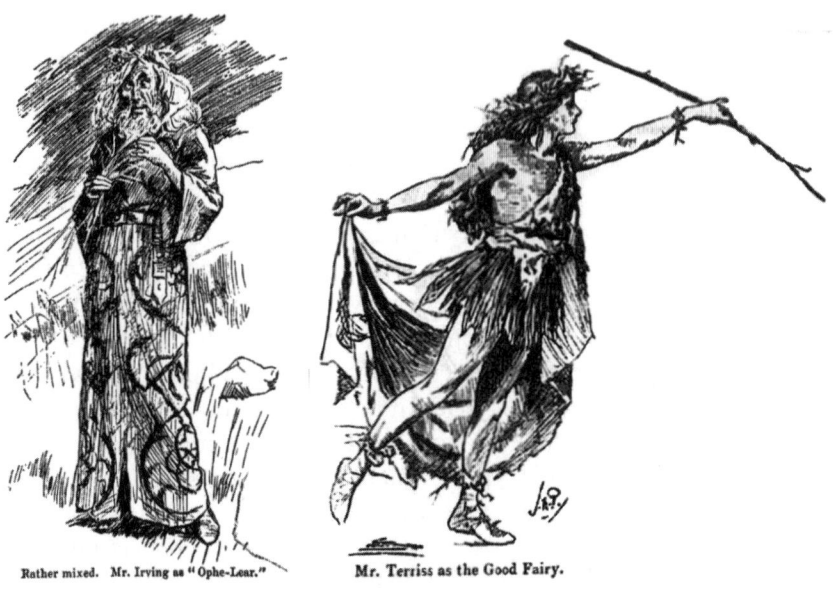

Figure 32. Bernard Partridge's depiction of Irving as King Lear and Terriss as Edgar. *Punch* (19 November 1892), 103:233.

Like other critics, Burnand obviously found this incident to be laughable, and, if Partridge's sketch is at all accurate (and it probably is), one can understand why. Terriss wore a short skirt and little else, and he is posed in the picture with his weight on one leg and arms outstretched like a ballerina. Partridge's other design depicts Irving as King Lear in his madness (Figure 32). He wears a somewhat exotic, feminine-looking robe, which apparently confused the audience. Was it a king's robe or a long dress? Furthermore, the figure has flowers and vegetation woven into his/her hair and holds vegetation to his/her breast. The punning caption comments indirectly on the androgynous figure, pointing out the parallel with the mad woman in *Hamlet*: 'Rather mixed. Mr. Irving as "Ophe-Lear"' (Young 2005b, 14).

Alluded to here is what some of Irving's contemporaries perceived as a feminine quality in his acting. In 1881, the now notorious Edward Vining, who believed that Hamlet was a woman, had stated that Irving's portrayal of the role was consistent with his own belief (Vining 1881, 78). In 1889, the popular comedian Fred Leslie wore female dress and imitated Irving at the Gaiety Theatre in *Ruy Blas; or, the Blasé Roué,* a burlesque of Hugo's *Ruy Blas*. Irving then pulled some strings at the Lord Chamberlain's office and the act was withdrawn. However, this was not quite the end of the matter, since a few nights later, Leslie reappeared in female ballet attire and mimicked Irving's gait and gesture (Irving 1951, 517). *Punch*, in spite of its generally respectful attitude to Irving, occasionally alluded to Irving's 'womanish' features. On 31 December 1881, for example, after providing a fanciful review of how Lillie Langtry might play Lady Macbeth at the Haymarket, it was mentioned in passing that Irving would make a 'respectable' witch (81:309). Then, on 10 February 1883, there appeared an engraving by Harry Furniss. It was entitled 'FÉDORA,' the name of the title-character in a play by Victorien Sardou (84:64). The engraving, which accompanied a review of Sarah Bernhardt in *Fédora*, showed Sarah Bernhardt and Henry Irving in identical poses and dresses confronting each other as if staring into a mirror. The caption, playing upon one of Hamlet's lines (I ii 236), was '"Very Like! Very Like!" – Hamlet' (reproduced in Young 2005b, 13).

A few years later, in the issue for 31 December 1887, *Punch* included an engraving, which purports to be an illustration of a work in an art exhibition catalogue (Figure 33). It depicts a woman in a grotesque posture walking from right to left, with her right arm extended in front of her. Her pose and physical characteristics are instantly recognizable as those of Irving in his performance as Hamlet, a point verified by comparison with the much-reproduced engraving of Irving as Hamlet that appeared in the *Graphic* on 14 November 1874 (p. 477) (Young 2005b, 7–9). The caption below the 1887 *Punch* engraving seems designed to make sure that readers do not miss the point: 'No. 534. After Six Lessons. Lady Amateur imitating eminent Tragedian' (92:251). Finally, and a few years after his design of Irving as King Lear, Partridge would further develop for *Punch* the mockery of Irving as female. On 31 May 1899, following Sarah Bernhardt's much-anticipated debut as Hamlet in Paris, *Punch* published an engraving designed by Partridge entitled 'GREAT ATTRACTION!' (116:258; Taranow 1996, Plate 3; Young 2002, 366). It depicted the 'Get thee to a nunnery' scene (III i) and showed Bernhardt in her Hamlet costume, including her blond wig (Figure 34). She is admonishing a cringing Ophelia, easily recognizable as Irving. As Ophelia, he wears a long white loose dress and a wig. This latter provides him with braids that hang over the shoulders in front, reaching to the waist. What had been hinted at in the King Lear design is now explicit, and one cannot help wondering what the effect would have been on Irving's relationship with *Punch*'s editor, Burnand.

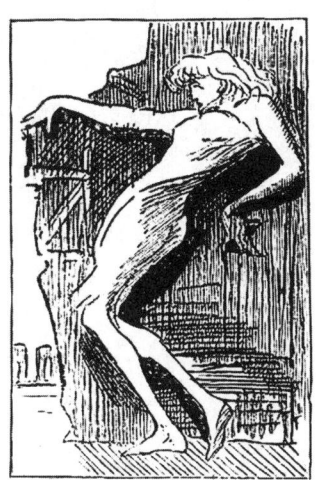

No. 534. After Six Lessons. Lady Amateur imitating Eminent Tragedian.

Figure 33. Unidentified artist's burlesque of Irving as Hamlet. *Punch* (21 May 1887), 92:251.

Between his production of *King Lear* and his next Shakespeare production in 1896, Irving was the recipient of a knighthood in recognition of his services to the theatre. He was the first actor ever to receive such an honour, and in this one gesture the acting profession was accorded a respectability and status that had always been denied it. There was general public acclaim, and Irving received innumerable congratulatory messages from around the world (Irving 1951, 578). Announced in the Birthday Honours list on 25 May 1895, the knighthood was conferred by the Queen at Windsor Castle on 18 July. The following day, Irving's fellow actors and actresses from London (and many from the provinces) assembled at the Lyceum to present Irving with a congratulatory address signed by over four thousand fellow actors (Irving 1951, 580; and Schoch 2004, 181)).

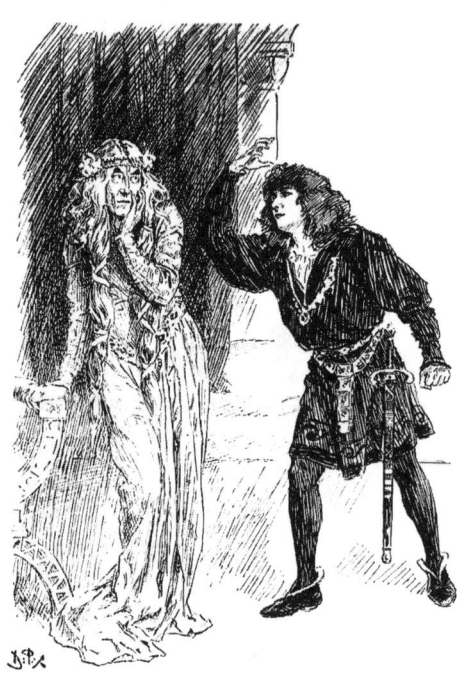

Figure 34. Unidentified artist's burlesque of Irving as Hamlet. *Punch* (21 May 1887), 92:251.

The week following the Lyceum event, *Punch* published its own gratulatory statement (dated Friday 19 July), a piece contributed by Arthur William à Beckett. For its title, *Punch* used a quotation from *Othello*: 'You are most apt to play the sir.' The event at the Lyceum, we are told, will be 'memorable in annals of British stage as a day set apart for one of the greatest triumphs of the Drama' (109:45). After describing the enthusiastic fervour of the assembled actors and actresses, Mr. Punch (à Beckett) then concludes by announcing that he 'takes this opportunity of joining in the demonstration, and drinks to Sir HENRY IRVING. May the Knight of the cheerful countenance prosper according to his deserts.'

During the remainder of Irving's career, *Punch* reviewed two of the actor/manager's final three Shakespeare production – *Cymbeline* and *Coriolanus*. As mentioned already, *Punch* ignored Irving's 1896 *Richard III*. *Cymbeline* opened on 22 September 1896 and played for eighty-eight performances. The *Punch* review, which was contributed by Burnand, appeared on 3 October. After noting that Irving's name had appeared on the playbills as plain 'Henry Irving', without 'Mr.' or 'Sir', the review began by pointing out that the production reflected Irving's view of the play as centered upon two characters: Imogen and Iachimo. For the Victorians, Imogen (played by Ellen Terry in Irving's production) was a paragon of virtue and faithfulness, representing womanhood at its most ideal, and Iachimo (played by Irving) was the cynical, evil tempter, who refused to believe that humans could sometimes be as virtuous as they seemed. Particularly striking in Irving's rendition of Iachimo (something noted by Burnand) was his profound contrition once he had been proved wrong, a contrition that provoked pity in the audience. Irving's acting text cut almost half the original and, of course, this enabled him to make his and Terry's roles as central as possible. Burnand's review proceeded in an almost jaunty tone, making jokes along the way about 'the modest, virtuous, retiring-to-bed-early *Imogen*,' about the chest that the long-legged Irving had to squeeze into, about the 'hearty, rough-and-ready *Belarius*,' and about 'the two "supposed" sons, Mr. B. WEBSTER and Mr. GORDON CRAIG, who were not wise enough to know their own father' (111:160). But laced in with this is praise for the actors, for the scenery by Hawes Craven and Joseph Harker, and for the contribution of Sir Lawrence Alma-Tadema, the Royal Academy artist, who was the design consultant regarding both sets and costumes.

Three engravings designed by Bernard Partridge accompanied the review, their captions suggesting the hand of the punning Burnand. Two of the engravings depict the chest in which Iachimo hides to spy on Imogen in her bedroom. The first of these shows Irving inside, doubled over, the caption noting that 'the lid is closed and he [Irving/Iachimo] is suffering from pains in the chest'. The second shows

Irving springing out of the hiding place in an action matching that described in the caption: 'Jackimo in the Boximo'. The third engraving depicts Frederick Robinson as Belarius and Ellen Terry as Imogen in her boyish disguise as Fidele. The accompanying caption is riddled with puns (I quote it as an example of the *Punch* punster at his most outrageous), but it should not detract the theatre historian from recognizing that the engraving is a useful record of two of the costume designs employed in the play:

> *Miss Imogen Terry (seeing Bill' Arry Oos).* Is it Mr. Fred Robinson Crusoe?
>   O Mr. Robinson Crusoe,
>   Why do you look at my trews so?
> My name is Norval – no, I mean Fidele.
> *British Bill 'Arry Oos Robinson Crusoe (heartily).* Fidele-de-dee! Avast, my hearty! Cave canem! There's the Cave (L. H.), and there's the Canem. *(Pointing to hound just off* R. H.) And now no more words. I believe *you*, my boy! (111:161)

Irving's final Shakespeare production was *Coriolanus*, which opened on 15 April 1901. Several times during his career, Irving had considered the play but for one reason or another had always put off doing it. Then, as now, it was not one of Shakespeare's more popular plays, so it is somewhat sad that it turned out to be both Irving's last Shakespeare production and perhaps his least successful. It ran for only thirty-three performances to increasingly smaller houses and was then withdrawn, being brought back only one more time for the final night of the season.

The *Punch* review by Burnand, perhaps mercifully free of comical engravings, appeared on 1 May with the title 'HENRICUS IRVINGIUS CORIOLANUS'. After some preliminary semi-amusing bluster about the correct pronunciation of the title-character's name, the reviewer notes the magnificent set designs by 'Sir ALMA TADEMA, Pictor Classicus, R.A.', and the specially composed music 'by that great classical commander ALEXANDER, yclept the melodious *eques* Sir A. C. MACKENZIE, *Compositor Dulcisonus*' (120: 328; see also 120:454, a separate article on the *Coriolanus* music). Though he finds that the play 'is wearisome to read', the hero being one who would have made a splendid soccer player 'in this "so-called" twentieth century', and though he acknowledges that the play is largely unfamiliar to the public, 'there being so few "quotations" in it', Burnand nonetheless finds plenty to praise in Irving's production. Without offering much detail, he remarks upon the ways in which the 'lights and shades of the character of the impulsive Roman are admirably brought out by Sir HENRY', and he notes how 'the violent tempest' of Coriolanus's wrath is tempered by the 'tenderly clinging *Virgilia* (Miss MABEL HACKNEY), his most sweet and gentle wife'. The effect is to introduce into the play 'that love interest of which, otherwise, it would be so entirely devoid'. High praise (as usual) is given to Ellen Terry, whom Irving cast as Volumnia, the mother of Coriolanus. Even so, the modern reader may wonder how to take the irony embedded in the following paragraph:

> Never could the clever, beautiful, and still youthful matron, mother of *Coriolanus* (we can gauge *Corey's* age by this), have been more perfectly represented than she is now by Miss ELLEN TERRY as *Volumnia*. Whether sewing at home, going out shopping with her charming companion *Valeria* (Miss MAUD MILTON), rousing her son up to the sticking point, on her knees beseeching him, Miss TERRY is admirable. (120:328)

To this the reviewer adds praise for the representation of the final scene ('a most effective finish to a severely classic play') and for the representation of the crowds, 'vigorously and artistically led by four thoroughly Roman citizens of the Leicesterus Squarus type'. Irving's son, Laurence, who played Junius Brutus, is singled out also for a touch of praise, though in this instance the plaudit may be either ironic or even sycophantic.

This is not a review, then, that points out directly that both Irving and Terry were miscast, and that, according to many other reviewers, Irving's reworking of the play into a three-act tragedy of filial love was unconvincing (Hughes 1981, 168). In retrospect, we know that Irving was a sick man. Possibly, as Odell suggested, he had lost heart (Odell 1920, 456). Three years earlier, a disastrous fire had destroyed all the valuable and irreplaceable painted scenery that had been such a feature of his Lyceum productions and that had enabled him to maintain his repertory of plays. For some time, he had been facing increased competition from other actor-managers (Herbert Beerbohm Tree emerged as a particularly vigorous rival) and other styles of dramatic entertainment. More difficult to take had been the growing financial difficulties in sustaining the Lyceum venture. In 1899 with the formation of the Lyceum Theatre Company, Irving had had to bow to the inevitable and hand over financial control to others. This last explains the final paragraph of the *Punch* review of *Coriolanus*. Referring to 'the report of the rather stormy meeting of the Lyceum Company', Burnand attempted to add his voice to those who had attempted to placate anxious shareholders worried about Irving's absences on account of sickness, provincial tours, and (in 1899–1900) a six-month tour in North America: 'The return of Sir HENRY "to his own again" is certain to mean "many happy returns". So let the shareholders cheer up'. Unfortunately, Burnand's optimism was misplaced, and the following year, the Lyceum was placed in receivership. Then, a few years later, Irving succumbed to sickness and died.

In following Irving's series of Shakespeare productions as recorded in the pages of *Punch*, I have largely ignored other competing, contemporaneous productions, apart from brief allusions to Edwin Booth's 1880–81 season at the Princess's Theatre, Wilson Barrett's 1884 *Hamlet*, and Mary Anderson's *Romeo and Juliet* of the same year. *Punch*, however, kept a close eye on other Shakespeare productions and reviewed or included notices of at least thirty of them between 1875 and 1901. In addition and during the same period, *Punch* reviewed or noted about a dozen productions in London by foreign actors and foreign theatre companies. It is not my intention to discuss in detail these fascinating resources, but I will point out certain features of them in order to indicate how *Punch* maintained its self-assumed role as guardian of Shakspeareanity.

Notices and Reviews: the Universities

During the 1880s and 90s, *Punch* regularly reviewed or alluded to student drama productions at Oxford and Cambridge. This may have reflected the particular interest of the *Punch* editor, Burnand, who in 1855 had founded the Cambridge University Amateur Dramatic Club (the A.D.C.) and had participated in its productions when he was a student at the university (Burnand 1880). His Cambridge connection was maintained when Footlights, the Cambridge theatre company founded in 1885, produced his *Cox and Box* in 1889 and his *Alonzo the Brave: Or Faust and the Fair Imogen* in 1891. Several Shakespeare productions at Oxford and Cambridge were among those referred to in *Punch,* and on one occasion the magazine included a review of *The Comedy of Errors* at Gray's Inn (109:289). In 1886, for example, the Cambridge A.D.C. put on *Henry IV* (whether Part I or II is not specified). A small article by Burnand in *Punch* on 4 December reported on its success and noted that the A.D.C. had imported some actors who were now alumni. The article, no doubt drawing upon Burnand's memories, also noted that thirty years earlier, actors had also been brought in from Oxford University (91:266).

Earlier in 1886, 'J. Penn Nibbs' had described a visit to Oxford on the occasion of the opening of the New Theatre and a performance of *Twelfth Night* by the Oxford University Dramatic Society (90:100–101). 'Nibbs' (here the fictional name for Burnand) explains that he had been given two tickets, so he took with him one of the *Punch* artists, the Irish-born Squib (the fictional name in this instance for Harry Furniss). That extra ticket allowed the review to be accompanied by several engravings designed by Furniss, though only one depicts the actual performance of the play in the form of a portrait of a Mr. Bourchier as Feste. In the review, Burnand reminisces about the Cambridge A.D.C. when he was an undergraduate, noting that at that time no women were permitted on the A.D.C. stage and Oxford students were forbidden even to form a drama society. Much had changed, and now Oxford's production can even draw upon the acting skills of women from Girton College. The review itself does not say a great deal, but the undergraduates are congratulated on their dramatic achievement. Burnand does, however, suggest that there was an element of burlesque woven into the production, particularly around the figure of Malvolio, who, we are told, 'gave an entertainment consisting of exceedingly clever imitations of IRVING, TERRY, ARTHUR CECIL and GEORGE GROSSMITH, which we all recognized in detail'. He also cannot resist jokingly pointing out that

Disraeli's nephew had a small part as an Illyrian Sheriff's Officer (90:101).

A later production of *King John* at Oxford also included a student with an illustrious relative, in this instance Henry Irving's son, also named Henry. The young man had had a troubled relationship with his father, one that was threatened even more when he insisted against the elder Irving's advice that he wanted to go on the stage. As a compromise, he had agreed to put his acting ambitions on hold and attend university (he went up to New College, Oxford). Evidently, once there, he could not resist the chance to act. Among the roles he undertook were Decius Brutus in *Julius Caesar* and the title role in *King John*. Rudolph Chambers Lehman reviewed this latter for *Punch* very positively on 21 February 1891 and noted that the older Irving had lent the chain mail and tapestries for the production and that the younger Irving did a very creditable job as King John. For this occasion, there appears to have been no second ticket made available, so none of the *Punch* artists was present to record the event.

Two years later, Lehmann also reviewed the Oxford University Dramatic Society's production of *The Two Gentlemen of Verona*, noting (as he had in the review of *King John*) that the Society was permitted by the university authorities to act only 'legitimate' drama. Shakespeare, presumably, was acceptable, but the burlesques so favoured at Cambridge were not. The point is underlined in John Priestman Atkinson's accompanying design that shows an Oxford don (he looks suspiciously like Mr. Punch) admonishing a young student, the accompanying caption being 'Teaching him his A. D. C.' However, as *Punch* had noted before, there was another difference between the Oxford and Cambridge productions: 'The Ladies here are real Ladies, not stuffed imitations, as at Cambridge' (104:77).

Notices and Reviews: the Elizabethan Stage Society

Quite different from the elaborate scenic ventures that characterized the Shakespeare productions of managers like Charles Kean, Henry Irving, and Herbert Beerbohm Tree, were productions that attempted to present Shakespeare in conditions that resembled the Elizabethan theatre. Where F. J. Furnivall, founder of the New Shakspere Society in 1873, had supervised the publication of photolithographic facsimiles of the Shakespeare quartos, William Poel, founder of the Elizabethan Stage Society in 1895, led a movement that sought to return the performance of Shakespeare's plays to something approximating Elizabethan stage conditions. The two forms of scholarly exploration converged on 16 April 1881 when Poel produced what was to be the first of a number of Shakespeare revivals, a *Hamlet* that employed the First Quarto text, copies of which were discovered in 1823 and 1856. With a cast of amateur actors, the production employed a platform stage in St. George's Hall in London that eliminated the kind of scenic effects and breaks between scenes that had become expected features in the commercial theatre. Though *Punch* did not send a reviewer to the performance, the event did not by any means go unnoticed. On 31 April appeared a short article entitled 'SHAKSPEARE AMENDED' by Edwin James Milliken (80:196). This records that 'MR. FURNIVALL is of opinion that the text of *Hamlet* known to commentators as "The First Quarto" furnishes a far better and more compact acting play than the modern stage-version. He, and "a strong body of amateurs", essayed, on the afternoon of Saturday, the 16th April, at St. George's Hall, to convert the public and the critics to their view of the case, – apparently with indifferent success.' The article then refers to a version of the 'To be, or not to be' soliloquy that Furnivall has sent to the *Daily News*. This opens the way for Milliken to offer his own burlesque version that wonders, among various other things, 'Who'd bear ... / Crass commentaries on Shakspearian quartos, / And all earth's ills, from FURNIVALL to toothache.'

The 1881 *Hamlet* was the first of some ten Shakespeare productions by Poel for which he was responsible up to 1901 (more followed in the thirty years after that). However, so far as I am aware, the only other Elizabethan Stage Society performance of Shakespeare that *Punch* ever mentions prior to 1902 is that of *The Two Gentlemen of Verona* at the Merchant Taylors' Hall on 28 November 1896. Accompanying the announcement of this event was an engraving designed by Archibald Chasemore (111:241). Entitled 'THE DRAMA IN THE DAYS OF ELIZABETH' and with the caption 'GRAND

SPECTACULAR SCENE FROM HENRY THE FIFTH. RETURN OF THE VICTORIOUS ARMY FROM AGINCOURT. SHAKSPEARE THEN COULD NOT VERY WELL "SPELL RUIN"', the engraving lightly mocks the goals of the Elizabethan Stage Society by depicting a scene from *Henry V* that employs the minimum of resources. The engraving takes its cue from the Chorus of *Henry V*, who tells the audience to apply the power of its 'imaginary forces' in order to 'Piece out [...] imperfections'. One man seen on stage must be imagined to be a thousand men, and if horses are mentioned, the audience must imagine them. To show this notion in action, Chasemore offers *Punch* readers his version of how the spectacular return of Henry V and his army might have been staged. Ironically, this is only described in Shakespeare's original (Chorus to Act V, 22–35). However, most notably in Charles Kean's production of 1859, which employed hundreds of extras and mounted Henry on a horse, and in George Rignold's lavish production at Drury Lane in 1878, the entry into London established itself as a spectacular and memorable set-piece and one of the highlights of both productions. Chasemore's engraving, however, shows a small, completely bare platform stage. At the rear is a blank wall. In place of any kind of scenic extravaganza in the Kean or Irving mould, there is a large sign attached to the wall: 'A STREET IN LONDON CITTIE'. There are three men on the stage. At the centre stands King Henry V. Behind him stands a soldier with a sign attached to his helmet: 'YE ENGLISH ARMY'. The third man at right waves his hat in the air to welcome Henry. Around his neck is yet another sign: 'THIS IS A CROUD'.

Notices and Revues: Foreign Visitors

During the latter half of the nineteenth century, London theatre-goers were regularly able to attend performances of Shakespeare given by visiting actors from Europe or the United States. In 1848, for example, the French actors of the Théâtre Historique performed at Drury Lane, an event that inspired an engraving in *Punch* that depicted Shakespeare imploring Mr. Punch to 'SAVE ME FROM SUCH FRIENDS,' the 'friends' in this instance being the angry and riotous audience at Drury Lane that expressed severe displeasure with the French venture (14:260). Then, in June 1852, a German company performed at the St. James's Theatre, alternating nightly with a French company starring the famous Rachel. It was during this season that Emil Devrient performed his Hamlet (in German), to be followed by a succession of other Hamlets, among them Tommaso Salvini (in Italian in 1875), Ernesto Rossi (in Italian in 1876), and Sarah Bernhardt (in French in 1899). Salvini also performed Othello in 1875, and in 1884 he returned to London and gave performances as Othello, King Lear, and Macbeth. Rossi also made a return visit and played King Lear at Drury Lane in June 1882.

In 1857, the celebrated Adelaide Ristori captivated London with her Lady Macbeth (a role that would be played in London by Sarah Bernhardt two years later), and in 1863, *Punch* called her 'the greatest of living actresses'. Lamenting that this 'bright southern star will be visible for a few nights only', *Punch* then stated that there are no 'words of sufficient strength to express his admiration of ADELAIDE RISTORI, or his compassion for the unhappy person who does not go and behold one or two of her performances' (44:261). However, on a much later return visit in 1882, she was, according to *Punch*, in a review by Burnand, a mere shadow of her former self (83:13). There were also a number of visiting Juliets, among them Stella Colas at the Princess's in 1863–64, and Helena Modjeska in 1881.

Edwin Booth's visits from America and the performances of the Frenchman Charles Fechter have already been mentioned earlier. To these examples can be added the visits of the Comédie-Française in 1879 (the company included Jean Mounet-Sully and Sarah Bernhardt), the Duke of Saxe-Meiningen's Company in 1881, the American Augustin Daly's company in 1888 and the years after, leading up to the opening of Daly's Theatre in Cranbourne Street, Leicester Square, in June 1893, and the visit of Sarah Bernhardt and her company to perform *Hamlet* at the Adelphi Theatre in 1899. To many of these visitors *Punch* responded positively, although the magazine never lost sight of the irony involved in presenting Shakespeare to English audiences in foreign translations. An engraving designed by Charles Keene for the 1883 *Almanack* (dated 7 December 1882), for example, forcibly expresses this point (Figure 35). Entitled 'THE BRITISH

DRAMA, 1883', it depicts a crowd of people at the entrance to a theatre. Many are looking at a poster advertising a performance of *Macbeth*. The cast list of the play shows that each major character is played by a non-English actor from Paris, Berlin, Rome, and Madrid respectively. They are joined by Mr. Epaminondas Twang of New York. At the centre of the crowd, a man is selling dictionaries. The

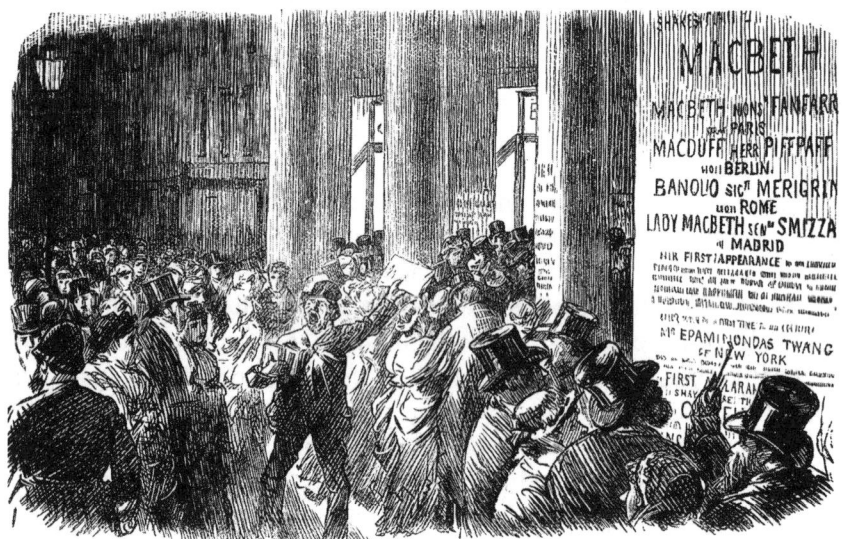

Figure 35. Charles Keene, 'THE BRITISH DRAMA, 1883'. *Punch Almanack* (7 December 1882), 84:n.p.

caption below states: 'ERE Y'ARE, GENTS! BILL O' THE PLAY AN' DIXH'NARY IN SIX LANGUAGES!' (*Almanack*, n.p.).

Three examples of *Punch* responses to the stream of foreign productions of Shakespeare – Salvini's 1875 *Othello* and *Hamlet*, the Duke of Saxe-Meiningen Company's 1881 *Julius Caesar* and *The Winter's Tale*, and Sarah Bernhardt's 1899 *Hamlet* – will suffice in what follows here to demonstrate the importance the magazine attached to what 'outsiders' might have to reveal concerning England's national poet.

When Tommaso Salvini presented a series of Shakespeare performances at Drury Lane in the Spring of 1875, he caused something of a sensation. His fiery Othello was especially praised. Tom Taylor reviewed it for *Punch* in the issue of 24 April and suggested that no actor since Macready had done so well in the role. Only the 'overvehemence' of the final scene received any negative comment. As far as Taylor was concerned, that Salvini delivered his lines in Italian was of no account: 'It is of secondary importance whether or not those who hear SALVINI understand Italian. They are sure to know the text of *Othello*; and SALVINI'S look, tone, and gesture speak the universal language' (68:181). Referring to a special performance that Salvini gave on a Monday morning so that other actors would be free to see it, Taylor suggested that those who attended would have seen

> a great artist, in the ideal sense of the word – one whose art 'in the very storm and whirlwind of his passion, can beget a temperance that gives it smoothness'; whose voice keeps its music even in rage or agony, and whose action can be graceful, even in its moments of utmost vehemence; and this without forfeiture of force, or sacrifice of truth.

There is more in this vein, and it is clear that the *Punch* reviewer was as excited by Salvini's work as everyone else.

That excitement also pervades Taylor's review of Salvini's *Hamlet*. Although he attempts to argue that the Latin Salvini cannot ever hope to capture the full Nordic nature of Hamlet, this all-too-familiar thesis about the differences between northern and southern temperaments is soon discarded. Also soon forgotten is the initial shock of the reviewer in discovering that Salvini had cut the opening Ghost scene, the entry of the Players and the recitation from their play, Hamlet's advice to the Player, the recorders episode, and the Second Gravedigger. Also a shock, it is claimed, is that Salvini's Hamlet has a heavy black moustache, which makes him 'almost as startling a *Hamlet* as FECHTER'S in a flaxen wig' (68:255). Those who see Salvini's Hamlet, Taylor says, will nonetheless be amazed: 'what consummate mastery of action, tone, and stage resource; what skill in finding visible means to indicate the Actor's currents of thought and changes of mood by gesture and "business"'. He then gives a number of examples of Salvini's effective stage business, including 'his manner of watching the *King* during the Play from behind his manuscript', his wild tossing of its loose leaves in the air, when his Uncle's 'occulted guilt' has 'unkennelled' itself. Actors who see the performance will likely imitate some of Salvini's stage business, Taylor suggests, but more important would be a different kind of benefit: 'If, with the Italian Actor's "business", they can carry away something of his distinction, grace of movement and gesture, measured and musical elocution, and finished art, it will be well for our Stage.' Praise from *Punch*, unlarded with burlesque or humour, does not come much stronger than this.

Six years later in the 11 June 1881 issue, *Punch* reviewed the Duke of Saxe-Meiningen Company's production of *Julius Caesar* at Drury Lane. The reviewer (Burnand) considered the *mise-en-scène* to be 'very nearly perfect', marred only by two interior scenes: the representation of Caesar's house in II ii and Brutus's tent in IV iii. This would have been suitable for toy theatre, but for the professional stage they would not do. What drew special praise, on the other hand, were the crowd scenes, something upon which the company prided itself (see also the *Telegraph* on 31 May and the *Athenaeum* on 4 June, quoted Odell 1920, II 424–5). The assassination scene is described as 'very impressive', and we are told that 'the effect in the celebrated funeral-oration situation was really thrilling' (80:268).

Irving apparently was to learn much from the German company's handling of such scenes (Odell 1920, II:377, 426), so Burnand's comment is of some interest. However, the lukewarm praise of the actors who played Julius Caesar, Antony, and Cassius tells us very little, and Burnand's review then degenerates into jests about Caesar's brightly-coloured nightgown and the crown of golden laurel leaves he appears to have been wearing in bed ('Hasn't the Bard expressly said, "Uneasy lies the head that wears a crown"?'). Burnand was also amused by the fact that no one at Drury Lane had any idea as to the identity of the small man in modern dress who somewhat resembled Shakespeare and was brought on to the stage at the conclusion of the play.

Everyone, however, applauded wildly, some of the less educated in the audience having indeed called for the author.

The joke about the man in modern dress is given particular prominence by one of two accompanying designs by Edward J. Wheeler. It depicts a very tall man in a toga presenting to the audience the very short Shakespeare look-alike in evening dress, the caption being 'Author! Author!' Wheeler's other engraving depicts Antony's funeral oration. A huge and wild crowd surrounds him, reaching up to the document (Caesar's will) in his hand. In the foreground lies Caesar's body on a bier. It is totally ignored, and no one has noticed that Caesar's hand is raised and points towards Antony and the document. The ambiguous punning caption (doubtless by Burnand) reads: 'The fine bold Roman Hand'.

At the conclusion of the review of *Julius Caesar*, Burnand explains that he has also seen the company's *Twelfth Night*, 'but, as we didn't think anything of it, we shan't say anything about it'. However, *Punch* did have a little to say about the production of *The Winter's Tale*, which opened on 13 June and which the magazine reviewed on 25 June. '*A Winter's Tale*', we are told (the *Punch* Ledgers do not name the reviewer), 'showed the Meiningen *troupe* at their united best and their individual worst. The Trial Scene was a masterpiece of military stage-drill, [...]' (80:289). Also praised were the pastoral scenes ('the idyllic portion of the play'): 'there is a babble of green fields, and Strephons and young Chloës, and pipes and tabors, and a smell of sweet hay, syllabubs, and an all-among-the-barley atmosphere, which is refreshing to the thirsty soul on a hot June night in London'. But that is all in the way of positive comments that *Punch* would venture. Two other comments, before *Punch* hastily moves on to review other London theatre offerings, are all that we get. 'Nobody', we are informed, 'acted particularly well', though only the comic figure Autolycus is singled out. He apparently 'was a very heavy personage', and the 'comic business was of the clown and pantaloon order'. As for the wonderful statue scene, the climax of the play, this 'was very tame and commonplace'. Given the glorious summer weather at the time and the attractions of dining out in places like Richmond, Greenwich, Epping Forest, or Hampton Court, *Punch* is led to conclude,

> We'd rather be a Dining 'un,
> Than a Dreary Lane-ing Meiningen.

Nonetheless, as George Odell was anxious to stress in his comments on the Saxe-Meiningen company (Odell 1920, 423–426), and reviewers other than *Punch* confirmed, the visitors from Germany left a strong and lasting impression on account of their ensemble work and the power of their crowd scenes, nothing approaching which had ever been seen before on the English stage. In addition, along with the example of the Comédie-Française who visited London in 1879, the Duke of Saxe-Meiningen's theatre company demonstrated ways of organizing a 'national' troupe, one that had the potential to earn theatre the status of a valued cultural institution (Jackson 1989, 240). It was Irving at the Lyceum who did most to achieve this. He earned a knighthood for his pains, but directly or indirectly he clearly owed much to the royal theatre of Saxe-Meiningen.

A final example of *Punch*'s response to visiting foreign Shakespeare productions is provided by the review of Sarah Bernhardt's *Hamlet*. Bernhardt had performed in England as early as 1879 when, as a member of the Comédie-Française, she had given an extract from Racine's *Phèdre*. The *Punch* reviewer had highly praised her for her 'feverish fire and passionate grace' while noting the perfection of the company's ensemble work (76:273). On 31 May 1884 (86:255), Burnand had commented on the report of the Parisian correspondent of the *Times* regarding Bernhardt's performance as Lady Macbeth at the Porte Saint-Martin theatre (she had left the Comédie-Française in 1880). Whereas the *Times* reviewer sent 'a glowing account,' Burnand's *Punch* article is unpleasantly disparaging, chiefly because of the language issue: 'Who over here at all events wants SHAKSPEARE in French?' Bernhardt, it is recommended, should take English lessons 'and play *Lady Macbeth* in the English as he is spoke'. However, when Bernhardt arrived in England shortly after and performed as Lady Macbeth at Drury Lane, the *Punch* reviewer (one 'Jerrold' and hence probably a son or grandson of Douglas Jerrold), though criticizing the unhistorical scenery and costumes, appears in a back-handed way to have been genuinely appreciative of Bernhardt's acting talents (86:270).

By 1899, Bernhardt was a familiar figure internationally, and she was idolized like a modern movie star. She had appeared in London almost every year since 1879 and would continue to do so until her death in 1923 (Taranow 1996, 53). Her decision to play Hamlet in 1899 at her own recently acquired theatre in Paris, as might be expected, was not something that *Punch* could ignore. Here was a woman, performing in French the premier male role among those created by England's national poet. The production at the Théâtre Bernhardt opened on 20 May 1899. When it was known that Bernhardt was shortly going to bring her production to London, *Punch* erupted on 31 May with a mocking preview, commenting on various features of the Paris production. Entitled 'HAMLET FOR LADIES', the article cites 'our trustworthy Paris Correspondent' regarding some of the features of the production that London theatre audiences will soon experience when they see Hamlet played by a woman. In I iv, for example, when Hamlet first sees the Ghost, 'masculine actors have usually spoken in a husky and awe-struck whisper'. However, Bernhardt 'will greet the mysterious phantom with a shrill scream, without which no lady, on the stage, has ever been known to receive a ghost' (116:256). Upon Hamlet's cry about a rat in the Closet Scene ('How now! A rat?'), Bernhardt 'will give a masterly representation of the terror which the presence of a rat or mouse invariably arouses in the breast of a lady on the stage' by 'springing lightly upon a chair and wrapping her cloak tightly about her ankles'.

In similar sexist vein, *Punch* reported that for the 'To be, or not to be' soliloquy, Bernhardt 'will be discovered working at a sampler', and when Hamlet refers to the 'bare bodkin', he 'will seize and brandish this implement, which, as may be supposed, will be lying on an adjoining work-table'. Two pages later appeared Bernard Partridge's design entitled 'GREAT ATTRACTION!' (Figure 34). As already mentioned earlier, this depiction of the 'Get thee to a nunnery' scene (III i) shows Bernhardt in her Hamlet costume, including her blond wig, admonishing a cringing Ophelia, easily recognizable as Irving (116:258). Although the emphasis is mainly upon the transformation of a legendary English Hamlet (Irving) into a frightened female, the engraving is also designed to emphasize in visual terms that *both* characters represented are the result of a gender switch by their respective actors.

When Bernhardt and her company arrived in London in early June to perform their *Hamlet* at the Adelphi Theatre, Burnand attended. Surprisingly, nothing is said in his review about the play being given in a prose French translation (that of Marcel Schwob and Eugène Morand), nor is anything said directly about the gender of the principal actor. Instead, and quite in keeping with its title ('SARAH'S YOUNG MAN'), the somewhat brief, one-column article that appeared on 21 June concentrates entirely upon an issue that engaged many other critics – Hamlet's youthfulness. Fifty-four years old at this time, Bernhardt presented what one American critic was shortly to call 'the most youthful Hamlet of recent years' (Taranow 1996, 104) and what another commentator called a 'spirited boy' (Robbins 1900, 908). Although her text retained the allusion to Yorick's skull having lain in the earth for thirty years (she later changed the number to sixteen), Bernhardt attempted to play Hamlet as though he was a youth of about twenty. This was the cue for *Punch*'s description of her Hamlet 'as a precocious child badly brought up by his injudicious mother' and (in his disrespectful treatment of Polonius) as 'a mischievous, spoilt Prince'. 'All other *Hamlets* – the male *Hamlets, bien entendu* – have been in comparison with "SARAH'S Young Man", eccentric middle-aged youths of from thirty to fifty.' With such a youthful, spoiled character, the business of the Play Scene in Bernhardt's production strikes one as possible, the reviewer says, 'otherwise, in any well-regulated Court, the monkey tricks of even so exalted a personage as the young Crown Prince would meet with severe and immediate rebuke from his mother' (116:289).

Hamlet's age also accounts in Bernhardt's production for what Burnand argues is a departure in the presentation of Ophelia. She is 'a knowing young lady just about a year or so older than *Hamlet*, and a past mistress of arts and crafts, an apt pupil of sly old Father *Polonius*'. Burnand praises Bernhardt's performance: 'With all her *gaminerie*', Bernhardt is 'far nearer the ideal *Hamlet* than any *Hamlet*, including FECHTER'S', that the reviewer has ever seen. He then singles out the manner in which Hamlet becomes more dignified as the play proceeds, so that 'when he is confronted with that egregious ass, *Osric*, he is as serious with *him* as he had been playful with *Polonius*'. Finally, Burnand gives particular praise to the manner in which Bernhardt performed the fencing scene. Her Hamlet 'is a master of the art and her business of whisking *Laertes*' sword out of his hand, and courteously proffering her own for his acceptance is the only rationally practical explanation of the exchange of weapons as devised by SHAKSPEARE. All this is excellent' (116:289). In his enthusiasm, Burnand may not have realized that this piece of stage business went back to the Théâtre Historique production of Alexandre Dumas's text in 1848 and was first introduced to English audiences by Salvini some twenty-four years previously in 1875 (Shakespeare 1999, 271). Today, reaching back over a much longer time span than that, we can still share something of what *Punch* recorded here since a 1900 film of Bernhardt's fencing scene still exists and shows the exchange of weapons just as Burnand described it.

Notices and Reviews: Herbert Beerbohm Tree

During the last decade of the nineteenth century, *Punch* reviewed a number of further Shakespeare productions. In 1890, there were reviews of the performances of Lillie Langtry as Rosalind at the St. James's Theatre and as Cleopatra at the Princess's (98:117, 161; 99:268). These were very positive, for the beautiful Langtry could do no wrong in the eyes of *Punch*. That same year, however, appeared disparaging reviews of F. R. Benson's productions of *The Taming of the Shrew, A Midsummer Night's Dream*, and *Hamlet* at the Globe Theatre. In 1881, Benson had organized a university production of Euripides's *Agamemnon*. After considerable debate among the university authorities, the performance took place. A number of leading London actors attended, including Henry Irving and Ellen Terry. Benson's acting ambitions subsequently received encouragement from Irving, and in 1882, Benson played Paris in Irving's Lyceum production of *Romeo and Juliet* (Irving 1951, 396–400). Then, the following year, he formed his own touring company with his wife as principal female actor. In 1888, Benson assumed the management of the Stratford Festival, and two years later, he brought his company to the Lyceum where he played an uncut version of *Hamlet*, and a succession of other plays. His pioneering efforts resulted in the increased popularity of Shakespeare's plays, but, like the Elizabethan Stage Society, he went against the ingrained taste for scenic spectacle by regularly playing with a minimum of scenery, although that was not the case with his Globe *Midsummer Night's Dream*. During his career, he produced almost all of Shakespeare's plays and served as governor of the Shakespeare Memorial Theatre and as a trustee of the Shakespeare Birthplace. His services to Shakspeareanity were to be considerable, but as the Victorian era drew to an end, *Punch* unaccountably ignored Benson's contribution. The magazine did, however, review George Alexander's 1896 *As You Like It* and his 1898 *Much Ado About Nothing* at the St. James's Theatre, and Johnston Forbes Robertson's 1895 *Romeo and Juliet* at the Lyceum Theatre. On the other hand, it ignored this latter's ground-breaking *Hamlet* in 1897, together with his 1898 *Macbeth*. Instead, *Punch* followed the fortunes of Irving's rival and disciple, Herbert Beerbohm Tree.

It was in January 1889 that Tree introduced the first of his sixteen productions of Shakespeare, the work chosen for this auspicious event being *The Merry Wives of Windsor,* in which he himself played Falstaff. Burnand or possibly Milliken (the Contributors' Ledgers are unclear as to who) attended the production at the Haymarket and on 12 January published a review in *Punch* that was tacked on to the detailed review of Irving's *Macbeth* at the Lyceum Theatre (96:16–17). The review was a mixed one that praised the staging and in very general terms the performances of Kemble as Dr. Caius, Mr. Righton as Sir Hugh Evans, Mr. Vollaire as Justice Shallow, and Mr. Brookfield as Master Slender. Lionel Brough as the Host of the Garter Inn 'is simply inimitable', we are told, and the production is worth seeing for his performance alone, along with that of Rose Leclercq as Margaret Page. Mrs. Tree's playing of Anne Page, however, is criticized as being 'far too melancholy' (96:16). She is more *Ophelia* than *Anne Page*, especially in the last Act, when she enters dressed all in white singing a sad ditty, and might be *Ophelia* on her way to the pond, or *Joan of Arc* going to execution, instead of a sprightly young lady, pretty sly too, about to take part in a merry practical joke, […].

When the reviewer turns his attention to Tree's Falstaff, memories of Mark Lemon's performances in the role inevitably come to mind. The reviewer dismisses Tree's efforts, suggesting that they are less than second rate, chiefly because the thin, adroit, and quiet Tree 'is no more physically fitted for *Falstaff* than he is for *Hercules*, and, keen as may be his perception of the humour of the fat old reprobate, he gives no evidence of it from the first scene to the last of his impersonation' (96:17).

Accompanying this comment is an engraving designed by Edward J. Wheeler that depicts Tree dressed in a beer barrel, his arms out to the side and the caption offering the rather feeble pun – 'The Beer-barrel Tree'. With the question of costume, the reviewer brings his commentary around to *Punch*'s own Falstaff: '[...] why did not he adopt the perfect and picturesque costume designed by JOHN TENNIEL for MARK LEMON when he appeared in the part? As far as appearance went, MARK LEMON was a model *Falstaff*, whereas Mr. TREE'S *Falstaff* looks like an obese, weak-kneed, overgrown Pantaloon.' Even so, Tree's Falstaff appealed to the public, and the role became his most popular part (Pearson 1956, 61). A few years later, Tree played Falstaff again, but this time in a revival of *King Henry IV*, Part I, in May 1896; however, *Punch* did not review this production.

Two years after the production of *The Merry Wives of Windsor*, Tree, who was still at the Haymarket, appeared as Hamlet on 21 January. The previous summer in the issue of 4 July, *Punch* had noted that Tree was to perform *Hamlet* in the provinces, marking the news with a small, unsigned engraving that depicted a tree at the centre of a village. The predicable caption was 'Tree in Hamlet' (101:12). Then, after *Hamlet* had opened, *Punch* included on 13 February an engraving designed by Bernard Partridge. It was entitled '"LOOK HERE, UPON THIS PICTURE AND ON THIS!" *(The Haymarket Hamlet as he is and ought to be.)*' (Figure 36). However, rather than depicting the episode of the two portraits in the Closet Scene, it shows, as was mentioned towards the end of the previous chapter, two Hamlets confronting each other – Beerbohm Tree at left and H. Kemble at right. Each is hatless and dressed in a very short tunic. Tree is tall and thin, and Kemble, a member of the Haymarket company, is short and fat. The caption below reads:

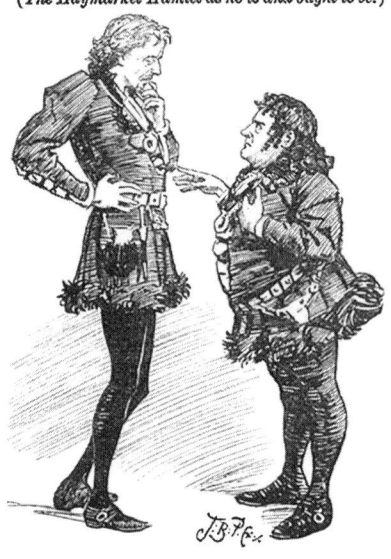

Figure 36. Bernard Partridge's portrait of Beerbohm Tree (left) and H. Kemble (right), both as Hamlet. *Punch* (13 February 1892), 102:73.

Mr. H. Kemble. My dear Tree. I ought to have played *Hamlet*. First my name – Kemble. Secondly, Shakspeare's authority – 'Oh, that this too too solid flesh would melt,' and again, 'Fat and scant of breath!' *Mr. B. Tree.* All right, my dear Kemble. Quite true what you say; and, any night, I am unable to play, you shall be my double! (102:73).

It was not until 16 April, however, that *Punch* reviewed the production. The reviewer, Burnand, who recalls 'the inauguration of startling new departures by CHARLES FECHTER', finds the production thought-provoking, but not always convincing. Of particular interest is his account of several pieces of stage business, chief of which is a pattern that ultimately he finds monotonous. He refers to Ophelia pausing on her exit and coming up quietly behind the absent-minded Prince 'as if to play bo-peep with him' (102:185). Later, after the 'Get thee to a nunnery' scene, Hamlet returns, and, 'while she [Ophelia] is stooping and in tears, he kisses her hair and runs away noiselessly as if this also were another part of the same game'. Later still, after the brawl with Laertes in the graveyard, Hamlet 'returns to weep and throw flowers into the grave'.

Why, Burnand wonders, does not the Second Gravedigger return with the drink he has been sent to get? A more positive response, however, is given to Tree's introduction of a young court jester, the successor to the elder Yorick of Hamlet's youth. Hamlet takes upon himself the task of teaching the jester. However, Hamlet's somewhat smug self-satisfaction in doing this is part of a larger pattern, 'consistent with the character of a Prince who takes upon himself to lecture the Actors on their own art. There is no subtler touch in SHAKSPEARE'S irony than his putting these instructions to players in the mouth of a noble amateur.' Curiously, Burnand refrained from any comparisons between Tree and Irving. As all London theatre-goers were aware, Hamlet had 'belonged' to Irving. Tree's taking on the role was one of a number of challenges he made to Irving's pre-eminence (Irving 1951, 482; Pearson 1956, 58–59), but on this occasion there was no acknowledgement of these matters from *Punch*.

A week later, *Punch* included a brief dramatic anecdote, contributed by Arthur William à Beckett, in which the spirit of Shakespeare and the Ghost of Hamlet's father appear before Beerbohm Tree in response to an announcement in one of the daily papers that due to the continued success of Hamlet, 'it has been decided (by arrangement with the Author)' to postpone another play. Shakespeare, it is revealed, has been to see *Hamlet* and has noted all the new 'business'. It does not trouble him, however, because his 'author's fees' ceased a long time ago (102:201).

A final comment on the production appeared on 7 May in the form of a short dramatic burlesque by one 'Browne' (102:225). Apparently, for the opening scene of *Hamlet*, which takes place at night, Tree turned down the theatre lights. This made matters very difficult for late-comers, who consequently had great difficulty in finding their seats. Irving had developed the practice of darkening the auditorium lights at the Lyceum during scene changes (Booth 1991, 84), which were effected in total darkness on stage by men in black clothing. According to Irving's business manager, Bram Stoker, when Irving developed his complex system of gas-lighting, he was also able to carry out 'a long-thought-of scheme: that the auditorium should be darkened during the play' (Jackson 1989, 189). However, a completely dark auditorium would have been considered socially inappropriate. Besides, it would have prevented patrons from following the action in their printed play scripts, a common practice during performances of Shakespeare. The *Punch* burlesque gently mocks (and probably exaggerates) what Tree did during the opening scene of *Hamlet*. Into the opening lines of the play are threaded various voices from the audience, the whole taking place in darkness. The following extract will suffice to give the sense of this particular reaction to the comparatively novel effect of a darkened theatre:

> HAMLET; OR, KEEPING IT DARK.
> SCENE I. – *At the Haymarket. – Darkness visible. Out of it come Voices.*
> *First Voice (probably on stage): 'Who's there?'*
> *Second V. (Probably in auditorium).* I can't see. Is it TREE?
> *Third V. 'Nay, answer me: stand and unfold yourself.'*
> *Fourth V.* I wish I could unfold the seat to let people pass.
> *Third V. 'You come most carefully upon your hour.'*
> *Fourth V.* Why on earth can't people be more punctual?

Tree reached a milestone in his career in 1897 when he took over the management of Her Majesty's Theatre in the Haymarket. Formerly a home to Italian opera, the theatre was rebuilt in 1897, Tree having invested some £10,000 of his Haymarket Theatre profits into the new venture across the street (Booth 1991, 32). Until his death in 1917, Tree remained at Her Majesty's, producing a series of Shakespeare's plays that rivalled and at times surpassed the visual splendours of Irving's work. Like Irving, however, he was often accused of obscuring Shakespeare with scenic excess (Odell 1920, II:390). His first Shakespeare production in his new theatre was a revival of *Julius Caesar* on 22 January 1898. A week later, *Punch* included a small item contributed by Arthur William à Beckett and entitled 'AN APPEAL TO CAESAR'. This consisted of a supposed letter from a young schoolboy. In it, the young student alludes to Tree's revival of *Julius Caesar* and to material on the play written by Tree, presumably for the program. Of particular concern was some biographical information concerning the play's title character. It seems that the Julius Caesar described by Tree did not match the man familiar to the young scholar, who had hitherto understood only that Caesar came to Britain in B.C. 55 'to eat oysters and to write a book to worry the lives out of the lower school' (114:48).

Regardless of the complaints of the fourth former, Smith Minor, that he hated having his 'fixed ideas shaken' by the learned Mr. Tree, *Punch* did not follow up with a review, even though Tree's production was a success and ran for over a hundred performances. With scenery and costumes designed by Sir Lawrence Alma Tadema, there was general agreement that no play of Shakespeare's had been mounted with such spectacular scenic effect and no crowd scene had been so effective as that in Tree's Forum scene. Even the much-praised production of the Saxe-Meiningen Company, for those who had seen it in 1881, was no match for Tree's. But *Punch* had nothing to say on this, possibly, one suspects, out of some kind of loyalty to Irving, who seems to have been particularly sensitive concerning Tree's rise to prominence as actor-manager at the very time when his fortunes at the Lyceum were beginning to fade. Nor did *Punch* trouble to send a reviewer to Her Majesty's in September 1899 for Tree's revival of *King John*. In January 1900, *A Midsummer Night's Dream* was also ignored. Later that year, when Tree put on both *Julius Caesar* and *Othello*, acknowledgment of Tree's work was restricted to a small notice entitled 'HER MAJESTY'S' in the issue for 1 August: 'In spite of Hamlet's having said "Great CAESAR dead and turned to clay", Mr. BEERBOHM TREE is going to revive him in the autumn. He has also taken Mr. SHAKESPEARE'S Moor for the grouse season and hopes to make some fine bags. We trust these bags will […] fill his treasury […]' (119:82).

A year later at what was now His Majesty's Theatre, Tree had a great success with a production of *Twelfth Night*, in which he played Malvolio. In a small article in *Punch* discussing the souvenir program that was issued for this play (3 April), Burnand noted that Tree's 'impersonation of *Malvolio* is a masterpiece of comicality' and reported that Maud Jeffries's Olivia had vastly improved since the opening night (120:258). The production, which had been playing to full houses, looked like having a long run, Burnand suggested. Of the souvenir program, Burnand remarked that it is 'very cleverly drawn by CHAS. BUCHEL and reproduced in colour by HENTSCHEL LTD,' and that it included likenesses of each of the actors and actresses in their respective dramatic characters, making it an attraction that warrants a re-visit to Her Majesty's.

Three weeks later, there appeared an article by Henry W. Lucy in the weekly 'ESSENCE OF PARLIAMENT. EXTRACTED FROM THE DIARY OF TOBY, M.P.'. In it, attention is focused on the passing of the budget, but there is also an engraving by Edward Tennyson Reed depicting the Chancellor of the Exchequer, Sir Michael Hicks Beach, as Malvolio. The engraving parodies Buchel's picture of Tree, a point noted in the caption, and the politician is given the following line from *Twelfth Night*: 'I SAY THIS HOUSE IS AS DARK AS IGNORANCE; … AND I SAY THERE NEVER WAS A MAN THUS ABUSED!' The title of the supposed play in which 'Sir Malvolio Hicks Beach' appears is a parody of that of *Twelfth Night; Or, What You Will*. Here it is given as *Budget Night; Or, Whether You Like It Or Not!!* This section of the article is dated Thursday, 18 April, but a further diary entry by Toby then follows. This records that the next night (Friday), affairs at Westminster were very dull, so he went to His Majesty's Theatre to see *Twelfth Night*. Then follows a review of Tree's production. One detail of stage business particularly caught Lucy's attention:

> when the clown [i.e. Feste] is prominently to the front in conversation with *Olivia*, the way the fussy, vain, pompous steward, touches him with his wand of office, in indescribable manner indicating possession and authority over some meaner thing, is a rarely devised bit of bye-play.

Of the performance as a whole, Lucy was very positive, noting that Tree's *Twelfth Night* is 'a peerless comedy, delightfully played' (120:315). After praising various of the principal actors, he then singled out Tree's Malvolio: 'BEERBOHM TREE crowns the success of his staging, the triumph of his getting together such a company, by his rendering of *Malvolio*.' Tree, it would seem, was finally receiving proper notice from *Punch*.

* * *

By the time Tree produced *Twelfth Night*, Queen Victoria was already dead and her theatre-loving son had succeeded her. During that part of her reign following the birth of *Punch*, English theatre had undergone extraordinary changes, and, partly as a result of the efforts of a succession of talented actor-managers, the performance of Shakespeare's plays had achieved great success and popularity, in spite of a popular saying among theatre managers that Shakespeare spelled death at the box office. As we have seen, the pages of *Punch*, particularly its theatre reviews, provide a chart, though not always a complete one and not always an unbiased one, of much of this theatrical activity. The early volumes of *Punch* allow one to witness the attempts of Macready to establish serious drama and create something akin to a national theatre where the plays of Shakespeare would have a central and lasting place. That dream was never fulfilled, but others, in their own different ways took up the cause, among them Samuel Phelps, Charles Kean, Henry Irving, F. R. Benson, and Herbert Beerbohm Tree, this last going on to produce a further nine major Shakespeare productions in the early years of the new century.

Chapter Four

Punch and Shakespeare Transposed

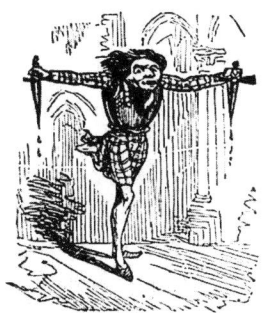

Throughout the Victorian era, as we have just seen, *Punch* writers and artists provided readers with a lively, ongoing commentary upon major Shakespeare productions, the performances of prominent Shakespearean actors, and the attempts by a number of actor-managers to create something akin to a national theatre where Shakespeare's plays would have a permanent home. The commentary in *Punch* on these matters would presumably have been viewed by the magazine as a serious contribution (however comic the format) to Shakspeareanity. However, when Shakespeare's works were appropriated by artists working in other theatrical media – the opera, the ballet, the hippodrama – *Punch* faced a challenge. Were such transformations of Shakespeare to be scoffed at and condemned as base perversions, or were they to be seen as part of the natural evolution of Shakspeareanity and hence to be accepted with good grace? And what of the work of graphic artists who often based drawings, paintings, and sculptures upon characters or situations in Shakespeare's plays? The annual Royal Academy exhibitions displayed many of these works, which were often submitted by leading national artists. Were these works to be made the butt for comedy, or were they to be seen as serious contributions to the ever-growing awareness and appreciation of Shakespeare?

Finally, there is the whole question of burlesque, a highly popular and highly developed form of Victorian entertainment. *Punch* repeatedly burlesqued lines, scenes, and even entire plays by Shakespeare. Like many other transformations of Shakespeare, this form of humour required readers to be familiar with Shakespeare's original texts, characters, and plot situations if the burlesques were to be effective. This process, it may be argued, enhanced Shakspeareanity by indirectly reinforcing and at times expanding readers' familiarity with Shakespeare's works.

Opera

As we saw in Chapter Two, *Punch* early on took aim at opera (see also Altick 1997, 690–709). In this, British chauvinism was an easy ally. Here was an art form, generally the work of foreign composers and librettists, usually presented in a foreign language (chiefly Italian or French), and employing most of its lead singers from Italy. Opera was also open to attack because of its frequently elaborate and near incomprehensible plots. Indeed, between 1842 and 1844, *Punch* capitalized on this by creating an entire series of comic burlesques of the plots of operas by such composers as Bellini, Donizetti, Pacini, and Rossini (2:34–35; 4:165, 175, 185; 5:25, 41–42, 217–218, 255; 6:145, 149, 165; 12:96). However, what especially troubled *Punch* in the 1840s, when Jerrold first began to talk about the sorry state of Shakspeareanity, was the apparent popular preference for opera over serious national drama, and in particular that of Shakespeare.

As was noted in Chapter Two, the situation was made worse by two matters that *Punch* found particularly irksome. First, there was the evident favour displayed by Queen Victoria and Prince Albert toward opera. In 1844, in Thackeray's 'GREAT NEWS! WONDERFUL NEWS!' the Queen is accused of having loved 'the Opera best' (6:189), while Prince Albert is said by Jerrold in 'DIFFUSION OF SHAKSPEAREANITY AT COURT' to have been a worshipper of 'the idols of the Opera' (6:199). A few years later, Thackeray was still following the same theme with regard to the Prince, ironically suggesting that, whereas the Prince was very familiar with Her Majesty's Theatre, the opera house in the Haymarket, perhaps he should cross the street and see a Shakespeare production by Benjamin Webster at the Haymarket Theatre:

> I was almost afraid that you did not care about your SHAKSPEARE; because you never, or scarcely ever, went to see him. I now look forward to the pleasure of hearing that you have called upon him at an early opportunity, which I dare say will be afforded you at MR. WEBSTER'S in the Haymarket. You know where it is, for you very often look in on the other side of the way. (13:52)

According to an item by Jerrold in *Punch* in 1847, so ingrained was Queen Victoria's and Prince Albert's love of opera over any interest in serious drama that none of the horses in the royal stables appeared to have been 'manageable one step beyond the Italian Opera'. Furthermore, there was not a single 'Royal horse that does not shy at an English play-bill' (13:141). In 1848, however, the Queen and the Prince pointedly ceased going to operas. As we have already seen, this was in response to growing political unrest and revolutionary threats, and following severe criticism of the royal family for exclusively favouring foreign entertainments. In a dramatic about face, Queen Victoria now became a regular patron of the theatre, attending benefit performances for the Keans and Macready, establishing theatricals at Windsor (see Chapter Three), and, through repeated visits to the theatre, helping to build a solid and faithful audience representative of all social classes (Schoch 1998, 127–134).

The second aspect concerning opera that particularly irked *Punch* in its early years was, as has also been discussed in Chapter Two, the disappearance of Shakespeare from the former two major patent theatres, Drury Lane and Covent Garden. This occurred as a direct result of the 1843 Theatre Regulation Act. No longer the exclusive home of the 'legitimate' drama, these two theatres could now attempt to cash in on the potentially more lucrative types of entertainment that had previously been so popular at some of the non patent theatres. At Drury Lane, as we have seen, the new manager, Alfred Bunn, opened the doors to a variety of popular fare, including opera. This enraged *Punch* and Douglas Jerrold in particular, especially since Bunn, as if to add insult to injury, himself wrote libretti for a number of Michael William Balfe's operas, including the very successful *The Bohemian Girl* in 1843, *The Daughter of St. Mark* (1844), and *The Enchantress* (1845). Increasingly, Covent Garden also provided a home to opera, and in 1847, the theatre officially became the Royal Italian Opera House, though, despite its new name, it shortly began to add French operas to its predominantly Italian repertoire. Soon, and perhaps to the chagrin of Jerrold, the Royal Italian Opera House developed a reputation as one of the finest opera houses in Europe.

Elsewhere, opera at Her Majesty's Theatre in the Haymarket under the management of Benjamin Lumley attracted a faithful clientele that included the aristocracy and well-to-do who could afford the relatively high ticket prices. If only, *Punch* (Percival Leigh) mused in 1844, that same clientele could be persuaded to attend performances of Shakespeare and pay for the privilege. Perhaps Samuel Phelps and Mary Warner, whose prices at Sadler's Wells were very affordable, should take Her Majesty's on off nights and 'charge opera prices for admission. The ladies will all rush to hear *dear* SHAKSPEARE; and, of course, the gentlemen will follow them. […] if the house is not nightly crowded by Rank, Fashion, and Beauty, to his realisation of a fortune by the end of the season,' *Punch* will 'not say that he will not shut up his Office' (7:32). *Punch*'s (Leigh's) suggestion was, as might be expected, not taken up by the enterprising Shakespeareans at Sadler's Wells, while opera continued its popularity.

The popularity of opera received an enormous boost when, as mentioned in Chapter Two, Jenny Lind broke her contract with Bunn and made her 1847 London debut at Her Majesty's in Meyerbeer's *Robert le diable*. Lumley suddenly found himself with an unprecedented success on his hands, one which even *Punch* applauded. Lind fever then gripped London and the provinces for two years until to the dismay of English opera-goers in general and Benjamin Lumley in particular, the 'Swedish Nightingale', as she became known, decided to cease acting (30:42). She declared that she would sing only in concerts and oratorios. Later, she left for America following her final concert on 30 June 1856 (30:234). Even so, the English thirst for opera would not dry up, and Lumley was fortunate in finding a superb replacement for Lind in Henrietta Sontag (Countess Rossi), who opened on 7 July in Donizetti's *Linda di Chamonix* and by the end of the 1849 season had come close to assuaging the grief at Lind's sudden departure. By this date, there were four London opera houses in competition with each other – German at Drury Lane, French at the St.

James's Theatre, and Italian (and some French) at both Her Majesty's and Covent Garden. London could justly claim to be one of the great European centres for opera. No doubt, the champions of Shakspeareanity at *Punch* were fully aware of this, but they would not be silenced or abandon their cause of promoting the national drama and England's national poet.

Then, in 1850, there appeared a quite unexpected challenge related to *Punch*'s fear that opera (along with other types of theatrical entertainment) might threaten the legitimate drama and the production of Shakespeare's plays in particular. On 8 June, a new opera, *La tempesta*, written for Her Majesty's, opened with a stellar cast of performers, who included Luigi Lablache and Henrietta Sontag. What was especially significant about the new opera was that it was based on a Shakespeare play – *The Tempest*. Now, for the first time in *Punch*'s as yet brief history, the London opera had appropriated a work of Shakespeare. What is more, the libretto for the opera had been written by Eugène Scribe, a leading French playwright and highly experienced librettist, who had worked with many of the major opera composers of the day, a writer the *Times* referred to as 'the first living dramatist of Europe' (10 June 1850, p. 5).

Scribe's original libretto was in French, but it had then been translated into Italian by Signor Giannone. The composer of the opera was Jacques-François Fromental Halévy. Along with such composers as Rossini, Donizetti, and Meyerbeer, who had taken up residence in Paris to compose for the French theatres, Halévy, together with his compatriot Daniel Auber, was considered at the time to be an operatic composer of considerable stature, although today he is largely remembered only for his *La juive* (another collaboration with Scribe). *La juive* coincidentally received its London debut at Covent Garden the same year as *La tempesta* was performed at Her Majesty's, and by another coincidence Halévy's *Le val d'Andorre* had opened earlier in the year at the St. James's Theatre. There was also a performance of one of Halévy's works as the Princess's (*Times*, 10 June 1850, p. 5). In London, it would seem, Halévy was very much in favour.

Reviews of *La tempesta* were highly positive. The *Daily News*, for example, commented:

we have no hesitation in thinking that *La tempesta* will be regarded as the 'chef d'oeuvre' of its celebrated author. It's the work of a poet as well as a musician, like all Halévy's work it is profound in thought and masterly in construction, while it is bold, free, imaginative and dramatic, with a great deal of expressive melody, set off by the most varied and elegant instrumentation. (Quoted Lablache 1999, n.p.).

Equally appreciative was the *Illustrated London News*: 'Such a truly artistic work has seldom been seen on any stage; it is full of charming contrasts, employs every resource of modern art, and is free from all that is meretricious, glaring and noisy' (quoted Lablache 1999). The *Times*, which had earlier given its readers a biography of Halévy, in which it talked about the high reputation he had in Europe and England (25 May 1850, p. 8), ranked *La tempesta* as 'higher than any previous effort of the composer and gave the opera a very detailed and laudatory review (10 June 1850, p. 5). Accounting in part for the popular success of the work was not only the high standard of the singing, with Sontag as Miranda and Lablache as Caliban, and the fine orchestral playing under Michael Balfe, but the dancing of the great ballerina, Carlotta Grisi. She had been a regular visitor to London since 1842 and had become a popular success at Her Majesty's. Today, she is chiefly remembered as the original Giselle in the ballet created for her by Adolphe Charles Adam (the composer), Théophile Gautier (the poet), and Vernoy de Saint-Georges (the dramatist). In *La tempesta*, she played Ariel, a role that permitted her to exploit her talents to the full. In addition to its star cast, the opera also contained some striking scenic effects. These included the dramatic arrival of a ship that coincided with the conclusion of the opera.

But what was *Punch*'s reaction to this apparently highly acclaimed re-working of Shakespeare's play? Unfortunately, one looks in vain for a review. Perhaps *Punch* missed the production, which only had six performances due to Grisi having to leave for Russia where she would begin a new dancing career. However, four items among the June and July issues of *Punch* did offer some comment. The first, which was contributed by Percival Leigh and which appeared in the issue of 15 June, is entitled 'SCRIBE *v.* SHAKSPEARE' (18:235). In it, only the librettist of *La tempesta* is referred to, and the work in question is misleadingly alluded to as a 'burlesque of the *Tempest*'. Leigh cites a report in the *Times* concerning a pamphlet, in which it was supposedly the author's object 'To show that SHAKSPEARE, if he had lived at the present day, would probably have made the *Tempest* an Opera, rather than a spoken drama, and that, therefore, M. SCRIBE is carrying out the English poet's intention.' Though this was a mode of argument often employed to defend the elaborate scenic spectacles employed in a number of Victorian productions of Shakespeare (i.e. Shakespeare would have employed nineteenth-century scenic resources had they been available to him), no such idea is here acceptable to *Punch*. That Shakespeare's 'thoughts, conceptions, and images' should be 'spun out into trills and quavers' is absurd, says Leigh:

> Or, the idea of SHAKSPEARE turning his drama into an opera, with all these his peculiar beauties omitted! The idea that SHAKSPEARE would not have left such a work to M. SCRIBE, unless he could have got an injunction against him to hinder it! The idea of comparing SHAKSPEARE with SCRIBE! And, lastly, the idea of saddling all these absurdities on a certain unfortunate individual, by name.

Leigh then concludes by suggesting that what has happened has a precedent in Shakespeare's *A Midsummer Night's Dream*, in which Puck confers a reward on Bottom. As *Punch*'s readers would recall, that 'reward' was an ass's head. This is not specifically mentioned here in the conclusion of the article, where it is explained that a 'similar trick must have been played on the author [i.e. Scribe], to whom his friends may exclaim, in the words of *Quince*: "Bless thee, BOTTOM! bless thee! thou are translated."' The gist of *Punch*'s opinion is none the less clear: the Scribe-Halévy venture is asinine.

The next week, *Punch* included another short article, this one by Jerrold, attacking Scribe (18:244). Again, Halévy was not mentioned. Was it that *Punch* chiefly objected to the re-working of Shakespeare's text rather than the musical setting of that text? Jerrold now attacked Scribe's libretto by comically comparing him to the famous French cook, Alexis Soyer, the renowned chef at the Reform Club and author of a best-selling book entitled *Gastronomic Regenerator* (1846), a work intended for the kitchens of the wealthy and by 1850 already in its seventh edition. Scribe, we are told, 'threatens to oust M. SOYER, and to surmount the laurels of the original dramatist with the paper-cap of the cook'. *La tempesta* is referred to as Scribe's 'first dish to an English audience'. That dish, Jerrold notes, has been

> relished with such delight, press scribes – their ink-bottles foaming with champagne – having declared the fricassee of wondrous spiciness and flavour, and fast men having smacked their mouths, and yelled their applauses of the treat, the new French Opera Cook, in the depths of his gratitude, is about to publish the recipe by which he has been able to lay before a thoughtful, SHAKSPEARE-loving audience, the savoury mess.

The recipe then follows and is entitled 'HOW TO COOK A SWAN (OF AVON)'. The swan (i.e. Shakespeare) must first be cut into pieces and the heart and brains thrown away. The pieces of the swan are then to be placed in a kettle over a fire that can be fanned with the poem *Venus and Adonis*. The contents of the kettle may be stirred with the toe of Mlle Grisi, the heat of the fire can be increased by using Lablache as bellows, and when cooling is required, a song by Sontag can be used as cold champagne. The recipe continues in the same vein until the final instruction: 'Serve hot to an enlightened public, who will be frantic with delight that a French cook should have made so admirable a *fricassée* of their adored Swan of Avon.' To this, Jerrold then adds an admonition that makes clear the magazine's view that Scribe should stick to writing plays of his own: 'Further, *Mr. Punch* may be allowed to advise M. SCRIBE, who can hatch such admirable French geese of his own, not to meddle with the Swan of Stratford.'

Two more comments then appeared in *Punch* in successive weeks. On 29 June, a small item by Jerrold appeared with the title 'DRAMATIC MOVEMENT'. Without mentioning either Scribe or Halévy by name, he alluded to the appearance of Shakespeare at Her Majesty's and the departure of Shakespeare from Drury Lane. Also indirectly alluded to was the fact that England's most important dramatist, commemorated in a statue at Drury Lane, was now in the hands of men from Paris: 'From Drury Lane to Her Majesty's Theatre, the

Statue of SHAKSPEARE in a new coat of Plaster of Paris' (19:8). A week later, on 6 July, *Punch* made one last allusion to *La tempesta* in the form of yet another not so subtle insult contributed by Percival Leigh. Once again, however, the magazine avoided referring to the opera by name. The brief item in question was entitled 'Shakspeare à la Française', and it developed further the gastronomical conceit just discussed, beginning with the statement that 'To some tastes SHAKSPEARE, like railway accounts, must be cooked in order to be made pleasant (19:12). We then hear about a culinary innovation by Alexis Soyer named 'Croustade Shakspearienne à la Halévy Scribe.' Finally, then, Halévy's name is mentioned but only as a prelude to Leigh's concluding and dismissive comment on *La tempesta*: '*Croustade*, friend SOYER? Oughtn't it to have been *salmi*? Surely, if you meant to concoct a Shakspearian dish in the style of SCRIBE and HALÉVY, you should have made a hash of it.'

Whereas the Haymarket Theatre, a near neighbour of Her Majesty's, responded to the Scribe-Halévy venture with a revised version of Robert and William Brough's burlesque *The Enchanted Isle* (1848), now revised as *La! Tempest! Ah!* and deliberately aimed at burlesquing the French work, *Punch* remained relatively quiet when brushing aside the Scribe-Halévy transformation of Shakespeare into opera (the short run of *La tempesta* perhaps encouraged this). However, the somewhat later challenge posed by Ambrois Thomas's opera version of *Hamlet* was not so easily dismissed.

Thomas's opera, with libretto by Michel Carré and Jules Barbier, was first performed at the Paris Opéra on 9 March 1868, with the renowned French baritone Jean-Baptiste Faure in the title role and the Swedish soprano Christine Nilsson, as Ophelia. Much was cut from Shakespeare's original text, including the roles of Rosencrantz, Guildenstern, and Fortinbras, and the episode of Hamlet's voyage to England. More radical changes to Shakespeare's original included the added love scene between Hamlet and Ophelia, the on-stage drowning death of this latter, an interpolated drinking song for Hamlet with which he welcomes the Players ('O vin, dissipe la tristesse'), an added scene in which Hamlet overhears the King speaking to Polonius and learns that Polonius was a party to the murder of Hamlet's father, a ballet-divertissement (an obligatory item at the Opéra during the nineteenth century), and the very different conclusion that involves the return of the Ghost, whom everyone present is able to see, and the survival of Hamlet who then becomes king (the Queen also survives and will live the remainder of her days in a convent).

Punch, which always kept a close eye on the French cultural scene, was quick to respond. Less than two weeks later on 21 March, Henry Silver contributed an article about Thomas's opera, entitled 'SHAKSPEARE IN PARIS' (54:130). This spoke very disparagingly about such matters as '*Hamlet* sweetly warbling "To be, or not to be", to the beat of a conductor, and accompanied by fiddles.' The added ballet, as might be expected, drew Silver's sarcasm, readers being told to imagine '*Hamlet* with a ballet introduced in the mad scene' and 'dancers draped transparently, all capering and frisking, while *Ophelia* sings a waltz, and then very picturesquely drowns herself by limelight!' Equally absurd to Silver is the thought of the '*Ghost* stalking on the stage to the sound of a dead march, and then singing a long solo, descriptive of his sufferings'. In passing, Silver alludes to *A Midsummer Night's Dream*, as *Punch* had done in its response to *La tempesta*: 'Alas, poor WILLIAM SHAKSPEARE! Bless thee, how thou art translated, to please our lively neighbours!'

Elsewhere in the article, Silver notes that, according to a Paris informant, 'If M. AMBROISE THOMAS has not created a *Hamlet*, he has given to the world an *Ophelia* who will never be forgotten.' Silver was clearly struck, as were many who saw Thomas's opera, by the effect of the enhanced role of Ophelia, the result of the chief focus of Shakespeare's tragedy being transformed into that of a tragic love story. However, he largely ignores this important and intriguing aspect of the opera, and instead reiterates his outrage at the idea of a French composer meddling with Shakespeare:

> Created a *Hamlet!* Imagine a French tune-maker creating a *Hamlet!* [...] Only we wish our lively friends, when they want to spoil a play, would keep their paws off SHAKSPEARE. Why can't they sing VOLTAIRE, or bring CORNEILLE out at the opera? It is bad enough to try to translate *Hamlet* into French: but we can *not* stand seeing '*Airs from Hamlet*' at the music-shops, and hearing them brayed forth by blatant German bands, or squeaked about the streets by beastly barrel-organs.

Nothing more was then said about what *Punch* appears to have considered an aberration, but then on 16 January the following year, a small item by Shirley Brooks appeared entitled 'Good News for Shakspearians' (56:13). This was a notice announcing that Christine Nilsson was going to sing the part of Ophelia in the forthcoming London premiere of Thomas's opera (56:13). The twenty-five-year-old Nilsson had made her Paris debut in 1864 and was fast becoming one of the most celebrated sopranos of her day. She had something of the same physical attractions and charisma as Jenny Lind, and she had won great acclaim in the Paris production of *Hamlet* for her brilliant coloratura and moving rendition of Ophelia's love, madness, and death. Though admitting that Nilsson '*can* sing', Brooks concludes his notice by expressing the hope that 'her delightful performance may direct English tastes towards the play whence her opera is taken, and some day – who knows – we may witness a good performance of *Hamlet!* Thus sweetly doth music become a patron of poetry.'

That June, the British premiere of Thomas's opera took place at Covent Garden. It was sung in Italian, with the English baritone, Charles Santley, in the title role and, as promised, Christine Nilsson as Ophelia. For Covent Garden, Thomas and his librettists wrote a shorter, alternate ending, in which the Ghost does not appear and Hamlet dies soon after killing Claudius. However, this 'tragic' version, a sop, perhaps, to English sensibilities that would have been upset by *Hamlet* of all plays being given a 'happy' ending, appears in the end not to have been used (Thomas 1993, 26).

The *Punch* response to this second performance in London of an appropriation of Shakespeare by the French appeared on 3 July in the form of a supposed letter to *Punch*, signed 'Ben Buskin' (56:270). The fictional letter, which was composed by Henry Silver at the suggestion of Percival Leigh (see Silver diary for 23 June 1869), was entitled 'The Opera of "Omelette"' and immediately suggested that Thomas's work was a burlesque of Shakespeare's play, which, of course, it was not: 'HAVE you seen the new French opera – I mean, burlesque of *Hamlet?*' The supposed author of the letter claims that he has not seen the opera out of his 'reverence for SHAKSPEARE', but he then goes on to ridicule Hamlet singing '"To be or not to be" turned into recitative, and emphasized at intervals with thumps of the big drum and thrums of the big fiddles'. After noting that the reports of the singing of both Santley and Nilsson are very positive, he sarcastically alludes to Hamlet's drinking song. Such a song is 'just what SHAKSPEARE would himself have put into *Hamlet*'s mouth – that is, at least, if SHAKSPEARE, like his eminent translator, had been writing a burlesque'. The supposed author of the article then concludes by offering two musical burlesques of his own: 'To drink, or not to drink? / That is now the question' etc., to be sung to the tune of the traditional song 'Bobbing Joan', and 'Champagne Hamlet is my name', a parody of the contemporary popular song ('Champagne Charlie') written and sung by the music-hall star George Leybourne to music by Alfred Lee

Much later, after the popularity of Thomas's opera had become well established, *Punch* had more to say about the French operatic version of Shakespeare's play. Following a performance of the opera in London in the summer of 1890, with the great French baritone Jean Lasalle in the title role, *Punch* published a review by Burnand in the issue for 2 August. 'The Opera-Goer's Diary (Last Week of Opera)' was somewhat hostile from the outset, suggesting that the composer and his librettists appear 'to have read *Hamlet* once through, after which they wrote down as a *libretto* what they remembered of the story' (99:53). Few operas, it is suggested, are 'less dramatic than this', and the work should have been called '*Ophelia*', since 'whatever interest there may be in the Opera – and there is little – is centred entirely in' her. The Ghost is 'utterly purposeless', as is his son, Prince Hamlet. This latter 'is always posturing, weeping, calling out *ma mère*, and blubbering on the ample matronly bosom of his mother' and as such is like a big overgrown schoolboy.

This last point then leads Burnand to suggest that the French librettists have managed to realize 'SHAKSPEARE'S own description of his jelly-fleshed hero, whose mind is as shaky as his well-covered body. *Hamlet* was, accordingly, a fat youth, very much out of condition, [...]' Presumably, Burnand is here alluding to the physical appearance of Lasalle. The review includes two main complaints, the first of which concerns the treatment of Shakespeare's plot:

But what is there of the story? Nothing. The King is not killed: the Queen isn't poisoned: *Polonius* is not stabbed behind the arras, having been, perhaps, killed before the Opera commenced, since his name appears in the book but not in the programme […]

Then there is the expected castigation concerning ballet: '[…] the whole point of the Opera is in the last Act, where there is a *ballet* that has nothing to do with the piece.' The review then concludes first with a complaint about the length of Thomas's work and then with a burlesque plot outline showing how the work could be cut down to a two-hour show.

Burnand's review is accompanied by three small comic engravings designed by Edward J. Wheeler (99:53). The first shows Hamlet standing at down stage centre immediately in front of the conductor of the orchestra (Figure 37). Baton in hand, this latter is obviously in full charge of an ongoing performance. The caption below makes the point: 'Hamlet Personally Conducted'. The second engraving accompanies Burnand's comments on the ballet and shows Hamlet *en pointe,* dancing in the company of a group of ballerinas, all wearing *tutus*. The caption reads: 'Hamlet is out of it in the last Act. Why wasn't he brought into the Ballet?' The third engraving shows Hamlet with his back to a hysterical-looking Ophelia and an angry-looking Queen. The engraving matches part of Burnand's burlesque of the plot. Its caption states: 'An awkward moment for Hamlet. Row with his Mother and Ophelia', while the accompanying text gives a summary of *Punch*'s proposed version of Act Two:

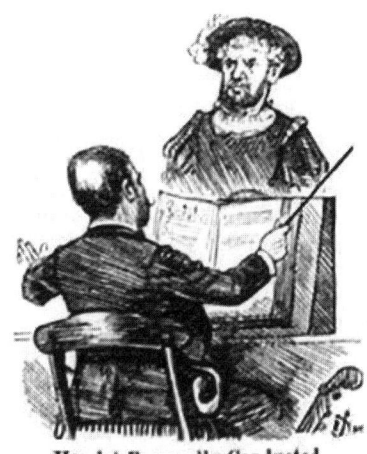

Figure 37. Edward J Wheeler, 'Hamlet Personally Conducted'. *Punch* (2 August 1890), 99:53.

Opening Chorus (anything; it doesn't matter if it's only pretty and bright). Enter HAMLET. Solo. 'Etre, ou ne pas être.' Enter OPHELIA, with book, pretends not to see HAMLET. Solo. Enter Queen. OPHELIA complains to her that HAMLET isn't behaving like a gentleman. Queen upbraids HAMLET: so does OPHELIA: HAMLET depressed. [etc.]

The comical engravings, the interpolated burlesque, and some of the other dismissive comments all express a degree of hostility to the French appropriation of Shakespeare's tragedy, but buried in the review are positive comments concerning Lasalle's singing, praise for the chorus at the end of Act 1, praise for Hamlet's drinking song, which was 'finely sung', an admission that it is a 'very hard-working Opera for the principals' and that there is 'good in it'. Is there, one wonders, a sign that *Punch* was drifting towards a realization that the transformation of Shakespeare into opera did not necessarily do harm to the original and might result in a work of art that could be enjoyed in its own terms? That seems to have been the case with another French opera that *Punch* had reviewed in the summer of 1889.

On 22 June of that year, *Punch* had published '"MODUS OPERANDI". *(The Covent Garden Government, and Her Majesty's Opposition.)*' by Arthur William à Beckett. This reviewed all the major opera productions for the week of 10 June at Covent Garden and Her Majesty's. Of concern here is à Beckett's brief review of the Saturday, 15 June, performance at Covent Garden of Charles Gounod's *Roméo et Juliette* in French, with Jean de Reszke and the Australian Nellie Melba in the title roles (96:301). This work had first been performed at the Théâtre Lyrique in Paris on 27 April 1867, and it had received its London premiere at Covent Garden that same summer. Sung at Covent Garden in Italian, it had received a favourable reception in *Punch*. A supposed 'John Beethoven Brown' (in reality Henry Silver), in a letter to the magazine published in the issue for 27 July, had said that it was the best new opera of the season. It was 'pleasanter than VERDI', for one can hear Gounod's Romeo 'without either being deafened or sent into a deep sleep' (53:39). Particular praise was given to the singing and acting of Giovanni Matteo Mario and Adelina Patti, who performed the title roles. Silver had given only a hint of any dissatisfaction regarding what had been done to Shakespeare's original: 'though a quantity of Shakspeare is stuffed into the libretto, it falls far short of what a Shakspeare-lover would have wished'. Two weeks later (10 August), *Punch* had then devoted a full page and a half to a very mild burlesque by Burnand of Gounod's work ('EVENINGS FROM HOME. AT COVENT GARDEN. PERFORMANCE OF GOUNOD'S NEW OPERA, ROMEO E GIULIETTA'). Here, however, the emphasis had not been directed at the opera so much as at the noisy audience, whose humming and discussion of details in the 'play text' had been a major distraction to the reviewer whose final comment were that a return visit would be worthwhile: 'But Somebody must hear it again when the Talkers and the Hummers are not present' (53:55).

By 22 June 1889, over twenty years later, Gounod's opera appears to have become familiar fare. The *Punch* article by à Beckett, although it jokes about Roméo's eccentric tights and the fact that the rendition of the marriage service ('fully choral') was 'calculated to cause the profoundest envy in the breast of the most accomplished curate attached to St. George's, Hanover Square', was very laudatory. Melba's singing of the waltz in Act 1, à Beckett notes, received a double encore, both De Reszke brothers (Edouard De Reszke sang the part of the Friar) were admirable, the smaller parts were 'well filled', and Signor Castelmary 'distinguished himself as *Le Duc de Vérone*'. What is more, the 'whole production (dresses, *mise-en-scène*, everything)' was 'worthy of the Poet, the Composer, and the Manager'. Assuming that by 'Poet', *Punch* means Shakespeare rather than the two librettists, Jules Barbier and Michel Carré, this is praise of a kind not yet encountered in the magazine in response to an opera based on Shakespeare (in this instance the French translation of the play by François-Victor Hugo). However, as already mentioned in Chapter Two, the review contains a not-so-laudatory engraving of a design by Edward J. Wheeler based on Hamlet's words to Horatio: 'Take him for all in all, we shall not look upon his like again.' The engraving depicts a version of Scheemakers's statue of Shakespeare, which, it is suggested, could be erected in the Royal Opera House. A telling detail consists of the scroll hanging down in front of Shakespeare and inscribed 'ROYAL ITALIAN OPERA COVENT GARDEN. GOUNOD'S ROMEO & JULIET. W SHAKSPEARE IN FRENCH.'

The implication is that at Covent Garden, at least, Shakespeare is not as he was and may be 'translated' for ever.

A week later (29 June), in another 'MODUS OPERANDI' article by à Beckett, *Punch* reported on a second performance of Gounod's work (96:311). We learn little new, except that real trees from Epping Forest were used for the Garden Scene, and that the house was 'crowded with an audience at once discriminating and enthusiastic'. Then, in the next 'MODUS OPERANDI' article (this one by Burnand), *Punch* again gave a brief review of *Roméo et Juliette*, this time of the performance that took place on Monday, 1 July. But again this tells us very little. Melba was 'charming', Jean De Reszke 'at his best', and Edouard De Reszke 'exemplary' (97:17). More fun is made of Roméo's tights, and there is a short burlesque of Roméo and Juliette's duet in Act IV concerning the morning lark. This is accompanied by an amusing unsigned engraving, probably designed by Wheeler, depicting the two characters gesturing towards a small bird outside the window. As might be expected, there is some rather obvious punning on the word 'lark'. The jokes are very light-hearted, and there is none of the unpleasant hostility that had greeted the London premiere of Thomas's *Hamlet*. Gounod's opera, it would seem, from the very first had won *Punch* over. It was to be considered 'worthy of the Poet' and was therefore to be left alone.

When further London performances of *Roméo et Juliette* were reviewed by *Punch* in April 1890 (98:181), in October 1891 (101:209), and in June the following year (102:208), there was a complete absence of any concern that Shakespeare's original had been appropriated and 'translated' into another media. This unquestioned acceptance seems to confirm that Gounod's now very familiar opera had been accepted on its own terms and deemed not to threaten the legitimate drama in any way. The review on 31 October 1891, written by Thomas Anstey Guthrie, is of the opening night of a revival at Covent Garden on 20 October. The singing of Emile Cossira and Mlle. Simmonet (both from the Opéra Comique) in the title roles is praised in very general terms, but the only detailed comment concerns Cossira's ample girth, which provided the reviewer with some mirth in the balcony scene in Act 4 when the singer was required to use a rather flimsy, unsecured ladder provided by Juliette. Thereafter, banal humour is reinforced with two engravings designed by Edward Tennyson Reed. One is captioned 'Two (Covent Garden) Gentlemen of Verona!!' and depicts caricatures of two men in Renaissance costume, one tall and thin, and the other short and decidedly stout. The other depicts Cossira in a very undignified position on his hands and knees, supposedly after he has climbed down from the balcony (Figure 38). The caption reads: 'Exit Romeo by the Rope Ladder, – a shrewd guess at what really happens'.

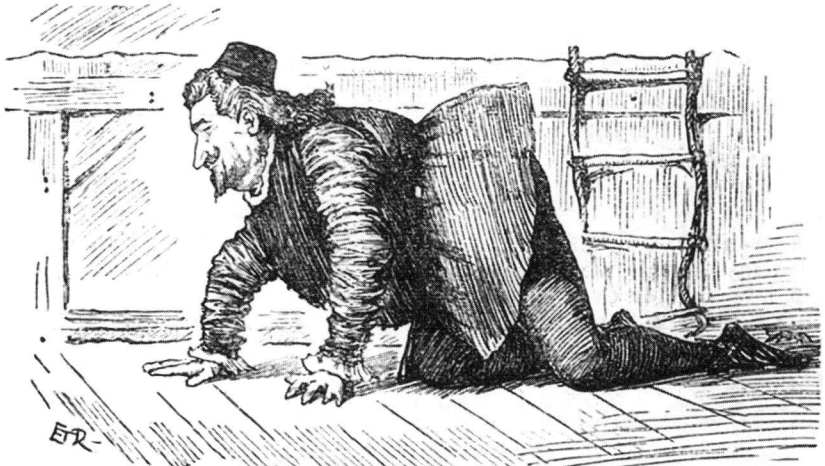

Exit Romeo by the Rope Ladder,—a shrewd guess at what really happens.

Figure 38. Edward Tennyson Reed's depiction of Emile Cossira's exit in the opera *Roméo et Juliette*. *Punch* (31 October 1891), 101:209.

The other review (by Burnand), published eight months later on 11 June in 'OPERA-GOER'S DIARY', a weekly, night by night summary of current opera productions, was of a performance on 30 May, with the familiar figures of Jean De Reszke as Roméo and his brother Edouard as the Friar. Both are praised, as is the American soprano Emma Eames, who was making her Covent Garden debut and had already made a name for herself when she sang Juliette with the De Reszke brothers in Paris two years before. However, Burnand appears to be mainly concerned to provide humour. Jean (here called

'Johnnie') should 'lighten' his part by wearing a 'flaxen-haired wig and light moustache', and Tybald should not die with his toes so close to the curtain, since 'friendly members of Capulet faction' consequently had to rescue his legs. As with the review the previous fall, the item was accompanied by two comic engravings, both, in this

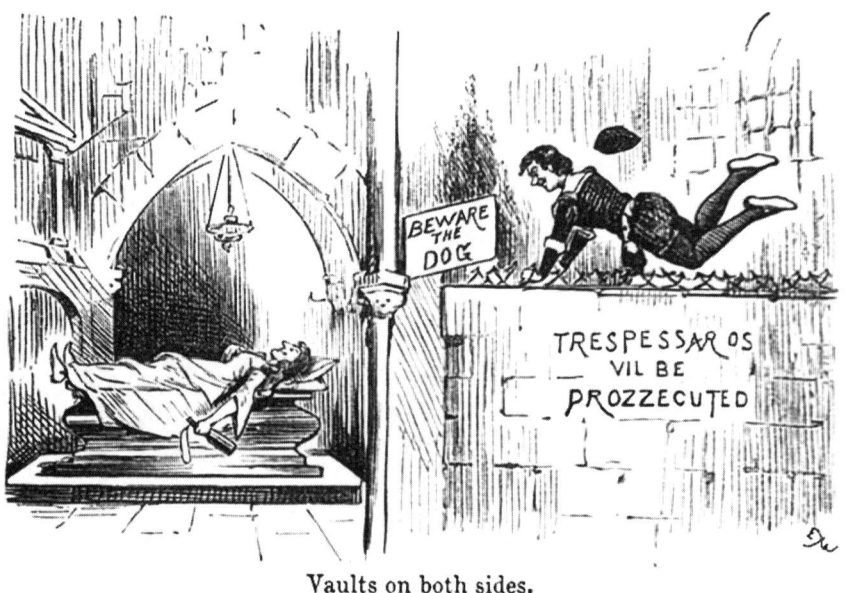

Vaults on both sides.

Figure 39. Edward J. Wheeler's burlesque of the tomb scene in the opera *Roméo et Juliette*. *Punch* (11 June 1892), 102:280.

instance, designed by Edward J. Wheeler. The first depicts the Friar with a mug of cider and dancing with Juliette. The caption reads: 'Hot weather. The Friar proposes cider-'cupping' as a remedy. Dance of joy in recompense.' The second engraving (Figure 39) depicts Juliette in the vault. She lies in a very undignified pose on her tomb with a bottle in her hand as though she has passed out from drinking. Roméo is vaulting over a wall topped with barbs, beside which is a notice, 'BEWARE THE DOG'. The punning caption reads: 'Vaults on both sides'. Light-hearted and amusing, perhaps, but hardly offering *Punch* readers anything particularly insightful concerning either Gounod's opera or Shakespeare's original play.

Punch's responses to the London premieres of Verdi's *Otello* and his *Falstaff* five years later were in somewhat the same vein. *Otello* was first performed in London on 5 July 1889 at the Lyceum Theatre, a few days after Irving had concluded his season there with a final performance of *Macbeth,* and *Falstaff* had its premiere at Covent Garden on 19 May 1894. The initial concern of the *Punch* reviewer (Burnand) was that the Lyceum was too small a theatre for the large orchestra the Verdi score required. In addition, the powerful tenor voice of Francesco Tamagno (he had sung at the Italian premiere of Verdi's work), it is suggested, would have filled a theatre twice the size. Her Majesty's Theatre, currently shut up, would have served far better. The point was probably a valid one, especially since Victorian audiences had great difficulty adjusting to the high volume of Verdi's music (Altick 1997, 692), frequently complaining that it was 'noisy' (see, *Punch* 20:186). However, members of the first-night audience were wildly enthusiastic, and the two lead singers, Tamagno and Victor Maurel (Verdi's original Iago), 'were rapturously encored in the declamatory dramatic pieces which do duty for songs' (97:17). 'As to *Iago*'s devilish kind of *Credo*, they would have had even this three times.' Burnand then remarks that there is no warrant in Shakespeare's text for Iago's 'Credo', but there, any analysis of what Verdi and his librettist had done in translating Shakespeare's tragedy into grand opera ends. The opera is left to rest upon its own merits, and it is obvious that *Punch* has largely dropped the kind of hostility that marked its response to the London debuts of Halévy's *La tempesta* and Thomas's *Hamlet*.

Five years later, and just over a year after its Milan premiere, Verdi's *Falstaff* received its London debut at Covent Garden. The *Punch* review by Burnand appeared three weeks later in the issue of 9 June in the series 'THE OPERA-GOER'S DIARY' (106:273). Arturo Pessina sang the title role, but though suitably rotund, the reviewer claims, he could not match Mark Lemon in his physical appearance, in that Lemon was the only Falstaff he had ever seen who did not look artificially 'stuffed.' Following this dutiful acknowledgment to *Punch*'s own Falstaff, Burnand then develops a comic analogy between Verdi's main character and a football, the principal character being 'to the other *dramatis personae* what the football is to the players'. Falstaff is 'about the same use as is a football in a scrimmage', best seen when he 'is being hustled about here, shoved away there, and finally jammed into the notable buck-basket to disappear over the balcony and fall splosh into the river below'.

Elsewhere, Burnand emphasizes that Pessina presents a very different Falstaff from that normally associated with Shakespeare: 'Signor PESSINA makes quite an Italian *Falstaff*, with such airs, –

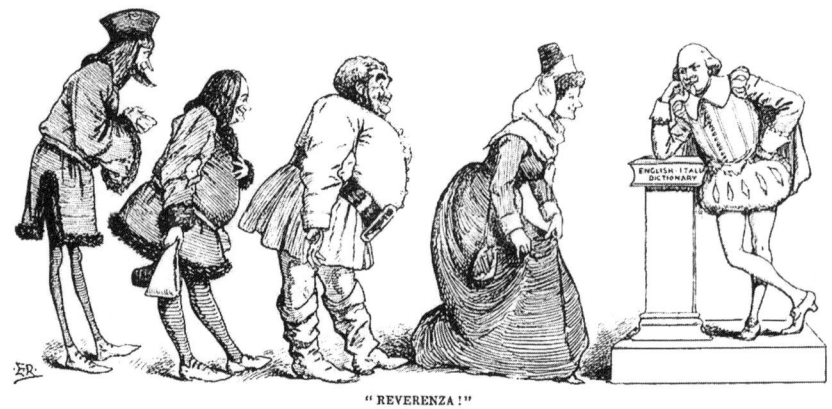

Figure 40. Edward Tennyson Reed's depiction of four characters from Verdi's *Falstaff*. *Punch* (9 June 1894), 106:273.

more or less taking, – graces and pantomimic action as are not associated with the English idea of SHAKSPEARE'S creation.' Furthermore, he writes, 'Why should this Op-erratic *Falstaff* "give" at the knees and shuffle in his walk?' As for the music, though much of it is delightful, it is 'rarely catching: not from beginning to end is there a phrase in it so immediately taking as is that well-known one in the overture to [Otto Nicolai's] *The Merry Wives of Windsor*'. The remainder of the cast is praised for their singing and acting, and the final scene is singled out as being 'most effective'. There is, of course, much more to Verdi's late style and to musical masterpieces than

Burnand seems to have grasped, but, as with the review of *Otello*, there is no attack upon the composer's attempt to translate Shakespeare into another medium. Whether or not Burnand thought Verdi's opera was 'worthy of the Poet' is not clear; however, an accompanying engraving by Edward Tennyson Reed adds a relevant gloss (Figure 40). Four of the characters from the opera, including Mistress Quickly and Falstaff, are lined up in front of Shakespeare. Mistress Quickly curtsies and the three male figures bow. Shakespeare stands upon a small dais and is posed, as in Scheemakers's statue, leaning upon a plinth. His elbow rests upon a large English-Italian dictionary, a small ironic reminder of the foreign roots of this particular tribute. However, Verdi's opera, we are invited to think, should be taken as a tribute to Shakespeare, a point reflected in the one-word caption: 'REVERENZA!'

Ballet

Whereas opera was seen as a largely alien Italian phenomenon, ballet (an integral part of many French operas) was identified as largely French and was perceived as effete and inappropriate as a medium for serious subjects. As we saw in Chapter Two, in 1843 when *Punch* was musing upon the discrepancy between the popularity of ballet and the neglect (in *Punch*'s view) of serious drama, the newly-passed Theatre Regulation Act was seen as a threat to the 'legitimate' drama. *Punch* was concerned that an unscrupulous entrepreneur of the likes of Albert Bunn could now use the former patent theatres to exploit for commercial gain popular preferences for entertainments such as opera and ballet. Thus, in one engraving (7:152), the artist depicted the portico of Drury Lane symbolically supported by four female ballet dancers, while on the roof were banners inscribed 'BALLET' and 'OPERA'. The same theme was present in the engraving depicting a medal that supposedly commemorated the expulsion of Shakespeare from England in 1845 (8:48) (Figure 7). One side of the medal depicts Bunn on the steps of Drury Lane, but behind him is a poster inscribed

'THEATRE ROYAL. BALLET.' Later that same year, John Leech designed the engraving entitled 'POET BUNN'S OPENING OF DRURY LANE THEATRE' (9:160). As we saw in Chapter Two, this showed Bunn being carried through the streets of London to Drury

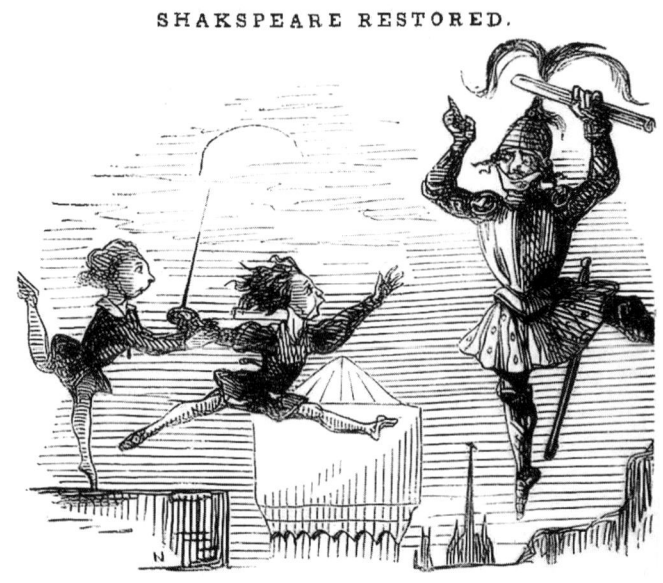

Figure 41. William Newman's burlesque of Hamlet following the Ghost in imaginary ballet version of Shakespeare's play. *Punch* (10 October 1846), 11:153.

Lane. Significantly special prominence is given in Leech's engraving to three female ballet dancers in Bunn's entourage (Figure 9).

Coupled to the fear that Shakespeare's plays would no longer have a theatre in which they could be performed was the concern that Shakespeare might still be made available but only if transformed into another medium such as ballet. In 1846, for example, *Punch* published Gilbert Abbott à Beckett's 'SHAKSPEARE RESTORED' (11:153). This referred to the Alexandre Dumas translation of Shakespeare into

French. À Beckett speculates that Dumas's *Hamlet* may soon be presented on the English stage in the form of a ballet for Drury Lane. 'The objection to [Shakespeare's] performance in this country will now be removed, since he will have passed the ordeal of appearance on the French stage, and has become qualified for re-translation in the English language.' To further make the point, the article is accompanied by an engraving designed by William Newman that depicts *Hamlet* being performed as a ballet (Figure 41). At right, the ghost in armour and a plumed helmet is in mid air, his right toe pointed to the ground in the manner of a ballet dancer. Hamlet at left, with his sword in his left hand, is also in mid air and appears to be leaping towards the Ghost, his legs fully extended. However, holding Hamlet's right hand is Horatio at far left. He stands on one point, his other leg extended behind him. We thus appear to be witnessing a ballet version of the dramatic moment when Hamlet attempts to follow the Ghost but is restrained from doing so by Horatio.

But *Punch*'s fantasy about *Hamlet* being transformed into a French ballet was not the first time such a thought had been expressed in the magazine. In 1843, *Punch* had published 'BALLET OF "LADY MACBETH"' (5:240–241). This was in response to a review in the *Times* of the ballet *Le diable amoureux* at Drury Lane. Attributed to 'Editor' in the Subscribers' Ledgers, this contained the suggestion that the only way to get a five-act tragedy performed might be to cut all the dialogue and 'give the heroine to a *première danseuse*'. The item in *Punch*, which is in the form of a purported letter, dated 21 November and signed 'AN ANCIENT FRIEND', commented indirectly on the low regard for serious drama and the popularity of ballet, and it offered the plot summary for a proposed full-length ballet based on *Macbeth*. A synopsis of the proposed ballet was provided, and this was illustrated by four small engravings to help readers envisage the new version of Shakespeare's tragedy (5:240–43). Among the suggested features is that Duncan be fascinated by Lady Macbeth and offer her an immodest proposal. One engraving shows this moment, while another illustrates the moment when Lady Macbeth (wearing a tutu and *en pointe*) hands her husband the dagger.

A further engraving portrays Lady Macbeth in the sleep-walking scene (Figure 42). Of this the supposed correspondent says: 'The

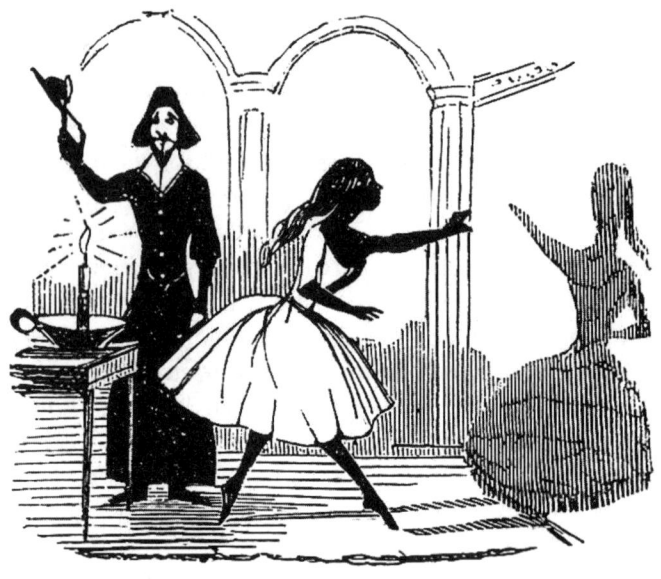

Figure 42. Unidentified artist's burlesque of ballet version of Lady Macbeth's sleep-walking scene. *Punch* (2 December 1843), 5:240.

walking in her sleep furnishes me with an admirable *pas seul*, which, I think, will eclipse the *pas de l'ombre* in *Ondine*. I shall call it the *pas de la chandelle*. Lady Macbeth will place a candle on a little table, which will cast a black deep shadow on the wall, and to this she may clamour with all the wildness of a distracted mind.' The author then discusses his proposed final scenes, which include Lady Macbeth appearing mad on the battlefield and being fatally wounded by an accidental blow from her husband. To conclude, Macbeth commits suicide and the scenery depicting Macbeth's castle dissolves to reveal Diana in her chariot with three fairies. Apart from the obvious fun derived from creating a burlesque of *Macbeth*, the article expresses an underlying concern that Shakespeare may become available only in some translated form, the ballet offering an extreme case. Forty-three years later, *Punch* was still making the same kind of point when it reviewed Thomas's opera of *Hamlet*. Like other French operas, that by Thomas included a ballet, as has already been noted, so, to show its disapproval, *Punch* included four engravings designed by Harry Furniss of an entire version of *Hamlet* ludicrously transformed into a ballet (91:209).

One can only imagine how *Punch* would have reacted had a full-length ballet based on a Shakespeare play appeared on the London stage, but for such a work, the world had to wait until the early twentieth century and the ballets of Alexander Krein (*Othello and Desdemona*), Constant Lambert (*Romeo and Juliet*), and Sergey Prokofiev (*Romeo and Juliet*). Instead, as was discussed in Chapter Two, *Punch* invented such an occasion and maliciously reviewed Charles Kean's 1856 production of *The Winter's Tale* as though it were a full-length ballet (30:198–199).

Much later, as we have already seen, when Herbert Beerbohm Tree had established himself at Her Majesty's Theatre and was putting on a series of spectacular Shakespeare productions, *Punch* could not resist noting in May 1900 that the production of *A Midsummer Night's Dream* contained a number of ballets. Taking its cue from this, *Punch* then suggests that Tree should take on *The Tempest* and reduce its text to the minimum (118:330). The article, which was by St. John Hankin, drama critic for the *Times*, then goes on to offer guidelines regarding such a text. It would now be reduced to three acts, the second of which would be largely taken up with 'a grand ballet *divertissement* in which Ariel appears in mid-air disguised as a harpy' (there are accompanying engravings of Julia Neilson in this role). In Act 3, Tree 'will evolve a Grand Masque of the Gods', and Prospero's great speech towards the end of Shakespeare's original will be re-written:

> Ye elves of hills, brooks, standing lakes and groves
> Ye quite invaluable concomitants
> Of SHAKSPEARE'S dramas, what a boon you are
> To any management! ... This rough magic   *[Waving the blue pencil.]*
> Never will I abjure. That heavenly music
> Which I have need of, and the dancers too
> I will commission from the best purveyors.
> I'll play *Macbeth, Othello,* and *The Dane*
> In such attractive guise you'll never know them;
> And deeper than did ever plummet sound
> I'll drown the 'Book'!

Thus, even at the end of the century, *Punch* still seems to feel that Shakespeare is under threat, his texts liable to be gutted, altered, or dispensed with, and productions transformed into spectacles involving other media (song and dance). No matter that the attack on Tree is as biased and as deliberately misleading as that on Kean's *The Winter's Tale* some forty-four years earlier. *Punch* still seems to believe that Shakspeareanity is under attack. Of course, the use of burlesque and humour provide some comic effects appropriate to the *raison d'être* of the magazine, and readers are assumed to understand how that humour works. Even so, below all this seems to be an underlying belief among the *Punch* staff that Shakespeare remains in need of defenders who will not be led astray by popular preferences for singing and dancing, and opera and ballet in particular.

Hippodrama at Astley's

Hippodrama was a popular Victorian form of entertainment that involved the mounting of plays on horseback. This required specially adapted theatres or arenas that included circus rings. The best-known example in London was Astley's. Although it underwent a series of official name changes in the course of its history, and although it was destroyed by fire at least four times, it survived in one form or another until 1893 when it was demolished, having been declared unsafe. Readers of Dickens will recall that he seems to have had a particular fascination with Astley's. There is a description of a visit to Astley's in Chapter 11 of *Sketches by Boz* (1836), and in No. 60 (Chapter 39) of *The Old Curiosity Shop* (September 1840) there is a description of Kit Nubbles's party at Astley's that has an accompanying illustration by Phiz (Hablot Knight Browne). Then, in *Bleak House* (1853) there is a description of Mr. George going to Astley's (Chapter 21), and in *Hard Times* (1854), Mr. Sleary proudly proclaims that his three-year-old 'Little Wonder of Theolathtic Equitation' is destined for 'Athley'th' (Book 3, Chapter 7).

Located on Westminster Bridge Road, just south of the Thames and only some two hundred yards from the Bridge, Astley's Amphitheatre was opened in the 1770s by Philip Astley, a former riding school owner who is often given credit (though not quite accurately) for being the father of the circus. From the beginning, horses provided an important part of the entertainments there, but with a circus ring in the amphitheatre (see *Punch*, 18:104) attached to a large stage, it was possible to create various kinds of hybrid entertainment. Astley's became renowned for its military extravaganzas involving hundreds of soldiers, horses, and cannons, as well as for providing a showplace for the kind of circus displays that horses could provide. Audiences were drawn from a wide social spectrum, tickets were affordable, and the entertainments were considered suitable for families.

Surviving play-bills give some indication of the nature of the entertainments. From its first performance on 19 April 1824, for example, the equestrian spectacle *The Battle of Waterloo* was a regular favourite, as was *Mazeppa*, another equestrian piece that was based on Byron's poem and first performed in 1831 (Altick 1997, 374, 596). The play-bill for 17 December 1855 is very typical. It announced the equestrian dramas *Rookwood* and *The Lottery Ticket*, with 'Scenes in the Arena.' That for 18 January 1858 listed the equestrian drama *The Storming and Capture of Delhi* with the equestrian pantomime *Don Quixote* and 'Scenes in the Circle', and that for 25 October 1858 announced *The Covenanters* and J. R. Planché's *Faint Heart Never Won Fair Lady,* with 'Scenes in the Court Imperial'. On 20 November (1865?) and during the week following, there was a grand revival of *Mazeppa*, together with *Ixion* by Burnand, who by this date was already an established member of the *Punch* table.

Punch was clearly aware of the threat to serious drama posed by the popularity of Astley's and the kind of entertainment offered there. In 1847, for example, appeared an article by Gilbert Abbott à Beckett entitled 'SHAKSPEARE AT ASTLEY'S' (12:269). Accompanied by an engraving (probably designed by William Newman) of an exotically-dressed performer standing on the back of one of three horses (Figure 43), the article laments the absence of Shakespeare's plays from Drury Lane and Covent Garden, an absence that 'threatens now to be permanent'. Humorously, à Beckett hopes that a place will be found for Shakespeare at Astley's in some kind of equestrian format: After all 'SHERIDAN has lately found a welcome' there, and '*Pizarro* has been literally "mounted", in fine style, at that Theatre.'

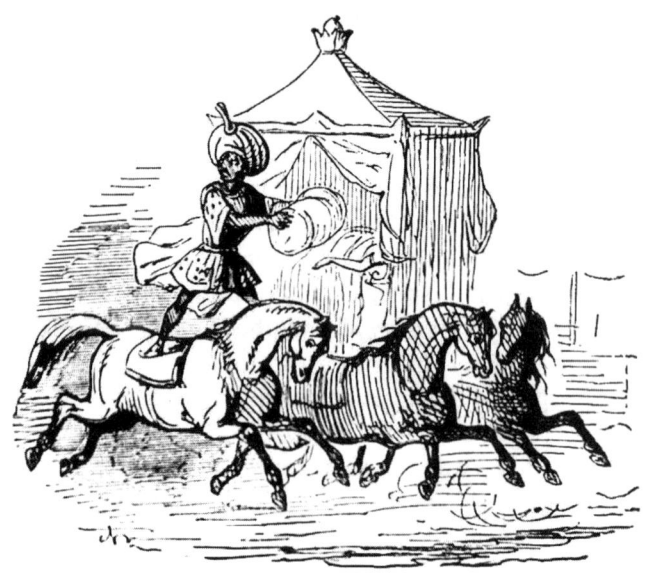

Figure 43. William Newman, 'SHAKESPEARE AT ASTLEY'S'. *Punch* (3 July 1847), 12:269.

The hope is 'that instead of seeing SHAKESPEARE only occasionally set to music, we may have the pleasure of seeing him very frequently set to harness and horsemanship'. À Beckett then playfully suggests that *'Othello*, as an Equestrian Tragedy, would be a very exciting novelty.' Other plays by Shakespeare also suggest 'that the immortal bard contemplated availing himself of the resources of the royal amphitheatre, Westminster Bridge, or some similar establishment for a perfect performance of his tragedies'. There is, for example, Richard III's 'ardent longing for "a horse! a horse"', while '*Hamlet's* philosophy could not come with better effect than spoken from the back of a horse at full gallop, which would finely illustrate the ups and downs of life that astonish and perplex the moralist.'

Ironically, *Punch* needed to wait only a few years before its comical suggestion became a reality when William Cooke, manager at Astley's from 1853 to 1861, put on equestrian versions of four of Shakespeare's plays during the 1850s: *Richard III* (in Cibber's version), *Macbeth, The Taming of the Shrew* (in Garrick's version entitled *Katherine and Petruchio),* and *Henry IV,* Part One. The first two of these – *Richard III* and *Macbeth* – were reviewed in *Punch.* On 16 August 1856, in 'THE LEGITIMATE DRAMA ON HORSEBACK', *Punch* noted: 'We have heard every body for some time complaining that the legitimate drama has gone to the dogs; but we are happy to find that SHAKSPEARE at all events has only gone to the horses, for we find *Richard the Third* in full play at Astley's' (31:62). Although the *Punch* reviewer (à Beckett) admits that he has not actually seen the performance, which opened on 4 August 1856 with James Holloway in the title part, he reports that the Battle of Bosworth has received praiseworthy accounts as have the antics of Richard III's highly-trained horse, which, 'by his picturesque *poses*, his intelligent snorts, and judicious bye-play, [...] seems almost to justify the apparently extravagant offer of his master to exchange his kingdom for such an animal'. With copious irony, à Beckett then expresses the hope that 'the experiment of SHAKSPEARE on horseback will prove sufficiently successful to induce the enterprising manager to make further experiments in the same direction'. Perhaps dogs 'might be found capable of enchaining the interest of our perishing five-act tragedies and comedies'. Although *Punch*'s reaction is negative in tone, other publications, including the *Times* (6 August 1856), were very positive. Cooke's production proved to be very popular and attained 97 performances by 22 November, with many more to follow, the last being for Cooke's final benefit on 30 January 1860. Among those who flocked to see the production was Queen Victoria (Saxon 1968, 155–156), something that would no doubt not have surprised *Punch.*

On 1 December 1856, William Cooke's equestrian version of *Macbeth* opened at Astley's where it would play fairly regularly until 9 February 1857. In 'THE HIPPODRAMA OF MACBETH AT ASTLEY'S', contributed by Percival Leigh, *Punch* noted in the issue of 13 December that this production of *Macbeth* was 'now in course of representation at Astley's (31:237). Various suggestions were then made as to how an actor might deliver Macbeth's lines about having 'no spur / To prick the sides of my intent'. Then, shortly after, on 10 January, the equestrian *Macbeth* was given a full review (32:12–13). The reviewer (his name is not revealed in the Ledgers) begins almost nostalgically by recalling how the smell of the sawdust brought back childhood memories of the place. Describing the entertainment as 'equestrian illustrations' of *Macbeth*, the reviewer, who admits to having arrived too late to see the witches at the opening (did they depart on horseback 'up a precipitous and well saw-dusted platform with cloud facings'?), begins by describing Macbeth and Banquo 'riding over the "blasted heath", and making no more fuss about it than if it had been that of Hampstead'. They were apparently then followed by 'six warriors in waterproof leggings smothered in buttons, mounted upon an equal number of "highly trained steeds"; and then twelve "supers" on foot, with their legs scored all over with red tape – which of course we know to be the Scottish army – and so the scene closed in',

The jocular and slightly bemused tone of this opening is then maintained for what follows. We hear about the arrival on horseback of Duncan 'under what we at first took to be a four-post bedstead, but which was in reality a regal canopy, supported by four retainers in crimson gaiters'. We hear about the scene in which Macbeth and his wife arrange the murder, and then the scene following the murder. The reviewer, however, feigns great disappointment that an opportunity to show Duncan's horses going wild was missed. After all, 'everybody who has seen *Mazeppa* knows perfectly well' what is 'the proper way of managing wild horses'. The reviewer also complains about a missed opportunity with regard to the scene of Banquo's murder. Why did his horses not 'go about' as mentioned in Shakespeare's text (see *Macbeth* III iii 11)? 'And why (in the name of all that is hippodramatic) did not the messenger who announces the coming of Birnam

Wood, gallop in on horseback?' However, the last scene, the reviewer playfully pretends, 'was very thrilling, and in every way a triumph':

> Dunsinane in a state of siege – terrific encounter of horse and foot – sortie of the garrison – *Macbeth* rushing about without his hat, like a maniac in the front garden – then the cream-coloured horse on the 'prompt side' was tapped under the knees till he fell down dead – and then the white horse on the O. P. Side was served in the same way, and fell down dead too – then *Macbeth* met *Macduff* in mid career, and a combat ensued, so terrible, that even to think about it takes one's breath away – and then *Macbeth* smeared some rose-pink over his countenance, and was finished off in a grim and ghastly manner – and then MR. W. COOKE, JUN., was hoisted on a shield – the warriors all shouted 'Hail, King of Scotland!' and the curtain came down, amid the 'deafening plaudits and reiterated acclamations of a crowded and fashionable audience'. (32:13).

This finale to the play is referred to in one of four accompanying unsigned engravings by John Tenniel (Figure 44). The other three

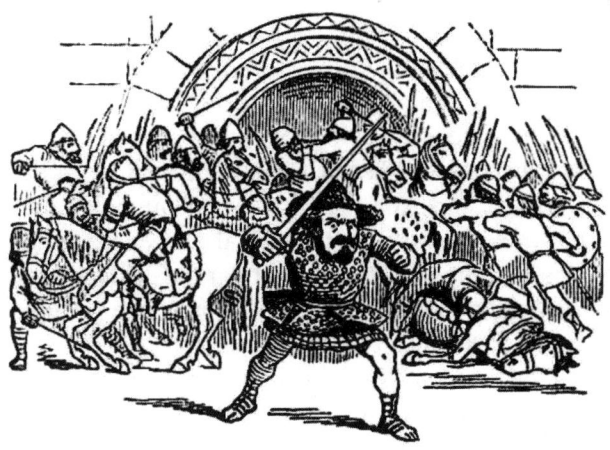

Figure 44. John Tenniel, 'MACBETH AT ASTLEY'S'.
Punch (10 January 1857), 32:13

present the scenes involving horses that *Punch* felt should have been included: the departure of the witches, Duncan's horses, and the arrival of the messenger with news about Birnam Wood. At no point does the reviewer display overt hostility to what has been done to

279

Shakespeare's play; however, indirectly and with fairly obvious irony, the reviewer states: '[...] we were a little disappointed; we felt that MR. COOKE scarcely made the most of his materials; in other words, that he gave us rather too much SHAKSPEARE, and not enough COOKE.' Furthermore, the reviewer argues, Cooke's 'new edition of the tragedy would be all the better for less letter-press, and more "equestrian illustrations"' (32:12).

A few months later, in the issue for 30 May 1857, *Punch* published 'SINGERS IN THE SAWDUST'. A small engraved initial letter 'A' by John Tenniel depicts a knight on horseback. In the ensuing article by Henry Silver, there is a reference to Macbeth having been 'hippodramatised' at Astley's and to the fact that 'we have grown somewhat accustomed to find SHAKESPEARE in the sawdust'. Also mentioned as an aside, although the allusion is no doubt intended to be negative, is that Charles Kean's recent production of *Richard II* at the Princess's included horses in the interpolated procession scene (see above, Chapter Three). Earlier in the play, though not mentioned by *Punch*, both Mowbray and Bolingbroke (this latter played by John Ryder, a veteran of Astley's) had mounted horses for the trial by combat in I iii, and it seems clear that Kean's use of horses in his version of the legitimate drama was influenced by the popular success of Astley's hippodramatic productions of Shakespeare (Saxon 1968, 168, 171), Kean's somewhat later staging in 1859 of a mounted Henry V's triumphal entry into London being another obvious example. The remainder of Silver's article on Astley's *Macbeth* then talks about the performance on horseback at Astley's of Verdi's *Il trovatore* (32:222).

A decade later, Astley's was still willing to present versions of Shakespeare's plays. As we have already seen in Chapter Three, in the spring of 1870, Samuel Phelps began a short engagement at Astley's in a production of *Othello*, with Hermann Vezin as Iago and that actor's wife as Desdemona (Phelps and Forbes-Robertson 1886, 304–305). *Punch* did not send a reviewer, so instead it published on 19 March two engravings by Linley Sambourne and a comic fantasy, consisting of suggestions as to how horses could be introduced into the Astley's production (58:108). That the Astley's *Othello* was not presented as a hippodrama is deliberately not made clear. As the

Punch author would have known, the reality was that Astley's was not at the time being used for circus acts. Neither the *Hamlet* presented there in 1864 with Alice Marriott in the title role nor the Phelps *Othello* were hippodramas (Saxon 1968, 208), and not until 1871 with the new management of George Sanger did Astley's return to circus acts and hippodramas.

The 'Translation' of Shakespeare

Although the *Punch* reviewers reacted in a fiercely hostile manner to a few of the works discussed so far in this chapter – the operas by Halévy and Thomas are the obvious examples, together with anything real or imagined that involved ballet – in the main, when a work of Shakespeare was 'translated' into some other stage medium, the response was often good-humoured and playful. One may see in this, I believe, a reaction closely allied to that associated with the appreciation of what can be variously defined as parody, burlesque, or travesty (this last a term often employed by the Victorians). If such works as those discussed in this chapter are viewed as in some way parodic (as seen above, *Punch* describes both *La tempesta* and Thomas's *Hamlet* as burlesques), then they can be appreciated as a form of tribute to the originals upon which they are based. Though *Punch* never discusses the point, 'translated' works have a value in that they belong to Shakspeareanity. They do not denigrate the original work but reinforce the viewer's knowledge and appreciation of that original. Indeed, for burlesque to work, the audience is required to be familiar with the original, while 'translation' into another medium (a Shakespeare play into an opera, for example), though not requiring prior familiarity with the original, nonetheless may benefit from that familiarity, at the same time as it may invite the viewer to return to the original. Issues pertaining to 'translation' and burlesque are of particular concern in the remaining two sections of this chapter. The first deals with *Punch*'s response to the representation of Shakespeare's works in the visual arts, and the second deals with *Punch*'s many textual burlesques of lines, scenes, and even entire plays of Shakespeare.

'Translations' – The Visual Arts

As Richard Altick has pointed out in his history of the first decade of *Punch*, the early years of the magazine coincided with a growing awareness of the fine arts of painting and sculpture among the general public. No longer the preserve of 'a small elite of collectors and connoisseurs', art works were increasingly prized by a growing middle class that was receptive to learning more about art and willing to exercise its spending power on 'aesthetic enjoyment and the purchase of visible domestic emblems of cultivation' (Altick 1997, 668). Significantly, just as in the late twentieth century the interiors of London Underground trains began to exhibit poetry alongside the long-familiar staple of advertisements, so in 1847 Henry Cole, the innovator and reformer, launched a proposal that the walls of railway stations be decorated with paintings, a scheme designed to disseminate culture among all classes of people. An off-shoot of such thinking was the later decoration of the interiors of railway compartments with reproductions of paintings, a practice that survived in Britain until well past the mid-twentieth century.

Advances in technology furthered the democratization of culture, enabling reproductions of art works to be marketed at relatively modest prices to a middle-class clientele that valued them both as a means of acquiring knowledge about high art and as a source of potential household decorations (Young 2002, 10–11, 92–93, 102–111). For Londoners and visitors to London, the annual exhibitions at the Royal Academy (for those who could afford the one-shilling entry fee) provided first-hand acquaintance with new art works, while shows at the British Institution often included older works. Then, there was the as yet modestly-sized collection at the National Gallery.

By 1841, there was a sufficiently broad knowledge of art that *Punch* could assume a degree of art-literacy among its readers sufficient enough for them to be able to recognize and enjoy burlesques of well-known art works (Altick 1997, 668). For example, *Punch* readers were entertained with comic burlesques in 1844, 1845, and 1896 of the *Laocoon* sculpture in the Musei Vaticani (7:28–29; 9:50; 81:244; and 110:81), the Elgin Marbles in 1852 (22:224), the *Apollo Belvedere* in 1846 (11:6), and Hiram Powers's sculpture *The Greek Slave* in 1844 and 1851 (7:28; and 20:236). Also burlesqued were John Singleton Copley's painting *The Collapse of the Earl of Chatham in the House of Lords* in 1847 (13:235), Jean Louis Géricault's *The Raft of the 'Medusa'* in 1851 (20:237), Henry Fuseli's *The Nightmare* in 1866 (50:101), Guido Reni's *Aurora* in 1874 (66:100–101), William Quiller Orchardson's *Napoleon on Board the Bellerophon* in 1880 (78:226) and his *Hard Hit* in 1885 (89:286), Albrecht Dürer's engraving *The Knight, Death, and the Devil* in 1887 (92:115) and his *Melancholia* in 1893 (104:194), and engravings from William Hogarth's *Marriage à la Mode* and *Industry and Idleness* in 1879 and 1891 respectively (77:163; 101:223).

Two artists particularly singled out by *Punch* for burlesque were the very popular Edwin Landseer and John Everett Millais. Of Landseer's works, *Punch* burlesqued *Islay and Tilco with a Red Macaw and Two Love Birds* in 1844 (7:38), his *Tethered Rams* in 1846 (10:36), his *The Challenge* in 1849 (16:180), his *Old Shepherd's Chief Mourner* in 1858 (34:24), his *Suspense* in 1871 (61:263), and his *The Cat's Paw* in 1880 (78:130). Millais was a friend to *Punch* and an especial friend of John Leech. He was also an occasional contributor and dinner guest (Spielmann 1895, 86, 517–518). From among his paintings, *Punch* burlesqued *Christ in the House of His Parents* in 1850 (18:198), *The Order of Release* in 1857 (33:98), *The North West Passage* in 1874 (67:239), and *Sowing Tares* in 1886 (90:13).

For many of its burlesques of the visual arts, *Punch* drew upon the annual London art exhibitions, particularly those of the Royal Academy each May and June. As already mentioned in Chapter 2, by the end of the century, the Royal Academy exhibition was attracting between 350,000 and 400,000 people. Increasingly, the one-shilling entry fee became affordable to more and more people, and for those who did not attend in person, there were printed commentaries (and sometimes reproductions) in newspapers and magazines. In addition there were reviews and reproduction of exhibit works in such specialized magazines as *The Graphic*, *The Art Journal* and *The Art*

Annual. The response of *Punch* to the interest, discussion, and publications generated each year was to offer its own reviews, often in the form of burlesques of the exhibition catalogues. All this is relevant to this chapter because, in keeping with Victorian tastes, the exhibitions frequently included compositions depicting Shakespearean characters and scenes (Altick 1985, 298–306; and Young 2002, 10, 11, 33, 47–48, 103, 110, 136, *et passim*). On a number of occasions, *Punch* burlesqued such works, either in its annual reports on the art exhibitions or in separate engravings or articles, especially when a work became particularly well known.

Among the works in this latter category was Sir Thomas Lawrence's portrait of John Philip Kemble as Hamlet, which is today in the Tate Gallery. This famous painting has been mentioned several times in previous chapters. It was first exhibited at the Royal Academy in 1801, forty years before the birth of *Punch*. Originally, it was the property of George IV, but in 1836, his successor, William IV, donated it to the nation. It then hung first in the National Gallery and then for a time in the National Portrait Gallery (Altick 1985, 305). It was thus familiar to many Londoners, but it had a much wider currency in the form of reproductions by painters and engravers who ensured that it became familiar during the century that followed among many who had never seen the original work (Garlick 1989, no. 451 [d]; Pressly 1993, no. 115; and Young 2002, 49 and 248).

Lawrence's portrait depicts Hamlet alone, an isolated, meditative figure, standing in a graveyard beside a newly-dug grave at night. He wears a long cloak and a dark plumed bonnet, and around his neck hangs the Order of the Elephant. In his left hand he holds a skull, but his gaze is upwards. In July of 1848, *Punch* included an unsigned wood engraving of this work to accompany an article by Jerrold aimed at goading the royal family (particularly the Queen) concerning undue neglect of the English theatre (15:32). The engraving (Figure 45) showed a mournful-looking Hamlet (Mr. Punch) standing, as in Lawrence's painting, with a skull in his left hand at his side. He wears a three-quarter length cloak and a plumed bonnet. The horizon is drawn very low (as in Lawrence's painting), and at top right is a crescent moon. Given the familiarity with Lawrence's work, *Punch*'s readership would surely have recognized the parody involved.

The same could also be said of a burlesque of Lawrence's painting that appeared in *Punch* the following year (17:147). The unsigned big cut, almost certainly the work of John Leech, was entitled 'HAMLET IN THE LONDON CHURCHYARD' (Figure 46). It accompanied a burlesque by Percival Leigh of Hamlet's meditation upon Yorick's skull, and the caption below the engraving consists of a telling quotation from *Hamlet*: 'Why man not imagination trace the remains of an alderman, till we find them poisoning his ward?' Around the neck of Hamlet (again transformed into Mr. Punch) hangs a chivalric order, but not the Order of the Elephant that Kemble had worn. The animal here represented appears to be a dog with its tail erect, presumably Punch's dog, Toby. Part of Punch's campaign against the unsanitary state of many graveyards, the engraving and Leigh's page-length parody of Shakespeare's graveyard scene satirically chastise the city and church authorities in London for allowing graveyards to become breeding places for disease, and specifically typhoid (see *Punch* 17:145). In burlesquing Lawrence's painting, *Punch* was clearly not in any way denigrating the original work of art. Rather, its transformation of the original invited viewers to exercise their wit and knowledge by recognizing the source and the comic-satiric effect achieved by the transformation. At the same time, we can note that no suggestion is given that Lawrence's original is a questionable form of Shakspeareanity. Indeed, quite the contrary would appear to be the case.

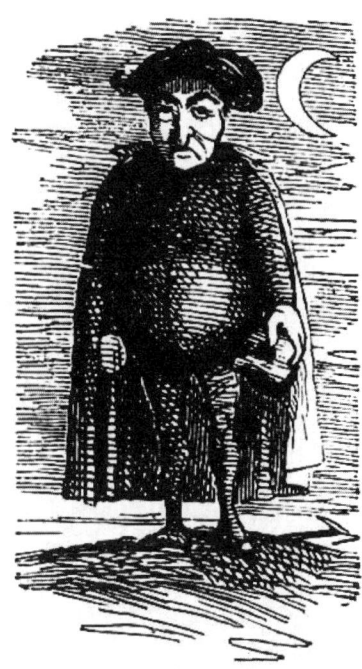

Figure 45. Unidentified artist's burlesque of Lawrence's portrait of J. P. Kemble as Hamlet. *Punch* (15 July 1848), 15:32.

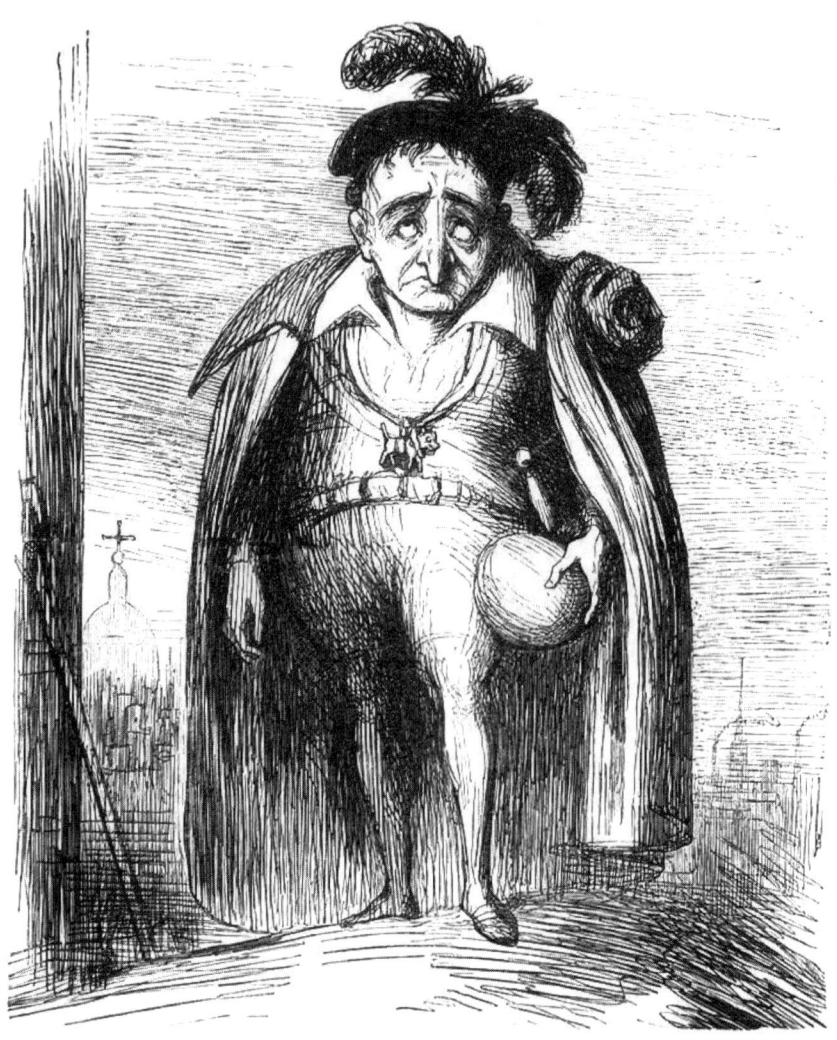

Figure 46. John Leech (unsigned), burlesque of Lawrence's portrait of J. P. Kemble as Hamlet. *Punch* (13 October 1849), 17:147.

Another well-known painting on a Shakespearean topic was William Hogarth's portrait of David Garrick as Richard III (c. 1745), now in the Walker Art Gallery, Liverpool. This depicted the episode

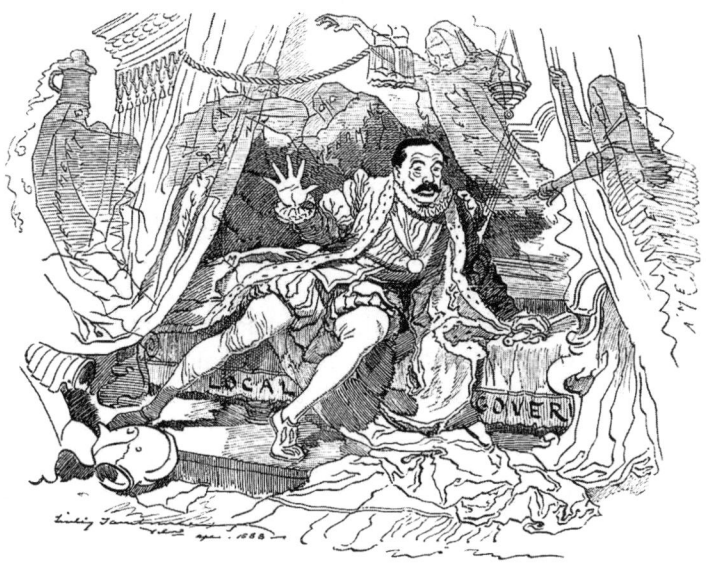

Figure 47. Linley Sambourne's burlesque of Hogarth's portrait of Garrick as Richard III. *Punch* (28 April 1888), 94:194.

in the final act of *Richard III*, in which the title character is visited the night before the Battle of Bosworth by a series of ghosts. In Hogarth's work, which has been described as 'the most frequently engraved and widely disseminated theatrical portrait of the eighteenth century' (Bate 2003, 12), Richard is depicted semi-recumbent upon a curtained bed. Terrified, he has started up, one hand raised, palm forward, with fingers spread as if to ward off the spectres that assail him. In the *Punch* issue for 28 April 1888, a full-page engraving designed by Linley Sambourne provided a witty burlesque of Hogarth's portrait. The engraving was part of a series of 'MR PUNCH'S PARALLELS', here with the added note 'After a Celebrated Picture'. Significantly, as with the burlesques of Lawrence's work, the original artist is not named. *Punch* could presumably expect that the original was well enough known not to need identification.

In Sambourne's design, Garrick was replaced by C. T. Ritchie, who had joined Lord Salisbury's cabinet as President of the Local Government Board in May 1887. Ritchie is shown dressed as Richard III and reclining on a bed that is inscribed 'LOCAL GOVERNMENT'. All around the bed are a number of ghosts. Several of these are inscribed 'AMENDMENT'. The caption reads: '"RITCHIE'S HIMSELF AGAIN!" – (*Till further notice.*)' (94:194). This is based on the famous interpolated line in Colley Cibber's version of the play: 'Richard's himself again.' Ritchie's chief task had been the Local Government Act of 1888 that created, for the first time, 62 county councils (Ensor 1936, 202–203). The ghostly amendments no doubt are reminders of the difficulties that had accompanied the passage of the quite radical bill as it was debated in Parliament.

Another painting that *Punch* felt assured would need no identification was Daniel Maclise's *The Play Scene in 'Hamlet'*. This had created something of a sensation at the Royal Academy exhibition in 1842. It was widely reviewed and acclaimed, and during the exhibition, there was constantly a crowd around it (*Daniel Maclise* 1972, 72; Forbes 1975, 102; Altick 1985, 302–302; Young 2002, 196–197). Later, it was bought from Maclise by Robert Vernon, who then gave 166 paintings and sculptures from his collection of British paintings to the National Gallery in 1847. Maclise's work was part of this donation and thus became available for all to see in the National Gallery. Today, it is in the Tate Gallery, which was opened in 1897 as the National Gallery of British Art.

When Vernon's gift was announced, *Punch* responded with an article by Tom Taylor in which some of the more prominent pictures in the Vernon Gallery held a meeting to discuss their imminent transfer to an institution often criticized for its shabby facilities, poor management, and questionable care of the works entrusted to it (see *Punch* 7:131, 8:246, 11:186, 11:193, 17:155, 17:231). According to Taylor's article, works by Joshua Reynolds, David Wilkie, Edwin Landseer, William Etty, William Turner, and John Constable all participated, and among the more prominent paintings to speak was

Daniel Maclise's *The Play Scene in 'Hamlet'*. In a burlesque of Hamlet's best-known soliloquy, Maclise's work

> [...] remarked, that 'to be or not to be' was now the question? He would ask the meeting whether 'twas nobler in a work to suffer the stench and crowding of a National Gallery, or to take steps with the Commissioners, and, by protesting, stop them? For who, he wished to know, would bear the smells and clouds of dust, the cleaner's wrong, the keeper's contumely, the ignorance of office, and the spurns that native talent from the Trustees takes, when he himself might his own place command, in a collection?' (13:108)

Twenty-four years later, in the issue for 2 September 1871, Charles Keene contributed a half-page design (Figure 48) that that was

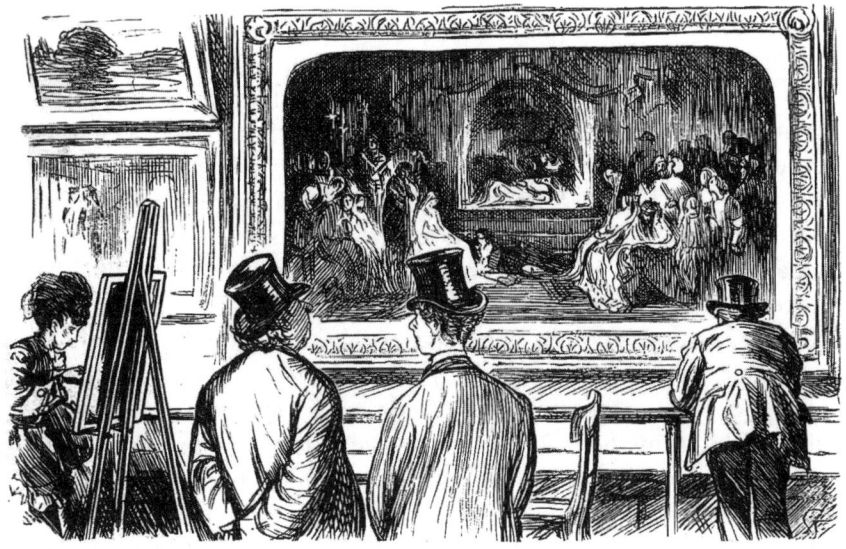

Figure 48. Charles Keene's depiction of the interior of the National Gallery and of Maclise's painting of the Play Scene in *Hamlet*. *Punch* (2 September 1871), 61:92.

entitled 'TECHNICAL' and depicted Maclise's painting on display in the National Gallery. The comedy is here not so much based upon a particular picture, which in this instance is not burlesqued, but upon the ignorance and naïveté of those looking at it. Keene's engraving shows a woman at left making a painted copy of the work. To the right, a man leans over the protective railing and peers intently at the picture. The main focus, however, is upon two men in the foreground whose dialogue is recorded below, a dialogue that reveals them to be actors whose appreciation of Maclise's artistry seems to be severely limited:

> *First Player ('Juvenile Lead').* 'PLAY SCENE – HAMLET. (*Deferentially.*) WHAT DO YOU THINK OF IT?'
> *Second Player ('First Heavy').* 'HOW PRECIOUS WELL THEM 'SUPERS' ARE PAINTED, AIN'T THEY?' (61:92)

The object of Keene's work is to poke fun at the ignorance and banality of the two men as they contemplate a well-known and much praised icon of Shakspeareanity, a representation of a scene from *Hamlet* that had earlier been made widely available in Charles Rolls's 1854 steel engraving for the *Art Journal* and in an 1863 steel engraving by Charles William Sharpe that had in turn been given to subscribers of the Art Union of London in 1868 (Young 2002, 103 and 196; Bate 2003, 27). Significantly, Rolls's engraving was later reissued in the 1872 Imperial edition of Knight's *Pictorial Shakspeare* and again in 1879 in J. S. Vertue's *Shakspere Gallery*. Other than Lawrence's 1801 portrait of Kemble as Hamlet, Keene could not have chosen a representation of Shakespeare that was better known.

Later, in the issue for 14 May 1892, *Punch* would make a similar point about the crass reactions of some viewers before paintings in public exhibitions (102:232), this time choosing among examples of celebrated and instantly recognizable works two Pre-Raphaelite paintings on Shakespearean topics: Millais's painting of the drowning *Ophelia*, and William Holman Hunt's *Claudio and Isabella*, first exhibited some forty years earlier at the Royal Academy in 1852 and 1853 respectively. Both paintings are now in the Tate Gallery.

On other occasions, *Punch* made fun of the exhibitors, examples being Thackeray's 'ROYAL ACADEMY' in 1846 (10:214), and Richard Doyle's 'IT IS OUR OPENING DAY' in 1848 (14:185). The first consisted of six humorous sketches of different types of artists, together with a satirical text, and the second was a depiction of a large crowd of artists jostling violently upon a grand staircase on opening day of the exhibition. A week after the second of these examples, Doyle burlesqued 'HIGH ART AND THE ROYAL ACADEMY' (14:197) by depicting two purported paintings of the dramatic moment in *Henry IV*, Part II, when Prince Hal strikes the Chief Justice (Figure 49). One painting (that on the left) supposedly employs the manner of

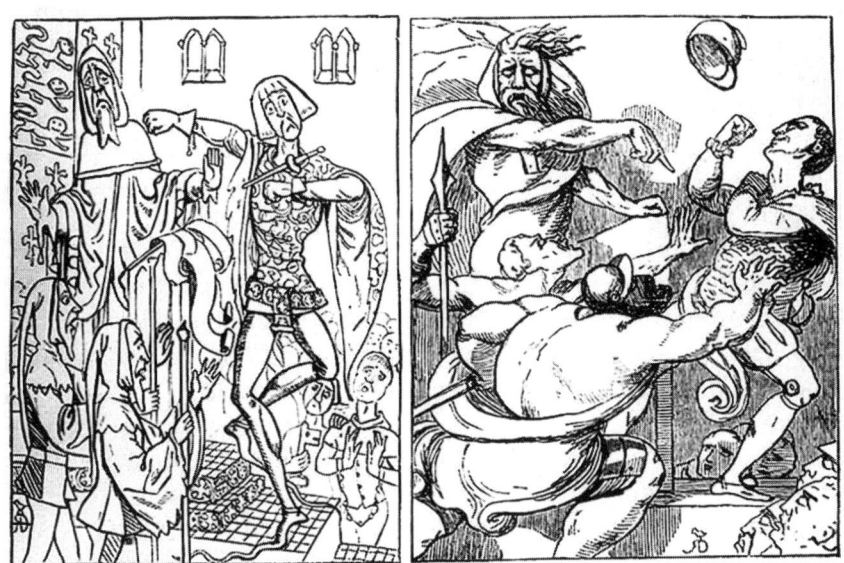

Figure 49. Richard Doyle, 'HIGH ART AND THE ROYAL ACADEMY'. *Punch* (13 May 1848), 14:197.

the Medieval and Gothic, of Fra Angelico, and of Pugin. It is done in the 'flat style,' an allusion to the outline technique used for the Westminster competition cartoons, a style associated with John Flaxman's engravings based on Homer and on Dante, and Moritz Retzsch's engravings based on Goethe and those in his *Outlines to Shakspeare* (Young 2002, 104–105). The other painting (that on the right) uses the style of Michelangelo and Henry Fuseli and includes what may be an allusion to Michelangelo's Sistine Chapel depiction of God creating human kind through the pointing of his finger. In this instance, however, the pointing finger is that of the Chief Justice and is directed towards an aggressive Prince Hal, whose fist is raised against him. Doyle's two burlesque designs are accompanied by a letter addressed to Mr. Punch from an artist ('ONE OF THE NINE HUNDRED REJECTED ONES') who submitted both works to the Royal Academy but was met with rejections. Doyle's burlesque compositions are a good-humoured comment on the current discussions about the merits or otherwise of outline art (Altck 1997, 676–679) and the doubtless annual complaints from artists whose submissions were rejected by the Royal Academy.

A *Punch* item containing a somewhat more complex allusion to a Shakespearean topic was John Tenniel's design entitled 'LITTLE VICTIMS' (79:91). This was published in the issue for 28 August 1880 (Figure 50). The full-page big cut is an amusing burlesque of a painting that had been exhibited at the Royal Academy two years before and is today owned by Royal Holloway College, University of London. Concerned, perhaps, that *Punch*'s readership might need a little help in recognizing the object of the burlesque, a caption is added: *'With Mr. Punch's apologies to "The Princes in the Tower", by J. E. Millais, R.A.'* Millais's painting had depicted the two boy princes (he had used his own children as models) in Shakespeare's *Richard III* standing at the foot of a stair case in a state of fear and bewilderment. As the viewer would recognize, they are in the Tower of London where they will shortly be murdered on the orders of their uncle, the Duke of Gloucester, in his quest to destroy all obstacles that stand between him and his ambition to become king.

In accordance with Shakespeare's text (III i 104), one prince is taller than the other. Tenniel's cartoon follows Millais's painting very closely, but the princes are changed into a hare (the taller of the two) and a rabbit. The caption contains a brief dialogue between the two animals. The 'terrified' hare says: 'WHAT'S THAT? – THE LORDS?' To this the 'shuddering' Rabbit responds: 'P'R'APS IT'S THE FARMERS!!' The engraving is thus transformed into political commentary, since, as the *Punch* reader discovers, Tenniel's big cut is linked to an item five pages earlier ('PUNCH'S ESSENCE OF PARLIAMENT'). This reports the deliberations in the House of Commons. Apparently, on the previous Thursday, there had been a debate

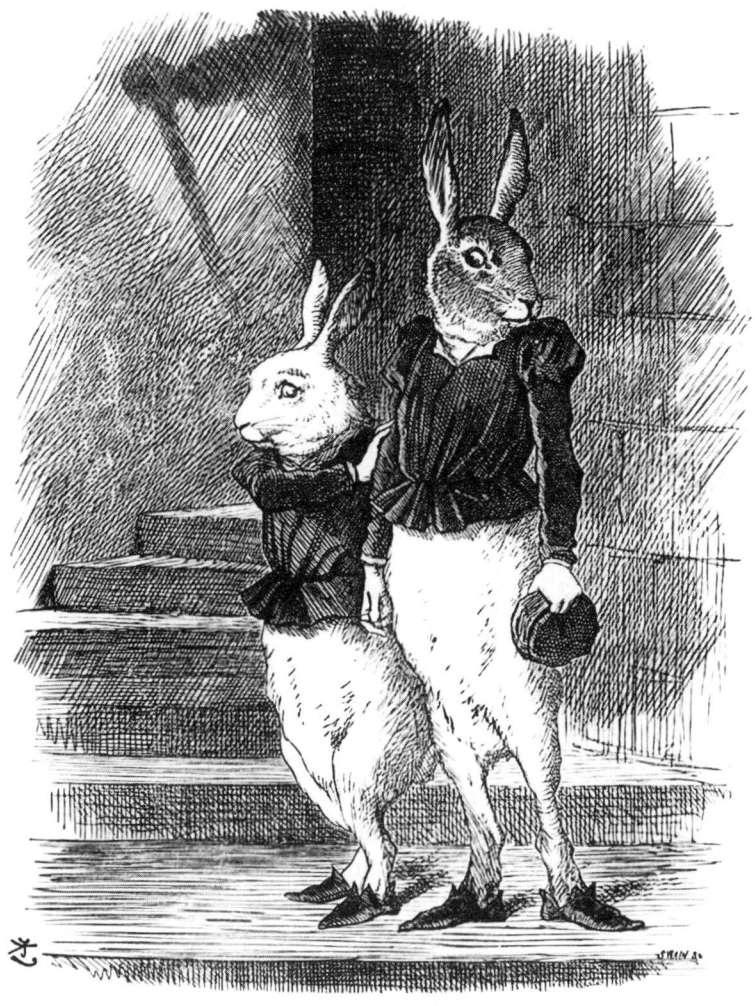

Figure 50. John Tenniel's burlesque of Millais's painting of the two princes in the Tower of London. *Punch* (28 August 1880), 79:91.

concerning the 'Hares and Rabbits Bill'. This had pitted farmers against sportsmen regarding hares and rabbits. Meanwhile, the 'Little Victims' (see Cartoon), by no means 'regardless of their doom', prick alarmed ears at the coming shadow, which, whether it be that of the Lord, who would preserve them for Sport, or the Farmer, who would pot them for crop-preservation, 'can bode but little good to Puss and Bunny' (79:86). When one has read this and returns to Tenniel's work, one notices that the 'coming shadow' (it is also there in Millais's painting) is depicted in the form of a menacing shadow on the wall beside the staircase behind the two animals.

Tenniel's full-page burlesque of Millais's *Little Princes* stands on its own, but most of the art works on Shakespearean topics that are referred to or that are burlesqued in *Punch* are named in *Punch*'s reviews of the annual Royal Academy exhibitions (Altick 1985, 298–306; and Young, *Hamlet and the Visual Arts*, 10, 11, 47–50, 110, 136, *et passim*.). In imitation of the often lengthy and detailed reviews that appeared each year in a number of newspapers and periodicals, *Punch* regularly provided its own humorous commentaries, beginning in 1842 with 'THE ROYAL ACADEMY' (2:215). Frequently, *Punch*'s accounts of the paintings, including those on Shakespearean subjects, would include small burlesque versions of the supposed pictures. Certain pictures on Shakespearean topics were among those burlesqued in this fashion. In its reviews, *Punch* frequently also provided what purport to be specific catalogue numbers so that those who had already been to the exhibition and had a catalogue to hand or those about to attend the exhibition could then enjoy *Punch*'s own descriptive entry. However, as will be noted below, *Punch* sometimes deliberately confused matters by not necessarily referring to actual works but instead creating imaginary substitutes. In such instances, the catalogue numbers as provided in *Punch* were then totally misleading.

The earliest *Punch* review of a painting on a Shakespearean subject was by Tom Taylor and appeared in connection with the Royal Academy exhibition in 1851 (20:219). The work in question was Millais's *Mariana in the Moated Grange*. A major figure in the Pre-Raphaelite Brotherhood, Millais had been bitterly attacked by *Punch* for his *Christ in the House of His Parents* the year before (18:198), an attack followed up by Dickens in *Household Words* in the issue for 15 June. Taylor begins his review of the 1851 exhibition, however, on a more conciliatory note by referring to an admonition of Prince Albert concerning critics and noting that because

> [...] genius draws itself up like a sensitive plant, at the harsh touch of satire, we are determined, this year, to water our artistic May-flowers, which blossom on the walls of the Academy, with the milk of human kindness, and not the bitter water from the well of Truth.

Even so, the review then proceeds to have some fun with *Convent Thoughts* by Charles Allston Collins, one of 'our dear and promising young friends, the Pre-Raphaelites'.

Taylor then directs readers' attention to Millais's work, now one of the artist's best-known works and since 1999 on display at the Tate Gallery. It was inspired by Tennyson's poetic portrait of the character Mariana in Shakespeare's *Measure for Measure*. Having been rejected by Angelo, to whom she was betrothed, she has been leading a lonely and desolate life in a moated grange. It appears that she still loves Angelo and longs to be reunited with him. The painting depicts Mariana in a blue dress standing before a stained glass window, apparently waiting for news of the man she loves. Her embroidery lies on a table in front of the window, and she is standing, her hands on the small of her back, as though she is too tired to continue her work. When the painting was exhibited, it was accompanied by lines from Tennyson that express her forlorn state:

> She only said, 'My life is dreary –
> He cometh not' she said;
> She said, 'I am aweary, aweary –
> I would that I were dead.'

The *Punch* critic, failing or perhaps simply refusing to engage with the subtleties of Millais's picture, its symbolism and its eroticism, instead reads the painting only in the most banal realistic terms. Quoting Tennyson's final stanza, 'Then, said she, I am very dreary', Taylor's review, which is accompanied by a small unsigned engraving (Figure 51), begins by suggesting that Millais's painting 'is obviously meant to insinuate a delicate excuse for the gentleman who wouldn't come –

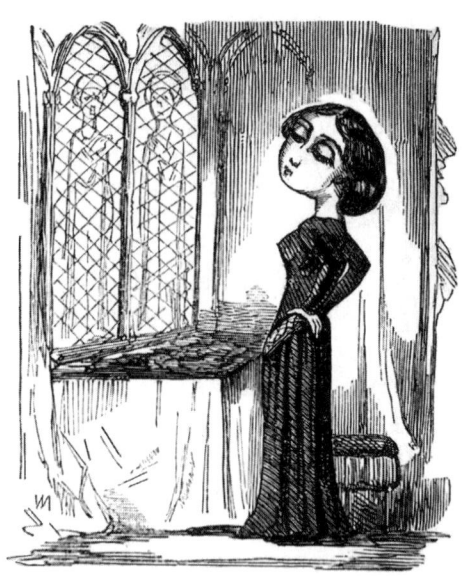

Figure 51. William McConnell's burlesque of Millais's *Mariana in the Moated Grange*. *Punch* (24 May 1851), 20:219.

and to show the world the full import of TENNYSON'S description'. In the *Punch* author's view,

Anything drearier than the lady, or brighter than her blue velvet robe, it is impossible to conceive. It is clear that that bit of crochet is too much for her. Her weary stretch and the yawn that is so finely foreshadowed in her face, say plainly, 'Oh, dear, how tired I am!' which is the vulgar English of TENNYSON'S world-famous *refrain*.

Years later, in 1892, *Punch* returned to Millais's painting with an engraving designed by George du Maurier (102:53). It was entitled 'ABOMINATIONS OF MODERN SCIENCE' (Figure 52). It depicts Mariana with candle-snuffers in one hand, apparently unsure about how to deal with a light bulb. The caption totally undercuts the romantic image created by Millais of the lonely woman who has been abandoned by her corrupt lover (Angelo) after her dowry has been lost at sea. Instead, we hear how Mariana arrived at the moated grange just in time to dress for dinner but found to her sorrow that her room was 'WARMED BY HOT WATER PIPES AND LIGHTED BY ELECTRICITY'.

During the last five decades of the nineteenth century, *Punch* reviews of Royal Academy exhibitions would allude to over twenty works on Shakespearean topics. Eight of these reviews were accompanied, as in the case of the comments on Millais's *Mariana*, with an engraving. Two of the Shakespearean works alluded to in the *Punch* reviews have already been mentioned in the previous chapter: Edwin Long's 1877 portrait of Irving as Richard III (74:265), and an unnamed artist's work that in *Punch*'s engraved version ('After Six Lessons. Lady Amateur imitating eminent Tragedian') provided an opportunity for a humorous joke concerning Irving's peculiar gait.

This latter work provides an example of a difficulty that confronts anyone who examines the *Punch* reviews of the Royal Academy exhibitions. According to *Punch*, the painting was No. 534 in the catalogue. However, Catalogue No. 534 in the 1887 exhibition was a painting by Henrietta Rae entitled 'Eurydice Sinking Back to Hades.' I have been unable to locate this painting, and it may, like so many other Victorian paintings, no longer be extant.

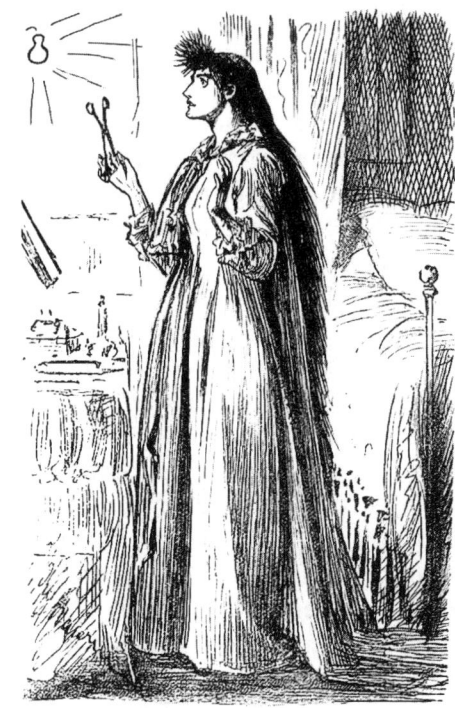

Figure 52. George du Maurier's burlesque of Millais's *Mariana in the Moated Grange*. *Punch* (30 January 1892), 102:53.

It has thus not been possible to determine whether *Punch* was burlesquing Henrietta Rae's painting or randomly selecting a supposed catalogue number that in reality had no connection with any actual painting. This latter possibility seems to apply to the *Punch* treatment of an item in the 1882 exhibition. On 24 June, after reporting on the exhibition in a series of previous issues, *Punch* included a small engraving (6 x 4 cms) of what was supposedly No. 29 in the catalogue. It portrayed a boy Hamlet wearing a plumed bonnet and holding a whip. He is standing on a stage with a dog (a collie). The caption reads 'Hamlet Junior. "The Colly-er Dog will have his day." Mrs. J. Collier.' However, although Mrs. J. Collier did exhibit a painting in 1882, it was No. 1475 in the catalogue and entitled 'A Coming Tragedian'. Item No. 29 was a portrait by John Everett Millais entitled 'Mrs. James Stern'.

Another example of this kind of confusion occurred in 'Mr. Punch's Royal Academy Guide' (102:221), a review by Burnand of the 1892 exhibition. Again, *Punch* included a catalogue number (No. 699) and a small picture. In this instance the picture was supposedly by C. N. Henry and appears to portray two men fishing from a small boat. There is something caught in the net that they draw in, and the caption below suggests what this is by quoting a familiar line from *Hamlet*: '"Very Like a Whale", only it's a buoy not caught yet.' The burlesque is clear; however, in 1892, no artist by the name of C. N. Henry exhibited, and No. 699 in the exhibition catalogue was in fact a painting by Alan J. Hook entitled 'Dear Life!'

Caution is thus required when reading some of the *Punch* reviews of Royal Academy exhibits. Even so, most of the remaining allusions are to works that we know many *Punch* readers must have seen for themselves. A few examples can be briefly mentioned here. The year after Millais exhibited his *Mariana,* the public was confronted by his depiction of *Ophelia* (1852). In '"OUR CRITIC" AMONG THE PICTURES', the *Punch* reviewer, Tom Taylor, threw aside all previous opprobrium and gave Millais the most fulsome praise for this latter's *Ophelia* and his *Huguenot on St. Bartholomew's Day*:

> I have this year experienced a new sensation at the Exhibition of the Royal Academy. And I hasten to record my sense of the obligation to MR. MILLAIS. I offer my hand to that Pre-Raphaelite brother. I bow down to him, and I kiss the edge of his palette. I have rapped him over the knuckles, in former years, with my pen. He is at liberty to return the compliment, this year, with his maulstick.
>
> Before two pictures of MR. MILLAIS I have spent the happiest hour that I have ever spent in the Royal Academy Exhibition. In those two pictures I find more loving observation of Nature, more mastery in the reproduction of her forms and colours, more insight into the sentiment of our greatest poet, a deeper feeling of human emotion, a happier choice of a point of interest, and a more truthful rending of its appropriate expression, than in all the rest of those eight hundred squares put together. (22:216)

In noting his pleasure and that of 'the thousands who have felt as I felt before these pictures', Taylor was acknowledging the instant popularity of both pictures and of Millais's *Ophelia* in particular. Made familiar through countless reproductions, Millais's *Ophelia*, now in the Tate Gallery, quickly became the received image of Ophelia's fate, almost as recognizable as Hamlet, the man with the skull (Young 2002, 340). The painting depicts, as Taylor records in some detail, the prone and fully-clothed Ophelia in the brook that is shortly to claim her life. Her mouth is open, and she appears to be singing, as is recorded in the description of her death in *Hamlet* (IV vii 177). The beautiful woman (Elizabeth Siddal was Millais's model) wears an elaborate silver embroidered antique dress that Millais is known to have purchased especially for use in the painting (*Millais* 1967, 33), and she is framed by flowers and vegetation that Taylor describes in some detail. As Taylor appears to have been aware, Millais had been criticized for the elaborate pains he had taken to capture the details of the peripheral vegetation. However, instead of following this vein, Taylor defends Millais and directs his readers' attention to the main focus of the painting – Ophelia's face and what it expresses:

> Talk as you like, M'GILP, eminent painter, to your friend MR. SQUENCE, eminent critic, about the needless elaboration of those water mosses, and the over making-out of the rose-leaves, and the abominable finish of those riverside weeds matted with gossamer, which the field botanist may identify leaf by leaf. I tell you, I am aware of none of these. I see only that face of poor drowning OPHELIA. My eye goes to that, and rests on that, and sees nothing else, till [...] the tears blind me, and I am fain to turn from the face of the mad girl to the natural loveliness that makes her dying beautiful. (22:216)

Taylor's review of Millais's *Ophelia* then concludes with a somewhat backhanded compliment, but one that is sincere nonetheless in implying the success of Millais's graphic representation of Shakespeare's lines describing Ophelia's death: 'If a painter were ever pardonable for painting after a poet – and such a poet – MR. MILLAIS may be forgiven for his picture of OPHELIA.'

In the same exhibition at which Millais's *Ophelia* was shown, the American-born Charles R. Leslie's *Juliet* was first displayed. This depicted Juliet about to take the potion in IV iii. In contrast to the praise heaped upon Millais's painting, Taylor gave it a short but scathing mention (22:232), mocking Leslie's efforts by suggesting that the Shakespearean context of the painting had been imposed upon a much lowlier subject: 'If MR. LESLIE choose to paint MISS SMITH of Clapham Rise, as she appeared when about to take her medicine, he is welcome to do so. But let him give the thing its right name, and not mislead my pretty country cousin in this way, and compel me to set her right, […].'

The following year, however, *Punch* found a work on a Shakespearean topic at the 1853 exhibition that its reviewer, Taylor again, appears to have liked almost as much as Millais's *Ophelia*. The work in question was by the Pre-Raphaelite painter William Holman Hunt. His *Claudio and Isabella*, according to the enthusiastic Taylor was '*the* book of this collection, though it records in colours what SHAKSPEARE has written in words; […]' (24:199). He favours this work over all the other exhibits, including pictures by Landseer and Millais, and he is 'glad to say, too, that notwithstanding the infallible judgment of the *Examiner* critic, who talks about "Pre-Raffaelite, and other follies", my *Claudio and Isabella* has quite a large reading public […]'. In saying this, *Punch* (Taylor) is attesting to a growing shift in public taste away from so-called 'high art' and its representations on a grand scale of historical, religious, and allegorical subjects. Instead, there had developed among the general populace an appreciation for art that treated domestic, anecdotal, and contemporary topics. As Richard Altick has noted, *Punch* appears to have shared the popular sentiment that 'history painting was outmoded and unsuited, in any case, to the national temper' (Altick 1997, 673). In the remainder of his review of Hunt's *Claudio and Isabella*, Taylor explains in considerable detail what he sees in the picture, concentrating upon the manner in which each of the two central figures is painted in such a way that their inmost feelings are revealed. Of Isabella he says:

> I see in those grave, tearful eyes, that set brow, the dawn of the suspicion – till now kept down – that this brother, for whom she would die without a fear or a regret, is about to choose his own life before his sister's honour. Do you see how she presses her hands on his heart, as if to quell the fluttering fear that is about to unman the poor wretch, and how he has clutched her wrists in the abject terror that the images of what he fears of death bring storming in upon him? How skilfully and delicately he has marked in the character of her head,

with all its beauty, that strong temper which will soon rise to her lips in scornful rejection of 'that warpèd slip of wilderness' – that unworthy *Claudio*. (24:199)

Taylor's commentary on Claudio is equally detailed and likewise designed, he says, to suggest that Hunt has depicted the facial expressions and gestures that any reader of the review would display if placed in the same circumstances as the two figures in the painting. In conclusion, he responds to the negative reviews of some of his 'daily and weekly brethren' by comparing Hunt's masterful technique with that of Bellini. Significantly, Shakespeare is barely mentioned. His characters (Claudio and Isabella), it seems, have attained a life of their own, independent of the printed page and independent of the theatre. They now belong in the realm of the poetic imagination, freely available to the graphic artist and to the viewer, between whom is assumed a common familiarity with Shakespeare's original.

Such praise of graphic representations of Shakespearean subjects is, however, relatively rare in the *Punch* reviews of the annual Royal Academy exhibitions. Augustus Egg's 1860 painting of a scene in *The Taming of the Shrew* is, for example, described by Charles Eastlake as a 'shindy' in which '*Petruchio* clutches the joint as though it were his wife's jointure. Everything will be smashed or crashed, except the doublets, which are *slashed*' (38:200). Humorous passing allusions are made to works by John Rogers Herbert, William Powell Frith, and Edward Matthew Ward in 1868 and 1876 (54:155; and 70:188). Keeley Halswelle's 1878 depiction of the Play Scene in *Hamlet* gives rise to a pun ('all work and no play. But "Halswelle that ends well"') (74:265), and Edwin Long's 1880 three-quarter length portrait of Henry Irving as Hamlet provokes another when *Punch*, Burnand in this instance, mocking Long's compositional choice, referred to its title as 'Henry Irving as Hamlet, or, Knee Plus Ultra' (78:240). Shown at the same exhibition, John Gilbert's painting of the murdered Duke Humphrey in *Henry VI*, Part II, provides an excuse for word-play by Burnand on 'Gloucester' (78:240), and Anna Lea Merritt's painting of *Ophelia* provokes a pun by Burnand on the artist's name and a comment on Ophelia's hair: 'What's in a name? Merritt undoubtedly. The theatrical perruquier, from whom this *Ophelia* hired her wig, ought to be ashamed of himself. Fortunately for him, his name is not in the Catalogue' (78:241). In the review of the 1894 exhibition, Burnand's humour took a racist slant in 'GEMS FROM THE ROYAL ACADEMY'. His article reviewing the pictures at the Royal Academy Exhibition included an engraving purportedly representing Catalogue No. 523, a work by Solomon Joseph Solomon. The illustration provides a portrait of a stereotypical Jewish man and has the caption 'The Coming Hamlet. "Aha! wait till I appear"' (106:227).

In 1896, the American artist Edwin Austin Abbey exhibited his *Richard Duke of Gloucester and the Lady Anne*, a work that is now in the Yale University Art Gallery. Although the *Punch* reviewer, Burnand, made an attempt at humour, there is also a vein of unmistakable praise for the innovative expatriate's work. Abbey had a lifelong interest in Shakespeare's works, and his composition was to be the first of seven large oil paintings on Shakespearean topics that he provided for the Royal Academy exhibitions between 1896 and 1900 (Oakley 1994, 22, 40–43; Young 2002, 199–201). There appears to have been no painted precursor to his 'Wooing Scene', in which Richard, Duke of Gloucester, woos the Lady Anne, whose husband he has killed. However, Burnand makes no comment on this, nor does the reviewer offer any kind of detailed comment on the dramatic situation portrayed, the use of 'historic' costumes, the large number of retainers who accompany the funeral procession, and the startling way in which they are in movement as Richard pursues Anne, a departure from Shakespeare's I i, where everything is brought to a halt prior to Richard's wooing of the newly-made widow. Instead, Burnand first indulges in some punning wordplay when he suggests an alternative title: '*Dick and Anne: or, the Double Gloucester who thinks himself quite the Cheese, and the Lady who has just lost a Sovereign*' (110:227). In what follows, however, Burnand lauds the painting as 'a marvellous work', and predicts (with a final punning flourish) that 'This will be the talk of the public. The scene is in London, probably in the vicinity of Westminster, […] and will entitle the American artist to be remembered ever after as "Westminster Abbey". This is *the* picture of the year. Most certainly it is the very Abbeyest of "Abbey Thoughts".'

The following year, Abbey exhibited a painting of the Play Scene in *Hamlet*. Again, this was a highly innovative composition in that it concentrated its focus upon the figures of Hamlet and Ophelia and omitted the performance of the play-within-the-play which the characters are watching, instead presenting events as though seen through the eyes of the itinerant actors (Young 2002, 200–201). *Punch*'s comment was limited to an engraving by Edward Tennyson Reed (Figure 53). This burlesqued Abbey's portrayal of Hamlet and Ophelia, and in particular Hamlet's recumbent pose with his head against a seemingly

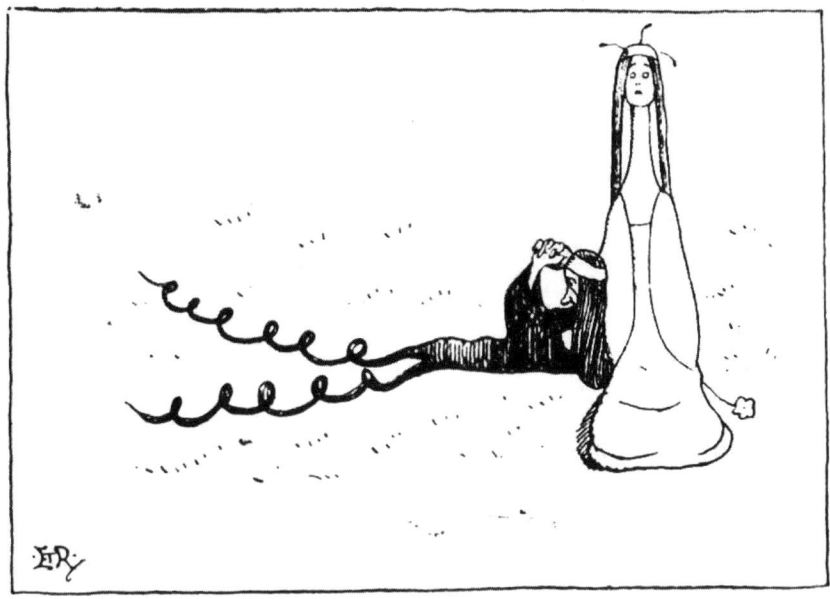

Figure 53. Edward Tennyson Reed's burlesque of Abbey's painting of the play scene in *Hamlet*. *Punch* (8 May 1897), 112:226.

unresponsive Ophelia. In the original, Hamlet lies on his back, his legs extended and apart. Reed exaggerates this and gives Hamlet corkscrews for legs. The caption below completes the burlesque: 'No. 477. Design for a Double Corkscrew: or, Gimlet, Prince of Denmark! E. A. Abbey, A.R.A.' (112:226). After this, and apart from a brief allusion to Sir Edward Poynter's *Helena and Hermia* in 1901 (120:356), *Punch* made no further allusions during the Victorian era to Royal Academy exhibits based on Shakespeare's works.

'Translations' – Burlesque Texts

One of the most common kinds of Shakespearean transformation during the nineteenth century was not opera, ballet, hippodrama, or pictorial art, but textual burlesque that in its most extended form found its way into the theatre. Michael Booth has noted that during this period 'Shakespearean burlesque was almost an industry of its own' (Booth 1981, 196), and more recently Richard W. Schoch has shown in telling detail just how extensive that industry was and how it belonged to an even larger swath of stage comedy where no area of culture was exempt from the satiric scrutiny of burlesque, whether opera, melodrama, poetic drama, mythology, English history and legend, or contemporary fiction and plays (Schoch 2002, 4). Vital to the effectiveness of burlesque was that the reader/viewer be familiar with the object being burlesqued. Some thirty-one years before the birth of *Punch*, John Poole, whose *Hamlet Travestie* was published in 1810 and first performed a year later, explained this very clearly when he defended his choice of Shakespeare's *Hamlet* as the object of his play:

> From the force of its sentiments, the beauty of its imagery, and, above all, the solemnity of its conduct, there is, perhaps, no tragedy in the English language better adapted to receive a burlesque than 'HAMLET'; and from its being so frequently before the public, so very generally read, and so continually quoted, it is, more than any other, calculated to give to burlesque its full effect, and which can only be produced by a facility of contrast with its subject work. [...] For a reader, therefore, to derive entertainment from a burlesque, but more particularly to be enabled to decide whether it be ill or well executed, a familiar acquaintance with the original is indispensable. (Poole 1978, 6)

As Poole's statement also implies, not only is familiarity with the original a requirement, but the more admired and revered that original the better. One may add, too, that the more earnestly Shakespeare was presented by actors and theatre managers as the apogee of high culture, the greater the subversive invitation of burlesque. It is thus no accident that coinciding with the great Shakespeare revivals of Macready, Phelps, Kean, and Irving that were discussed in the previous chapter, there was also a notable increase in Shakespearean burlesques (Schoch 2002, 5–6), many of which burlesqued those Shakespeare plays being revived in the theatre. In addition, such works often burlesqued the accents, mannerisms, and stage business of specific actors, used men in women's roles or women in men's roles, put women in costumes that revealed what polite society would normally conceal, and set Shakespeare's best-known speeches to popular tunes of the time. Burnand's *Lord Lovel and Lady Nancy Bell or the Bounding Brigand of the Bakumboilum* (1856), for example, contained a scene burlesquing *Romeo and Juliet*, which then merged into a mocking rendition of the Statue Scene in Charles Kean's current production of *The Winter's Tale*, all accompanied by music familiar from Kean's *The Corsican Brothers* (Wells 1978, 1:xiv–xv). When Irving was enjoying his phenomenal success as Hamlet in 1874 at the Lyceum, Poole's *Hamlet Travesty* was put on at the Globe with Odell as Hamlet, 'and shortly afterwards with Mr. Leonard Boyne as the Prince, both actors indulging in an imitation of Mr. Irving's performance' (Adams 1891, 122). A year later, Salvini's *Othello* was countered by the anonymous *Salthello Ovini*, and when the young Wilson Barrett dared to play Hamlet at the Princess's during Irving's absence in 1884, J. Comyns Carr wrote *A Fireside Hamlet* for the Prince of Wales Theatre, and William Yardley supplied *Very Little Hamlet* for the Gaiety (Hamilton 1885, 2:164), both of which were reviewed by Arthur William à Beckett in *Punch* (87:292).

However, though specific actors and performances might often be mocked, fundamental to the whole enterprise of nineteenth-century Shakespearean burlesque is that the value and status of the original textual object are not undermined. The youthful Barrett's pretensions were subjected to ridicule in *Very Little Hamlet* by having Nellie Farren depict him as a child vowing to play Hamlet. Hilarious it may be to rewrite the plot and text of plays like *Hamlet, Macbeth, Romeo and Juliet, Othello, Richard III*, and *The Tempest*, to mention the most commonly-burlesqued plays, but respect for them remained untarnished. Indeed, burlesque indirectly strengthened their cultural status. At the same time, by testing audiences' memories of the original works, burlesque strengthened and widened knowledge of Shakespeare. Burlesque was in effect an instrument of Shakspeareanity.

Such a positive view of burlesque as an agent of high culture did not, of course, go unchallenged. There were those who felt that burlesque in itself was a debased form of art that in turn debased its subjects. In fact, there was a fairly lively debate during the Victorian era concerning these matters (Schoch 2002, 19–20, 57–58, 70–73), one that flared up, for example, when it was announced in the *Daily News* in August 1883 that John Hollingshead (he was an 'outside' salaried staff member of *Punch*) would be producing burlesques of *Hamlet* and *The Tempest* at the Gaiety Theatre. One reader wrote to complain that the announcement was made 'uncoupled with any word of disapproval or disgust'. In his view,

> [...] the English stage may well be thought by Englishmen to have reached its lowest point of degradation, and one strangely in contrast with the honour we profess to pay to it, when two of the finest plays and finest works in all literature are to be sacrificed to the passion for burlesque. We had better consider ourselves no longer the same nation, and cease to pride ourselves on having produced the foremost man in all literature when we descend to this without protest. (Quoted Hamilton 1885, 2:144).

Vigorous defenses of burlesque then followed in the *Daily News* and the *Times*, and included lengthy statements by the editor of *Punch*, Burnand. This latter happened to be the author of the forthcoming burlesque of *The Tempest*, which, as was mentioned in Chapter One, was entitled *Ariel, a Burlesque Fairy Drama in Three Acts and Four Tableaux*. On 20 October, Burnand's play was reviewed in *Punch* by its author (the reviewer's name, of course, was not revealed). In the review, Burnand went out of his way to refer without the slightest qualms of conscience to the very positive notices the play had had in other publications (85:184–185). That *Punch* articles were never signed was clearly advantageous in this particular situation.

If we accept that burlesque was one means by which bardolatry was paradoxically supported and reinforced during the Victorian era, the implications for *Punch* are considerable. After all, within its pages, Shakespeare's words were constantly burlesqued. Lines, scenes, and (on occasion) entire plays were subjected to textual transformations intended to provoke among readers the same kinds of amusement that they experienced when attending burlesque performances at the theatre. Particular sources of delight and amusement were derived from the employment of Shakespeare's words and characters to parallel topical issues and persons in the news; from humorous allusions to familiar local places; from the transformation of Shakespeare's words into mundane, modern idiom to reduce the high-flown and poetic to the lowly speech of the everyday; and from the reduction of Shakespeare's characters into familiar modern citizens, who seem far from their original and often heroic and elevated counterparts. Of course, Shakespeare was by no means the only writer burlesqued in the pages of *Punch*. Dickens was an especially favourite target. Among others were Isaac Walton, Jonathan Swift, Thomas Gray, Samuel Coleridge, Edgar Allan Poe, Robert Louis Stevenson, Alfred Tennyson, Edward Bulwer-Lytton, and Lewis Carroll, this last on occasion permitting some additional fun in house since John Tenniel was Carroll's illustrator for the *Alice* books. However, in spite of the wealth of burlesque based on the works of such writers, Shakespeare was by far the most frequently burlesqued author, an obvious sign of his stature within the national consciousness and a sign that familiarity with his works could be expected among *Punch*'s readers. Lines from *Hamlet* provided by far the most frequent source for burlesque, with *Macbeth* a distant though robust second. *As You Like It, Richard III, Othello*, and *The Tempest* then followed. Familiar lines, passages, and scenes from Shakespeare's remaining plays also on occasion provided ammunition for burlesque.

Most commonly, burlesque in *Punch* of Shakespeare's text focuses upon a single, well-known line. Typically, that line is applied to a context far removed from its original place in Shakespeare. Oberon's 'I know a bank', for example, provides the titled for a short article by Horace Mayhew about farthing banks that have been established in 'connection with the Ragged Schools' (36:207). Showing off this same technique, a short article by Henry Silver appeared on Christmas Eve 1859, in which several one-liners of this kind were dovetailed together:

Is it reasonable to suppose that *Othello* was out fishing when he remarked to *Desdemona,* 'Perdition catch thy sole?'

'Then let the kettle to the trumpet speak!' Is this reading correct? Should it not be rather, 'Then let the trumpet to the kettle speak!' Speaking-trumpets are, and long have been, quite common. But what grounds have we for believing that in the time when SHAKESPEARE wrote, any more than in our own, there was such an instrument as a speaking kettle?

'My tables! meat it is, I set it down.' May this be cited as a proof that *Hamlet* was a butcher?

What authorities can you quote for the popular belief that the man *Macbeth* called 'whey-face' was in reality a Kurd? (37:254)

Elsewhere, John Hollingshead used the Witches' line in *Macbeth* ('Fair is foul, and foul is fair'), which alludes to both the weather and the Witches' deceptions, to comment on the founding of the National Fair Trade League. Apparently, the League proposed a tax on food, something that the *Punch* author clearly did not feel was 'fair' (81:71).

Often, too, a line may be altered in some way to fit a new context. Commenting on the noxious smells emanating from Covent Garden, for example, Burnand offered a version of a familiar line from *Hamlet*: 'Break, break, my heart, for I must hold my – nose' (69:57). When the military commander Sir Garnet Wolseley was given a peerage and thus became a member of the House of Lords but ineligible to sit in the House of Commons, Hollingshead recalled his namesake in Shakespeare's *Henry VIII*, in which the Cardinal comments on his fall from grace by saying 'Had I but serv'd my God with half the zeal / I serv'd my king, He would not in mine age / Have left me naked to mine enemies.' The report in *Punch* on Sir Garnet Wolseley's good fortune is ironically entitled 'THE FALL OF WOLSELEY' and accompanied by a note that states that 'WOLSELEY is to be banished to the House of Lords for the remainder of his natural life.' This is then followed by a burlesque of Shakespeare's famous line: 'If I had served my country with half the zeal that I have served my Chief [i.e. the Prime Minister], he would not have peeraged me in middle-age' (80:129).

Often changes to a line were made to create a pun to further add to the humour. For example, in an article on the opera singer, Jean de Reszke, who was to have sung in *Faust,* Burnand reported that the singer had suddenly experienced pain in the bottom of his foot while doing a pole vault. Upon further examination, he had discovered that he had injured his ankle. Burnand then re-worked the well-known line in *Hamlet* ('O, my prophetic soul, my uncle') that expresses Hamlet's response when he first realizes that his uncle has murdered his father: 'O my prophetic sole, my ankle.' Elsewhere, burlesquing the first two lines of the song 'Sigh no more ladies' in *Much Ado About Nothing*, *Punch* (the actual author is not listed in the Contributors' Ledgers) alluded to the common Victorian situation in which a man would guarantee a friend's loan from a money-lender but then get caught out when that friend did not pay off what had been borrowed. The *Punch* writer then introduced a quotation that was 'to be borne in mind when you have to meet that little Bill you backed for a Friend' (71:187). The original Shakespeare text, however, is slightly amended:

> SIGN no more * * *
> Men were deceivers ever.

Shakespeare's couplet was a favourite in *Punch*, eliciting such self-explanatory versions as 'SIGH no more, dealers, sigh no more, / Shares were unstable ever'(53:129) and 'BUY no more Ladies; buy no more; / Shops were deceivers ever' (105:264).

As a final example of the technique, we may take Burnand's comment on the announcement in June 1894 that the Duchess of York had been 'safely delivered of a son', a piece of news that apparently coincided with a change in the weather 'from cold and uncertain to very warm' (106:306). Quoting (with a small omission) the famous opening two lines of *Richard III* that contain a pun on 'sun' and 'son', Burnand kept that same pun but applied it to a very different topical situation: 'Now is the winter of our discontent / Made glorious by this *Son* of York.'

As already noted, *Punch*'s burlesque transformations of Shakespeare's text were by no means limited to a line or two at a time. The *Punch* writers seemed to have found irresistible the challenge of creating more extended burlesques. By far the most prolific creator of such material was E. J. Milliken, who provided some thirty-two examples; Tom Taylor and Percival Leigh each contributed nine;

St. John Hankin wrote eight; Shirley Brooks five; and Gilbert Abbott à Beckett and Arthur William à Beckett each composed four. Other writers, such as Henry Silver, Francis Burnand, Charles Mortimer, H. Savile Clarke, John T. Bedford, and John Hollingshead contributed only one or two each. Among all the authors just named, two particularly tempting passages from Shakespeare were the 'To be, or not to be' soliloquy in *Hamlet* and that favourite of anthologists, Jaques's 'All the world's a stage' speech in *As You Like It*.

As might be expected, the speech from Hamlet was ideal for reflecting upon social and political issues currently under debate: the pros and cons of temperance ('To drink, or not to drink' 1:190), of vaccination ('To vaccinate or not' 80:245), or of taking morning baths ('TUBBING or not tubbing' 91:171). In 1847, when the announcement of Robert Vernon's gift of pictures to the National Gallery was announced, *Punch* published, as we have already seen, a fanciful report by Tom Taylor that burlesqued the 'To be, or not to be' soliloquy (13:108). In 1884, some thirty-seven years later, the speech remained as potent as ever as a vehicle for burlesque. On this occasion, the speech was used by John T. Bedford to express Sir William Harcourt's concerns as Home Secretary concerning a parliamentary bill that would reform the various governing authorities of London to make an expanded and unified city corporation the main governing authority (86:72). Bedford's burlesque begins as follows:

> SCENE – *The Home Office. Tables covered with huge heaps of official returns, from the Corporation, the Metropolitan Board of Works, and the Thirty-Eight Districts of the Metropolis. The* HOME SECRETARY *discovered, looking weary and worn. He throws himself back in his uneasy chair, and soliloquises –*
> To be, or not to be, that is the question; –
> Whether 'tis better for a while to suffer
> The harmless follies of the Corporation;
> Or to bring on myself a sea of troubles,
> Much easier raised than ended. To pass my Bill, –
> No more; and by a Bill, to say we end
> The headache, and the thousand natural worries
> That place is heir to. 'Tis a consummation
> Devoutly to be wish'd. [etc.]

Equally varied were the uses to which *Punch* applied burlesques of Jaques's 'All the world's a stage' speech, with its account of the seven steps that mark the passage in human life from birth to death. In 1845, when speculation in railway stocks was at its height, *Punch* published Tom Taylor's 'JAQUES IN CAPEL COURT'. The burlesque talked about an entrance to the London Stock Exchange in Capel Court, which was a popular meeting-place for stockbrokers and their clients, and it also referred to 'stags', who in stock-market slang were those who bought shares in a newly formed company but planned to sell the allotment at a premium. 'ALL the world are stags!' we are told, 'Yea, all the men and women merely jobbers' etc. (9:197). The following year, Jaques's speech became the vehicle for a comment by Taylor on the industrial revolution and the central role of steam power: 'The world's ruled by steam / And all the men and women are its subjects' etc. (11:40). Two years later, when much of the world's attention was upon events in France and the downfall of Louis-Philippe, Jaques's speech was transformed (again by Taylor) into a commentary on the seven ages of the Republic: 'FRANCE is a stage, / And all her heroes little more than players' etc. (15:224). Then, during a particularly cold winter in 1850, *Punch* published Gilbert Abbott à Beckett's 'ALL the town's a slide, / And all the men and women merely skaters' etc. (18:27). Later that year, as a comment on what it felt were the inadequacies of the attempt to catalogue the books in the British Museum, a huge task begun by Antonio Panizzi, *Punch* offered à Beckett's 'ALL the thing's a farce, / And all the time and labour merely wasted' etc. (19:190).

Some years after this, appeared 'THE SEVEN AGES OF A PUBLIC MAN', which detailed the various stages in the life of a man who eventually rose through the ranks of public life to become a minister of the crown before declining in old age to 'childish Red-tapism, and mere Routine: / Sans heart, sans brains, sans pluck, sans everything' (28:195). There were two predictably sexist versions on 'THE SEVEN AGES OF WOMAN' (82:230 and 102:230), two on different types of luggage (113:39 and 119:456), and in 1894 a version that details all the roles that a regular theatre-goer may observe during a theatre season: 'ALL the world's upon the stage, / And here and there you really get a player' (107:25). This last, perhaps, was also

311

mindful that the first line of Jaques's speech was the motto of the Garrick Club (several of the *Punch* staff were members), a place filled with paintings, sculptures, and various other memorabilia related to Shakespeare (Gager 1996, 41).

Alongside *Punch*'s burlesque versions of such familiar set speeches, there were others from a variety of plays, among them Macbeth's 'Is this a dagger that I see before me?' Antony's 'Friends, Romans, countrymen', Othello's 'O now, for ever / Farewell the tranquil mind!' and the description of the death of Falstaff in *Henry V*. Elsewhere, the reader of *Punch* might encounter burlesques of even more extended passages of text, even whole scenes, among the many examples being the Closet Scene in *Hamlet* (65:236), the encounter between Julius Caesar and the Soothsayer (90:126), the scene before the battle towards the end of *Macbeth* (90:150), the Cauldron Scene from the same play (92:246), the opening scene of *Romeo and Juliet* (106:90), and the Trial Scene in *The Merchant of Venice* (118:320). For the 1864 Shakespeare tercentenary issue, as mentioned in Chapter Two, Burnand contributed a two-page burlesque, purportedly a newly-discovered Shakespeare manuscript containing a fragment of a lost Shakespeare play (Tercentenary Issue, 9–10).

As the century neared its close, even more ambitious burlesques offered entire plays. In 1892, there was Arthur William à Beckett's 'HAMLET IN HALF AN HOUR' (102:281), followed six years later by St. John Hankin's 'OPHELAINE AND HAMELETTE' (114:268–269). Hankin also contributed burlesque *Macbeth*s in 1898 and 1901 (115:121 and 121:193–194, 203, 221, 235), a *Tempest* in 1900, and in 1901 a *Coriolanus*. As an amusing variation in 1901, *Punch* then introduced a series by Hankin intended to dramatize what happened after certain Shakespeare plays ended. Both *Hamlet* and *Much Ado About Nothing* were featured (120:50–51, 68, 70) that year. The series, which included comic sequels of such other plays as Tom Robertson's *Caste* and Henrik Ibsen's *A Doll's House*, were then published in book form as *Punch's Dramatic Sequels* (1901) and *Lost Masterpieces* (1904).

As may be inferred from a number of the examples given above, *Punch* frequently employed Shakespearean burlesque in one form or another to comment upon social and political issues, with topics ranging from the relatively trivial to those of vital importance. Humorous social commentaries, at their lightest, might burlesque Shakespeare in order to deal with relatively trivial social issues, such as cab fares, the foul language of cabbies, women's hats, the fashionable pastime of ferning, or the regulation that Kentish policemen had to be clean-shaven. On many occasions, however, burlesques of Shakespeare also direct readers' attention to far more serious matters such as the miseries caused by protectionist trade laws, the dangers posed by unsanitary graveyards, the problem of unclean drinking water, the need to muzzle dogs as a precaution against rabies, and concerns about unions and strikes.

A single example must here suffice to represent this considerable body of material. It derives from one of *Punch*'s long-standing concerns about the railways. For *Punch*, the revolution brought about by the development of railways during the Victorian era was of enormous benefit. As noted in Chapter One, rapid distribution of each newly-published issue of the magazine permitted *Punch* to appear in drawing rooms and libraries in towns and villages throughout Britain almost as soon as anyone in London obtained a copy. Furthermore, some of *Punch*'s initial commercial success was probably due to its suitability for casual railway reading and its availability from news vendors at railway stations (Altick 1997, 541). *Punch* found that the phenomenon of passenger rail travel supplied plenty of light-hearted comic material that could readily involve burlesque applications of Shakespeare: jokes about female travellers misinterpreting the conversations of men in a station waiting room (50:246); male worries about being alone with a female in a railway carriage compartment (51:43); the huge size of Bradshaw's railway timetable guide (85:109); the social stigma attached to travelling in either second-class or third-class accommodations if one felt that one was really a first-class traveller (103:245); and the amount of luggage that some chose to take on a train journey (113:39).

However, *Punch*'s commentary on the development of the railways also had a dark side when, again in many instances making use of Shakespeare burlesque, it turned its attention to more serious issues: the widespread financial speculation that took place in raising venture capital to fund proposed railways the length and breadth of

Britain (9:172; 9:197; 12:79; 13:5. See also Altick 1997, 450–466); the neglect of safety in favour of profit that made accidents numerous and often deadly (11:46; 11:220; 15:214; 18:4; 23:129; 24:125; 65:197. See also *Mr Punch's Victorian Era* 1887, 1:142, 145; 2:251–252); unjustifiable high fares (15:214; 28:42); the abominable conditions of third class travel (15:214); and noise and smoke pollution, particularly in London close to the major railway terminals (49:222; 83:293). A typical example is a burlesque of Act 4 scene 1 in *Macbeth*, when Macbeth revisits the three weird sisters (here transformed by *Punch* into the directors of the Great Western, the South Western, and the North Western Railways). An unsigned big cut of the scene by John Leech (Figure 54) was accompanied by a separate text by Tom Taylor, a burlesque version of the weird sisters' chant as they dance around the cauldron. This latter rehearses such evils as the financial speculation in railways, high fares, the abominable conditions of third class travel, and threats to the availability of return tickets, all to the chorus: 'Bubble, bubble, without trouble, / Fares increase and profits double!' (15:214). Towards the end of the sisters'/directors' chanting, the subject of railway accidents is introduced, with particular reference to crashes and the dire effects of the release of high pressure steam in such a situation. Stokers are cheap and 'smashes plenty':

> For sole bye-law our high pleasure;
> Engines at low price and high pressure
> (No matter though they smash and scald one)
> Add to the ingredients of our cauldron.

When Macbeth (John Bull) enters, nothing more is said. He stands for the British public and is regarded by the three sisters as an idiot, ripe for exploitation:

> Now for picking up our crumbs! –
> Something stupid this way comes!
> Open strong box, to buy our stocks!

Mac-Bull is perhaps not quite as foolish as the sisters think, however, for he recognizes them for what they are: 'How now, you secret, sharp, and downright stags, / Who is't you'd *do*?' The profiteering by

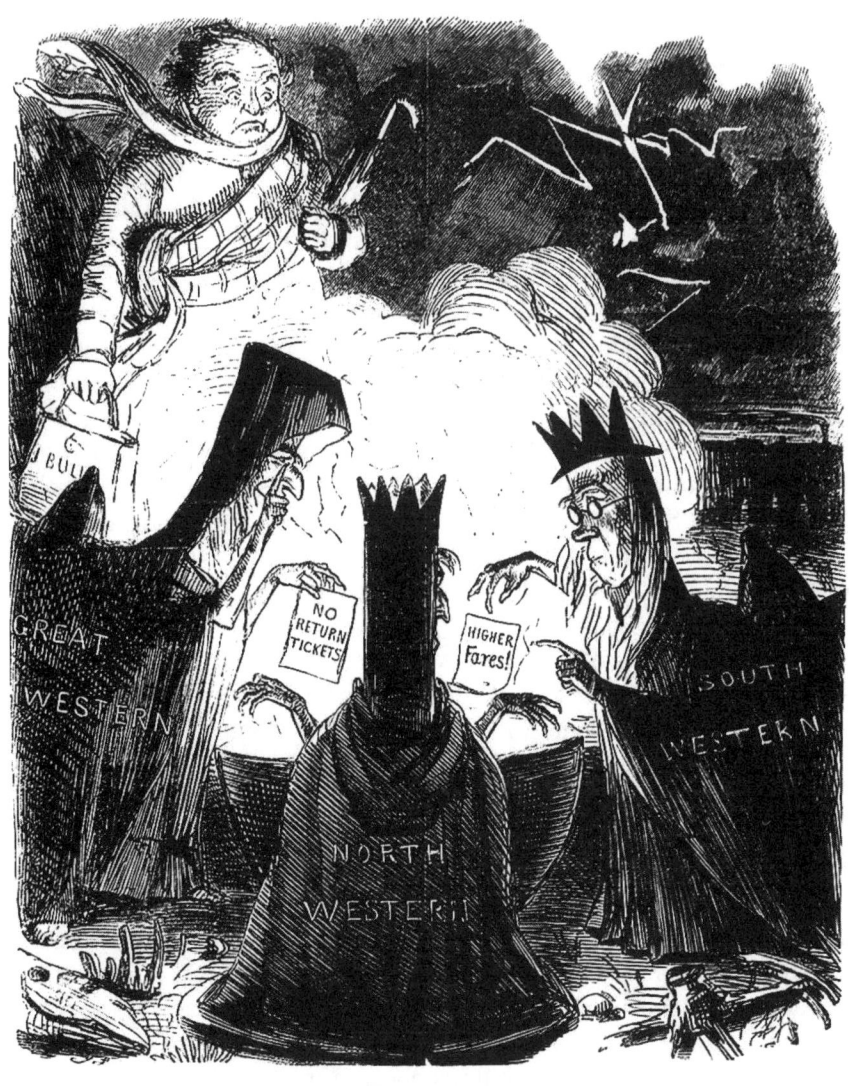

MAC—BULL AND THE RAILWAY WITCHES.

Figure 54. John Leech's comment on the irresponsible management of the railways. *Punch* (18 November 1848), 15:215.

speculators (the 'stags') and the unscrupulous management of the railway companies thus results not just in the sufferings of foolish investors but in the deaths and injuries of those who travel on the railways once they are built.

Where politics were concerned, *Punch* frequently burlesqued Shakespeare to comment on all the major issues of the times. These items often portrayed important political figures, doing much to fix in readers' minds visual images of parliamentary personages such as Sir Robert Peel, William Gladstone, Benjamin Disraeli, Lord Salisbury, Joseph Chamberlain, Randolph Churchill, William Harcourt, and important international personages such as Louis Napoleon, Adolphe Thiers, Abraham Lincoln, Giuseppe Garibaldi (Young 2005, 233–234), Kaiser Wilhelm of Prussia, Prince Bismarck, and Paul Kruger. Important political matters that *Punch* dealt with by creating burlesques of Shakespeare included such topics as the Corn Laws, the Jewish Emancipation Act, the suffragette movement, the government of London, and home rule for Ireland. Major international issues included slavery in the United States, French republicanism, the Crimean War, the American Civil War, the Franco-Prussian War, various international treaties and alliances among the dominant European powers, events in Egypt, and the Anglo-Boer Wars. One example of Shakespeare burlesque as applied to such serious issues must here suffice.

In 1886, William Gladstone was defeated in the Parliamentary election that followed the failure of his efforts to pass a Home Rule bill for Ireland. Except for a brief triennium from 1892 to 1894, Gladstone's Liberals were out of office for the next nineteen years. Between 1886 and the end of the Victorian era, however, Ireland remained a preoccupation, something that can be traced in a number of *Punch* items based on Shakespearean scenes and characters. One such item is a Tenniel big cut that appeared in *Punch* on 12 December 1891 (101:283). Entitled 'KATHLEEN AND PETRUCHIO', it depicted the scene (IV iii) in *The Taming of the Shrew*, in which the strangely dressed Petruchio prevents his new wife Kathleen (Katherina in Shakespeare's original) from accepting a fashionable-looking hat from the Haberdasher (Figure 55). *Punch*'s reader/viewers would quickly have recognized that Tenniel's graphic burlesque was

Figure 55. John Tenniel's comment on the issue of Home Rule for Ireland. *Punch* (12 December 1891), 101:283.

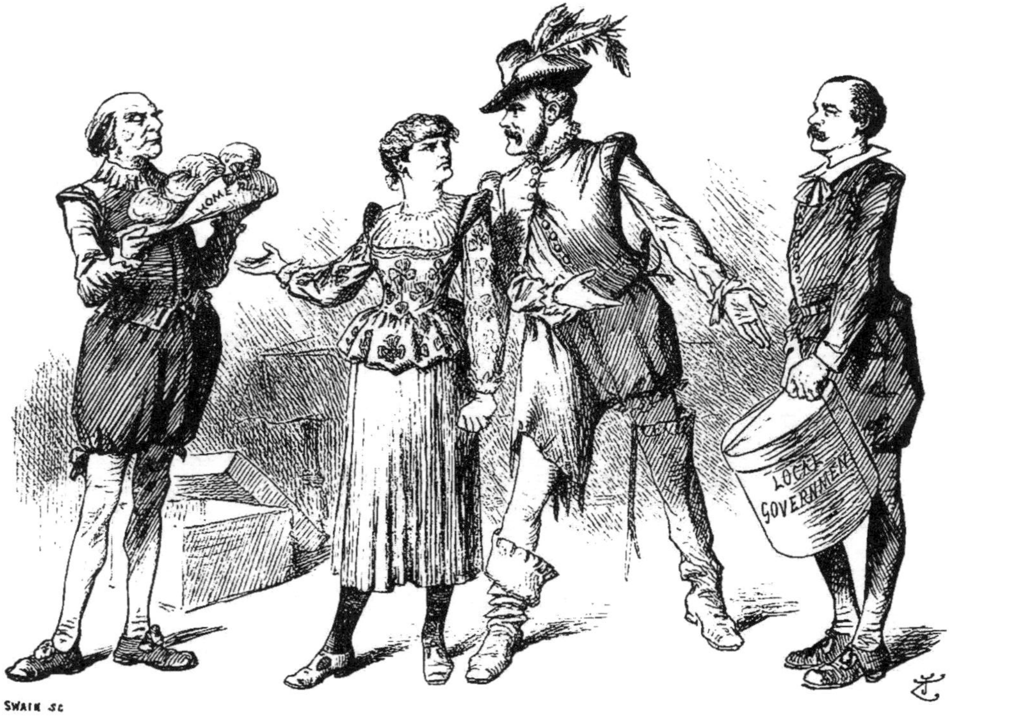

KATHLEEN AND PETRUCHIO.

Kathleen. "I'LL HAVE NO SMALLER; THIS DOTH FIT THE TIME, AND GENTLEWOMEN WEAR SUCH HATS AS THESE."

Petruchio. "WHEN YOU ARE GENTLE, YOU SHALL HAVE ONE TOO, BUT—OF ANOTHER FASHION."—*Shakspeare Balfourised.*

an allegory. Petruchio is Arthur. J. Balfour, who in 1891 was Secretary for Ireland in Lord Salisbury's cabinet but as of October had become First Lord of the Treasury. The Haberdasher at left is William Gladstone, leader of the opposition Liberals, who offers Kathleen a hat inscribed 'HOME RULE'. The figure at right, who holds an unopened hat box, here represents W. L. Jackson, who had taken over from Balfour as Secretary for Ireland. Kathleen (the name is presumably chosen for its 'Irishness') is a personified figure of Ireland (Hibernia), as is apparent from the shamrock emblems on her dress. Irish Home Rule, which would continue as an issue until 1914, is here rejected by Balfour in favour of a much less radical scheme for local government. But, as the caption makes clear, even that choice is conditional upon Kathleen (Hibernia) becoming 'gentle.'

In Shakespeare's original text, Katherina says of the hat, 'I'll have no bigger, this doth fit the time, / And gentlewomen wear such caps as these' (IV iii 69–70), but in Tenniel's caption, to suit the allegory, 'bigger' is changed to 'smaller', since the Irish wanted nothing less than Home Rule. A further re-writing of the text, which Tenniel refers to as '*Shakspeare Balfourised*', occurs in the caption in Petruchio's response. In Shakespeare, he says to Katherina, 'When you are gentle, you shall have one too, And not till then' (I viii 71–72), but in the *Punch* burlesque there is a barbed promise that seems to imply that Ireland may never attain full Home Rule: 'WHEN YOU ARE GENTLE, YOU SHALL HAVE ONE TOO. BUT – OF ANOTHER FASHION'.

As so often with regard to Tenniel's big cuts, on the opposite page is an extended dramatic burlesque by Milliken. It is entitled 'KATHLEEN AND PETRUCHIO; OR, SHAKSPEARE BALFOURISED', and its cast list identifies the same four persons as appear in the engraving. The text begins with a burlesque version of Petruchio's famous soliloquy (IV i 188–211), in which he compares his planned 'taming' of Katherina to training a falcon. As in the original, Petruchio (here A. J. Balfour) begins: 'Thus have I politicly begun my reign' (here as First Lord of the Treasury). The next eight lines also remain the same, but what follows is then a re-writing of Shakespeare concerning the need to control the 'stormy spirits' of the Irish with 'Resolute government'. Balancing this, there follows a ten-line burlesque of Katherina (Kathleen/Hibernia's) complaint to Grumio (W. L. Jackson) about the treatment she is receiving from her new husband (A. J. Balfour). However, there are significant departures from the original. Katherina's 'The more my wrong, the more his spite appears' (IV iii 2) becomes Kathleen's 'The more my wrong the more his smile appears!' The line 'He does it under name of perfect love' (12) is retained, as is "Twere deadly sickness, or else present death', but the remaining lines are changed to comment on Ireland's subjection to Law and Order by a power that claims to have her best interests at heart. The burlesque then jumps ahead to Petruchio's promise that they will shortly return to her father's house, dressed in 'silken coats, and caps, and golden rings / With ruffs, and cuffs, and farthingales and things', but then Milliken adds a topical allusion to colours that are obviously politically very significant: 'With orange tissue trimmed with true-blue / Eschewing wearing of the green, – that's knavery'.

The burlesque then proceeds with an extended version of the text that provides the caption for Tenniel's big cut. Kathleen (Hibernia) is about to be offered a cap (Local Government) by Balfour, but she expresses her preference for that she has already ordered from the Haberdasher (Gladstone). Petruchio (Balfour) assures her that the Haberdasher (Gladstone) 'loves thee not', but Kathleen (Hibernia), as in the original text, declares: 'Love me or love me not, I like the hat, / And it I will have, or I will have none.' This opens the way for the concluding aside in the burlesque when Grumio comments, 'Then is she like to be bareheaded long!' In this *Punch* was prescient. Gladstone's second Home Rule bill was rejected by the Lords in 1893, and Ireland did not achieve any significant form of Home Rule until 1914, and even this was put on hold because of the outbreak of war.

A comprehensive survey of this rich body of burlesque material is endlessly fascinating in what it reveals about the use of Shakespeare by *Punch* as a medium shared with its readers – a medium that can readily be applied to social and political commentary. However, such a survey would not here add substantially to what has already been demonstrated in this book regarding the ubiquitous presence in *Punch* throughout the nineteenth-century of allusions to Shakespeare and of burlesques of Shakespeare. Burlesque, as I have tried to indicate, was ubiquitous in *Punch*, but it was also inseparable from a love and respect for Shakespeare. Writers and readers who knew their Shakespeare could share a common enjoyment in a kind of subversive deconstruction of a familiar and revered original text, but in the end the appreciation of that original remained untouched. Indeed, its status was arguably enhanced. Like the other forms of transformation discussed in this chapter – opera, ballet, hippodrama, the graphic arts – burlesque contributed immensely to Shakspeareanity and its dissemination within Victorian popular culture. However, whereas in dealing with the transformation of Shakespeare into other media, *Punch* was directing its gaze outside itself to what was happening in theatres and art galleries, in the case of textual and graphic burlesque the situation is different. Although burlesque theatre productions were regularly reviewed in *Punch*, burlesque was also central to *Punch*'s own workings as a comic magazine, and, as a result, burlesques of Shakespearean material were among *Punch*'s chief contribution to Shakspeareanity.

In Conclusion

Lamentably, *Punch* has now ceased publication, and a once vibrant link with Victorian culture has become silent. Two of my Victorian grandparents, who died a half century ago in the 1950s, were loyal subscribers to *Punch*. To them I attribute my first acquaintance with Mr. Punch. This happened during my childhood, on those interminable Sunday afternoons when my parents brought me to my grandparents' house on family visits. Always advised to be seen but not heard too much, I found those visits severely testing. But my grandmother, who had had four boys of her own, understood my plight and always had on hand for me plenty of back issues of *Punch*, along with a surreptitious supply of ginger biscuits. With these two aids, I was able to survive until teatime and the long walk home. These same grandparents were strong believers in the benefits of education, but mercifully, given my young age, they did not thrust the family Shakespeare upon me. They trusted in schooling and my father and mother to see to it that I was appropriately imbued with what *Punch* in its early years referred to as Shakspeareanity. Their faith was not misplaced, and I hope that their spirits will be gladdened by my attempts here to write of two of the principal cultural icons in their lives – *Punch* and Shakespeare.

As I have tried to show, *Punch*, once established within the fabric of Victorian culture, mirrored the ubiquitous presence of Shakespeare within that culture. At the same time, to the credit of its numerous authors and artists, *Punch* contributed in all manner of small ways to the furtherance of the Victorian knowledge and love of Shakespeare. Whether Shakspeareanity is today as pervasive a cultural force as it was in the Victorian era is doubtful, although the easy availability of significant numbers of theatre, television, and film productions of Shakespeare's works appears to signify that Shakespeare remains valued. And though, for whatever reasons, we may regret that Shakespeare's text is (like the Bible) not now so widely familiar as it was during the Victorian era, though knowledge of Shakespeare is chiefly nurtured through the institutions of formal education, and though Shakespeare may often seem to be the exclusive preserve of high culture, Shakspeareanity appears to be alive and supremely hearty in our own time, constantly reinvented, perhaps, but far from being submerged by competing cultural forces. In the very different world of Victorian Britain, when Christian evangelicalism and the quest for empire flourished hand in hand, *Punch*, I believe, played a role in positioning and maintaining the symbolic place of Shakespeare's works alongside the Bible. That is the story I have tried to tell. What has happened since and where Shakespeare is sited within contemporary culture is a different tale and one I leave for others to ponder.

Bibliography

Allen, Shirley S. *Samuel Phelps and Sadler's Wells Theatre*. Middletown, Conn.: Wesleyan University Press, 1971.

Altick, Richard D. *Paintings from Books: Art and Literature in Britain, 1760–1900*. Columbus, Ohio: Ohio State University Press, 1985.

—— *Punch. The Lively Youth of a British Institution 1841–1851*. Columbus, Ohio: Ohio State University Press, 1997.

Anstey, F. *A Long Retrospect*. London: Oxford University Press, 1936.

Appelbaum, Stanley, and Richard Kelly (eds). *Great Drawings and Illustrations from Punch, 1841–1901*. New York: Dover, 1981.

Auerbach, Jeffrey A. *The Great Exhibition of 1851: A Nation on Display*. New Haven: Yale University Press, 1999.

Bate, Jonathan. 'The Shakespeare Phenomenon.' In *Shakespeare in Art*. Edited by Jane Martineau and Desmond Shawe-Taylor. London: Merrell, 2003. Pp. 9–19.

Booth, Michael R. *Theatre in the Victorian Age*. Cambridge: Cambridge University Press, 1981.

Briggs, Asa and Susan (eds). *Cap and Bell: Punch's Chronicle of English History in the Making, 1841–1861*. London: MacDonald, 1972.

Burnand, Francis C. *The 'A.D.C.', Being the Personal Reminiscences of the University Amateur Dramatic Club Cambridge*. Second edition. London: Chapman and Hall, 1880.

Cole, John William. *The Life and Theatrical Times of Charles Kean, F.S.A. Including a Summary of the English Stage for the last Fifty Years*. Second edition. 2 vols. London: Richard Bentley, 1859.

Dalziel, Edward and George. *The Brothers Dalziel: A Record of Fifty Years Work, 1840–1890*. 1901; rpt. London: Batsford, 1978.

Daniel Maclise 1806–1870. Catalogue of exhibition at National Portrait Gallery (London, 3 March–16 April 1972) and National

Gallery of Ireland (Dublin, 5 May–18 June 1972). London: Arts Council of Great Britain, 1972.

Davis, Jim, and Victor Emeljanow. *Reflecting the Audience: London Theatregoing, 1840–1880*. Hatfield, Herts.: Hertfordshire University Press, 2001.

Dexter, Walter (ed.). *The Unpublished Letters of Charles Dickens to Mark Lemon*. London: Halton & Truscott Smith, 1927.

Dixon, Diana. 'Children and the Press, 1866–1914.' In *The Press in English Society from the Seventeenth to Nineteenth Centuries*. Edited by Michael Harris and Alan Lee. Rutherford, N.J.: Fairleigh Dickinson University Press, 1986.

Downer, Alan Seymour. *The Eminent Tragedian, William Charles Macready*. Cambridge, Mass.: Harvard University Press, 1966.

Campbell, Oscar James (editor). *The Reader's Encyclopedia of Shakespeare*. New York: MJF Books, 1966.

Dobson, Michael. *The Making of the National Poet: Shakespeare, Adaptation and Authorship, 1660–1769*. Oxford: Clarendon Press, 1992.

Ellis III, Ted. R. 'Burlesque Dramas in the Victorian Comic Magazines.' *Victorian Periodicals Review* 15 (4) (Winter 1982): 138–143.

Engen, Rodney K. *Dictionary of Victorian Engravers, Print Publishers, and Their Works*. Cambridge: Chadwick-Healey, 1979.

—— *Sir John Tenniel: Alice's White Knight*. Aldershot, Hants: Scolar Press, 1991.

Ensor, Sir Robert C. K. *England, 1870–1914*. Oxford: Clarendon Press, 1936.

Forbes, Christopher. *The Royal Academy (1837–1901) Revisited*. New York: Forbes Magazine Collection, 1975.

Foster, R. F. *Paddy & Mr. Punch: Connections in Irish and English History*. Harmondsworth: Penguin, 1995.

Foulkes, Richard. *The Shakespeare Tercentenary of 1864*. London: Society for Theatre Research, 1984.

—— (ed.) *Shakespeare and the Victorian Stage*. Cambridge: Cambridge University Press, 1986.

—— *Performing Shakespeare in the Age of Empire*. Cambridge: Cambridge University Press, 2002.

Gager, Valerie L. *Shakespeare and Dickens: The Dynamics of Influence*. Cambridge: Cambridge University Press, 1996.

Garlick, Kenneth. *Sir Thomas Lawrence: A Complete Catalogue of the Oil Paintings*. Oxford: Phaidon, 1989.

Grafton, Carol Belanger (editor). *Fanciful Victorian Initials: 1,142 Decorative Letters from 'Punch'*. New York: Dover, 1984.

—— (ed.) *Humorous Victorian Spot Illustrations*. New York: Dover, 1985.

Graves, Algernon. *The British Institution, 1806–1867: A Complete Dictionary of Contributors and Their Work from the Foundation of the Institution.* 1875; rpt. Bath: Kingsmead Reprints, 1969.

—— *The Royal Academy of Arts: A Complete Dictionary of Contributors and Their Work from Its Foundation in 1769 to 1893.* 3rd edition. 1901; rpt. Bath: Kingsmead Reprints, 1973.

—— *Society of Artists of Great Britain, 1760–1791 / The Free Society of Artists, 1761–1783 / A Complete Dictionary of Contributors and Their Work from the Foundation of the Societies to 1791.* London: Bell, 1907.

Graves, Charles L. *Punch's History of Modern England.* 4 vols. London: Cassell, 1921.

Halliday, F. E. *The Cult of Shakespeare.* London: Duckworth, 1957.

Hamilton, Walter. *Parodies of the Works of English and American Authors.* 6 vols. London: Reeves & Turner, 1884–1889.

Hamlet Through the Ages (see Mander and Mitchenson).

Hancher, Michael. *The Tenniel Illustrations to the 'Alice' Books.* Columbus, Ohio: Ohio State University Press, 1985.

Harrison, J. F. C. *A History of Working Men's Colleges.* London: Routledge & Kegan Paul, 1954.

Hatton, Joseph. *With a Show in the North: Reminiscences of Mark Lemon.* London: W. H. Allen, 1871.

Hodgson, W. B. *Life and Letters of W. B. Hodgson.* Edited by J. Meiklejohn, 1883.

Horrocks, Clare. 'The Personification of "Father Thames": Reconsidering the Role of the Victorian Periodical Press in the "Verbal and Visual Campaign" for Public Health Reform.' *Victorian Periodicals Review,* 36 (1) (Spring 2003): 2–19.

Huggett, Frank E. *Victorian England as Seen by Punch*. London: Sidgwick and Jackson, 1978.

Hughes, Alan. *Henry Irving, Shakespearean*. Cambridge: Cambridge University Press, 1981.

Irving, Laurence. *Henry Irving, The Actor and His World*. 1951; rpt. London: Columbus Books, 1989.

Jackson, Russell (ed.) *Victorian Theatre: The Theatre in Its Time*. Franklin, NY: New Amsterdam, 1989.

Jacobs, Henry E, and Claudia D. Johnson. *An Annotated Bibliography of Shakespearean Burlesques, Parodies, and Travesties*. New York: Garland, 1976.

Jones, John Bush, and Priscilla Shaw. 'Artists and "Suggestors": The *Punch* Cartoons 1843–1848.' *Victorian Periodicals Newsletter* 11 (1) (March 1978): 3–14.

Kelly, Richard. *Douglas Jerrold*. New York: Twayne, 1972.

Kelly, Thomas. *The History of Adult Education in Great Britain*. Liverpool: Liverpool University Press, 1962.

Kimberley, Michael. *Lord Ronald Gower's Monument to Shakespeare*. Stratford-upon-Avon Papers No. 3. Stratford-upon-Avon: The Stratford-upon-Avon Society, 1989.

Knight, Charles. *Passages of a Working Life During Half a Century: With a Prelude of Early Reminiscences*. 3 vols. London: Bradbury & Evans, 1865.

Knight, Jacqueline. 'The Theatre of John Tenniel.' *Theatre Arts Monthly*. 12 (1928):111–118.

Lablache, Clarissa. 'Halévy's *La tempesta.*' Online essay, 1999. Http://www.meyerbeer.com/halvysla.htm.

Lanier, Douglas. *Shakespeare and Modern Popular Culture*. Oxford: Oxford University Press, 2002.

Layard, George Somes. *A Great 'Punch' Editor: Shirley Brooks of Punch, His Life, Letters, and Diaries*. New York: Henry Holt and Co., 1907.

Leary, Patrick. 'Table Talk and Print Culture in Mid-Victorian London: The "Punch" Circle, 1858–1874.' Diss. Indiana University, 2002.

Mantell, Gideon. *The Journal of Gideon Mantell*. Edited by E. Cecil Curwen. London: Oxford University Press, 1940.

Manvell, Roger. *Ellen Terry.* London: Heinemann, 1968.
Marly, Diana de. *Costume on the Stage.* London: Batsford, 1982.
Marston, John Westland. *Our Recent Actors.* Boston: Roberts Brothers, 1888.
Merchant, W. Moelwyn. *Shakespeare and the Artist.* London: Oxford University Press, 1959.
Merlo, Carolyn. 'John Everett Millais's "Portia".' *Gazette des Beaux-Arts,* 104 (September 1984): 77–85.
Millais. An Exhibition Organized by the Walker Art Gallery, Liverpool, & the Royal Academy of Arts, London (January–April 1967). London: Royal Academy, 1967.
Moody, Richard. *Astor Place Riot.* Bloomington, Ind.: Indiana University Press, 1958.
Moran, James. *Printing Presses: History and Development from the Fifteenth Century to Modern Times.* London: Faber and Faber, 1973.
Morley, Sheridan (ed.). *Punch at the Theatre.* London: Robson Books, 1980.
Morris, Frankie. 'John Tenniel, Cartoonist: A Critical & Sociocultural Study in the Art of the Victorian Cartoon (Britain).' Diss. University of Missouri, 1985.
—— *Artist of Wonderland: The Life, Political Cartoons, and Illustrations of Tenniel.* Charlottesville: University of Virginia Press, 2005.
'Mr. Punch at Dinner: Centenary of a Famous Printery.' *British and Colonial Printer and Stationer*, 28 (January 1926): 63.
Nineteenth-Century Shakespeare Burlesques. Selected and introduced by Stanley Wells. 5 vols. Wilmington, Del.: Glazier, 1978.
Oakley, Lucy. 'The Evolution of Sir John Everett Millais's "Portia".' *Metropolitan Museum Journal,* 16 (1982): 181–194.
—— *Unfaded Pageant: Edwin Austin Abbey's Shakespearean Subjects From the Yale University Art Gallery and Other Collections.* New York: Miriam and Ira D. Wallach Art Gallery, Columbia University, 1994.
Odell, G. C. D. *Shakespeare from Betterton to Irving.* 2 vols. 1921; rpt. New York: Blom, 1963.

Patten, Robert L. *Dickens and his Publishers*. Oxford: Oxford University Press, 1978.

Pearson, Hesketh. *Beerbohm Tree: His Life and Laughter*. New York: Harper, 1956.

Pettitt, Clare. 'Shakespeare at the Great Exhibition of 1851.' In *Victorian Shakespeare, Volume 2: Literature and Culture*. Edited by Gail Marshall and Adrian Poole. Basingstoke: Palgrave Macmillan, 2003. Pp. 61–83.

Phelps, W. May, and John Forbes-Robertson. *The Life and Life-Work of Samuel Phelps*. London: Sampson Low, Marston, Searle & Rivington, 1886.

Plant, Marjorie. *The English Book Trade. An Economic History of the Making and Sale of Books*. Third edition. London: George Allen & Unwin, 1974.

Poole, Adrian. *Shakespeare and the Victorians*. Arden Critical Companions. London: Arden Shakespeare, 2004.

Prager, Arthur. *The Mahogany Tree: An Informal History of PUNCH*. New York: Hawthorn Books, 1979.

Pressly, William L. *A Catalogue of Paintings in the Folger Shakespeare Library*. New Haven and London: Yale University Press, 1993.

Price, R. G. G. *A History of Punch*. London: Collins, 1957.

[*Punch*]. *Mr Punch's Victorian Era: An Illustrated Chronicle of Fifty Years of the Reign of Her Majesty the Queen*. 3 vols. London: Bradbury, Agnew, 1887.

Ray, Gordon. *Thackeray: The Uses of Adversity 1811–1846*. 2 vols. London: Oxford University Press, 1955.

Reid, Forrest. *Illustrators of the Eighteen Sixties: An Illustrated Survey of the Work of 58 British Artists*. 1928; rpt. New York: Dover, 1975.

Robins, Elizabeth. 'On Seeing Madame Bernhardt's Hamlet.' *The North American Review*, 171, no. 529 (December 1900): 908–919.

Sarzano, Frances. *Sir John Tenniel*. New York: Pellegrini & Cudahy, 1948.

Saxon, A. H. *Enter Foot and Horse: A History of Hippodrama in England and France*. New Haven: Yale University Press, 1968.

Schlicke, Paul. *Dickens and Popular Entertainment*. London: Allen and Unwin, 1985.

Schoch, Richard W. *Shakespeare's Victorian Stage: Performing History in the Theatre of Charles Kean*. Cambridge: Cambridge University Press, 1998.

—— *Not Shakespeare: Bardolatry and Burlesque in the Nineteenth Century*. Cambridge: Cambridge University Press, 2002.

—— *Queen Victoria and the Theatre of Her Age*. Basingstoke: Palgrave Macmillan, 2004.

Schoenbaum, Samuel. *Shakespeare's Lives*. Oxford: Clarendon Press, 1970.

Schouvaloff, Alexander (compiler). *The Theatre Museum*. London: Scala, 1987.

Scott, Clement. *Drawing-Room Plays and Parlour Pantomimes*. London: Stnaley Rivers, 1870.

Shakespeare, William. *The Riverside Shakespeare*. Edited by G. Blakemore Evans. Second edition. Boston: Houghton Mifflin, 1997.

Shakespeare, William. *Hamlet, Prince of Denmark*. Edited by Robert Hapgood. Cambridge: Cambridge University Press, 1999.

Sherson, Errol. *London's Lost Theatres of the Nineteenth Century, with Notes on Plays and Players Seen There*. London: John Lane, 1925.

Simpson, Roger. *Sir John Tenniel: Aspects of His Work*. Rutherford, Madison, Teaneck: Fairleigh Dickinson University Press, 1994.

Slater, Michael. *Douglas Jerrold, 1803–1857*. London: Duckworth, 2002.

Spencer, Terrence John Bew (ed.) *Shakespeare: A Celebration 1564–1964*. Harmondsworth: Penguin, 1964.

Spielmann, Marion Harry. (a). *The History of "Punch"*. New York: Cassell, 1895.

—— (b). 'Our Graphic Humorists: Sir John Tenniel,' *Magazine of Art* (1895), 18:201–207.

Stoker, Gill. 'John Tenniel.' Undated online essay containing biography (http://oufcnt2.open.ac.uk/~gill_stoker/biog.htm).

Taranow, Gerda. *The Bernhardt Hamlet: Culture and Context*. New York: Peter Lang, 1996.

Taylor, Gary. 1991. *Reinventing Shakespeare: A Cultural History from the Restoration to the Present.* Oxford: Oxford University Press.

Taylor, George. *Players and Performances in the Victorian Theatre.* Manchester: University of Manchester Press, 1989.

Thackeray, William Makepeace. Review of John Leech's *Pictures of Life and Character.* In *Quarterly Review,* 96 (December 1854): 81–82.

Thackeray, William Makepeace. *The Letters and Private Papers of William Makepeace Thackeray.* Collected and edited by Gordon N. Ray. 4 vols. Cambridge, Mass.: Harvard University Press, 1945–1946.

Thomas, Ambroise. *Hamlet.* Booklet to accompany recording. EMI France, 1993.

Toynbee, William (editor). *The Diaries of William Charles Macready.* 2 vols. London: Chapman and Hall, 1912.

Trewin, John Courtenay. *The Night Has Been Unruly.* London: Robert Hale, 1957.

—— *The Journal of William Charles Macready.* London: Longmans, 1967.

Vining, Edward P. *The Mystery of Hamlet: An Attempt to Solve an Old Problem.* Philadelphia: Lippincott, 1881.

Wells, Stanley (compiler). *Nineteenth-Century Shakespeare Burlesques.* 5 vols. Wilmington, Delaware: Michael Glazier, 1978.

Welsh, Alexander. *The City of Dickens.* 1971; rpt. Cambridge, Mass.: Harvard University Press, 1986.

Woodward, Llewellyn. *The Age of Reform: England 1815–1870.* Second edition. Oxford: Oxford University Press, 1962.

Young, Alan R. *Hamlet and the Visual Arts, 1709–1900.* Newark: University of Delaware Press, 2002.

—— (a). 'Sir John Tenniel's Emblematic Shakespeare Cartoons for Punch.' In *Emblem Scholarship, Directions and Developments. A Tribute to Gabriel Hornstein.* Edited by Peter M. Daly. Turnhout, Belgium: Brepols, 2005. Pp. 229–47.

—— (b). 'Henry Irving's Hamlet: Some Visual Sources.' *Nineteenth Century Theatre and Film,* 32 (2) (Winter 2005): 3–19.

Index of *Punch* Artists Cited

Atkinson, John Priestman (1864–1894 fl.) 120, 139, 228

Chasemore, Archibald (1868–1901) 229–230
Corbould, Alfred Chantrey (1853–1920) 50

Doyle, Richard (1824–1883) 10, 42, 43, 92, 290–292
Du Maurier, George (1834–1896) 42, 44, 48, 50, 53, 296, 297

Furniss, Harry (1854–1925) 54, 119–120, 134–135, 204–205, 207, 213–215, 220, 227, 273

Galter, William (1830s–1840s fl.) 50
Gilbert, John (1817–1897) 35, 62, 301

Harrison, L. (1898–1900 fl.) 117,
Harvey, William (1796–1866) 58
Henning, Archibald (?–1864) 50

Keene, Charles (1823–1891) 42, 50, 58, 60, 77, 124–125, 231–232, 289–290

Landells, Ebenezer (1808–1860) 24, 41, 50, 58
Leech, John (1817–1864) 30, 41, 42, 43, 44, 46, 47, 49, 50, 54, 55, 64, 71–72, 80, 81, 104, 112, 113–114, 151–155, 157–158, 285–286, 314–315

McConnell, William (?–1867) 296
May, Philip William 'Phil' (1864–1903) 44, 54,

Meadows, Kenny (1790–1874) 35, 41, 50, 58, 62

Newman, William (1842–1864 fl.) 81, 89, 144, 270, 271, 275–276

Partridge, J. Bernard (1861–1945) 44, 54, 115–116, 135, 218–220, 221–222, 223–224, 237–238, 241–242

R., G. 146
Reed, Edward Tennyson (1860–1933) 44, 148, 246, 265

Sambourne, Linley (1844–1910) 44, 50, 114, 116, 122–123, 174, 206, 280, 287–288
Scott, Clement (1841–1904) 50

Tenniel, John (1820–1914) 11, 30, 40, 43, 44, 45, 48, 49, 50, 53, 54, 58–66, 77–79, 97, 98, 103, 104–105, 183, 192, 241, 279–280, 292–294, 307, 316–319
Thackeray, William Makepeace (1811–1863) 34, 88, 290–291 (see also under 'Index of *Punch* Authors')

Wheeler, Edward J. (1872–1902 fl.) 114, 115, 207, 208–210, 211–212, 217, 235, 241, 261–262, 263–264, 266–268, 269
Wilson, Thomas Harrington (1842–1886 fl.) 179

Index of *Punch* Authors Cited

À Beckett, Arthur William (1844–1909) 49, 50, 51, 52, 125, 138–139, 142, 198, 222–223, 243, 244–245, 262, 263–264, 305, 310, 312

À Beckett, Gilbert Abbott (1811–1856) 41, 42, 49, 50, 52, 54, 55, 81, 82, 83, 131, 133, 140–141, 146, 178, 270–271, 275–276, 310, 311

À Beckett, Gilbert Arthur (1837–1891) 49

Ashby-Sterry, Joseph (1836–1917)

Bedford, John T. (1881–1884 fl.) 310
Bennett, Charles H. (1865–1867 fl.) 53
Brooks, Shirley (1816–1874) 42, 45, 46, 47, 50, 53, 83, 95, 97, 100, 105, 133, 179–180, 181, 184–185, 259, 310
Browne, (?) (1892–1897 fl.) 243–244
Burnand, Francis C. (1836–1917) 42, 43, 50, 51, 52, 53, 55, 65, 99, 104, 105, 119–120, 127, 128, 129, 132, 134, 142, 147, 173–174, 193–194, 198, 203, 204–205, 206–207, 208, 209, 210–215, 216–218, 221, 223, 224–228, 231, 234–236, 238–239, 240–241, 242–243, 245–246, 260–261, 263, 265–269, 275, 301–302, 305, 306, 308–309, 310, 312

Clarke, H. Savile (1881–1885 fl.) 52, 310
Coyne, Joseph Stirling (1803–1868) 24, 42, 51, 52, 85, 102

Edwards, (?Sutherland) (1901 fl.) 52

Guthrie, Thomas Anstey (1856–1934) 50, 147, 264–265

Hankin, St. John (1869–1909) 273, 310, 312
Hollingshead, John (1827–1904) 141, 306, 308, 310
Hood, Thomas (1799–1845) 29

Jerrold, Douglas (1803–1857) 29, 35, 41, 49, 51, 53, 54, 56–58, 68–70, 72, 73, 83, 85–86, 88, 89–90, 91, 92–93, 109, 110, 111, 113, 129–130, 144, 145, 146, 150–155, 156, 157–158, 159, 162–163, 165, 166, 167–168, 175, 176, 177, 178, 179, 181–183, 185, 187, 236–237, 250, 251–252, 255–257, 284

Lehmann, Rudolph Chambers (1856–1929) 228
Leigh, Percival (1813–1889) 34, 41, 42, 45, 49, 54, 56, 88, 90, 95, 99, 104, 105–106, 121–122, 128, 132, 146, 162, 192, 252, 255, 257, 259, 278–280, 285, 309
Lemon, Mark (1809–1870) 24, 25, 29, 41, 42, 46, 47, 50, 52, 53, 54, 55, 77, 79, 83, 95, 104, 105, 150–151, 241, 267
Lester, Horace Frank (1884–1887 fl.) 123, 208–209
Lucy, Henry W. (1843–1924) 126, 246

Mayhew, Henry (1812–1887) 24, 41, 42, 43, 46, 49, 50, 52
Mayhew, Horace (1816–1872) 43, 45, 50, 53, 179, 190, 307
Milliken, Edwin James (1839?–1897) 43, 124–126, 129, 205–206, 229, 240–241, 309, 318–319

333

Morris, (?) (1881 fl.) 141, 143

Oxenford, John (1812–1877) 52, 53

Reach, Angus (1821–?1850) 53

Seaman, Owen (1861–1936) 50

Silver, Henry (1828–1910) 43, 46, 47–49, 51, 53, 63, 95, 97–99, 101, 102, 104, 105, 106, 145, 169–171, 173, 185, 186, 189–190, 190–192, 192–193, 258, 259–260, 262–263, 280, 307–308

Smith, Albert (1816–1860) 41, 49, 52, 83, 146

Taylor, Tom (1817–1880) 42, 49, 50, 53, 58, 89, 91–92, 95, 97, 105, 106, 107–108, 159, 164–165, 174, 176–177, 186, 192, 195–197, 199–200, 201–202, 204, 233–234, 288–289, 294–296, 298–299, 299–300, 309, 310, 311, 314

Thackeray, William Makepeace (1811–1863) 25, 29, 31, 40, 41, 42, 44–45, 49, 67–68, 83, 96–97, 123, 250–251, 290–291 (see also under 'Index of *Punch* Artists')

Thompson, Alfred (1877 fl.) 52

Wills, W. H. (1810–1880) 146

General Index

Abbey, Edwin Austin 302–303
Abergeldi Castle 79
Adam, Adolphe Charles 254
Addison, Miss. 93
Albert, Prince 30, 54, 57, 69, 76, 82, 85–86, 88, 92, 154, 159, 250–251, 295
Alexander, George 240
Alice, Princess 86
Alma-Tadema, Sir Lawrence 223, 224
Altick, Richard 30, 282, 300
American Civil War 316
Anderson, James 173
Anderson, Mary 209, 211–212, 226
Angelico, Fra 291
Anglo-Boer Wars (see Boer Wars)
Antiquarian Society 154
Arbuthnot, Rev. George 127
Arnold, Matthew 70
Art Annual, The 38, 283–284
Art Journal, The 38, 283, 290
Art Union 290
Ashby-Sterry, Joseph 55
Astley, Philip 275
Astor Place Riots 110, 158
Athenaeum 48, 66, 94, 96, 100, 134, 161, 234
Auber, Daniel 253
Austen, Jane 32, 39

Bacon, Delia 121–122, 126, 128
Bacon, Francis 121–125
Bailey, Samuel 132
Balfe, Michael William 82, 251, 254
Balfour, Arthur J. 318–319
ballet 12, 73, 75, 160, 162, 184, 220, 249, 257–258, 261–262, 269–274
Balmoral 79

Barbier, Jules 263
Barnum, P. T. 56, 86–87, 91
Barrett, Elizabeth 30
Barrett, Thomas 60
Barrett, Wilson 209–211, 226, 305
Bateman, H. L. 195, 198
Bateman, Isobel 197, 199, 200
Bateman, Kate 199, 200, 212, 213
Bateman, Mrs. 199
Bath 161
Beach, Sir Michael Hicks 246
Bedford, Paul 192
Beethoven, Ludwig van 111
Belville, Walter 110–111
Benson, F. R. 239–240, 247
Bentley's Miscellany 28
Bernhardt, Sarah 220, 221, 231, 232, 236–239
Bewick, Thomas 24
Bible 11, 70
Birch, William John 130–131
Birmingham 194
Bismarck, Prince 316
Blondin, Charles 138
Boer Wars 11, 316
Bonaparte, Eugene 61
Booth, Edwin 170, 194, 203–204, 226, 231
Booth, Michael 304
Boston Mail 157
Boston Museum of Fine Arts 60
Boyne, Leonard 305
Bright, John 105
Britannia 79, 104
British Institution 38, 282
British Library 123
British Museum 60, 63, 107, 311

335

Brontës, the 30
Brooke, Gustavus 170, 192
Brough, Lionel 240
Brough, Robert 257
Brough, William 257
Brown, Ford Maddox 218
Browne, Hablot Knight (Phiz) 274
Browning, Robert 30
Bryant, R. 24
Buchell, Charles 245
Buckingham, James Silk 89
Buckingham Palace 67, 68, 105
Buckstone, John Baldwin 93, 192
Bull, John 104, 314–315
Bunn, Alfred 72–73, 75–76, 81–84, 87, 90, 111, 151, 160, 162, 175, 251, 269–270
Burbage, Richard 134
burlesque 11, 12, 60, 114, 127, 249–320
Bury 195
Butler, Mrs. 93
Byron, Lord 139

Calvert, Charles 194
Cambridge Amateur Dramatic Club (A.D.C.) 43, 226–227, 228
Cambridge University 226
Carew, John Edward 109
Carlyle, Thomas 30, 32, 122
Carr, Alice Comyns 212, 215
Carr, J. Comyns 305
Carré, Michel 263
Carroll, Lewis (see Dodgson, Charles)
Castelmary, Signor 263
Cecil. Arthur 227
Chace Act (1891) 146
Chamberlain, Joseph 316
Charivari, Le (Paris) 23
Charles, Maria 143
Chatterton, F. B. 172, 188
Chippendale, William Henry 201
Churchill, Randolph 316
Cibber Colley 34, 110, 132, 161, 164–165, 181, 200, 277

Clarke, Charles Cowden 35, 36, 106
Clarke, Mary Cowden 35, 36, 37, 93, 106
Clipstone Street Artists' Society 63
Clough, Arthur Hugh 31
Coglan, Charles 203
Colas, Stella 231
Cole, Henry 282
Cole, John 176–177, 178
Coleridge, Samuel Taylor 186, 307
Collier, Mrs. J. 297–298
Collier, John Payne 93, 127, 130
Collins, Charles Allston 295
Cologne 111
Comédie-Française 231, 236, 264
Congress of Paris 62
Constable, John 288
Cooke, William 277, 278–280
Copley, John Singleton 283
Corn Laws 316
Cornwall, Barry (Bryan Waller Proctor) 35, 58
Cossira, Emile 264
Courier and Enquirer (New York) 158
Craig, Gordon 223
Craven, Hawes 205, 209, 223
Creswick, William 142
Crimean War 316
Crystal Palace 112, 113, 117, 196
Cushman, Charlotte 153, 154
Cuthbert, William 205

Daily News, The 253–254, 306
Daily Picayune (New Orleans) 156
Daily Telegraph, The 116
Dalrynple, Captain 79
Dalrymple, Marcia 79
Daly, Augustin 116, 138, 231
Dalziel Brothers 60
Daumier, Honoré 23
Davenant, William 181
Delane, John 104
De Quincey, Thomas 106
Derby, Earl of 105

De Reszke, Edouard 263, 264–266
de Reszke, Jean 115, 262, 263, 264–266, 308
de Saint-Georges, Vernoy 254
Devrient, Emil 231
Dickens, Charles 25–26, 54, 55, 96, 139, 151, 166, 168, 175, 274, 294, 307
Dickinson, Emily 31
Disraeli, Benjamin 104, 105, 316
Dixon, W. Hepworth 48–49, 94, 97, 99, 103
Dodd, William 37
Dodgson, Charles (Lewis Carroll) 30, 58, 307
Donizetti, Gaetano 252, 253
Donnelly, Ignatius 123–126, 129
Douglas Jerrold's Weekly Newspaper 167
Dowdeswell Galleries 60
Dramatic Authors' Society 51, 52, 73
Dryden, John 127
Duke of Saxe-Meiningen's Company 231, 232, 234–236
Dumas, Alexandre 144, 239, 270–271
Dürer, Albrecht 283

Eames, Emma 265
Eastlake, Charles 301
Edinburgh 157
Edward, Prince of Wales 71–72, 79, 86, 247
Egg, Augustus 301
Elgin Marbles 283
Elizabeth I, Queen 75, 123
Elizabethan Stage Society 228–230, 240
Ellesmere, Earl of 108
Emerson, Ralph Waldo 31
Emmanuel, Victor 105
Era 189
Etty, William 288

Fairholt, Frederick William 63
Falconer, Edmund 172
Farren, Nellie 305

Farren, William 93
Faucit, Helen 38, 93, 100, 103, 133, 173, 192
Faure, Jean-Baptiste 257
Fechter, Charles 100, 105, 170, 172, 188–192, 231, 242
Fitzgerald, Edward 30
Flaxman, John 291
Flower, Charles Edward 103
Flower, Edward Fordham 100–101
Folger Shakespeare Library 123
Fontana, Signor 107
Forbes Robertson, Johnston 206, 240
Forrest, Edwin 110, 156–159
Forster, John 175
Foulkes, Richard 96
Franco-Prussian War 316
Franklin, John 30
Frith, William Powell 301
Furnival, F. J. 229
Fuseli, Henry 283, 291

Garibaldi, Giuseppe 104, 105, 316
Garrick Club 49, 69, 311
Garrick, David 73, 107, 159, 277, 287–288
Gaskell, Elizabeth 30
Gautier, Théophile 254
George IV, King 284
Géricault, Jean Louis 283
Gervinus, G. G. 106
Giannono, Signor 253
Gillray, James 48–49
Girton College 227
Gladstone, William 105, 316, 318–319
Glover, Mrs. 93
Glyn, Isabella 193
Goethe, Johann Wolfgang von 212, 291
Gounod, Charles
    Roméo et Juliette 115, 262–266
Grant, Albert 107
Graphic, The 38, 221, 283
Gray, Thomas 307
Gray's Inn 227

337

Great Exhibition (1851) 103, 111
Greenwood, Thomas 160
Grisi, Carlotta 254, 256
Grossmith, George 227
Guild of Literature and Art 54, 55, 93

Hackney, Mabel 225
Halévy, Jacques-François Fromental 253, 255–257, 281
　La tempesta 253–257, 281
Halswelle, Keeley 301
Handel, George Frederick 94, 101, 151
Hanmer, Sir Thomas 184
Hannard, William John 52
Harcourt, Sir William 310, 316
Harker, Joseph 223
Harley, John Pritt 93
Harper's New Monthly Magazine 31, 146
Harris, Augustus 189
Hart, Joseph C. 121
Harvard Library 123, 196
Hathaway, Anne 101, 123
Hawthorne, Nathaniel 122
Heath, Charles 38
Hemming, Jr., Henry 59
Henry, C. N. 298
Henry, Prince of Battenberg 79
Hentschel Ltd. 245
Herbert, John Rogers 301
Hibernia 318–319
Hills, E. 134
Hippodrama 12, 249, 274–281
Hogarth, William 113, 283, 287–288
Holloway, James 277
Holmes, Nathaniel 121
Homer 291
Hook, Alan J. 298
Horne, R. H. 166
Horton, Priscilla 93
Hugo, François-Victor 263
Hugo, Victor 220
Hunt, Leigh 30
Hunt, William Holman 290, 300

Ibsen, Henrik 312
Illustrated London News 53, 117, 187, 218, 254
Ingelby, Clement Mansfield 127, 129
Ireland 62, 316–319
Irving, Henry 11, 81, 128, 134, 138, 147–149, 155, 188, 194–226, 227, 237–238, 239, 240, 243, 247, 296–297, 301, 305
Irving, Henry Brodribb 228
Irving, Laurence 225

Jackson, W. L. 318–319
James, Henry 31
Jameson, Anna Brownell 37, 38
Janssen, Gheerart (see Shakespeare, bust of)
Jeffries, Maud 245
Jewish Emancipation Act 63
Johnson, Samuel (the actor) 201
Jones, George 85, 89, 90, 91, 97
Jonson, Ben 151

Kean, Charles 72, 76, 105, 138, 144, 149, 150, 152, 154, 155–156, 165, 167, 170, 171, 175–188, 190, 199, 228, 230, 247, 251, 273, 280, 305
Kean, Edmund 51, 109, 159, 186, 190
Kean, Ellen (Ellen Tree) 155, 186, 251
Keeley, Robert 59
Kemble, Charles 67–69, 162
Kemble, Fanny 85
Kemble, H. 135, 242
Kemble, John Philip 51, 73, 101, 159, 194, 284–286, 290
Knight, Charles 29, 30, 33–36, 58, 87, 93, 128, 130, 132, 290
Knowles, John 53
Kossuth, Lajos 58,
Krein, Alexander 273
Kruger, Paul 316

Lablache, Luigi 253, 254
Lamb, Charles and Mary 37, 129, 215

Lambert, Constant 273
Landseer, Edwin 283, 288, 300
Langtry, Lillie 220, 239
Lasalle, Jean 260, 262
Last, Joseph 24
Laurie, Peter 89
Lawrence, Sir Thomas 101, 194, 284–286, 290
Leclercq, Rose 240
Lee, Alfred 260
Leslie, Charles R. 299–300
Leslie, Fred 220
Leybourne, George 260
Lincoln, Abraham 52, 105, 316
Lind, Jenny 81, 82–83, 252, 259
Liverpool 122
Lloyd's Weekly London Newspaper 168, 179
Local Government Act (1883) 288
Locke, Matthew 181, 200
London
    Albert Memorial 117
    Belgravia 113, 154
    Bouverie Street 42, 47
    Capel Court 311
    Green Park 100
    Hanover Square 263
    Hyde Park 113
    Islington 161, 162, 172
    Leicester Square 107–108, 231
    Mayfair 154
    New River 163
    Park Lane 117
    Pentonville 109, 171
    Primrose Hill 102
    Rotten Row 113
    Stock Exchange 311
    Temple Garden 95
    Tower of London 63, 292
    Westminster Abbey 83, 107, 181, 302
    Westminster Bridge 275, 276
London County Council 115, 147–149
London Tavern 57

Long, Edwin 198, 296, 301
Longfellow, Henry Wadsworth 31
Loraine, Henry 193
Louis Philippe, King of France 74–76, 163, 311
Lowell, James Russell 31
Lucette, Catherine 171
Lumley, Benjamin 81, 252
Lytton, Edward Bulwer 54, 96, 307

Mackenzie, Sir Alexander C.ampbell 224–225
Maclise, Daniel 151, 288–290
Macready, William Charles 47, 57, 59, 73–76, 93, 110, 114, 140, 144, 147, 149–160, 160–161, 167, 172, 174, 175, 177, 185, 190, 195, 199, 204, 251, 305
Madam Tussaud's 138, 176
Maddox, J. M. 153
Manchester 194, 195
Mansfield, Richard 198
Mario, Giovanni Matteo 262
Marshall, Frank 128
Marston, Henry 171
Mantell, Gideon 113
Marriott, Alice 281
Massey, Gerald 125
Matthews, Charles 51
Maurel, Victor 267
Maxwell, Caroline 37
Mead, Thomas 197
mechanics institutes 131
Meiningen (see Duke of Saxe Meiningen)
Melba, Nellie 115, 262, 263
Melville, Herman 31
Merritt, Anna Lea 301
Meyerbeer, Giacomo 142, 252, 253
Meyrick, Samuel Rush 63
Millais, John Everett 283, 290, 292–296, 298–299, 300
Milton, John 97, 109, 123, 124
Milton, Maud 225

339

Modjeska, Helena 206, 231
Montague, Miss 153
Montgomery, Walter 173
Morand, Eugène 238
Morning Chronicle, The 179–180
Morning Herald, The 105
Mounet-Sully, Jean 231
Musei Vaticani 283

Napoleon, Louis 64, 104, 105, 316
National Fair Trade League 308
National Gallery 282, 284, 288, 289–290, 310
National Portrait Gallery 54, 102, 108, 284
National Shakespeare Committee (see under Shakespeare)
Neilson, Julia 273
Nesbitt, Mrs. 93
Neville, Henry 193
New Gallery 215
New Orleans 156
New Shakspere Society (see Shakespeare, New Shakspere Society)
New York 110, 122, 145, 156–159, 195, 232
Nicolai, Otto 268
Nineteenth Century 134
Nilsson, Christine 259
North London Railway 142
Notes and Queries 136

Oakes, James 157
Odell, George 180–181, 225, 236
Opera 12, 69, 73, 81, 82, 115, 142, 153, 160, 162, 249, 250–269
Opéra Comique 264
Orchardson, William Quiller 283
Osborne House 79
Oxford 86, 149, 195,
Oxford English Dictionary
Oxford University 226
Oxford University Dramatic Society 149, 227–228

Palmerston, Viscount 104
Panizzi, Antonio 311
Pantomime 12
Paris 59, 117
Paris Exhibition (1889) 103
Parton, James 31
Paton, Allan Park 134
Patti, Adelina 262
Pauncefort, Georgina 201
Paxton, Joseph 113
Peel, Sir Robert 75, 105, 316
Pessina, Arturo 267–268
Phelps, Edmund 171
Phelps, Samuel 59, 100, 102, 108, 137, 145, 149, 154, 160–175, 177, 188, 190, 192, 193, 199, 204, 215, 247, 252, 280, 281, 305
Philadelphia 157
Philipon, Charles 23
Phiz (see Hablot Knight Browne)
Planché, James Robinson 63, 154, 275
Poe, Edgar Allan 307
Poel, William 229
Poole, John 304
Potter, Paul 52
Powers, Hiram 283
Poynter, Sir Edward 303
Prokofiev, Sergey 273
Pugin, Augustus Welby 291
Punch, or The London Carivari Almanack 24, 231–232
  Artists (see Index of Artists)
  Bradbury & Evans (Frederick Evans and William Bradbury, proprietors) 24–26, 30, 28, 41, 45, 47, 50, 54
  burlesque 249–320
  circulation 29
  Contributors' Ledgers 46, 141, 142, 150, 187. 188, 190, 235, 240, 271, 309
  dinners 41–42, 44–46
  dinners (smutty humour at) 47–49
  early history 23–26

identity of Mr. Punch 39–41
'*Punch*'s Illustrations to Shakspeare' 61–63
readership 28–31
readership and Shakespeare 32–39
Shakespeare, knowledge of by *Punch* artists and writers 56–58
Shakespeare Tercentenary special issue 100, 103–107, 192
technology and mass production of 26–28
theatre, involvement in by *Punch* artists and writers 51–56
Toby, Mr. Punch's dog 9–10, 83, 285
writers (for individual writers see Index of Writers)
writers and artists 41–50, 49–50
Putnam's Monthly 122

Quarterly Review 40

Rachel 231
railways 311, 313–316
Rae, Henrietta 297
Reform Club 255
Reni, Guido 283
Retzsch, Moritz 291
Reynolds, Joshua 288
Richie, C. T. 288
Rignold, George 230
Ristori, Adelaide 231
Robertson, Tom 312
Robin's London Auction House 89
Robinson, Frederick 224
Rolls, Charles 290
Roselle, Master Percy 173
Rossi, Ernesto 231
Rossini, Gioachino 253
Royal Academy 38, 198, 249, 282, 283–284, 290–292, 294–303
Royal Holloway College 292
Russell, Earl John 104
Ryder, John 142

Saintsbury, George 127
Sala, George Augustus 83
Salisbury, Lord 288, 316
Salvini, Tommaso 114, 116, 200, 231, 232–234
Sandringham 80, 81
Sanger, George 281
Santley, Charles 259
Sardou, Victorien 220
Sargent, John Singer 212, 215–216
Scheemakers, Peter (see Shakespeare, statue by Peter Scheemakers)
Schob, Marcel 238
Schoch, Richard W. 304
Schoenbaum, Samuel 130
Scott, Clement 55
Scott, Sir Walter 120, 127, 139
Scribe, Eugène 253–256
Selous, Henry Courtney 35
Shakespeare, William
  authorship debate 121–126
  biography 129–131
  birthplace 69, 84–93, 110, 127, 240
  bust by C. J Allen (Aldermanbury) 117
  bust by Charles Bacon 117
  bust by Gheerart Janssen (Stratford-on-Avon) 48, 107, 110, 118
  bust by Louis-François Roubiliac 107
  Chandos Portrait 108
  critical works on 128–131
  effigy in Madame Tussaud's
  exhumation 126–128
  Kesselstadt Death Mask 106, 118
  National Shakespeare Committee 48, 94, 97–100
  New Shakspere Society 58, 127
  Northern Shakespeare Society 110
  People's Central Committee of the Shakespeare Memorial Fund 85, 89

341

plays
All's Well That Ends Well 62
Antony and Cleopatra 55, 128, 193
As You Like It 72, 77, 101, 128, 150, 155, 178, 240, 307, 310, 311–312
Comedy of Errors, The 62, 101, 173, 227
Coriolanus 11, 197–198, 224–225, 312
Cymbeline 67–68, 100, 114, 150, 162, 173, 223–224
Hamlet 59, 63–64, 92, 100, 115, 124, 128, 132, 133, 134–136, 138, 140, 141, 142, 147–149, 150, 161, 171, 172, 175, 176, 178, 187, 188, 189–190, 191, 192, 194–197, 201–202, 208, 210–211, 212, 220, 221–222, 226, 229, 232–234, 236–239, 240, 241–243, 257, 259–261, 270, 273, 281, 288–290, 301, 302–303, 305, 306, 307, 308, 309, 310, 312
Henry IV (Parts 1 and 2) 51, 64–65, 85, 138, 142, 169–170, 173, 178, 227, 241, 291
Henry V 146, 168, 180, 230, 280, 312
Henry VI (Part 1) 95, 172
Henry VI (Part 2) 62, 102, 172, 301
Henry VI (Part 3) 172
Henry VIII 154–155, 173, 180, 182–183, 202, 217, 308
Julius Caesar 59, 131, 133, 150, 155, 171, 178, 228, 232, 234–236, 244–245
King John 55, 150, 163, 173, 178–179, 180, 182, 228, 245
King Lear 49, 92, 111, 114, 128, 159, 192, 217–220
Macbeth 48, 92, 105, 106, 114, 131, 133, 134, 148, 150, 153–154, 156–157, 159, 161, 166, 171, 173, 179–180, 181, 182, 192, 193, 199–200, 212–216, 240, 271–272, 277, 278–280, 307, 308, 312, 314–315
Measure for Measure 62, 290, 295–296, 300
Merchant of Venice, The 48, 81, 101, 102, 150, 161, 171, 173, 178, 192, 198, 203, 208, 312
Merry Wives of Windsor, The 55, 85, 93, 128, 178, 240–241
Midsummer Night's Dream, A 90, 167–168, 170, 192, 245, 255
Much Ado About Nothing 101, 103, 150, 193, 207–208, 216–217, 240, 309, 312
Othello 64, 92, 101, 114, 131, 141, 145, 147–148, 150, 151, 153, 156, 161, 171, 173, 174, 190–191, 198, 200, 204, 205, 222, 232, 233, 245, 273, 280–281, 305, 307
Pericles 62
Richard II 172, 180–181, 185, 187, 280
Richard III 34, 46, 55, 110, 128, 132, 161, 164–165, 167, 181–182, 192, 198, 200, 208, 223, 277, 287, 292–294, 302, 305, 307, 309
Romeo and Juliet 100–101, 102, 128, 148, 149, 175–176, 205–207, 209–210, 211–212, 226, 239, 240, 273, 299–300, 305, 312
Taming of the Shrew, The 99, 193, 277, 301, 316–319
Tempest, The 55, 128, 253, 273, 305, 306, 307
Titus Andronicus 62, 172
Troilus and Cressida 128, 172
Twelfth Night 85, 102, 116, 178, 192, 202, 209, 227–228, 235, 245–246

Two Gentlemen of Verona, The 150, 228, 229
Winter's Tale, The 77–79, 150, 180, 184–185, 232, 235, 273, 305

poetry
Passionate Pilgrim, The 194
Sonnets 47, 126
Venus and Adonis 100, 256

portrait of Shakespeare by Martin Droeshout (First Folio) 108
Shakespeare's Cliff 70, 74
Shakespeare Club (Stratford-on-Avon) 94
Shakespeare Memorial Library 196
Shakespeare Memorial Theatre (Stratford-on-Avon) (see under Theatres)
Shakespeare's Head, The 56
Shakespearean Monumental Committee (Stratford-upon-Avon) 84
statue by Henry Hugh Armstead (Albert Memorial) 117
statue by John Bell (Great Exhibition) 111–114
statue by John Cheere (Stratford-on-Avon Town Hall) 107
statue (Drury Lane) 256
statue by Fontana (Leicester Square) 107
statue by Paul Fornier (Paris) 119
statue by Ronald Gower (Stratford-on-Avon) 117–121
statue by Peter Scheemakers (Westminster Abbey) 83, 100, 107, 109, 139, 263, 269
statue by John E. Thomas (International Exhibition, 1862) 117
statue by William Hamo Thornycroft (Poets' Fountain, Park Lane) 117
Tercentenary (1864) 10, 48, 94–107, 188, 194
tomb (Stratford-on-Avon) 86, 126, 128

Shakspeareanity 11, 12, 68–70, 81, 85, 97, 174
Sharpe, Charles William 290
Shaw, Capt. Eyre M. 143
Siddal, Elizabeth 299
Simmonet, Mlle. 264
Smirke, Robert 106
Smith, William Henry 121, 126
Society for the Diffusion of Useful Knowledge 131
Solomon, Solomon Joseph 302
Somerset County Gazette 28
Sontag, Henrietta (Countess Rossi) 252, 253, 254
Southampton Art Gallery 218
Soyer, Alexis 255–256
Spielmann, Marion Harry 43, 46, 56, 58,
Standard, The 105
Standfust, W. G. 38
Standing, Herbert 211–212
Staunton, Howard 35
Stephens, George 108
Stirling, Fanny 205, 207
Stevenson, Robert Louis 307
Stoker, Bram 243
Stratford-on-Avon 55, 84, 100–101, 106, 118, 188
Sullivan, Barry 103
Swift, Jonathan 307
Sydenham 117

Tamagno, Francesco 267
Tate Gallery 215, 284, 288, 290, 299
Taylor, Gary 121
Telbin, William 205
Telegraph, The 234
Tennyson, Alfred 295, 307
Terriss, William 209, 219–220
Terry, Ellen 54, 81, 129, 148–149, 200, 201–202, 204, 205, 207–208, 212–216, 223, 225, 227, 239
Terry, Kate 54, 193
Thackeray, Anne 96
Theatre, legislation 144–149

343

Theatre, problems when attending 140–149

Theatre Regulation Act (1843) 71–72, 110, 144, 152, 160, 162, 251

Theatres
  Adelphi 51, 54, 102, 193, 231, 238
  Astley's 174, 185, 193, 274–281
  Astor Place (New York) 156, 157–158
  Covent Garden 52, 72, 81, 92, 110, 115, 137, 143, 144, 151, 159, 160, 175, 185, 251–252, 253, 259, 262–264, 267, 275
  Daly's Theatre 116, 138, 231
  Drury Lane 72, 73, 81, 87, 109, 110, 111, 120, 133, 137, 144, 150, 152, 154, 155, 159, 172–174, 175, 185, 188, 192, 230–231, 236–237, 251, 252, 256–257, 269–270, 275
  Gallery of Illustration 51
  Gaiety 220, 305, 306
  Garrick 110
  Globe (Elizabethan and Jacobean) 134
  Globe (Victorian) 198, 239, 305
  Haymarket 52, 54, 72, 102, 137, 140–141, 144, 149, 153, 155, 160, 175, 192, 241, 244, 250–251
  Her Majesty's 81, 138, 244–246, 250, 253, 256–257, 267, 273
  Lyceum 11, 81, 108, 129, 138, 147, 148, 172, 188, 192, 195–209, 211–220, 222–226, 239, 243, 267
  Merchant Taylors' Hall (occasional) 229
  Miss Kelly's (the Royalty) 54
  Olympic 160, 192, 193
  Pavilion 143
  Porte Saint-Martin (Paris) 236
  Prince of Wales 203, 305
  Princess's 72, 102, 138, 153, 154, 160, 170, 177, 179, 187, 188, 189, 190, 193, 195, 204, 209, 226, 231, 239, 253, 280, 305
  St. George's Hall (occasional) 229
  St. James's 54, 160, 239, 253
  Sadler's Wells 72, 73, 102, 137, 160–172, 188, 192, 193, 252
  Shakespeare Memorial Theatre 103, 117, 118, 240
  Standard 142
  Strand 52
  Surrey 102, 150
  Théâtre Bernhardt (Paris) 237
  Théâtre Historique 230, 239
  Théâtre Lyrique (Paris) 262
  Theatre Royal (Exeter) 144
  Victoria 73
  Windsor Castle (Rubens Room) (occasional) 167, 177–178, 187, 251
  Winter Garden (New York) 195

Theatrical Journal 161
Thiers, Adolphe 316
Thomas, Ambroise 257, 281
  Hamlet 194, 257–262, 264, 272–273
Thomas, Moy 134
Thorne, Sarah 142
Thumb, General Tom 56, 57, 67–68, 87
Tilbury, Harries 94
Times, The 28, 65, 97, 104, 119, 161, 173, 217, 236, 253, 254, 255, 271, 273, 277, 306
Timmins, Samuel 127
Tomkins 139–140
Tree, Miss. Beerbohm 150
Tree, Herbert Beerbohm 135, 138, 226, 228, 240–246, 273
Tupper, Martin 105
Turner, William 288

Vanderhoff, George 59
Verdi, Giuseppe 262, 267–269, 280

Vernon, Robert 288, 310
Vernon Gallery 288
Vestris, Mme Eliza
Vezin, Herman 174, 280
Vezin, Mrs 174, 280
Victoria, Queen 11, 30, 54, 56, 57, 67–69, 72, 75, 76, 85–86, 88, 90, 92, 104, 118, 137, 150, 153, 154–155, 159, 163, 168, 177, 186, 222, 247, 250–251, 277, 284
Vining, Edward 220
Vining, Mrs. H. 150
Virtue, J. S. 290
Vizetelly, Henry 58
Von Bunsen, Baron Christian 155

Walker Art Gallery (Liverpool) 287
Wallack, James 59, 150
Walton, Isaac 307
Ward, Edward Matthew 301
Warner, Mary 72, 108, 137, 160, 161, 162, 165, 252
Webster, Benjamin 51, 53, 93, 99, 105, 141, 160, 223, 250–251
Whitman, Walt 31
Whittington Club 152
Wigan, Alfred 192
Wilde, Oscar 115–116, 118
Wilhelm II, Kaiser 111, 316
Wilkie, David 288
William IV, King 284
Windsor Castle 67, 76, 79, 222
Wingfield, Lewis 209
Wise, John 106
Wolseley, Sir Garnet 308
Wordsworth, Charles 106

Yardley, William 305